LEVITES AND PRIESTS
IN BIBLICAL HISTORY AND TRADITION

Society of Biblical Literature

Ancient Israel and Its Literature

Steven L. McKenzie, General Editor

Editorial Board

Suzanne Boorer
Victor H. Matthews
Thomas C. Römer
Benjamin D. Sommer
Nili Wazana

Number 9

LEVITES AND PRIESTS
IN BIBLICAL HISTORY AND TRADITION

LEVITES AND PRIESTS
IN BIBLICAL HISTORY AND TRADITION

Edited by

Mark A. Leuchter
and
Jeremy M. Hutton

Society of Biblical Literature
Atlanta

LEVITES AND PRIESTS
IN BIBLICAL HISTORY AND TRADITION

Copyright © 2011 by the Society of Biblical Literature

All rights reserved. No part of this work may be reproduced or transmitted in any form or by any means, electronic or mechanical, including photocopying and recording, or by means of any information storage or retrieval system, except as may be expressly permitted by the 1976 Copyright Act or in writing from the publisher. Requests for permission should be addressed in writing to the Rights and Permissions Office, Society of Biblical Literature, 825 Houston Mill Road, Atlanta, GA 30329 USA.

Library of Congress Cataloging-in-Publication Data

Levites and priests in biblical history and tradition : edited by Mark Leuchter and Jeremy M. Hutton.
    p. cm. — (Society of Biblical Literature ancient Israel and its literature ; v. 9)
    Includes bibliographical references and index.
    ISBN 978-1-58983-606-8 (paper binding : alk. paper) — ISBN 978-1-58983-607-5 (electronic format)
    1. Priests, Jewish—History. 2. Priests, Jewish—Biblical teaching. 3. Levites. 4. Bible. O.T.—Criticism, interpretation, etc. I. Leuchter, Mark. II. Hutton, Jeremy Michael.
    BS1199.P7L48   2011
    296.4'95—dc23

2011042390

Printed on acid-free, recycled paper conforming to
ANSI/NISO Z39.48-1992 (R1997) and ISO 9706:1994
standards for paper permanence.

Contents

Abbreviations ix

Introduction 1
Mark Leuchter and Jeremy M. Hutton

Part I
Priests and Levites in Social Context

Covenant Priesthood: Cross-cultural Legal and Religious Aspects
of Biblical and Hittite Priesthood 11
Ada Taggar-Cohen

Who Is Sacrificing at Shiloh? The Priesthoods
of Ancient Israel's Regional Sanctuaries 25
Susan Ackerman

The Levitical Diaspora (II): Modern Perspectives
on the Levitical Cities Lists (A Review of Opinions) 45
Jeremy M. Hutton

The Social Status of Priestly and Levite Women 83
Sarah Shectman

Part II
Priests and Levites in Scriptural Context

The Violent Origins of the Levites: Text and Tradition............. 103
Joel S. Baden

Between Shadow and Substance: The Historical Relationship
of Tabernacle and Temple in Light of Architecture and Iconography 117
Cory D. Crawford

What Do the "Levites in Your Gates" Have to Do
with the "Levitical Priests"? An Attempt at European-North American
Dialogue on the Levites in the Deuteronomic Law Corpus............. 135
Peter Altmann

Those Stubborn Levites: Overcoming Levitical Disenfranchisement..... 155
Stephen L. Cook

Part III
Priests and Levites in Exegetical Context

Middle-Tier Levites and the Plenary Reception of Revelation 173
Mark A. Christian

The Cultic Status of the Levites in the *Temple Scroll*:
Between History and Hermeneutics 199
Jeffrey Stackert

From Levite to Maśkîl in the Persian and Hellenistic Eras 215
Mark Leuchter

Contributors 233

Index of Passages 235

Index of Authors 250

Abbreviations

AB	Anchor Bible
ABD	*Anchor Bible Dictionary*. Edited by David Noel Freedman. 6 vols. New York: Doubleday, 1992.
AnBib	Analecta biblica
AoF	*Altorientalische Forschungen*
AOAT	Alter Orient und Altes Testament
AS	Assyriological Studies
ATD	Das Alte Testament Deutsch
AThANT	Abhandlungen zur Theologie des Alten und Neuen Testaments
BA	*Biblical Archaeologist*
BASOR	*Bulletin of the American Schools of Oriental Research*
BBB	Bonner biblische Beiträge
BDB	Brown, F., S. R. Driver, and C. A. Briggs. *A Hebrew and English Lexicon of the Old Testament*. Oxford: Clarendon, 1907.
BETL	Bibliotheca ephemeridum theologicarum lovaniensium
BHK	*Biblica Hebraica*. Edited by R. Kittel. Stuttgart: Württembergische Bibelanstalt, 1905–6; multiple editions.
BJS	Brown Judaic Studies
BKAT	Biblischer Kommentar. Altes Testament
BN	*Biblische Notizen*
BO	*Bibliotheca orientalis*
BWANT	Beiträge zur Wissenschaft vom Alten und Neuen Testament
BZ	*Biblische Zeitschrift*
BZABR	Beihefte zur Zeitschrift für altorientalische und biblische Rechtsgeschichte
BZAW	Beihefte zur Zeitschrift für die alttestamentliche Wissenschaft
CBC	Cambridge Bible Commentary
CBQ	*Catholic Biblical Quarterly*
CC	Continental Commentaries
CHANE	Culture and History of the Ancient Near East
ConBOT	Coniectanea biblica: Old Testament Series
COS	*The Context of Scripture*. Edited by William W. Hallo. 3 vols. Leiden: Brill, 1997–2002.
CTH	Catalogue des Textes Hittites
DJD	Discoveries in the Judaean Desert
DSD	*Dead Sea Discoveries*
Eothen	Eothen: Collana di studi sulle civiltà dell'Oriente antico

ErIsr	Eretz Israel
FAT	Forschungen zum Alten Testament
FRLANT	Forschungen zur Religion und Literatur des Alten und Neuen Testaments
GAT	Grundrisse zum Alten Testament
HALOT	Koehler, L., W. Baumgartner, and J. J. Stamm, *The Hebrew and Aramaic Lexicon of the Old Testament*. Translated and edited under the supervision of M. E. J. Richardson. 4 vols. Leiden: Brill, 1994–99.
HAT	Handbuch zum Alten Testament
HBM	Hebrew Bible Monographs
HdO	Handbuch der Orientalistik
HKAT	Handkommentar zum Alten Testament
HSM	Harvard Semitic Monographs
HThKAT	Herders theologischer Kommentar zum Alten Testament
HTR	*Harvard Theological Review*
HUCA	*Hebrew Union College Annual*
IBHS	*An Introduction to Biblical Hebrew Syntax*. B. K. Waltke and M. O'Connor. Winona Lake, Ind.: Eisenbrauns, 1990.
ICC	International Critical Commentary
JANER	*Journal of Ancient Near Eastern Religions*
JANES	*Journal of the Ancient Near Eastern Society*
JAOS	*Journal of the American Oriental Society*
JB	Jerusalem Bible
JBL	*Journal of Biblical Literature*
JHS	*Journal of Hebrew Scriptures*
JJTP	*Journal of Jewish Thought and Philosophy*
JNES	*Journal of Near Eastern Studies*
JSJ	*Journal for the Study of Judaism in the Persian, Hellenistic, and Roman Periods*
JSOT	*Journal for the Study of the Old Testament*
JSOTSup	Journal for the Study of the Old Testament: Supplement Series
JSP	*Journal for the Study of the Pseudepigrapha*
JSPSup	Journal for the Study of the Pseudepigrapha: Supplement Series
KHAT	Kurzer Handkommentar zum Alten Testament
KUB	*Keilschrifturkunden aus Boghazköi*
LHBOTS	Library of Hebrew Bible/Old Testament Studies
NAB	New American Bible
NCB	New Century Bible
NEAEHL	*The New Encyclopedia of Archaeological Excavations in the Holy Land*. Edited by E. Stern. 4 vols. Jerusalem: Israel Exploration Society and Carta; New York: Simon & Schuster, 1993.

NEB	New English Bible
NET	New English Translation
NICOT	New International Commentary on the Old Testament
NIDB	*The New Interpreter's Dictionary of the Bible*. Edited by Katharine Doob Sakenfeld. 5 vols. Nashville: Abingdon, 2006–9.
NJB	New Jerusalem Bible
NJPS	*Tanakh: The Holy Scriptures. The New JPS Translation according to the Traditional Hebrew Text*
NLT	New Living Translation
NRSV	New Revised Standard Version
OBO	Orbis biblicus et orientalis
ÖBS	Österreichische biblische Studien
OEANE	*The Oxford Encyclopedia of Archaeology in the Near East*. Edited by E. M. Meyers. New York: Oxford University Press, 1997.
OLA	Orientalia lovaniensia analecta
OTE	*Old Testament Essays*
OTL	Old Testament Library
OTM	Oxford Theological Monographs
OTS	Oudtestamentische Studiën
PEQ	*Palestine Exploration Quarterly*
PJ	*Palästina-Jahrbuch*
RB	*Revue biblique*
RBL	*Review of Biblical Literature*
REB	Revised English Bible
RevQ	*Revue de Qumran*
RGG	*Religion in Geschichte und Gegenwart*. Rev. ed. Edited by Hans Dieter Betz et al. 8 vols. Tübingen: Mohr Siebeck, 1998–2005.
RSV	Revised Standard Version
SAHL	Studies in the Archaeology and History of the Levant
SAOC	Studies in Ancient Oriental Civilizations
SBLABS	Society of Biblical Literature Archaeology and Biblical Studies
SBLAIL	Society of Biblical Literature Ancient Israel and Its Literature
SBLDS	Society of Biblical Literature Dissertation Series
SBLEJL	Society of Biblical Literature Early Judaism and Its Literature
SBLRBS	Society of Biblical Literature Resources for Biblical Study
SBLStBL	Society of Biblical Literature Studies in Biblical Literature
SBLWAW	Society of Biblical Literature Writings from the Ancient World
SBT	Studies in Biblical Theology
SBTS	Sources for Biblical and Theological Study
SEÅ	*Svensk exegetisk årsbok*
SHANE	Studies in the History of the Ancient Near East

SJOT	*Scandinavian Journal of the Old Testament*
SOTSMS	Society for Old Testament Studies Monograph Series
StBoT	Studien zu den Boğazköy-Texten
STDJ	Studies on the Texts of the Desert of Judah
StPohl	Studia Pohl
SubBi	Subsidia biblica
SWBA	Social World of Biblical Antiquity
TA	*Tel Aviv*
TDOT	*Theological Dictionary of the Old Testament.* Edited by G. J. Botterweck and H. Ringgren. Translated by J. T. Willis, G. W. Bromiley, and D. E. Green. Grand Rapids: Eerdmans, 1974–.
THeth	Texte der Hethiter
TRE	*Theologische Realenzyklopädie.* Edited by G. Krause and G. Müller. Berlin: de Gruyter, 1977–.
TynBul	*Tyndale Bulletin*
VT	*Vetus Testamentum*
VTSup	Vetus Testamentum Supplements
WBC	Word Biblical Commentary
WC	Westminster Commentaries
WMANT	Wissenschaftliche Monographien zum Alten und Neuen Testament
ZABR	*Zeitschrift für altorientalische und biblische Rechtsgeschichte*
ZA	*Zeitschrift für Assyriologie*
ZAH	*Zeitschrift für Althebräistik*
ZAW	*Zeitschrift für die alttestamentliche Wissenschaft*
ZBK	Zürcher Bibelkommentare
ZDPV	*Zeitschrift des deutschen Palästina Vereins*

Introduction

Mark Leuchter and Jeremy Hutton

Ancient Israel's priestly functionaries have always occupied a paramount position in the study of the Hebrew Bible, both in antiquity and in modern scholarship. Already in Julius Wellhausen's groundbreaking study of Israelite religion, attention was drawn to the central position of Aaronides, Zadokites, and Levites in the formation of the biblical corpus and the historical development of Israelite religious ideology and identity,[1] and countless important studies have followed in Wellhausen's wake. The antiquity and authenticity of the textual sources concerned with priests and Levites have time and time again been subjected to detailed scrutiny, the relationship between the various priestly houses serves as a point of departure for reconstructed histories of Israel's monarchic politics, and the distinctions between ranks and gradations of priests in a variety of compositions has fueled intense speculation regarding the various iterations of sacral activity as Israelite communities formed, dissolved, and reformed over time.[2] In recent decades, the study of Priestly language and ideology have further clarified the nuanced distinctions between different schools of Priestly thought;[3] these forays not only have provided important entrees into the understanding of ritual and concepts of holiness in Israelite religion but have contributed to new ways of understanding the growth of the biblical literature more broadly. They have also more clearly delineated the role of Priestly ideology in the shaping of

---

1. Julius Wellhausen, *Prolegomena to the History of Israel* (trans. J. S. Black and Allan Menzies, with a preface by W. Robertson Smith [1885]; repr., with a foreword by Douglas A. Knight; Atlanta: Scholars Press, 1994), 121–67.

2. See among others Kurt Möhlenbrink, "Die levitischen Überlieferungen des Alten Testaments," *ZAW* n.s. 11 (1934): 184–231; A. H. J. Gunneweg, *Leviten und Priester: Hauptlinien der Traditionsbildung und Geschichte des israelitisch-jüdischen Kultpersonals* (FRLANT 89; Göttingen: Vandenhoeck & Ruprecht, 1965); Aelred Cody, *A History of Old Testament Priesthood* (AnBib 35; Rome: Pontifical Biblical Institute, 1969); Frank Moore Cross, *Canaanite Myth and Hebrew Epic: Essays in the History of the Religion of Israel* (Cambridge, Mass.: Harvard University Press, 1973), 195–215.

3. Jacob Milgrom, *Leviticus: A New Translation with Introduction and Commentary* (3 vols.; AB 3, 3A, 3B; New York: Doubleday, 1991–2000); Israel Knohl, *The Sanctuary of Silence: The Priestly Torah and the Holiness School* (Minneapolis: Fortress, 1995).

major literary collections such as the Pentateuch, the Psalter, and the historiographic texts spanning Joshua–Kings.[4]

Yet despite more than a century of critical research, many problems continue to stand in the way of our understanding of the diversity, function, origins, influence, and legacy of priests and Levites as depicted in the Hebrew Bible. Virtually all scholars accept the broad division between Aaronide priests, on one hand, and Levites, on the other, with long-standing sacral and political rivalries defining the boundaries between them. Similarly, many have accepted a model seeing a relatively late, Persian-era reconciliation and orchestration of the priestly ranks, with Aaronides serving as the dominant priestly house governing temple affairs and Levites functioning as scribal and administrative mediators between the public and the ruling Aaronides.[5] However, there is little agreement regarding the topography of the road leading up to this late hierarchical ordering, and questions abound regarding the social location of the various priestly groups, the discrepancies in the depictions of their origins, the inconsistencies in sources regarding their ritual functions, the relationship between prophecy and the priesthood, and of course the thorny matter of dating the texts housing these collective data.

The impasse facing scholars studying Israel's priesthood in its manifold forms is, to some degree, rooted in the presuppositions and related limitations in defining the very terms "priest" and "Levite." The idea of priests representing a common ancient Near Eastern social typology set apart for cultic authority, ritual and ceremonial training, intercessory responsibility, and legal expertise is generally recognized, and studies into Israelite religion commonly accept that Israel's priestly figures should be viewed as part of the spectrum of ancient priesthood in cross-cultural perspective. However, while some scholars have worked from the position that priesthood was from the outset an exclusively hereditary status deriving primarily from Levite "tribal" ancestry,[6]

---

4. On the Pentateuch, see the collection of essays in Gary N. Knoppers and Bernard M. Levinson, eds., *The Pentateuch as Torah: New Models for Understanding Its Promulgation and Acceptance* (Winona lake, Ind.: Eisenbrauns, 2007); Eckart Otto and Reinhard Achenbach, eds., *Deuteronomium zwischen Pentateuch und Deuteronomistischem Geschichtswerk* (FRLANT 206; Göttingen: Vandenhoeck & Ruprecht, 2004). For a brief but illuminating examination of the Psalter, see Mark S. Smith, "The Levitical Redaction of the Psalter," *ZAW* 103 (1991): 258–63. On Joshua–Kings, see the recent study by Jeffrey C. Geoghegan, *The Time, Place and Purpose of the Deuteronomistic History: The Evidence of "Until This Day"* (BJS 347; Providence, R.I.: Brown Judaic Studies, 2006).

5. On the long process leading up to this ostensible reconciliation, see Joachim Schaper, *Priester und Leviten im achämenidischen Juda: Studien zur Kult- und Socialgeschichte Israels in persischer Zeit* (FAT 31; Tübingen: Mohr Siebeck, 2000).

6. Such, for example, is the view of Cody, *History of Old Testament Priesthood*, 29–38, 51, 58–60. More recently, Stephen L. Cook has advanced a similar position (*The Social Roots of Biblical Yahwism* [SBLStBL 8; Atlanta: Society of Biblical Literature, 2004], 55–57).

others have pointed to permeability as a hallmark of the priesthood.⁷ The term לוי ("attached [to]") is itself highly suggestive of this meaning,⁸ indicating the method whereby local priesthoods grew over time through the incorporation of new members into their ranks,⁹ as well as how these priestly clans amalgamated into larger social entities. At what point, then, does a firm distinction between "priest" and "Levite" emerge in Israelite religion? Who is responsible for creating this distinction, and what purpose does it serve? How does such a division in rank or typology reflect larger sociopolitical trends implicit in the biblical sources?

Related to these matters is the fact that priestly function is evident in one form or another among ostensibly lay figures as well throughout the Hebrew Bible, and thus a strict dichotomy between Israelite laity and Israelite priests is difficult to sustain. Recent important works on family religion in ancient Israel, for example, demonstrate the depth of cultic life within family units that complement (or in some cases, rival) the cultic authority of priests at a regional or even state sanctuary.¹⁰ Textual/linguistic, anthropological, and archaeological evidence points to different priestly roles not only within the more familiar typological categories ("altar priests" versus "lector priests,"¹¹ or the depiction of Levites as scribes/librarians on one hand, militiamen on the other, or authoritative cultic functionaries on yet another), but also among

---

7. The fluidity of priestly status was discussed in the context of royal/administrative appointment by Gösta W. Ahlström, *Royal Administration and National Religion in Ancient Palestine* (SHANE 1; Leiden: Brill, 1982), 48–49. For a different approach to the issue of permeability and fluidity in priestly status, see Jeremy M. Hutton, "The Levitical Diaspora (I): A Sociological Comparison with Morocco's Ahansal," in *Exploring the Longue Durée: Essays in Honor of Lawrence E. Stager* (ed. J. David Schloen; Winona Lake, Ind.: Eisenbrauns, 2009), 227–30.

8. The etymology of the term is discussed by Karel van der Toorn, *Family Religion in Babylonia, Syria, and Israel: Continuity and Change in the Forms of Religious Life* (Studies in the History and Culture of the Ancient Near East 7; Leiden: Brill, 1996), 304; but cf. Cody, *History of Old Testament Priesthood*, 29–33.

9. See especially the brief discussion by Lawrence E. Stager, "The Archaeology of the Family in Ancient Israel," *BASOR* 260 (1985): 28.

10. Van der Toorn's monumental study *Family Religion in Babylonia, Syria, and Israel* set the agenda for contemporary discussion on this topic. See also Saul M. Olyan, "Family Religion in Israel and the Wider Levant of the First Millennium BCE," in *Household and Family Religion in Antiquity* (ed. John Bodel and Saul M. Olyan; Malden, Mass./Oxford: Blackwell, 2008), 113–26.

11. See especially the parallels discussed by Diana V. Edelman, "Of Priests and Prophets and Interpreting the Past: The Egyptian ḤM-NṮR and ḤRY-ḤBT and the Judahite NABI?," in *The Historian and the Bible: Essays in Honour of Lester L. Grabbe* (ed. Philip R. Davies and Diana V. Edelman; LHBOTS 530; New York: T&T Clark International, 2010). A version of this paper was presented in the Priests and Levites in History and Traditions consultation at the 2009 annual meeting of the Society of Biblical Literature in New Orleans, Louisiana.

the elders of a village or clan and the male and female heads of individual households.[12] Religious life in ancient Israel was not simply left in the charge of priests—Levite, Aaronide, or otherwise—but was a far more textured and complicated phenomenon in which priests played an important but by no means exclusive role. Where, in this network of cultic interaction, may one situate a dedicated priestly caste? How do the textual sources regarding this caste evidence awareness, acceptance, or repudiation of these features?

In addressing these textual sources, one encounters the persistent problem of literacy and scribal authority and the role that Aaronide priests and Levites played in the production of Israel's literature. The last two decades of research have yielded a picture of ancient Israel as a largely pre- or nonliterate culture, with only the priestly and royal/administrative elite possessing the facilities to produce significant and complex written materials.[13] For many scholars, even this becomes a possibility only fairly late in Israel's history, accompanying the rise of Judah in the late eighth century into full-fledged statehood capable of supporting a scribal infrastructure that could produce the materials currently found in the Hebrew Bible.[14] Others still place the production of these materials later, in the Persian period, when the influence of the Persian imperial system provided a suitable background for the transmission of written tradition.[15] In either case, these studies make the case that only within a complex state-sponsored matrix could Israelite priests draw from resources that would allow for the composition of texts. However, more recent research has challenged this paradigm and has demonstrated that scribalism existed beyond the confines of the royal court, the Jerusalem temple, or the offices of imperial administrators and was present already throughout the hinterland in the late Iron I–Iron IIa period.[16] This raises many questions regarding the role of texts in different

---

12. See Cook's discussion of the sacral role of elders (*Social Roots*, 195–230). On male and female leadership in the household cult, see Olyan, "Household Religion"; and Susan Ackerman, "At Home with the Goddess," in *Symbiosis, Symbolism, and the Power of the Past: Canaan, Ancient Israel, and Their Neighbors from the Late Bronze Age through Roman Palaestina. Proceedings of the Centennial Symposium, W. F. Albright Institute of Archaeological Research and American Schools of Oriental Research, Jerusalem, May 29/31, 2000* (ed. William G. Dever and Seymour Gitin; Winona Lake, Ind.: Eisenbrauns, 2003), 455–65.

13. Ian M. Young, "Israelite Literacy: Interpreting the Evidence," *VT* 48 (1998): 239–53, 408–22; William M. Schniedewind, *How the Bible Became a Book: The Textualization of Ancient Israel* (New York/Cambridge: Cambridge University Press, 2004); David M. Carr, *Writing on the Tablet of the Heart: Origins of Scripture and Literature* (New York/Oxford: Oxford University Press, 2005), 116–21.

14. Scholars adopting this view routinely defer to the conclusions draw by David W. Jamieson-Drake, *Scribes and Schools in Monarchic Judah: A Socio-Archaeological Approach* (JSOTSup 109; Sheffield: Sheffield Academic Press, 1991).

15. Philip R. Davies, *Scribes and Schools: The Canonization of the Hebrew Scriptures* (Library of Ancient Israel; Louisville: Westminster John Knox, 1998), 65–71.

16. Ryan Byrne, "The Refuge of Scribalism in Iron I Palestine," *BASOR* 345 (2007):

historical and social contexts and the purpose of literature widely regarded as possessing priestly interest (the P document, Deuteronomy, various prophetic works, etc.). Were these works composed and cultivated by priests for their own literate circles (as is often thought) or with a larger audience in mind? Are the compositional techniques and hermeneutical strategies associated with the production of these texts solely the province of the scribes of the Jerusalem temple, or did they originate and continue to develop in other social environments? How do the "official" texts of the Jerusalem priestly establishment countenance the function of texts deriving from competing scribal circles?

The present volume emerged from the papers presented at the Society of Biblical Literature meetings in New Orleans (2009) and Atlanta (2010) in a newly formed program unit entitled "Priests and Levites in History and Tradition" and devoted to the aforementioned unresolved issues. The unit was formed to revisit some of the axiomatic assumptions that have led to scholarly impasses in research over the last several decades, as well as to establish new avenues of inquiry that have surfaced in recent scholarship both within and beyond the field of ancient Israelite religion and the Hebrew Bible. The papers presented at these sessions explored the place of priests and Levites in relation to the cult, kinship, literacy, sexual politics and gendered space, warfare, mythology, administration, and other components of Israelite life from a multitude of positions and perspectives, demonstrating the benefit of and indeed the need for interdisciplinary approaches to untying the knots that have hindered progress in the past. The present volume incorporates many of the papers presented at those SBL sessions as well as others traversing similar and closely related territories, with the aim of defining fruitful trajectories for further research.

Four essays under the rubric "Priests and Levites in Social Context" discuss historical and sociological aspects of Israel's religious functionaries. Ada Taggar-Cohen provides a comparison of Israelite (derived primarily from the so-called Priestly tradition) and Hittite models of priesthood, arguing for a number of functional and ideological parallels between the two. Susan Ackerman asks, "Who is sacrificing at Shiloh?" This question prompts an investigation into the ritual dynamics of ancient Israel's sanctuaries, with the conclusion that it was not the priests but rather the common folk ("non-elites"), who were engaged in the sacrificial acts. This conclusion indicates that there may have been more space for women in the ritual process than is often supposed. Jeremy Hutton provides a history of scholarship on the so-called Levitical cities, arguing that, although Wellhausen anticipated (and even established)

1–31; Jeremy M. Hutton, *The Transjordanian Palimpsest: The Overwritten Texts of Personal Exile and Transformation in the Deuteronomistic History* (BZAW 396; Berlin/New York: de Gruyter, 2009), 169–75; Seth L. Sanders, *The Invention of Hebrew* (Traditions; Champagne, Ill.: University of Illinois Press, 2009).

the major foci of the study of Josh 21 and 1 Chr 6, a variety of methodologies will be needed—including social-scientific criticism—to solve the enigmatic puzzle of the cities. Sarah Shectman explores the complicated status (or, better, *statuses*) of women descended from and married to priests and other members of the tribe of Levi. She demonstrates ancient Israelite women's complex network of social relations in both everyday and ritual contexts, including sexuality, mourning, and eating taboos.

A second group of four essays examines "Priests and Levites in Scriptural Context." Joel Baden analyzes the pentateuchal traditions concerning the origins of the Levites' claims to special status as devotees of Yhwh. He argues that the Yahwistic author utilized two complementary traditions of the Levites' violent origins—in one tradition, they were landless; in the other, they were completely dedicated to the service of Yhwh—to build up the J source's picture of that tribe. Cory Crawford probes the similarities and differences between the literary recollections of the temple in Jerusalem and the tabernacle in order to further understand the relationship between these two structures. Peter Altmann contrasts American and (Continental) European approaches to texts dealing with the Levites and priests, focusing on Deut 18:1–8. He concludes that each group has something to learn from the methodologies and conclusions of the other. In an excellent example of Altmann's "American approach," Stephen L. Cook combines biblical research with social-scientific investigation in order to interrogate the interaction between Deuteronomy (esp. 18:1–8) and the book of Jeremiah. He examines some of the tensions between these books' respective attempts to deal with Levites' disenfranchisement, discovering that Jeremiah's denunciation of the centralized cult in Jerusalem threatened to undo the Levites' economic and political gains that had only recently been made by the dissemination of Deuteronomy, with its pro-Levitical agenda.

Finally, the third group of essays focuses on "Priests and Levites in Exegetical Context." These essays have in common an interest in textual appropriations of Levitical and priestly traditions during the Persian and Hellenistic periods. In an essay inspired by what Altmann has called "European approaches" to priestly and Levitical texts, Mark Christian examines three biblical pericopae (Neh 8; Lev 17–26; and Deut 16:18–18:22) in redaction-critical perspective, teasing out their respective presentations of the complicated interactions among priest, prophet, and layperson. Jeffrey Stackert compares the perquisites assigned to the Levites in a few passages from Deuteronomy (notably, e.g., Deut 18:1–8) and in those passages' reformulation in the *Temple Scroll*. Stackert argues that the latter text has made several innovations, elevating the Levites' status while at the same time maintaining the strict distinction between Levites and Aaronide priests found in other biblical traditions. Finally, Mark Leuchter's concluding essay provides a reflection on the streams of tradition both received and augmented in the book of Daniel. He argues that the book occupies a medial position in a cultural development moving from a more temple-based (i.e., Levitical) mode of religious engagement to one that is more scribally centered, wherein exegesis of an increasingly solidified biblical text serves as the locus of religious engagement and authority.

The contributions to the present volume demonstrate that while the foundations laid by earlier generations of scholars remain the basis for contemporary study, new avenues of inquiry are long overdue. It is essential that the methods and perspectives informing cross-disciplinary research be brought to bear on the study of the sacerdotal cultures of ancient Israel and early Judaism as advances in archaeology, the study of law, hermeneutics, sociology and anthropology, and literary criticism forge new mechanisms for exploring the record of the past refracted through the text of the Hebrew Bible. At the same time, conversations among these disparate methods and approaches are essential. The contents of the present volume offer complementary insights even as they offer challenges to the axioms and paradigms informing each investigative enterprise. In the end, it is our hope that this volume provides not only a representative look at the state of the field regarding the study of priests and Levites but also a point of departure for future research into the place of Israel's priestly caste within the miasma of ancient Near Eastern religion, the role that these figures played in their own socio-cultural universe, and the impact they had on subsequent authors and audiences.

Part I

Priests and Levites in Social Context

Covenant Priesthood: Cross-Cultural Legal and Religious Aspects of Biblical and Hittite Priesthood

Ada Taggar-Cohen

I. The Study of Hittite Priesthood

Hittite religion existed for several centuries and during this time underwent many developments. Population migrations within the Hittite kingdom during the late fifteenth through the fourteenth/thirteenth centuries B.C.E. drastically influenced the religious configuration within the core Anatolian Hittite kingdom, as well as its territories in northern Syria. Strong Hurrian as well as Luwian influences are detected, some of which continued into the first millennium. However, these new influences did not cause the elimination of previous cultural-religious beliefs and practices of the population of Anatolia, but rather created an entwined cultural sphere for what we now term "the Hittites."[1]

In the last decade, the study of Hittite priesthood has advanced in two main directions. One is manifested in the study of texts focusing on the ancient religious centers of the old Hittite kingdom, such as the towns of Nerik, Zippalanda, Arinna, and the capital Ḫattuša, and by combining archaeological and textual evidence.[2] The other is manifested in various studies of cultic function-

---

1. In the last decade, two major volumes on Hittite religions have been published. Each attempts in its own way to outline the complicated state of evidence regarding the emergence of different religions within the Hittite Empire. See Maciej Popko, *Religions of Asia Minor* (Warsaw: Academic Publications Dialog, 1995); and Volkert Haas, *Geschichte der hethitischen Religion* (HdO; Leiden: Brill, 1994). To these books should be added several other works that include new insights into political and religious changes during Hittite history. See the short description in Billie Jean Collins, *The Hittites and Their World* (SBLABS 7; Atlanta: Society of Biblical Literature, 2007), 157–95.

2. See, e.g., Volkert Haas, *Der Kult von Nerik: Ein Beitrag zur hethitischen Religionsgeschichte* (StPohl 4; Rome: Pontifical Biblical Institute, 1970); Maciej Popko, *Zippalanda: Ein Kultzentrum im hethitischen Kleinasien* (THeth 21; Heidelberg: Winter Verlag, 1994); idem, *Arinna: Eine heilige Stadt der Hethiter* (THeth 50; Heidelberg, Winter Verlag, 2009); Peter Neve, *Hattusa: Stadt der Götter und Tempel* (Mainz: Philipp von Zabern, 1996).

aries' titles and in the editing of a large number of Hittite ritual texts.³ The great majority of Hittite texts are of a religious nature, in particular, prescriptive rituals. Historical texts regarding the priesthood are very rare, and therefore much of the description of the priesthood is based on reconstructions from cultic texts such as rituals and festivals, as well as from some administrative texts, which in most cases relate to festivals. Owing to the nature of the texts very few priests are identified by name except for the "royal priesthood," that is to say, the king, the queen, and the princes.⁴ The Hittite royal house and the kingdom's administration were responsible throughout Hittite history for the creation of a system administrating the particular Hittite amalgam of religious beliefs and practices.

II. The Main Characteristics of Hittite Priesthood

The Hittite priesthood was composed of a designated group of cultic functionaries who were held responsible for the daily care of the gods and their needs. Their designation was decided through divine selection, such as choosing by lots or by oracular means, followed by the king's approval for high-ranking priests.⁵ That is to say, the Hittite priesthood was a post appointed by the king himself or his administration. The installation of the priest manifested a special relation with his god, and it took place in a ritual context.⁶ There was a clear hierarchy within the priesthood recognized by titles such as higher- and lower-rank priests, as well as by the definition of "holy" or "sacred" priests.⁷ The rank of priests was also indicated by different kinds of

---

3. For recent publications, see the series Studien zu den Boğazköy-Texten (Wiesbaden: Harrassowitz) = StBoT; Texte der Hethiter (Heidelberg: Winter Verlag) = THeth; Eothen: Collana di studi sulle civiltà dell'Oriente antico (Florence: LoGisma Editore) = Eothen. All of these series include monographs and collections of papers. In 2006 I published a comprehensive work on Hittite priesthood with an attempt to present the basic scope of its study: Ada Taggar-Cohen, *Hittite Priesthood* (THeth 26; Heidelberg: Winter Verlag, 2006).

4. See Taggar-Cohen, *Hittite Priesthood*, 369–83.

5. For the few texts providing evidence of this procedure, see ibid., 217–26.

6. For an edition of the Hittite text of installation of a new priest, see Ada Taggar-Cohen, "The EZEN-*pulaš*: A Hittite Installation Rite of a New Priest in Light of the Installation of ᵈIM Priestess in Emar," *JANER* 2 (2002): 127–59. The installation of a Hittite priest does not indicate anointment. The only mention of anointment is that of the king as part of the ritual of his installation as a priest, as well as his coronation. See Taggar-Cohen, *Hittite Priesthood*, 226; also Ilya Yakubovich, "Were Hittite Kings Divinely Anointed?" *JANER* 5 (2005): 107–37.

7. For the title *šuppiš* ᴸᴼSANGA, see Taggar-Cohen, *Hittite Priesthood*, 148–52. The title might designate them as high priests of the main cult centers Zippalanda, Arinna and Ḫattuša as determined by Popko, *Arinna*, 68, as "Tempelherr." However, this title exists also

clothing;[8] the "holy" high priests wore a special headdress in the shape of a horned helmet, also worn by the deities.[9] The priesthood elite came from the core Anatolian towns of Zippalanda, Arinna, Nerik and Ḫattuša, which were originally Ḫattian religious centers.[10] They therefore seem to have belonged to the ancient stratum of the Anatolian religious system. Thus, the Hittites may have adopted the local priesthood when they took over central Anatolia in the seventeenth century B.C.E.[11] One of the most important aspects of Hittite priesthood, however, was the fact that they were regarded as part of the state administrative system and as such had specific obligations to the king, as well as owing dedication to the gods.

III. The Legal-Administrative Status of Hittite Priesthood as Reflected in the *Išḫiul*-Instructions Texts

As already mentioned, the Hittite priesthood was an institution that was headed by the royal family, with the king and queen as high priests, and that descended hierarchically down to the different temples throughout the kingdom.[12] It was state-controlled, and therefore priests had an obligation of loyalty to the king and were obliged to go through special legal procedures prescribed for all members of the kingdom's administration.

To induce and ensure loyalty of the administration toward them, the Hittite kings developed a device called *išḫiul-*, which dated from the late old Hittite kingdom. This was a written text prescribing the obligations of the state administration both civil and military, and upon which all had to take an oath.[13] This text was a commitment of loyalty, validated by an oath under the supervision of the gods. The *išḫiul-* procedure, which included a

---

for low-ranking sacred priests and might therefore indicate a cultic state of the priest such as that mentioned for biblical priests in Exod 19:22.

8. See regarding a priest's ranking, Taggar-Cohen, *Hittite Priesthood*, 211–14.

9. See Theo P. J. van den Hout, "Tudḫaliya IV und die Ikonographie hetitischer Grosskönige des 13. JHS," *BO* 52 (1995): 545–73. The biblical high priest headdress (מצנפת; Exod 29:6) might be compared with this special Hittite headdress.

10. See Popko, *Religions of Asia Minor*, 67–80.

11. The Hittite religion absorbed into its core the authoritative ideology of the ancient Ḫattian religious beliefs. This had implications relating to the Hittite concept of authority. See Frank Starke, "Ḫalmašuit im Anitta-Text und die hethitische Ideologie vom Königtum," *ZA* 69 (1979): 47–120.

12. See Jörg Klinger, "Zum 'Priestertum' im hethitischen Anatolien," *Hethitica* 15 (2002): 109.

13. For a new general description of these texts, see Franka Pecchioli Daddi, "Classification and New Edition of Politico-Administrative Texts," in *Acts of the Vth International Congress of Hittitology, Çorum, September 02–08, 2002* (ed. Aygül Süel; Ankara: Nokta Ofset, 2005), 599–611; idem, "Die mittelhethitischen *išḫiul*-Texte," *AoF* 32 (2005): 280–90.

detailed description of professional duties, created a bond between the servant of the state and his master the king, via a solemn oath on a written text. In Hittite research these texts describing the legal procedure for creating and maintaining loyalty are called "instructions and protocol" texts; however, they were termed *išḫiul-* by the Hittites themselves, so I therefore entitle them "*išḫiul-*instructions texts." The term *išḫiul-* meaning "obligation," "duty," "regulation," "law," or "treaty," is derived from the verb *išḫai-*, "to bind, wrap, obligate, impose upon."[14] When appearing in Hittite treaties it has been translated by the word RIKSU in Akkadian and was correlated in biblical scholarship with the word ברית, "covenant."[15] The term *išḫiul-* correlates with ברית on the basis of the hierarchical status of servitude that it implies, as seen in the terminology "master–servant."[16]

The main purpose of the biblical covenant was to make the Israelites servants of YHWH (Lev 25:22; 26:13). Similarly, the other biblical covenants indicate the status of servitude to YHWH regarding both the Israelite king and the priesthood.[17] The Hittite texts indicate this by the word written with the Sumerograph ARAD, meaning "servant/slave"; the biblical text uses the word עֶבֶד or the verbal form עָבַד, and the verb שֵׁרֵת is used in relation to the priesthood.[18] This idea of servitude has a significant correlation in the Hittite *išḫiul-*texts.

IV. The *išḫiul-*Instructions Texts for the Priesthood

The subject of interest here is the *išḫiul-*texts specifically written for the Hittite priesthood. From over twenty texts categorized today as *išḫiul-* of the administrative instruction category, four are *išḫiul-*texts for the priesthood in major cities of the Hittite kingdom: Nerik (KUB 31.113/KUB 57.36), Zippalanda (KUB 55.21/KUB 57.29), Šamuḫa (KUB 32.133), and the capital Ḫattuša (CTH 264). The longest and most complete of the four is the one for the priesthood of Ḫattuša. The first three include instructions on priestly duties, while the text for the Ḫattuša priesthood emphasizes, as well as the duties of the priests, their special relation to the divine world, which gives them the status

---

14. Jaan Puhvel, *Hittite Etymological Dictionary*, vol. 2 [E/I] (Berlin/New York: Mouton, 1984), 398–403.

15. M. Weinfeld, "*bᵉrith*," *TDOT* 2 (1975): 253–62.

16. For this statement, see Ada Taggar-Cohen, "Biblical *Covenant* and Hittite *išḫiul-* reexamined," *VT* 61 (2011): 461–88. According to the Hittite administrative system, members of the royal family owed loyalty to the king and queen, through the same device of *išḫiul-* as other people or groups, and if they received any kind of an administrative appointment such as the positions of governor or sub-king, they too had to have an *išḫiul-* with the king.

17. See the use of the term עבד for Moses (Exod 14:31; Num 12:7; Josh 12:6; etc.), David (2 Sam 7; 1 Kgs 8:24–26; Jer 33:21), and Levites (Num 8:11; etc.).

18. Exod 28:35 and passim.

of "servants of the divine." The *išḫiul*-text identifies the priesthood according to location—the city of the religious center (in the cases of Nerik and Ḫattuša), or according to the temple of the divine entity (in the case of Šamuḫa). Below is a short description of these four texts and their contents.[19]

1. The Nerik *išḫiul*- (KUB 31.113): four paragraphs can be read on the obverse of this tablet. The first paragraph instructs the priests to use water from the forest outside the city for the preparation of the god's bread. The next paragraph instructs the priests on procedures for opening and closing the temple: in the morning they must go around the temple, clean the temple grounds, and then set out bread for the god. When darkness falls they should light a lamp, close the temple, and remain in front of the door to sleep.[20]

This text, which goes back to an old tradition of the priestly duties in Nerik, includes duties and regulations dictated by the king himself. Although unfortunately the beginning of the text is missing, its language and the remaining word *išḫiul*- clearly place it in the category of *išḫiul*-instructions texts.

2. The Zipalanda *išḫiul*-text (KUB 55.21) details the priests' obligations even more clearly: "They will spread the bed for the SANGA-priest, of the Sun-goddess of the Earth, at the courtyard. He sleeps over there regularly. And this (is) his obligation [*išḫiul*-]: (making) accurately the spreading (and) sleeping. He (will) eat in front of the Sun-goddess [of Earth]."[21]

These obligations include the activities expected of the priests, but the Hittite king judiciously incorporated them in a written text, as part of the obligations his servants were required to perform toward him.

3. The *išḫiul*- to the priesthood of the temple of IŠTAR in Šamuḫa presents a case of direct involvement of the king in setting up procedures for worship to replace previous ones. The text is broken, but the remaining parts reveal detailed ritual prescriptions (KUB 32.133 lines 7–11): "Muršili the great king on the spot rewrote it: In the future when either the king or the queen or a prince or a princess come to the temple of the Deity of the Night of Šamuḫa let them perform these ceremonies. . . ." In the subsequent paragraphs of the text all ingredients and material for the rituals are listed in detail, followed by a prescriptive ritual for a priestess and a priest to be carried out in the case of the arrival of members of the royal family. The king thus set down for the priests

---

19. Even though the colophon of the first three texts was not preserved and did not include the title *ishiul*- (although the term did appear in the text), on the basis of their contents and conceptual phrasing they are clearly instructions texts. One can compare these texts with, for example, the very detailed instructions text for the Hittite king's bodyguards (CTH 262); see Hans G. Güterbock and Theo P. J. van den Hout, *The Hittite Instructions for the Royal Bodyguard* (AS 24; Chicago: The Oriental Institute of the University of Chicago, 1991).

20. For the text, see Taggar-Cohen, *Hittite Priesthood*, 179.

21. For the text, see ibid., 180–81.

the exact procedures to be followed for rituals, festivals, and daily activities in the service of this goddess.²²

4. A more detailed instructions text of *išḫiul-* is the one for the temple personnel of Ḫattuša (CTH 264), which I have entitled "Instructions for Temple Personnel."²³ This text probably represents the most elaborate *išḫiul-*text for the priesthood and should be seen as a developed edition of earlier analogue texts. Although the beginning of the text is unfortunately missing, on the basis of the genre of these *išḫiul-*texts, we surmise that it was the king who delivered these instructions. The instructional part begins by demanding the ritual purity of those who prepare the food for the gods, so as to please the gods. A special passage follows these instructions explaining the meaning of pleasing the gods. It reads as follows (lines i 21–26, 28–31):

> Is the soul of a human and of the gods any different? No!
> [Th]is certainly (is) not the case! The soul is one and the same. When a slave is present in front of his master, he (is) washed, and he has dressed in clean (clothes). Either he gives his master to eat, or he gives him to drink. Since that master of his eats or drinks, he is relaxed in his soul, [.....]
> Is the soul of the gods any different? If at some point the slave angers his master, either they kill him, or they may maltreat (= injure) his nose, his eyes (and) his ears. Or the master [will sei]ze him, his wife, his children, his brother, his sister, his in-laws, his family, his male slave or his female slave (and will punish him).²⁴

The Hittite word used here to represent the idea that I translated as "soul" is written with the Sumerogram ZI standing for "soul," "will," or "desire." The servant must please his master's ZI, that is, the will and the desire of the divine. The opposite of pleasing the divine is to anger him, and thus the Hittite text continues (lines i 34–38):

> If [som]eone angers the soul of a go[d],
> does the god seek it from that person alone?
> Does he not seek it from his wife, [his children] his [s]eed, his family,
> his male slaves, his female slaves, his cattle, his sheep, and together with his grain!
>   (Along) with everything he will ruin him.
> Be ver[y mu]ch afraid regarding a matter of a god.

---

22. For the text, see Taggar-Cohen, *Hittite Priesthood*, 307–8; see also J. L. Miller, *Studies in the Origins, Development and Interpretation of the Kizzuwatna Rituals* (StBoT 46; Wiesbaden: Harrassowitz, 2004), 312–19. For an interpretation of this text in light of Exodus 19–24 see Ada Taggar-Cohen, "Violence at the Birth of Religion: Exodus 19–40 in Light of Ancient Near Eastern Texts," *Journal of the Interdisciplinary Study of Monotheistic Religions* 1 (2005): 101–16.

23. For the latest edition of the text, see Taggar-Cohen, *Hittite Priesthood*, 33–107, and on its legal aspects, ibid., 129–35.

24. For the text, see ibid., 41, 71.

The "Instructions for Temple Personnel" continues with the following topics relating to the priestly office: the importance of celebrating festivals on time, providing a list of festival names; the priests' responsibility to care for food and beverages for the gods; the responsibility of guarding the temple; permission to enter the temple precinct; prohibition regarding the misuse of the temple's wealth, including warnings regarding any kind of cheating having to do with temple possessions, which also belong to the gods; and permission to prepare sacrifices and eat of them (the priests serving the gods should eat the sacred food). There are also instructions regarding fire, fields, animal breeding for sacrifices, and so on.[25]

The Hittite texts show that the priest holds his position, on the one hand, because he was chosen by the divinity whom he is to serve, but, on the other hand, because he was also nominated by the Hittite king himself, validated through the *išḫiul-* procedure. The Hittite priest thus had a special status, being a direct servant of the gods, and in many cases a servant of a specific god as well; the priest was committed to the service of the divine world but received orders regarding duties from the king, who was acting as the highest authority, an authority he received from the gods themselves.

V. Biblical Priesthood in Comparison

Just as the description of the Hittite priesthood relies on textual evidence from a period of some four hundred years, the description of biblical priesthood is based on various sources and reflects different historical periods. In both cases we find characteristics that relate to the status, formation, and practices of the respective priesthoods. In the Bible we find texts dealing with the designation and dedication of the priests, as well as texts describing historical events in which priests were involved. For our purpose these texts will be considered as evidence derived from a single source.[26]

In contrast to the Hittite institution, biblical priesthood has already been studied and described in great detail. Biblical priests represent a separate group of divinely chosen people, whose status is determined by oracular means and by divine decree (Num 17), declared in two ways: a legal endowment in which the word ברית is used (Num 18), and a ritual of dedication to their work (Exod 29 and Num 8). In Num 3–4 the duties of the Levites concerning care of the tent of meeting are prescribed, and in different chapters in Leviticus the priests are instructed in great detail on how to conduct rituals and sacrifices. Among the biblical texts, only Num 18 seems to suggest clearly the special covenantal status of both groups, priests and Levites, indicating their relations with the

---

25. For a summary of the priestly duties as instructed in CTH 264 in comparison with other Hittite texts, see Tagger-Cohen, *Hittite Priesthood*, 437–44.

26. Most of the material compared derives from the biblical Priestly texts (P).

divine. In this regard, biblical priesthood shares similar characteristics with the Hittite institution, as follows:

1. The priests, being a privileged group serving the divine, have as their duty to please the deity. The Hittite priests' duty is to please the god's soul, written with the Sumerogram ZI, meaning "will" or "desire." The biblical text has an interesting parallel to this concept with the word רצון, which also means the "will" or "desire" of God, such as sacrifices that will be favored by him (Exod 28:38; Lev 22:20–21; Isa 56:7; 60:7; Jer 6:20; Ps 40:9; 143:10).

2. Biblical priests are expected to fear and show reverence to the divine, as evident in Mal 2:5: "I had with him a covenant of life and well-being, which I gave to him, and of reverence, which he showed me. For he stood in awe of my name."[27]

3. The opposite of the biblical רצון is חמה קצף or כעס—that is, the "anger" or "wrath" of God. In the Hittite text, if reverence is not shown to the gods and the priests sin by not fulfilling their obligations, their punishment might be severe, even as severe as death to the sinner and all his seed. In Exod 30:17–21 the priests were warned that they would die unless they purified themselves before making the sacrifices: "they shall wash their hands and feet that they may not die. It shall be a law for all time for them, for him and his offspring, throughout the ages." Similarly, in Num 18, a text that should be regarded as representing the instruction of the temple personnel in the Bible, the last phrase warns "but you must not profane the sacred donations of the Israelites, lest you die" (v. 32).

In the Hittite instructions text we find: "If some wooden or clay utensils you hold, (and) a pig (or) a dog somehow touches (them), but the kitchen attendant does not dispose of it, so that, that man, from a defiled (vessel) gives the gods to eat; to that one the gods will give excrement (and) urine to eat (and) drink" (CTH 264 iii 64–68).[28] Compare this with Mal 2:2–3: "If you do not obey, and you do not honor my name . . . I will put your seed under a ban, and I will strew dung upon your faces, the dung of your festal sacrifices."

4. The fact that punishment is mentioned in the biblical text makes the biblical priesthood similar to the Hittite priesthood, in the sense that in both cultures breaking loyalty to the divine, on the one hand, and the king, on the other, by not fulfilling the instructions, is regarded as a sin and deserves punishment. There are various degrees of punishment in the Hittite text, from a warning or fine, to injury, and up to capital punishment for the sinner and even the annihilation of his house.

---

27. The Hittite text CTH 264 warns several times "be very much afraid of the will of the god" (Hittite verb naḫḫ-; i 38, ii 29, 34, ii 57), and once instructs, "maintain great reverence (regarding) the thick bread and the libation vessel of the gods" (iii 58).

28. For the text, see Taggar-Cohen, *Hittite Priesthood,* 61–62, 80–81.

In the biblical text we find punishment delivered by god in the terminology יָמוּת, "he shall die," whereas, when the sin is one of violation of authority (which Jacob Milgrom puts under "encroachment"[29]) the verb used is (pausal) יוּמָת, "he shall be put to death," equal to the Hittite "it is a capital penalty" (CTH 264 ii 50, 55; iii 83).[30]

In the Bible, the story of Ahimelek, the priest of Nob (1 Sam 21) who was punished for disloyalty to King Saul, is one example.[31] Another is Abiathar, the priest of David who was expelled by the latter's son Solomon for being loyal to Adonijah (1 Kgs 2:26). The punishment of the house of Eli of Shiloh is a case of disloyalty to the divine and of not acting according to משפט הכהנים (1 Sam 2:13).[32] The Hebrew word משפט is used in parallel meaning to ברית, in presenting the way the ברית is processed (Lev 26:15; Deut 7:12; Josh 24:25). Thus, the combination מִשְׁפַּט הַמְּלֻכָה (1 Sam 10:25) stands in parallel to the ברית of the kingship (2 Kgs 11) and has been translated as the "protocol" or "regulation" of kingship, or the "laws of kingship." The term *išḫiul-*, too, is translated "treaty," "laws," or "regulations," and has even been translated as "protocol."[33]

5. Both Hittite and biblical priests have their ritual activities prescribed by the divine, through the highest political authority: the king in the case of the Hittites, and, in the Pentateuch, Moses, who functioned as the political leader to whom the priesthood owed obedience. Moses appointed Aaron and his sons to the priesthood,[34] and the Levites to support them.

In the Israelite historical context, the priesthood is clearly an administrative post and part of the kingdom's administration. David, Solomon, and Jeroboam all install priests at the beginning of their kingship (respectively, Abiathar and Zadok together [2 Sam 8:17], the reappointment of Zadok alone [1 Kgs 2:27, 35; 1 Chr 18:16; but cf. 1 Kgs 4:4], and unnamed priests in 1 Kgs

---

29. Jacob Milgrom, *Numbers* במדבר: *The Traditional Hebrew Text with the New JPS Translation* (JPS Torah Commentary; New York: Jewish Publication Society, 1990), 40.

30. For more on the similarity of the concept of punishment in both cultures, see Jacob Milgrom, "The Shared Custody of the Tabernacle and a Hittite Analogy," *JAOS* 90 (1970): 208–9.

31. The punishment was the annihilation of the entire priesthood of Nob. See Ada Taggar-Cohen, "Political Loyalty in the Biblical Account of 1 Samuel xx–xxii in Light of Hittite Texts," *VT* 55 (2005): 251–68.

32. For a parallel to the Hittite priestly "law" or "regulations" regarding the duty to sleep overnight next to the divine, note 1 Sam 3:3.

33. Translating the term *išḫiul-* regarding the rules applied to Kurunta king of Tarḫuntašša as a sub-king to the great king of Ḫatti; Gary Beckman, *Hittite Diplomatic Texts* (2nd ed.; SBLWAW 7; Atlanta: Society of Biblical Literature, 1999), 108.

34. Although it seems that Aaron had already been some kind of a priest in Egypt, and Moses appointed him as a priest for Yhwh. See the reference to Aaron "the Levite" (Exod 4:14), as well as the origins of the house of Eli in Egypt according to 1 Sam 2:27. For an ancient priestly house adopted by a new regime, compare my note above regarding the ancient religious centers of Ḫatti.

12). Another occasion on which the servile relationship of the priesthood to kingship is apparent is the coup d'état of Jehoiada the high priest against Queen Athaliah (2 Kgs 11; 2 Chr 23). The priest showed the young prince Jehoash to the other priests and formalized a ברית with them. After the prince was enthroned, another ברית was formalized between the people and the king and between the king and the people and their god. The priest Jehoiada remained loyal to the line of David.[35]

VI. Priesthood as an Administrative Post

I offer here a specific example to illustrate the status of the priesthood in the two cultures as an administrative nomination, although clearly chosen by the divine.

The Hittite king was chosen by the gods for kingship, but first he had to be chosen as a servant of the gods, thus becoming a priest. As a prince, he was the priest of a specific god or goddess, who was regarded as his divine guardian, and who would guide him throughout his political life.[36] As he assumed different positions in the kingdom, he became priest to other gods as well. Ḫattušili III tells of being chosen at a young age by the goddess Ištar, who informed his father, the great king of Ḫatti, of her choice through a dream to his brother Muwatalli. Ḫattušili served as a priest to the goddess, who in exchange facilitated his way to the throne of Ḫatti. When he became the king of Nerik and Ḫakmiš, a post given to him by his brother, who was then the great king, he also became a priest to the important Storm God of Nerik.[37] As the great king of Ḫatti, Ḫattušili himself chose the next priest to the goddess Ištar, declaring his son, the future king Tudḫaliya IV, as the priest. His investiture is announced as follows:

> This son whom I [gav]e for priestship and a house (I gave) for the service of Ištar of [Šam]uḫa, let him, with his son, his grandson, and his descendants, my seed, hold it (as) the priestly office for Ištar of Šamuḫa.

This investiture is followed by a warning to anyone who would dare to reject this installation for priesthood. The king then allots land to the temple of the goddess:

---

35. For whether there is one covenant bond or two, see the commentary for these verses in Mordechai Cogan and Hayim Tadmor, *II Kings: A New Translation with Introduction and Commentary* (AB 11; New York: Doubleday, 1988), 132–33.

36. For a detailed description of the Hittite princes who appear in the texts as priests, see Taggar-Cohen, *Hittite Priesthood*, 373–77.

37. Following the text "The Apology of Ḫattušili III," translated by Theo J. P. van den Hout (*COS* 1.77:199–204).

The property of Armatarḫunta, which I gave to her (i.e., the goddess) and whatever settlements were Armatarḫunta's, behind every single cult monument they will erect her (statue) and they will pour a vessel. (For) Ištar (is) my goddess and they will worship her as Ištar the High. The mausoleum which I made myself, I handed it over to the goddess, (and) I handed over to you in subservience my son Tudḫaliya as well. Let Tudḫaliya, my son, administer the house of Ištar! I (am) the servant of the goddess, let him be servant of the goddess as well!³⁸

In the Bible, the case of Aaron and Moses is similar to that of the Hittite king and his chosen son. Moses, to whom Yhwh was revealed first, imposes the priestship to Yhwh on his own kin, a brother rather than a son, and builds a special place for that purpose.³⁹ The hereditary line continues through Aaron's offspring (e.g., Num 25:10–13): "Phinehas, son of Eleazar son of Aaron the priest, has turned back My wrath (חמה) from the Israelites. . . . Say, therefore, 'I grant him My covenant of friendship. It shall be for him and his descendants after him a covenant of priesthood for all time (ברית כהנת עולם), because he took impassioned action for his God, thus making expiation for the Israelites." It was Moses who decreed the bequest of this priesthood.

The issue of priestly prerogatives, including allotment of lands to the temple to be used by the priests, has been previously examined in the aforementioned cases by Moshe Weinfeld.⁴⁰ Biblical priesthood is presented as exclusively hereditary (although likely was not, at first⁴¹), as seen in the history of the Judean kingdom, and probably in the northern kingdom as well (Judg 18:30). In the Hittite texts there is no direct mention regarding legal rights in the priesthood transferred by heredity; however, this can be assumed on the basis of priestly houses mentioned as belonging to several generations, as well as the Hittite usage of the title "son/daughter of the priest." It seems likely that priestly families belonged to a certain temple and remained in their towns of origin.⁴²

---

38. Ibid., 204. The appointment ends with a "vindication clause" assuring the decedents of Tudḫaliya, or more precisely, of Ḫattušili and Puduḫepa, the role of priesthood administrating the temple of Ištar, granting them freedom from levy and corveé. Similarly, the Aaronide priests are protected from encroachers (Num 18:4, 7).

39. Challenging Moses and Aaron was considered to be a rebellion against God, and a sin to be punished by annihilation, as is clear from Num 16.

40. Moshe Weinfeld, *Social Justice in Ancient Israel and in the Ancient Near East* (Publications of the Perry Foundation for Biblical Research in the Hebrew University of Jerusalem; Jerusalem: Magnes, 1995), 97–139.

41. See, e.g., Lawrence E. Stager, "The Archaeology of the Family in Ancient Israel," *BASOR* 260 (1985): 1–35.

42. Popko describes the cult centers of the Hittite kingdom in relation to the priesthood of the capital Ḫattuša (*Religions of Asia Minor*, 144–47). These cult centers, regarded as gods' cities, had temples that owned much land and were exempted from taxes.

VII. A Word of Caution Concerning the Comparative Approach

Comparing the biblical and Hittite texts might also have its pitfalls. In a couple of cases Jacob Milgrom has compared the "Instructions for Temple Personnel" (CTH 264) to the biblical texts. Regarding the priesthood, Milgrom's attempt to show that the biblical division into priests and Levites had its roots in the second-millennium priestly conduct of the Hittites[43] has to be reconsidered. His most elaborate comparison was in using the text to explain the different tasks of the groups of priests and Levites as guards of the tabernacle. According to Milgrom's reading of the Hittite text, the Hittite priests, like their biblical counterparts, were divided into two groups of guards, those who guarded inside the precinct—the priests—and those who guarded outside the precinct—the Levites—thus suggesting that a certain group was not allowed to enter the precinct.

The Hittite text indicates two kinds of guarding tasks: the guarding of the inner parts of the temple by the priests, patrolling the temple grounds in shifts and sleeping through the night inside the temple at the door to the shrine (indicated in the texts as "sleeping with the god"), and guard duty outside the temple by the *ḫaliyatalla-men* ("watchers"), who were troops assigned by the king to guard the temples in certain towns.[44] These troops did not belong to the temples and may not have been located in every city in the country, but only in big towns where there were a large number of temples, such as Ḫattuša. The priests were responsible for admitting the *ḫaliyatalla-men* to their posts every evening, while they themselves guarded the temple's inner parts. This text, therefore, does not make a distinction between the two priestly groups, that is to say, those who protected the temple from the outside and took care of the utensils, and those who protected it from the inside, but distinguishes between priests and professional guardsmen. According to the Nerik *išḫiul*-text, the priests had to walk around the temple to check it in the morning before they opened it, but there is no mention of them guarding it through the night from the outside, only the inside.

The Hittite priesthood according to this text (CTH 264) identifies the priesthood using a general term "Temple Men," under which there are three types of priests: two male priests (SANGA-priest and GUDU$_{12}$-priest), and a female type of priestess (AMA.DINGER^{LIM}-priestess). All three were responsible

---

43. Milgrom, "Shared Custody," 204–9.

44. See Richard H. Beal, *The Organisation of the Hittite Military* (THeth 20; Heidelberg: Winter Verlag, 1992), 252–54. The temples were the property of the gods donated by the king, and they housed treasures that were administered by the royal court, as clearly described in CTH 264 ii 34–47.

for the protection of the temple, but only the male priests were responsible for the night guard.⁴⁵

Another division between temple personnel arises from the colophon of this text. The colophon declares that the *išḫiul-* is for the following groups: "Temple-Men," "kitchen attendants of all the gods," "farmers of the gods," and "cowherds and shepherds of the god." There was a division between the priests, termed in this text "Temple-Men"⁴⁶ and those who prepared and served food during the rituals. The cult functionaries called "kitchen attendants," including the "cupbearer, table-man, cook, baker, and beer brewer," were neither guards of the temple nor priests, but participated in all rituals inside the precinct and before the gods. In Hittite temples the cult functionaries differed on the basis of hierarchy, and not, as in the biblical text, on the basis of graded holiness.⁴⁷

The Hittite texts do not mention a concept of a sacred precinct but rather stress the threshold of the temple as indicating the entrance to a sacred area.⁴⁸ Worshipers were allowed to enter that area to present their sacrifice to the gods, as well as foreigners.⁴⁹ In this regard the biblical rules were the same.⁵⁰

VIII. Conclusion

The Hittite *išḫiul-* was a legal procedure for organizing the administration of the Hittite kingdom. It reflected hierarchical authority, where the Hittite king was first and all others were in his service, be they vassal kings or the core Hittite administration, which included the priesthood. The priesthood however, had a special task because the priests came into contact with the divine world and served it personally, thus guaranteeing the safety of the king and the prosperity of the Hittite kingdom. Its regulations therefore had to be strict and clear, and thus were prescribed in detail in the different texts of *išḫiul-* as mentioned above. Their commitment to the king could not be separated from their commitment to the gods, since all temples were regarded as royal property. Their punishment too would come from the divine, but if caught cheating they would be punished by the royal court, as clearly indicated in the text.

Biblical covenants with the priesthood had exactly the same idea of servitude directly to the god, while the appointment and installation into priesthood

---

45. A detailed explanation appears in Taggar-Cohen, *Hittite Priesthood*, 126.
46. For this title, see ibid., 279–311.
47. For biblical holiness, see Philip P. Jenson, *Graded Holiness: A Key to the Priestly Conception of the World* (JSOTSup 106; Sheffield: JSOT Press, 1992), 115–48.
48. The Hittite word *ḫali-* translated in the past as "precinct" should be translated "(night) watch." See Puhvel, *Hittite Etymological Dictionary*, vol. 3 [Ḫ], 24–26; and Johannes Friedrich and Annelies Kammenhuber, *Hethitesche Wörterbuch*, vol. III/2 [Ḫ] (Heidelberg: Winter Verlag, 1991), 41–43.
49. Taggar-Cohen, *Hittite Priesthood*, 127.
50. Milgrom, "Shared Custody," 205, 207–8 n. 25.

were conducted by the political authority, the leader Moses or, in later historical texts, by the kings.

The ברית of the priesthood, as it is termed in Num 18 and 25, is not to be compared legally with a "royal grant," as has long been argued in biblical scholarship;[51] it was more an administrative appointment with the expectation of total loyalty in return, as required from all the king's servants. Although the priests were loyal to the king, they were fulfilling their obligations to his God. All prerogatives they received were part of their priestly status. This post of priesthood included fear of the divine and its wrath. Although the Hittite procedure of the *išḫiul-* includes the taking of an oath, it is not described in the Hittite text itself. Nor is taking an oath mentioned in the biblical texts regarding the priesthood; however, it is implied in both cultures with the notion of punishment should the covenant, or the *išḫiul-*, be violated: "be very much afraid of the will of the god," demands the Hittite text repeatedly.

---

51. Moshe Weinfeld, "The Covenant of Grant in the Old Testament and in the Ancient Near East," *JAOS* 90 (1970): 202–3. The conditional aspect of the post is evident in the administrative appointments of royalty in the Hittite kingdom. For a long discussion denying the unconditionality of land grants in the ancient Near East, see already Gary N. Knoppers, "Ancient Near Eastern Royal Grants and the Davidic Covenant: A Parallel?" *JAOS* 116 (1996): 686–94.

Who Is Sacrificing at Shiloh?
The Priesthoods of Ancient Israel's Regional Sanctuaries

Susan Ackerman

I. The Anomalies of the Shilonite Priesthood

Scholars have often noted that in 1 Sam 1:1–2:26, the story of the birth of the great priest-prophet Samuel and of his being dedicated to cultic service at the hill-country shrine of Shiloh, the nature and duties of the Shilonite priesthood are characterized in somewhat curious ways. For example, and most obviously, 1 Sam 1:1–2:26 assumes that Hannah's son Samuel can be allowed to join the ranks of Shiloh's priests, even though he does not come from the Levitical lineage that biblical tradition otherwise insists is required of priestly authorities.[1] Likewise anomalous is the mechanism that 1 Sam 2:13–14 presumes for determining the part of the sacrificial animal allotted for priestly consumption. According to that text, the priest (or his attendant) would come to someone who was boiling the animal's meat for the post-sacrificial meal, stick a fork into the cooking pot, and fish out whatever piece providence might provide. Elsewhere in the Bible, though, the portions of a sacrificial animal that are to be allotted to a priest are specified: for instance, the animal's shoulder, its two jowls, and its stomach, according to Deut 18:3. Leviticus 7:28–36 also designates specific, albeit different, parts of the animal as the priestly share.[2]

Elsewhere in the Bible, too, one of the main duties assigned to the priesthood is to perform the altar rituals of blood and fat manipulation that dedicate these portions of a sacrificial animal to Yahweh. This is especially attested in texts that stem from Jerusalem's priestly communities, for example, texts in Lev 1–7 that are attributed to P and texts in the related Holiness Code in Lev 17–26 (see, e.g., Lev 1:5, 8, 11–12, 15; 3:1–17; 7:22–27; 17:1–7; see also, elsewhere in P and in related sources, Num 18:17 and Ezek 44:7, 15).[3] Texts from

---

1. See, e.g., Hector Avalos, *Illness and Health Care in the Ancient Near East: The Role of the Temple in Greece, Mesopotamia, and Israel* (HSM 54; Atlanta: Scholars Press, 1995), 330.
2. Ibid., 331.
3. Patrick D. Miller, *The Religion of Ancient Israel* (Library of Ancient Israel; London: SPCK; Louisville: Westminster John Knox, 2000), 165, 170–71. On the precise nature of

Deuteronomy, although they are not as overwhelmingly emphatic, similarly suggest that the parts of the sacrificial ritual enacted at Yahweh's altar were a priestly obligation. Thus, according to Deut 10:8, it is the members of Israel's priestly tribe, the Levites, who have been designated by divine decree "to stand before Yahweh and minister to him" (see similarly Deut 18:5, 7), and Deut 26:4 specifically speaks of a Levite's taking a basket of vegetative offerings that an Israelite brings to the sanctuary and placing it beside Yahweh's altar on that worshiper's behalf. The so-called Last Words of Moses, a poetic text embedded in Deuteronomy's prose in Deut 33:1–29, further affirms the Levites' role in presenting burnt offerings on Yahweh's altar (v. 10). In the Deuteronomistic History,[4] too, the special role of the Levites (or, more specifically, of Moses as the Levites' progenitor) as the ones who perform the rites of altar service that are part of the sacrificial ritual is articulated. Most notably for our purposes, this role is stressed in 1 Sam 2:28, a text that is part of a fairly heavy-handed editorial addition (1 Sam 2:27–36) that was appended to 1 Sam 1:1–2:26 in the late seventh century B.C.E. by the Deuteronomistic Historian(s), as part of the Historian's/Historians' project of bringing the Samuel narratives in line with the book of Deuteronomy's agenda of cult centralization:[5] "I chose

---

the relation of Ezekiel to the Priestly writer(s) and the larger Priestly school, see Menahem Haran, "Ezekiel, P, and the Priestly School," *VT* 58 (2008): 211–18.

4. As a major strain in biblical scholarship would posit, I understand the so-called Deuteronomistic History to have been rendered in a "first edition" at the end of the seventh century B.C.E., in ca. 620–610, and in a "second," or "revised edition" a few decades later, in ca. 580 B.C.E. See Frank Moore Cross, "The Themes of the Book of Kings and the Structure of the Deuteronomistic History," in idem, *Canaanite Myth and Hebrew Epic: Essays in the History of the Religion of Israel* (Cambridge, Mass.: Harvard University Press, 1973), 274–89; Richard Elliot Friedman, "From Egypt to Egypt: Dtr^1 and Dtr^2," in *Traditions in Transformation: Turning Points in Biblical Faith* (ed. Baruch Halpern and Jon D. Levenson; Winona Lake, Ind.: Eisenbrauns, 1981), 167–92; idem, *The Exile and Biblical Narrative: The Formation of the Deuteronomistic and Priestly Works* (HSM 22; Chico, Calif.: Scholars Press, 1981), 1–26; and Richard D. Nelson, *The Double Redaction of the Deuteronomistic History* (JSOTSup 18; Sheffield: JSOT Press, 1981), passim, but esp. 13–28, 119–28. For other scholars who hold this view, see the bibliography assembled by David Miano, *Shadow on the Steps: Time Measurement in Ancient Israel* (SBLRBS 64; Atlanta: Society of Biblical Literature, 2010), 5 n. 10.

5. See P. Kyle McCarter, who writes of 1 Sam 2:27–36 as "replete with the devices and clichés of the . . . historian" (*I Samuel: A New Translation with Introduction and Commentary* [AB 8; Garden City, N.Y.: Doubleday, 1980], 92); see similarly Marc Brettler, "The Composition of 1 Samuel 1–2," *JBL* 116 (1997): 665: "2:27–36 is . . . a secondary, Deuteronomistic addition . . . full of Deuteronomistic language and ideology"; also John T. Willis, who lists 1 Sam 2:27–36 as among "relatively the latest passages" in 1 and 2 Samuel, texts that he further characterizes as having "*some* affinities in thought and expression with Dt [i.e., Deuteronomy]" ("An Anti-Elide Narrative Tradition from a Prophetic Circle at the Ramah Sanctuary," *JBL* 90 [1971]: 288 n. 3). But see, specifically in response to Brettler, Gary Rendsburg, "Some False Leads in the Identification of Late Biblical Hebrew Texts: The

him [Moses]," Yahweh is said to proclaim, "out of all the tribes of Israel to be my priest [and] to go up to my altar." Yet in the preceding account in 1 Sam 1:1–2:26, there is no description of a priest being present at the Shiloh sanctuary's altar in any context, and certainly not in order to perform the rite of blood manipulation that is a key priestly function according to other texts (perhaps this was not a part of Shilonite ritual?). Priestly engagement with a sacrificial animal's fat is, conversely, mentioned in 1 Sam 1:1–2:26, but only in a passage that recounts the scandalous behavior of Hophni and Phinehas, the two priestly scions of Shiloh's chief priest, Eli. More specifically, this text, 1 Sam 2:15–16, describes Hophni and Phinehas as attempting inappropriately to claim the priestly allotment of the sacrificial meat before the fat owed to Yahweh had properly been burned.

Moreover, even if the fat-burning ritual had been properly engaged in 1 Sam 2:15–16, the text does not seem to presume that priestly agents would have performed this act. To be sure, it might initially appear that the third-person masculine plural verb used twice (in both 2:15 and 2:16) to describe the burning (יַקְטִרוּן; "and they burned...") associates the fat-burning responsibility with Eli's two sons, since they are the subjects of the larger pericope of 1 Sam 2:12–17. But upon closer inspection, the referent of "they" in 2:15 and 2:16 seems less than grammatically clear, so much so that translators often avoid the pronoun's ambiguities by using the passive voice (see, e.g., the NRSV rendering of 2:15, "Before the fat had been burned...," or P. Kyle McCarter's rendering of 2:16 in his Anchor Bible commentary on 1 Samuel, "Let the fat be burned...").[6] McCarter also points out that in the Dead Sea Scrolls, the ambiguity of 2:16 was addressed through expansion, in order to read decisively יקטר הכהן, "let the priest burn [the fat]."[7] Yet this clarifying expansion seems almost special pleading in the Dead Sea Scrolls tradition, whose parent community's priestly biases are well known: an admission on the part of the Dead Sea Scrolls' priestly transmitters that, without further elaboration, the ambiguities of 1 Sam 2:15 and 16 might allow these verses to be interpreted as assigning the responsibility for the burning of the fat of Shiloh's sacrificial offerings to non-priestly worshipers. And in fact, the nearest plural antecedent of יַקְטִרוּן in 1 Sam 2:15 and 16 is not the priestly pair Hophni and Phinehas, but

---

Case of Genesis 24 and 1 Samuel 2:27–36," *JBL* 121 (2002): 35–45. For further discussion of Brettler's and Rendsburg's arguments, see Mark Leuchter, "Something Old, Something Older: Reconsidering 1 Sam. 2:27–36," *JHS* 4 (2002–3): art. 6: published online at http://ejournals.library.ualberta.ca/index.php/jhs/article/view/5855.

6. McCarter, *I Samuel*, 77. Other translators who render in the passive in 2:15 include the JB, the NEB, the REB, the NJPS, and the RSV; in both 2:15 and 2:16, Hans Wilhelm Hertzberg, *I and II Samuel* (OTL; Philadelphia: Westminster, 1964), 32; David Toshio Tsumura, *The First Book of Samuel* (NICOT; Grand Rapids/Cambridge, U.K.: Eerdmans, 2007), 153–54 and n. 91 on p. 153.

7. McCarter, *I Samuel*, 79.

כל־ישראל, or the Israelites. Thus, Georg Braulik concludes that 1 Sam 2:15–16 does not "create the impression that it was a priest who usually 'smoked' [i.e., burned the fat] as if it was his right."[8]

More generally, Richard D. Nelson writes in his study of the Israelite priesthood that at Shiloh, "Eli and his sons ... played no special role in the sacrificial ritual except to collect their tariff (1 Sam 2:13–14),"[9] and Aelred Cody similarly remarks, "The priesthood at Shiloh ... had no monopoly on sacrifice, for we know that Samuel's father Elkanah sacrificed as a pilgrim to the sanctuary they frequented."[10] Indeed, 1 Sam 1:4–5 speaks of Elkanah *only* in its comments describing the offering of a שלמים sacrifice and the subsequent apportioning of the slaughtered animal's meat,[11] and 1 Sam 2:13 similarly speaks of a non-priestly agent—a כל־איש, or "someone," whom the passage clearly differentiates from Shiloh's priests—as making a שלמים sacrifice at Shiloh and then overseeing the cooked meat's distribution.[12] Likewise, 1 Sam 1:25 (although this is a textually confused verse) recounts how a bull that had been brought to Shiloh on behalf of Elkanah's household as an offering was slaughtered without there being any mention of a priest's presence. Furthermore, even after the slaughter, no priest is said to be present to attend to the presentation at Shiloh's altar of the animal's fat and (if this was included in the Shilonite ritual) its blood. Nor is any priest on hand to attend to the grain offering of an ephah of flour that 1 Sam 1:24 identifies as a sacrificial offering that accompanied the bull's slaughter, even though other biblical texts (e.g., Lev 2:2, 8) require a priest to bring such an offering to Yahweh's altar and burn a designated portion of it there. Certainly, the priest Eli is not on hand to deal with these altar rites according to 1 Sam 1:25, as he is sought out only after the sacrifice and, presumably, its attendant rituals had been completed.[13]

How might we explain these anomalies in 1 Sam 1:1–2:26 regarding priestly altar service and the priesthood's sacrificial responsibilities? The most

---

8. Georg Braulik, "Were Women, Too, Allowed to Offer Sacrifices in Israel? Observations on the Meaning and Festive Form of Sacrifice in Deuteronomy," *Hervormde teologiese studies* 55 (1999): 921.

9. Richard D. Nelson, *Raising Up a Faithful Priest: Community and Priesthood in Biblical Theology* (Louisville: Westminster John Knox, 1993), 46–47.

10. Aelred Cody, *A History of Old Testament Priesthood* (AnBib 35; Rome: Pontifical Biblical Institute, 1969), 72.

11. Elkanah's sacrifice is described in 1 Sam 1:3 using the term לזבח, which means, literally, "to slaughter [an animal for sacrifice]," but even more specifically means "to slaughter [an animal as a שלמים offering]": see Gary A. Anderson, "Sacrifice and Sacrificial Offerings (OT)," *ABD* 5:873b, 878b; similarly Jacob Milgrom, *Leviticus: A New Translation with Introduction and Commentary* (3 vols.; AB 3, 3A, 3B; New York: Doubleday, 1991–2000), 1: 218.

12. The sacrificer is described as זָבַח זֶבַח, which we can render most literally (see preceding note) as "slaughtering a שלמים sacrifice."

13. Contra Philip F. Esler, "The Role of Hannah in 1 Samuel 1:1–2:21: Understanding a Biblical Narrative in Its Ancient Context," *Kontexte der Schrift* 2 (2005): 33.

common answer is to respond by reference to time. Thus, many scholars argue that the priesthood seems significantly divorced from the execution of sacrifices at Shiloh because this sanctuary space dates—or at least is presented in the biblical text as dating—from the earliest period of Israelite history, during which it could be supposed that an organized priesthood had not fully established its rights pertaining to sacrificial service. Nelson, for example, cites the Shiloh account in 1 Sam 1:1–2:26 specifically when he writes, "The priestly role changed considerably over the course of... historical development," and "at first, the principal priestly function was not sacrifice."[14] Saul M. Olyan likewise mentions 1 Sam 1:1–2:26 in conjunction with his suggestion that texts that he would date to the period of the "early monarchy" "are not much concerned about whether professional priests performed every priestly function," including the rites of sacrifice. But "over the course of the monarchic period and the exile (the 10th through 6th centuries B.C.E.)," Olyan continues, "the relatively open priesthood... became a closed, strictly hereditary elite exercising greater control of the cult."[15] For example, by the early sixth century B.C.E., Ezek 44:11 has even assigned to priests the role of slaughtering the sacrificial animal before the portions to be devoted to the deity were brought to the altar.[16]

I certainly agree that the priesthood's responsibilities and roles developed and evolved during the era of Israel's preexilic history to which Nelson's and Olyan's comments are directed. Nevertheless, it is my contention in what follows that the operative category for explaining the Shilonite priesthood's lack of engagement with sacrificial ritual in 1 Sam 1:1–2:26 is not *time*, but *space*. More specifically, it is my contention that throughout the course of Israel's preexilic history, priests at ancient Israel's regional or provincial sanctuaries (which I would define as sanctuaries located within a reasonable distance—about a day's walk, give or take—from worshipers' homes) were significantly divorced from the execution of these sanctuaries' sacrificial rituals, and this in contradistinction to priests' engagement in these same sacrificial rituals at large, state-sponsored temples.[17] These would include, preeminently, the state-sponsored temple in Jerusalem that is the subject of both our priestly sources'

---

14. Nelson, *Raising Up a Faithful Priest*, 11; see similarly Cody, *History of Old Testament Priesthood*, 73–74.

15. Saul M. Olyan, "Religious Personnel: Israel," in *Religions of the Ancient World: A Guide* (ed. Sarah Iles Johnston; Cambridge, Mass./London: Harvard University Press, 2004), 298.

16. Saul M. Olyan, *Rites and Rank: Hierarchy in Biblical Representations of Cult* (Princeton: Princeton University Press, 2000), 19.

17. See similarly Phyllis Bird: "The local shrine represents the simplest form of cultic leadership, invested in a resident priest—and his family—while the Temple cultus occupies the other end of the spectrum, with its elaborate, graded system of special orders and offices" ("The Place of Women in the Israelite Cultus," in *Ancient Israelite Religion: Essays in*

and Deuteronomy's sacrificial injunctions, but also the two state-sponsored temples of the northern kingdom at Dan and Bethel and state-sponsored temples that were located within border fortresses and/or in border towns such as Arad, Beersheba, Geba, and Benjaminite Mizpah.[18]

II. Ancient Israel's Regional Sanctuaries

As is surely clear from what I have so far intimated, I would take Shiloh to be among preexilic Israel's regional or provincial sanctuaries, although I must admit that the biblical evidence in this regard is mixed, as there are countervailing traditions that identify Shiloh as the central sanctuary of "all Israel" during the Israelites' premonarchic era. Let us turn first, then, to what I would consider a more clear-cut example of a preexilic place of worship that is (at best) regional in its scope, the small-scale shrine (according to 1 Sam 9:22, only about thirty people worshiped there) at which Samuel is described as ministering in 1 Sam 9:11–14, 19, 22–25. This shrine is located perhaps—if it is to be equated with the shrine that Samuel is said to found in 1 Sam 7:17—in Samuel's family's hometown of Benjaminite Ramah.[19]

Honor of Frank Moore Cross [ed. Patrick D. Miller, Paul D. Hanson, and S. Dean McBride; Philadelphia: Fortress, 1987], 403).

18. Regarding state-sponsored temples at border fortresses and/or within border towns, see Miller, *Religion of Ancient Israel*, 88 and 254–55 n. 230.

19. First Samuel 7:17 describes Samuel as erecting an altar in Ramah, which that text takes to be Samuel's hometown; 1 Sam 9:11–14, 19, 22–25 describe Samuel as coming to preside over a sacrifice that commentators most typically interpret as taking place at that same shrine (although this is, in fact, not specified). See, e.g., Peter R. Ackroyd, *The First Book of Samuel* (CBC; Cambridge: Cambridge University Press, 1971), 77; Yairah Amit, "Literature in the Service of Politics: Studies in Judges 19–21," in *Politics and Theopolitics in the Bible and Postbiblical Literature* (ed. Henning Graf Reventlow, Yair Hoffman, and Benjamin Uffenheimer; JSOTSup 171; Sheffield: JSOT Press, 1994), 32; Menahem Haran, *Temples and Temple-Service in Ancient Israel: An Inquiry into the Character of Cult Phenomena and the Historical Setting of the Priestly School* (Oxford: Clarendon, 1978), 309, 311; Ralph W. Klein, *1 Samuel* (WBC 10; Waco, Tex.: Word Books, 1983), 70, 87; Tsumura, *First Book of Samuel*, 107; and Willis, "An Anti-Elide Narrative Tradition," 308; idem, "Cultic Elements in the Story of Samuel's Birth and Dedication," *Studia Theologica* 26 (1972): 45. Cf., however, McCarter, *I Samuel*, 163 and 174–75, notes on 1 Sam 9:4 and 9:5. While he unequivocally locates the shrine mentioned in 1 Sam 7:17 in Benjaminite Ramah (see p. 148), McCarter understands the shrine in 1 Sam 9 to be located in Ephraimite Ramathaim, the town that he understands one strand of the Samuel tradition (based on 1 Sam 1:1) as identifying as Samuel's hometown. See also McCarter, "Annotations to First Samuel," in *The HarperCollins Study Bible: New Revised Standard Version, including the Apocryphal/ Deuterocanonical Books with Concordance* (rev. and updated ed.; ed. Harold W. Attridge; San Francisco: HarperSanFrancisco, 2006), 401, note on 1 Sam 9:12; and Miller, *Religion of Ancient Israel*, 162. Hertzberg somewhat similarly sees two strands of tradition in 1 Sam 9, one of which concerns (and originally stemmed from) Benjaminite Ramah and the other of

According to 1 Sam 9, Samuel comes only occasionally to this shrine to minister as priest. First Samuel 9:12, for example, describes Samuel as coming to the shrine specially on the day of this text's setting, because the people were sacrificing. Despite William McKane's claim, moreover, that "Samuel is . . . represented as enjoying priestly authority and performing priestly duties" in 1 Sam 9,[20] and despite Patrick D. Miller's similar sense that in 1 Sam 9:11–14, "Samuel is depicted as carrying out priestly responsibilities, specifically sacrifice, at what seems to be a local shrine at Ramathaim [which Miller, based on 1 Sam 1:1, takes to be Samuel's family's hometown, as opposed to Ramah],"[21] Samuel's role in the sacrificial cult while he is present at the 1 Sam 9 shrine in fact seems negligible. He blesses (יְבָרֵךְ; 1 Sam 9:13) the sacrifices before the people feel able to eat of them, and he also seems able to designate how certain portions of the animal's meat are to be apportioned at the post-sacrificial meal (1 Sam 9:23). Samuel is not, however, said to have been present during the slaughter of the sacrifice, nor to have performed ritual manipulations of its fat or (if this was a requisite part of the 1 Sam 9 ritual) its blood.[22] Neither—except for directing that a certain portion of the sacrificial meat be set specially aside (see again 1 Sam 9:23)—does he engage in preparing the animal's flesh for consumption. Rather, this task is assigned to a different (cultic?) agent: the טבח, or the "butcher," "cook."

To be sure, this account in 1 Sam 9 does not necessarily contradict the theses of Nelson and Olyan that I have questioned above, given that it presents itself as set in the premonarchic period of Israelite history and so could be said to represent one of those early monarchic texts that, in Olyan's words, "are not much concerned about whether professional priests performed every priestly function."[23] Biblical tradition, however, suggests that a situation very similar to that described in 1 Sam 9 prevailed at certain ninth-, eighth-, seventh-, and early sixth-century B.C.E. sites that I would understand to be local or regional sanctuaries of ancient Israel's northern and southern kingdoms. Such sanctuaries would presumably include at least some of the shrines that share with the

---

which concerns (and originally stemmed from) the tradition that located Samuel's hometown in Ramathaim (*I and II Samuel*, 79).

20. William McKane, *I and II Samuel: A Commentary* (Torch Bible Commentaries; London: SCM, 1963), 73.

21. Miller, *Religion of Ancient Israel*, 162; see similarly ibid., 176; and also, on Samuel's priestly role in 1 Sam 9:11–14, 19, 22–25, Willis, "Cultic Elements in the Story of Samuel's Birth," 45. On Samuel's priestly role more generally, see ibid., 44–48, with other references listed at 47 n. 50, but cf. Cody, who rejects the view that Samuel in 1 Sam 9 or, indeed, anywhere in 1 Sam 1–16 is understood as a priest (*History of Old Testament Priesthood*, 72–80). For more on the distinction Miller posits here between Ramah and Ramathaim, see n. 19 above, and my discussion below.

22. Similarly, Tsumura, *First Book of Samuel*, 273.

23. Olyan, "Religious Personnel: Israel," 298.

shrine of 1 Sam 9:11–14, 19, 22–25 the designation במה (see 1 Sam 9:12, 13, 14, 19, and 25).²⁴ This is not to say, however, that all במות can be counted as regional sanctuaries, as certain במות are better classified as more centralized and even national shrines (e.g., the בית במות of Bethel established as one of the two national shrines of the northern kingdom of Israel by King Jeroboam I [1 Kgs 12:30–31] and the archaeological complex that excavators have labeled as a במה at the other of Jeroboam's two national sanctuaries, at Tel Dan).²⁵

---

24. The terms במה (singular)/במות (plural) are typically rendered in English as "high place(s)," a translation that comes via the Vulgate, which rendered במה as *excelsus* (W. Boyd Barrick, "High Places," *ABD* 3:196b; idem, BMH *as Body Language: A Lexical and Iconographical Study of the Word* BMH *When Not a Reference to Cultic Phenomena in Biblical and Post-Biblical Hebrew* [LHBOTS 477; New York: T&T Clark, 2008], 1). But this translation is misleading in many respects: for example, while biblical texts do speak of hills and mountains as the sites of במות, this is not a universally attested sensibility, as the במה at the Tophet in Jerusalem was in the *Valley* of Hinnom (Jer 7:31; 19:5–6; 32:35) and Ezek 6:3 speaks of the במות of both the hills and *valleys*. Nor is it necessarily the case, whatever some have argued (e.g., Haran, *Temples and Temple-Service in Ancient Israel*, 18–25; Patrick H. Vaughan, *The Meaning of "bāmâ" in the Old Testament: A Study of Etymological, Textual and Archaeological Evidence* [SOTSMS 3; Cambridge: Cambridge University Press, 1974], 31, 55; and Roland de Vaux, *Ancient Israel: Its Life and Institutions* [London: Darton, Longman & Todd, 1961], 284–88), that במות are always associated with man-made elevations (Barrick, "High Places," 197a). Overall, as Miller points out (*Religion of Ancient Israel*, 236 n. 21), "there is much that is still unclear" regarding the במות, despite "a considerable literature that seeks to figure out what a *bāmâ* is, its type of structure and its use." In addition to a 1980 article by Barrick ("What Do We Really Know about the 'High Places'?" *SEÅ* 45 [1980]: 50–57), Miller points readers, as would I, to J. A. Emerton, "The Biblical High Place in the Light of Recent Study," *PEQ* 129 (1997): 116–32; and Matthias Gleis, *Die Bamah* (BZAW 251; Berlin/New York: de Gruyter, 1997).

25. On the בית במות of Bethel, see W. Boyd Barrick, "On the Meaning of *bêt-ha/(b) bāmôt* and *bāttê-habbāmôt* and the Composition of the Kings History," *JBL* 115 (1996): 623–25. The Tel Dan material has never been fully published: a popular account of the remains is available in Avraham Biran, *Biblical Dan* (Jerusalem: Israel Exploration Society, 1994); Biran also published preliminary reports of his findings in Avraham Biran, "The Temenos at Dan" (in Hebrew), *ErIsr* 16 (1982): 252*–53*; idem, "Dan," *NEAEHL* 1:323–32; idem, "A Chronicle of the Excavations 1966–1992," in *Dan I: A Chronicle of the Excavations, the Pottery Neolithic, the Early Bronze Age and the Middle Bronze Age Tombs* (ed. Avraham Biran et al.; Annual of the Nelson Glueck School of Biblical Archaeology; Jerusalem: Nelson Glueck School of Biblical Archaeology, Hebrew Union College–Jewish Institute of Religion, 1996), 9–62; and idem, "A Chronicle of the Excavations 1993–1999," in *Dan II: A Chronicle of the Excavations and the Late Bronze Age "Mycenaean" Tomb* (ed. Avraham Biran; Annual of the Nelson Glueck School of Biblical Archaeology; Jerusalem: Hebrew Union College–Jewish Institute of Religion, 2002), 5–32. Other recent discussions of the Tel Dan site can be found in Eran Arie, "Reconsidering the Iron Age II Strata at Tel Dan: Archaeological and Historical Implications," *TA* 35 (2008): 6–64; William G. Dever, *Did God Have a Wife? Archaeology and Folk Religion in Ancient Israel* (Grand Rapids/Cambridge, UK: Eerdmans, 2005), 139–51, esp. 139–45; David Ilan, "Dan," *OEANE* 1:107–12; Philip J. King

Still, 1 Kgs 13:32 and 2 Kgs 17:9; 23:5, 8, and 19 identify במות that were sites of Israelite worship located in towns or cities (depending on how one translates Hebrew עיר) that were roundabout the northern and southern kingdoms: that is, it seems to me, במות that served as provincial or regional sanctuaries.[26] The במות sanctuaries in both Israel and Judah that are mentioned in the eighth-, seventh-, and early sixth-century B.C.E. oracles of the prophets Amos, Hosea, Jeremiah, and Ezekiel (Amos 7:9; Hos 10:8; Jer 7:31; 19:5; 32:35; Ezek 6:3, 6; 20:29) might be taken as regional sanctuaries as well. Thus, although Miller notes that there may have been provincial or regional shrines during the monarchic era that were not called by the designation במה, he concludes that "the *bāmôt* or 'high places,' served as geographical or regional cult centers."[27]

At these regional במות, the priesthood's role in the sacrificial cult again seems to be minimal. For example, even though King Jeroboam I of the northern kingdom of Israel is said in 1 Kgs 13:33 to have appointed priests to serve at the north's במות shrines already at the beginning of his reign (ca. 932 B.C.E.), 2 Kgs 17:9–11, which purports to describe the general history of Israel's north-

---

and Lawrence E. Stager, *Life in Biblical Israel* (Library of Ancient Israel; Louisville/London: Westminster John Knox, 2001), 323–30; Beth Alpert Nakhai, *Archaeology and the Religions of Canaan and Israel* (ASOR Books 7; Boston: American Schools of Oriental Research, 2001), 184–85; and Ziony Zevit, *The Religions of Ancient Israel: A Synthesis of Parallactic Approaches* (London/New York: Continuum, 2001), 180–91, esp. 185–89.

26. Barrick, who in addition to objecting to the translation of במה as "high place" (see n. 24 above), also objects to the characterization of במות as local sanctuaries: in his recent *BMH as Body Language*, for example, he criticizes Emerton, Gleis, and J. T. Whitney for holding this view, and, in an unpublished paper, he similarly faults King and Stager, Miller, Nakhai, and Zevit for the same (W. Boyd Barrick, "Why Do We Associate Biblical Bamoth with Israelite 'Popular' Religion?" [paper presented at the joint meeting of the Midwest Region of the Society of Biblical Literature, the Middle West Branch of the American Oriental Society, and the American Schools of Oriental Research at Bourbonnais, Illinois, February 20–22, 2004]; cf. Emerton, "Biblical High Place in the Light of Recent Study," 129–30; Gleis, *Die Bamah*, 32–234 [chs. 4–6]; and J. T. Whitney, "'Bamoth' in the Old Testament," *TynBul* 30 [1979]: 138; King and Stager, *Life in Biblical Israel*, 319; Miller, *Religion of Ancient Israel*, 76, 236 n. 22; Nakhai, *Archaeology and the Religions of Canaan and Israel*, 163–64; and Zevit, *Religions of Ancient Israel*, 262–63). But if I read Barrick correctly (and I am grateful to Professor Barrick for having provided me with a copy of his unpublished paper), what really concerns him is the association he believes all these scholars presume between "local" and "popular" religious practices, by which Barrick means, at a minimum, practices that were engaged independent of royal sanction and that could be, more maximally, described as non-normative in the sense of being "neo-Canaanite" and "non-Yahwistic." Yet I see no reason to assume this equation (although I do not doubt that many have made it), which is to say: I see no reason not to think that the במות can be "local" in the sense I have described (shrines used by worshipers who live within a twenty-five- to thirty-kilometer [15.5–18.5 mile] radius or so, who come there to engage in ritual practices that are certainly for them a part of normative Yahwistic cult).

27. Miller, *Religion of Ancient Israel*, 76–77.

ern kingdom from its establishment to its fall, describes only the *people* of Israel as those worshiping and making offerings at במות sanctuaries. To be sure, these verses do not specifically document the people's (as opposed to the priests') performing of the sort of sacrificial rituals that are my particular interest here, but this point is explicitly (and repeatedly) made in texts that purport to describe the religious practices of the במות of the southern kingdom of Judah in the ninth and eighth centuries B.C.E. Thus, it is the Judean *people* (עם) who are described as performing sacrifices (מזבחים) and making offerings at the במות in the following texts:

- 1 Kgs 22:44 (in most of the Bible's English versions, 1 Kgs 22:43), which purports to date from the first half of the ninth century B.C.E.
- 2 Kgs 12:4 (in most of the Bible's English versions, 2 Kgs 12:3), which purports to date from the second half of the ninth century B.C.E.
- 2 Kgs 14:4, which purports to date from the first half of the eighth century B.C.E.
- 2 Kgs 15:4, which also purports to date from the first half of the eighth century B.C.E.
- 2 Kgs 15:35, which purports to date from the second half of the eighth century B.C.E.

This situation may even have persisted during the seventh and early sixth centuries B.C.E., despite the fact that, by the late seventh century B.C.E., the Deuteronomistic redactors of 1–2 Kings had clearly come to envision that it was a cadre of Levitical priests who had presided over sacrifice at the במות of both the northern kingdom of Israel, from its beginnings until that kingdom's destruction, and the southern kingdom of Judah (see in this regard the two Josianic-era [that is, late seventh century B.C.E.] passages of 1 Kgs 13:2 and 2 Kgs 23:8–9).[28] According, however, to Ezek 20:28–29, which dates from ca. 591 B.C.E., it was the *people* of Israel, throughout their history, who had offered sacrifice at a sanctuary that "is called Bamah to this day."

Of course, one must grant that Ezekiel's intent in his description of the people's במה worship is to speak polemically, and even more one must grant that the Deuteronomistic passages from 1–2 Kings that I have cited above about the במות are—given the challenge that the במות present to the Deuteronomists' core theology of centralized worship—some of the most polemically laden texts in the entire Hebrew Bible. It is thus difficult indisputably to assign to these texts historical reliability. Yet I would suggest that while polemically laden texts can hardly be taken as straightforward depictions of Israel's religious history, these polemics nevertheless must, in terms of their underlying

---

28. On the Josianic-era date of the Deuteronomistic History's first redaction, at least as I understand it, see n. 4 above.

portrayal of Israelite religious practice, present a picture that was generally believable to their ancient Israelite audience. This is because, like any polemic, the polemical texts of the Bible were generated in an attempt to persuade their listeners to take the side of the polemicists in very real and live arguments that were taking place within the Israelite community at the time of these polemics' production. Or, to put the matter somewhat more colloquially: polemics aren't about beating a dead horse. It follows, therefore, that while there is certainly room for exaggeration, the polemics of the authors and/or redactors of the Deuteronomistic History and Ezekiel against במות worship, if they were to compel, would have needed to "ring true" to their audience in at least their broad outlines, regarding, for example, their intimations that priests were significantly detached from the sacrificial rites of ancient Israel's regional sanctuaries. From this it further follows that these intimations would have "rung true" because they reflected an experience of priestly detachment at regional sanctuaries similar to that audience's own. Consequently, Baruch Halpern rather flippantly describes regional shrines as sites of "back-yard-barbeque cult," characterized by a "rejection of the absolute need for ritual specialists to execute offerings."[29]

III. Shiloh

So what now of Shiloh? Could we characterize it, as I have characterized the במה sanctuary described in 1 Sam 9:11–14, 19, 22–25 and the במות sanctuaries of 1 Kgs 22:44 (Eng. v. 43); 2 Kgs 12:4 (Eng. v. 3); 2 Kgs 14:4; 2 Kgs 15:4; 2 Kgs 15:35; and Ezek 20:28–29, as a regional sanctuary where the priesthood's lack of participation in the shrine's key sacrificial rituals is to be explained by its localized scale?

The major impediment here, of course, is those biblical sources to which I have alluded already that suggest that Shiloh was not a sanctuary of only local or regional importance, but instead was the premier place of worship for *all* of Israel's tribes during the premonarchic period of Israelite history,[30] before the

---

29. Baruch Halpern, "Sybil, or the Two Nations? Archaism, Alienation, and the Elite Redefinition of Traditional Culture in Judah in the 8th–7th Centuries B.C.E.," in *The Study of the Ancient Near East in the Twenty-First Century: The William Foxwell Albright Centennial Conference* (ed. Jerrold S. Cooper and Glenn M. Schwartz; Winona Lake, Ind.: Eisenbrauns, 1996), 303.

30. Certain biblical scholars also promote this understanding: see, e.g., Miller, *Religion of Ancient Israel*, 79; Gordon J. Wenham, "Deuteronomy and the Central Sanctuary," in *A Song of Power and the Power of Song: Essays on the Book of Deuteronomy* (ed. Duane L. Christensen; SBTS 3; Winona Lake, Ind.: Eisenbrauns, 1993), 98–99; Willis, "Cultic Elements in the Story of Samuel's Birth," 44, 46; also, although he expresses some caveats, McKane, *I and II Samuel*, 35, citing Lucas H. Grollenberg, *Atlas of the Bible* (London: Nelson, 1956), 162.

site was seemingly destroyed by the Philistines in ca. 1050 B.C.E.[31] The sources that promulgate this view, however (e.g., Ps 78:60; Jer 7:12; 26:6–9), all come from a date that is far later than the premonarchic period that 1 Sam 1:1–2:26 purports to describe; more important, these sources come from a date quite late in Israel's monarchic era (the late seventh century B.C.E.).[32] They thus reflect the seventh-century B.C.E. theological ideal of Yahweh's one "chosen place" that is particularly associated with the book of Deuteronomy: in the seventh century B.C.E., the Jerusalem temple and, in the premonarchic period of Israelite history, the shrine at Shiloh.[33] That this "posture of the Deuteronomistic movement in the late 7th century" reflects the actual status of the premonarchic Shiloh sanctuary, however, seems unlikely,[34] if for no other reason than pragmatism: "[I]t is absurd to assume," in the words of the noted scholar of Deuteronomic thought Moshe Weinfeld, that worshipers would routinely travel to a sanctuary that was, for those who lived in Israel's farthest reaches, "some three, or more, days' journey distant."[35] Rather, we must posit, to quote Weinfeld again, "the existence of provincial sanctuaries" within a reasonable distance (about a day's walk, I would once more suggest) from worshipers' homes.[36]

To understand Shiloh as such a provincial sanctuary, let us return to 1 Sam 1:1–2:26, and especially its opening verses, 1:1–2, where we are introduced to Elkanah, the father of the yet-to-be-born Samuel, and Elkanah's two wives, Hannah and Peninnah. In these introductory verses as they stand, and more specifically in 1:1, we are also told that this family comes from a village called Ramathaim-zophim, in the hill country of Ephraim. Somewhat later in 1 Sam 1:1–2:26, however, in 1:19 and 2:11, the family is described as coming

---

31. On the date of Shiloh's destruction, see further n. 46 below.

32. On the seventh-century B.C.E. date of Ps 78, see Richard J. Clifford, "In Zion and David a New Beginning: An Interpretation of Psalm 78," in *Traditions in Transformation: Turning-Points in Biblical Faith* (ed. Baruch Halpern and Jon D. Levenson; Winona Lake, Ind.: Eisenbrauns, 1981), 139–41 (this reference was brought to my attention by Baruch Halpern, "Shiloh," *ABD* 5:1214a), but cf. Mark Leuchter, "The Reference to Shiloh in Psalm 78," *HUCA* 77 (2006): 1–31. On the date of Jer 7:12, a part of Jeremiah's so-called temple sermon, and the related passage 26:6–9, see Susan Ackerman, *Under Every Green Tree: Popular Religion in Sixth-Century Judah* (HSM 46; Atlanta: Scholars Press, 1992), 6 and n. 3 on that page.

33. This Deuteronomic sense of a "cultic succession" is well described by John Day, "The Destruction of the Shiloh Sanctuary and Jeremiah vii 12, 14," in *Studies in the Historical Books of the Old Testament* (ed. J. A. Emerton; VTSup 30; Leiden: Brill, 1979), 89–90, 90 n. 13, where Day cites as well R. E. Clements, "Deuteronomy and the Jerusalem Cult Tradition," *VT* 15 (1965): 312.

34. Halpern, "Shiloh," 1214a.

35. Moshe Weinfeld, *Deuteronomy and the Deuteronomic School* (Oxford: Clarendon, 1972), 218.

36. Ibid., 219.

from Ramah, typically understood as referring to a hill-country town that lay in the tribal territory of Benjamin. This town of Ramah (modern er-Ram), which is near the Benjaminite–Ephraimite border, about 8.5 kilometers (5.3 miles) north of Jerusalem, is, moreover, identified as the home of Elkanah's son Samuel at several other points in 1 Samuel—in 7:17; 8:4; 15:34; 16:13; 19:18; 25:1; and 28:3—and McCarter in addition notes (citing Samuel R. Driver's 1913 work on the text and topography of the books of Samuel) that the place-name of Ramathaim-zophim that is found in 1 Sam 1:1 is "grammatically impossible."[37]

Many scholars have suggested, therefore, that the seemingly geographical designation צוֹפִים, "zophim," in the place-name Ramathaim-zophim is better read as צוּפִי, or "Zupi," a reference, that is, to Elkanah's family's membership in a clan called the Zuphites (as is reflected later on in 1:1, in the name of Elkanah's ancestor Zuph, and also in the ancient Greek translation of the Hebrew Bible, which reads a gentilic term, Σειφα, instead of צוֹפִים).[38] Some commentators have in addition argued that the territory of this Zuphite clan lay on the border of Benjamin and Ephraim, proximate to, if not encompassing, Benjaminite Ramah.[39] According to this reconstruction, the Ramathaim (or the "height") of 1 Sam 1:1 is thus identical to the Ramah (or the "height") of 1:19; 2:11; and elsewhere, and as a result, there is no contradiction among the various 1 Samuel texts regarding Elkanah's family's hometown. An alternative reconstruction suggests, however, (1) that there was in fact a Zuphite Ramathaim of Ephraim, separate from Ramah of Benjamin and possibly to be identified with New Testament Arimathea/modern Rentis (as it was by

---

37. McCarter, *I Samuel*, 51, referring to Samuel R. Driver, *Notes on the Hebrew Text and the Topography of the Books of Samuel, with an Introduction on Hebrew Paleography and the Ancient Versions and Facsimiles of Inscriptions and Maps* (2nd ed.; Oxford: Clarendon, 1913), 1; see similarly Henry Preserved Smith, *A Critical and Exegetical Commentary on the Books of Samuel* (ICC; Edinburgh: T&T Clark, 1899), 6.

38. See, e.g., Ackroyd, *First Book of Samuel*, 18; Driver, *Notes on the Hebrew Text*, 1; Hertzberg, *I and II Samuel*, 21; Klein, *1 Samuel*, 1–2; McCarter, *I Samuel*, 51; and Smith, *Critical and Exegetical Commentary on the Books of Samuel*, 6. As Driver, Klein, McCarter, and Smith all point out, the mistaken reading of צוֹפִים, or "zophim," arose when the מ of the following phrase מהר אפרים, "from the hill country of Ephraim," was mistakenly copied twice and thus appended to the original צוּפִי (Driver, *Notes on the Hebrew Text*, 1; Klein, *1 Samuel*, 2; McCarter, *I Samuel*, 51; and Smith, *Critical and Exegetical Commentary on the Books of Samuel*, 6). For somewhat different explanations, each of which deals with the grammatically difficult צוֹפִים, "zophim," yet preserves the integrity of the consonantal text as it has come down to us, see Karel van der Toorn, *Family Religion in Babylonia, Syria, and Israel: Continuity and Change in the Forms of Religious Life* (Studies in the History and Culture of the Ancient Near East 7; Leiden/New York: Brill, 1996), 190 and n. 39 on that page; and Tsumura, *First Book of Samuel*, 106–7.

39. See, e.g., Patrick M. Arnold, "Ramah," *ABD* 5:613b; Tsumura, *First Book of Samuel*, 107, 124–25.

the church historian Eusebius in the third–fourth centuries c.e.), or possibly to be identified (as has been argued by Diana Edelman)[40] with Khirbet Raddana; and (2) that at least one strain of the Samuel tradition understands this Ramathaim of Ephraim, rather than Ramah of Benjamin, to be Elkanah's (and Samuel's) hometown.[41]

Fortunately, resolving this conundrum is not essential for our analysis here, as it just so happens that both Benjaminite Ramah (modern er-Ram) and Ephraimite Ramathaim (assuming that it indeed existed, and regardless of whether it is identified with New Testament Arimathea/modern Rentis or with Khirbet Raddana) lie about 25–30 kilometers (15.5–18.5 miles) from Shiloh (Ramah/er-Ram lies about 22.5 kilometers [14 miles] south and just a little west of Shiloh as the crow flies, or, as near as I can figure, about 24.9 kilometers [15.5 miles] if one were to travel by ancient roads; Arimathea/Rentis lies about 26.2 kilometers [16.3 miles] to the west and a little south of Shiloh as the crow flies, or again, as near as I can figure, about 30.5 kilometers [19 miles] if one were to travel by ancient roads; Khirbet Raddana lies about 18.1 kilometers [11.2 miles] south and a little west of Shiloh as the crow flies, or, once more, as near as I can figure, about 25.2 kilometers [15.7 miles] if one were to travel by ancient Israelite roadways). The story told in 1 Sam 1:1–2:26 thus describes how Elkanah and his family embark annually, according to 1:3, 7, 21, and 2:19, from either their Benjaminite hometown of Ramah (which according to one group of scholars was also known as Ramathaim) or from their Ephraimite hometown of Ramathaim (if we take Ramathaim to denote a location other than Ramah) to travel approximately 25–30 kilometers (15.5–18.5 miles)— that is, one day's, or just a little over one day's walk—to visit what I would again propose we understand as a regional sanctuary at Shiloh.[42] There they engage in worship together with other locals (note the communal context implied

---

40. Diana Edelman, "Saul's Journey through Mt. Ephraim and Samuel's Ramah (1 Sam 9:44–5; 10:2–5)," *ZPDV* 104 (1988): 54–57; see also Karel van der Toorn, "Saul and the Rise of Israelite State Religion," *VT* 43 (1993): 522. These references were both brought to my attention by Barrick, "Why Do We Associate Biblical Bamoth with Israelite 'Popular' Religion?"

41. So, e.g., Hertzberg, *I and II Samuel*, 23; Klein, *1 Samuel*, 5; McCarter, *I Samuel*, 58, 61–62; and Carol Meyers, "An Ethnoarchaeological Analysis of Hannah's Sacrifice," in *Pomegranates and Golden Bells: Studies in Biblical, Jewish, and Near Eastern Ritual, Law, and Literature in Honor of Jacob Milgrom* (ed. David P. Wright, David Noel Freedman, and Avi Hurvitz; Winona Lake, Ind.: Eisenbrauns, 1995), 85–86.

42. A similar understanding of Shiloh as a regional sanctuary is well articulated by van der Toorn, *Family Religion*, 244 and n. 39 on that page; see also idem and Cees Houtman, "David and the Ark," *JBL* 113 (1994): 226; Milgrom, *Leviticus*, 1:31–32; and Yigael Shiloh, "Iron Age Sanctuaries and Cult Elements in Palestine," in *Symposia Celebrating the Seventy-Fifth Anniversary of the Founding of the American Schools of Oriental Research (1900–1975)* (ed. Frank Moore Cross; Zion Research Foundation Occasional Publications 1–2; Cambridge, Mass.: American Schools of Oriental Research, 1979), 153.

by 1 Sam 2:12–17), who, like Elkanah's family, presumably came periodically to the shrine at Shiloh from villages in Ephraim and in Benjamin and more generally from sites around Israel's central hill country that were about a day's walk away.[43] Indeed, Shiloh's position just east of a major highway that led from Jerusalem through the important center of Bethel to the equally important city of Shechem (Judg 21:19) well positioned it to serve as a religious hub at which central hill-country worshipers might gather.

Interestingly enough, our archaeological data concur, although no Israelite-era shrine has been found at Shiloh owing to erosion and destruction by later occupation.[44] The extant archaeological remains (in particular, large pillared buildings in which a rich ceramic assemblage was found, including vessels with animal reliefs) do imply, however, that there was some major, non-residential complex—probably a shrine, according to the most recent excavator of Shiloh, Israel Finkelstein, who worked at the site from 1981 to 1984—on Shiloh's summit during the Iron Age I period of Israelite history.[45] Finkelstein's excavations, moreover, have also intimated that just as 1 Sam 1:1–2:26 (at least as I have interpreted) suggests, Shiloh served as a *regional* shrine for Israel's central hill-country residents during the Iron I era (or at least until the site's destruction, as Finkelstein would have it, in ca. 1050 B.C.E.).[46] In fact, Finkelstein theorizes, Shiloh's role as a regional sanctuary dates back even to the Canaanite period of the late Middle Bronze Age (sixteenth century B.C.E.), when Shiloh, although it was relatively small, seems to have served

---

43. See similarly Milgrom, *Leviticus*, 1:32: "The distance to Shiloh from any point in the central hill-country of Benjamin, Ephraim, and Manasseh is just a one-day's journey."

44. Israel Finkelstein, "The History and Archaeology of Shiloh from the Middle Bronze Age II to Iron Age II," in *Shiloh: The Archaeology of a Biblical Site* (ed. Israel Finkelstein; Tel Aviv: Monograph Series of Tel Aviv University, 1993), 384–85; idem, "Seilun, Khirbet," *ABD* 5:1072a.

45. Finkelstein, "The History and Archaeology of Shiloh," 384–85; see also Nakhai, *Archaeology and the Religions of Canaan and Israel*, 171.

46. There is some debate over the date of Shiloh's destruction. According to Danish archaeological excavations of Shiloh in 1926, 1929, 1932, and 1963, and according especially to the 1963 excavators' reevaluation of the 1926, 1929, and 1932 results, Shiloh was destroyed during the Assyrian invasions of the second half of the eighth century B.C.E. According to the most recent excavator of the site, Israel Finkelstein, however, Shiloh was destroyed already in ca. 1050 B.C.E., perhaps by the Philistines. Finkelstein further argues, contra the Danish excavators' conclusions, that there was no significant resettlement after this destruction. For discussion, see further Marie-Louise Buhl and Svend Holm-Nielsen, *Shiloh, The Danish Excavations at Tell Sailun, Palestine, in 1926, 1929, 1932 and 1963*, vol. 1, *The Pre-Hellenistic Remains* (Publications of the National Museum, Archaeological Historical Series 12; Copenhagen: National Museum of Denmark, 1969); Finkelstein, "History and Archaeology of Shiloh," 388–89; idem, "Seilun, Khirbet," 1072a; idem, "Shiloh," *NEAEHL* 4:1368; and Leslie Watkins (based on material submitted by Israel Finkelstein), "Shiloh," *OEANE* 5:29.

local worshipers as a cultic gathering site, probably even one that housed a temple. (Although no sanctuary has been identified among Shiloh's Middle Bronze Age remains, the presence of some religious structure is suggested by the discovery of other monumental architecture, including storage rooms that contained cultic objects such as offering stands, bowls for making dedicatory offerings, and a bull-shaped zoomorphic vessel.)[47]

Unfortunately, no architectural remains from the succeeding Canaanite period of the Late Bronze Age were unearthed at Shiloh; instead, archaeologists discovered only a thick deposit (1.5 m) of earth, ashes, and stones, in which pieces of (deliberately?) broken pottery, animal bones (mostly sheep and goat), and nearly intact vessels containing ashes and more animal bones were found. Still, Finkelstein has proposed that this means that the memory of the sixteenth-century B.C.E. temple persisted among Late Bronze Age worshipers who lived in Shiloh's vicinity, who, despite the site's lack of a shrine building in their day, nevertheless came to this sacred ruin to leave dedicatory offerings and, more important, to participate (as is indicated by the preponderance of animal bones) in the rite of animal sacrifice.[48] That Shiloh remained a regional center, and probably a sacred center, for the Canaanites-*cum*-Israelites who inhabited the surrounding hill country during the subsequent Iron Age I period, is further suggested to Finkelstein by two factors: (1) the remarkable number of other Iron Age I sites surrounding Shiloh (twenty-six sites within a 5–6 kilometer [3.1–3.7 mile] radius),[49] in a density "two and even three times greater," as Finkelstein writes, than is found elsewhere in the Ephraimite hills,[50] and (2) the evidence noted above that points to the presence of a sanctuary building at twelfth- and eleventh-century B.C.E. Shiloh.

Thus, in Finkelstein's estimation, "In the beginning of the Iron Age, Shiloh was the outstanding candidate to become the sacred center of the hill-country population, since it was an ancient cultic site . . . in an area with . . . a high concentration of 'Israelite' sites."[51] Concomitantly, in my estimation, Shiloh was

---

47. Finkelstein, "History and Archaeology of Shiloh," 377; see also idem, "Seilun, Khirbet," 1071a; idem, "Shiloh," 1367; Nakhai, *Archaeology and the Religions of Canaan and Israel*, 104; and Watkins (based on material submitted by Israel Finkelstein), "Shiloh," 29.

48. Finkelstein, "History and Archaeology of Shiloh," 382; see also idem, "Seilun, Khirbet," 1071a–b; idem, "Shiloh," 1367; Nakhai, *Archaeology and the Religions of Canaan and Israel*, 141–42; and Watkins (based on material submitted by Israel Finkelstein), "Shiloh," 29.

49. Finkelstein, "History and Archaeology of Shiloh," 386; see similarly Jacob Milgrom, who reports the number of sites as twenty-two ("Priestly ['P'] Source," *ABD* 5:460a; this reference brought to my attention by Nakhai, *Archaeology and the Religions of Canaan and Israel*, 171).

50. Israel Finkelstein, "Seilun, Khirbet," 1072a; see also idem, "History and Archaeology of Shiloh," 386.

51. Finkelstein, "Seilun, Khirbet," 1072a.

a regional hill-country shrine that would have been staffed by a priesthood whose obligations in relation to the sanctuary's sacrificial rituals would have been negligible. This conclusion stands in agreement with the same argument I have made above concerning the priesthood's obligations at regional sanctuaries throughout Israel's preexilic history. In sum, I propose that because of Shiloh's status as a regional sanctuary, its priesthood is depicted as either absent or significantly disengaged in the passages in 1 Sam 1:1–2:26 that describe the slaughter of a sacrificial animal, the conducting of the post-sacrificial meal, and (most important) the altar ritual of fat and (if this were a part of Shilonite rite) blood manipulation.

IV. Concluding Reflections

These data regarding the priesthood's (non-)participation in sacrificial ritual at Shiloh and other regional sanctuaries have, I propose, important implications regarding a topic that has concerned me elsewhere in my work: the nature of women's religious experiences in ancient Israel. More specifically, I might propose that because it was the worshiping community's non-elites, as opposed to its priests, who executed key parts of sacrificial rituals at ancient Israel's regional sanctuaries, more opportunities were available for women to be involved.

Nevertheless, I must immediately admit that to assign a worshiping community's non-elites the responsibility for executing a regional sanctuary's sacrificial rites need not mean that *all* that community's members would be equally involved, and, given the male-dominated nature of ancient Israelite society, we can easily imagine a scenario whereby only a worshiping community's men would actually perform sacrificial functions. In fact, this is precisely what is suggested by 1 Sam 2:13, where the non-priestly "someone" who makes the שלמים sacrifice at Shiloh and then oversees the cooked meat's distribution is specifically gendered as male (איש). Likewise, in 1 Sam 1:4, as we have seen, Elkanah alone is described as offering up an animal for slaughter. Elkanah is also described in 1:4 and in the subsequent verse as taking sole responsibility for the distribution of the meat that was consumed at the post-sacrificial meal. We should probably also envision Elkanah as cooking that meat, as "the cooking of meat" is "the aspect of food production men are most likely to take on,"[52] especially in sacrificial contexts (in Gen 18:7, it is Abraham's male servant, or נער, who prepares the calf that Abraham serves to Yahweh and the deity's two divine attendants when they visit him at the oaks at Mamre that were near his

---

52. Carol Meyers, *Discovering Eve: Ancient Israelite Women in Context* (New York/Oxford: Oxford University Press, 1988), 147; this quotation brought to my attention by Nathan MacDonald, *What Did the Ancient Israelites Eat? Diet in Biblical Times* (Grand Rapids: Eerdmans, 2008), 126 n. 5.

and Sarah's tent, and in 1 Sam 9:23, as noted above, it is a male butcher or cook [טבח] who is described as having prepared at least one portion of the sacrificial meal that is described in that text).[53]

Still, according to 1 Sam 1:4–5, Elkanah distributes portions of the sacrificial meat to his two wives, Hannah and Peninnah, and to Peninnah's sons and possibly her daughters,[54] showing that this text's author(s) and/or redactor(s) envisioned women as engaged participants in at least the ritual meal that followed the offering of the sacrifice.[55] Carol Meyers, moreover, has published two different articles on Hannah's importance as a religious actor in the sacrificial ritual described in 1 Sam 1:24–25.[56] Unfortunately, as I mentioned briefly already, these two verses are textually confused, and so the exact nature of Hannah's engagement remains uncertain. Still, there can be no doubt that according to 1 Sam 1:24, Hannah assumed the responsibility for delivering sacrificial offerings to Shiloh—an animal for slaughter,[57] flour, and wine—and

---

53. This contra Bird, "Place of Women in the Israelite Cultus," 417 n. 37; eadem, "Women's Religion in Ancient Israel," in *Women's Earliest Records from Ancient Egypt and Western Asia: Proceedings of the Conference on Women in the Ancient Near East, Brown University, Providence, Rhode Island, November 5–7, 1987* (ed. Barbara S. Lesko; BJS 166; Atlanta: Scholars Press, 1989), 293; and Braulik, "Were Women, Too, Allowed to Offer Sacrifices?" 919.

54. The daughters are a part of Elkanah's family's party according to v. 4 of the Masoretic Text, but are not mentioned in the LXX. McCarter (*I Samuel*, 51) suggests that the Greek preserves the better reading here (meaning that the daughters were not originally included in the Samuel account), but Klein raises the possibility that the LXX's lack of reference to the "daughters" results from a deliberate omission, "represent[ing] a correction by someone who felt daughters would/should not participate in the sacrifices" (*1 Samuel*, 2, note on 1 Sam 1:4).

55. This contra Hertzberg, who seems to take Elkanah's apportioning of food to Hannah, Peninnah, and to Peninnah's sons and (perhaps) daughters as an atypical act, a "kind gesture" on Elkanah's part, as opposed to what Hertzberg takes to be the norm of "women and children ... remain[ing] in the background during a feast and wait[ing] until the mealtime proper was over" (*I and II Samuel*, 24).

56. Carol Meyers, "Hannah and Her Sacrifice: Reclaiming Female Agency," in *A Feminist Companion to Samuel and Kings* (ed. Athalya Brenner; Feminist Companion to the Bible 5; Sheffield: Sheffield Academic Press, 1994), 93–104 (= eadem, "The Hannah Narrative in Feminist Perspective," in *"Go to the Land I Will Show You": Studies in Honor of Dwight W. Young* [ed. Joseph E. Coleson and Victor H. Matthews; Winona Lake, Ind.: Eisenbrauns, 1996], 117–26); eadem, "Ethnoarchaeological Analysis of Hannah's Sacrifice," 77–91.

57. The Greek and Dead Sea Scroll readings of 1 Sam 1:24 that have Hannah bringing "a three-year-old bull" to Shiloh, as opposed to the Masoretic Text's "three bulls," are surely the better renderings, given that only one bull is killed in 1:25. As Driver and McCarter (among others) point out, the Masoretic Text has suffered a simple corruption here, as the מ of the original reading בפר משלש, a "three-year old bull," has been mistakenly repositioned to yield בפרם שלש, "three bulls." See Driver, *Notes on the Hebrew Text*, 20; McCarter,

that, at a minimum, she stood alongside Elkanah in 1:25 as he killed the sacrificial bull.[58] And should we envision Hannah as being at Elkanah's side as well when he (presumably) approached Yahweh's altar to dedicate the deity's assigned portion of the offering, the fat and (if this is a part of Shilonite ritual) the blood? It is certainly plausible that the man Elkanah and the woman Hannah, having been jointly present for the slaughter, might also have been jointly present for the subsequent altar ritual.

Thereby is suggested a role of some significance for Hannah as a ritual agent at Shiloh, and perhaps my argument in this paper helps us understand whence this significance stems. At regional sanctuaries, where priestly functions in the enactment of sacrificial ritual are occluded, opportunities arise for Israel's non-elites, including Israel's women, to be more centrally involved.

I Samuel, 56–57. But Braulik argues that "three bulls" is the correct reading, as one bull was to be sacrificed for each of the three people involved (Elkanah, Hannah, and Samuel; see Braulik, "Were Women, Too, Allowed to Offer Sacrifices?" 920 n. 38, drawing on the work of Stanley D. Walters, "Hannah and Anna: The Greek and Hebrew Texts of 1 Samuel 1," *JBL* 107 [1988]: 402). See also, on retaining the Masoretic reading as it stands, Tsumura, *First Book of Samuel*, 130–31.

58. In 1:25 according to the Masoretic tradition, Hannah seems to be envisioned as standing alongside her husband, Elkanah, and acting in tandem with him when the sacrificial animal is killed; the text reads: "And they [presumably Hannah and Elkanah] slaughtered the bull." The Greek Codex Vaticanus, however, describes Elkanah alone as killing the sacrificial animal. I would suggest, moreover, that Vaticanus, and also the fragmentary manuscript 4QSam^a from the Dead Sea Scrolls, is more reliable than the Masoretic Text in envisioning Elkanah alone as actually performing the slaughter, this as opposed to the arguments of some other scholars that the Greek shows "'patriarchalizing' of the text in removing Hannah's agency in performing the sacrifice" (Lillian R. Klein, "Hannah," in *Women in Scripture: A Dictionary of Named and Unnamed Women in the Hebrew Bible, the Apocryphal/Deuterocanonical Books, and the New Testament* [ed. Carol Meyers, with Toni Craven and Ross S. Kraemer; Boston: Houghton Mifflin, 2000], 91; see similarly Meyers, "Hannah Narrative in Feminist Perspective," 123 [= "Hannah and Her Sacrifice," 100–101]; somewhat similarly [although without accusing the Greek of deliberate "patriarchalizing"], see Walters, "Hannah and Anna," 400–409). The Greek and Dead Sea Scroll renderings, though, seem to me the more probable, in part, for logistical reasons (for two people jointly to wield a knife and slaughter a bull, as the Masoretic Text would have it, seems awkward). More important, understanding the man Elkanah as solely executing the slaughter seems consistent with the description of Elkanah alone sacrificing in 1 Sam 1:4 and of a male agent (כל־איש) sacrificing in 1 Sam 2:13. It is also consistent with biblical traditions elsewhere that describe only men killing sacrificial animals (e.g., Gen 31:54; 46:1; Judg 6:19), even when, as in Judg 13:19, a woman stands alongside.

The Levitical Diaspora (II): Modern Perspectives on the Levitical Cities Lists (A Review of Opinions)

Jeremy M. Hutton

Julius Wellhausen's short study of the Levitical cities in his *Prolegomena* called into question the previous scholarly consensus concerning the institution's authenticity, inaugurating a productive line of inquiry over a century ago. Not counting obligatory mention in commentaries on Joshua and 1 Chronicles and in other large-scale reference works (for example, biblical encyclopedias), the Levitical cities have been handled by literally dozens of treatments dedicated both specifically to the Levitical Cities Lists themselves (i.e., Josh 21 and 1 Chr 6) and, more generally, to Levitical genealogy and social function as a whole, in which short discussions of the cities is a necessity. The problems associated with the historical Levitical cities and their literary description have aroused the interest of the luminaries of the field: William Foxwell Albright, Albrecht Alt, Yehezkel Kaufmann, Benjamin Mazar, and Menaḥem Haran all contributed incisive studies between 1945 and 1961. Although critical investigations of the Levitical Cities Lists have never achieved a particularly central role in biblical studies, the various methodologies employed to deal adequately with the biblical text and the results of the individual studies have evolved over the course of the ensuing decades. This evolution has at times very closely mirrored emerging trends in the study of Hebrew Bible, and at other times has harked back blissfully to a more conservative, theoretically unified era of investigation. In the past five decades, articles dedicated specifically to the nature and history of the Levitical Cities Lists have appeared with some regularity. It is thus an opportune time to consolidate this scholarship, to reexamine the questions and problems it has generated, and to bring to bear other models and methodologies on the question of the Levitical Cities Lists. The present chapter attempts to provide a concise overview of the interrelationship

---

This essay continues a study begun in 2009 as Jeremy M. Hutton, "The Levitical Diaspora (I): A Sociological Comparison with Morocco's Ahansal," in *Exploring the* Longue Durée: *Essays in Honor of Lawrence E. Stager* (ed. J. David Schloen; Winona Lake, Ind.: Eisenbrauns, 2009), 223–34. In that essay, I referred to the present study as forthcoming under the title "The Levitical Diaspora (II): A Review of Opinions."

of only three of the many significant and interrelated questions permeating the study of the Levitical Cities Lists.

I. Wellhausen and the Established Lines of Inquiry

Wellhausen's challenge to the status quo raised several pertinent concerns that now form the central points of disagreement in the argument concerning the Levitical Cities Lists.[1] Wellhausen began his critique of previous commentators' historical consensus by pointing to the schematic nature of the underlying list, in which each Israelite tribe dedicated four of its cities to the Levites (although compare the prescription in Num 35:8 that the cities should be distributed in numbers consonant with tribal size). The schematic nature of the system already casts doubt on the system's historical practicability as a whole, argued Wellhausen.[2] Also instructive in this regard, for Wellhausen, was the geographic precision of Num 35:4–5, which delineates and assigns a preestablished pastureland to each city, irrespective of topographic realities.[3] Furthermore, archaeological and historical considerations preclude the assignment of several of the named cities to Israelite possession, whether because of their clear biblical identifications as non-Israelite enclaves (e.g., Gibeon, Shechem, Gezer, and Taanach), or because of complete nonexistence in the period under investigation.[4] Some cities simply could not have been dedicated solely to Levitical habitation, since they themselves functioned as central locations in their respective tribe's political system (e.g., Shechem, Hebron, and Ramoth).[5] Moreover, the Deuteronomic Code assumes a wider distribution of Levites throughout the land in cities otherwise unidentified as specifically Levitical (e.g., Gibeath-Phinhas[6]), and indicated by appeals to all Israelites to care for "the Levite in your gates" (e.g., Deut 12:12, 18; 14:27; 16:11). Far from removing any geographical lot from Levi (cf. Num 18:20–23), argued Wellhausen, the Levitical Cities Lists instead dedicated a large portion of land to the otherwise non-materialist tribe.[7] Finally, Wellhausen traced the earliest demon-

---

1. Julius Wellhausen, *Prolegomena to the History of Israel* (trans. J. S. Black and Allan Menzies, with a preface by W. Robertson Smith [1885]; repr., with a foreword by Douglas A. Knight; Scholars Press Reprints and Translations; Atlanta: Scholars Press, 1994), 159–64.
2. Ibid., 159.
3. Ibid.; cf. the rebuttal of Jacob Milgrom, "The Levitic Town: An Exercise in Realistic Planning," in *Essays in Honour of Yigael Yadin* (ed. Geza Vermes and Jacob Neusner; Totowa, N.J.: Allanheld & Osmun, 1983), 185–88.
4. Wellhausen, *Prolegomena*, 160.
5. Ibid.
6. Wellhausen adds here Anathoth, on the grounds that "Jeremiah had his holding there as a citizen and not as a priest, and he shared not with the priests but *with the people* (xxxii. 12)" (ibid., 160; emphasis original).
7. Ibid., 161–62.

strable mention of a geographic inheritance to be given to the Levites to the book of Ezekiel (45:5).[8] The schematic nature of the lists, the idealized nature of the cities' pastureland, and the conflicting testimony offered by the biblical texts all contributed to Wellhausen's skeptical assessment of the lists' value for historical reconstruction and to his tacit dating of the Levitical Cities Lists in the late-exilic or Persian period. The one allowance Wellhausen permitted was that the lists may contain "an echo of the general recollection that there were once in Israel many holy places and residences of priesthoods."[9] This concession was predicated on the acknowledgment that four of the cities of refuge—Hebron, Shechem, Qedesh, and Ramoth, all of which were "demonstrably famous old seats of worship"[10]—were inextricably linked with the Levitical cities as a subset of the latter.[11] Wellhausen's concession, however, did not require that all the enumerated cities had ever been Levitical at some point in time, and it certainly did not compel a favorable valuation of the lists' historicity.

Wellhausen's trenchant analysis has endured as the benchmark position from which studies of the Levitical Cities Lists begin, and justifiably so. The issues Wellhausen articulated and his arguments opposing the lists' historicity strike at the very heart of the problem. In a scant five pages, Wellhausen erected the arena within which all subsequent debates concerning the Levitical cities have played out. The parameters set in the *Prolegomena* can be separated into five discrete topics, each of which merits attention individually before a comprehensive understanding of the Levitical Cities Lists may be reached.

1. First, one must deal with the present forms of the two lists (Josh 21; 1 Chr 6)—both with their common elements, and with those elements in which they diverge. These differences may be encountered both in the structural framework surrounding the lists and in the elements of the lists themselves. As will be seen in the following discussion, establishing an "original" text of the list, or finding the sources from which the list was cobbled together, has become a major thrust of scholarship on the cities.

2. Second, one must reckon critically with what is manifestly a utopian schema assumed in the apportioning of the enumerated cities. Failure to do so results in the overestimation of the lists' value in reconstructing a historical system of Levitical cities. Similarly, the idealism of the delineation of Levitical territorial possession in Num 35:4–5 must be dealt with adequately. In both these cases—the form of the text and

---

8. Ibid., 162–64.
9. Ibid., 162.
10. Ibid.
11. This assessment has not, however, persisted uncontested; see below for further discussion.

the schematic nature of the text—analysis of the pertinent passages is dependent to a great extent on the interpreter's hermeneutical orientation to the text itself. For example, those embracing conventional text-critical methodology will be satisfied with tracing the lists back to a single precursor (perhaps with only mild methodological reservations), while those holding a more progressive model of text-critical work will seek to account for the differences in a more nuanced manner. Likewise, those whose primary orientation is to the history behind the text will often make allowances or concessions to the ideal or utopian nature of the lists, while at the same time upholding the lists' *general* plausibility; conversely, those whose primary object of study is the text itself tend to argue for the text's confabulatory tendencies.
3. Related to the problem of utopianism is the list's date and historical verisimilitude. For those claiming the purely literary construction of the Levitical Cities Lists, a date of the list's (/lists') composition and inclusion in the books of Josh 21 and 1 Chr 6 is mandatory. For those for whom the historical background of the text is at stake, the date of the historical referents takes precedence, while a date of the lists' composition, which is often provided, takes diminished priority.

The scope of the present venue requires that this discussion be limited to the three preceding questions. Although only these three questions will be handled below, we cannot but recognize that they are obviously intricately intertwined with one another, as they are with still other problems. Once the preceding interpretations regarding the textual integrity of the lists, the degree of utopianism in the lists, and the historicity of the lists have been made, commentators are potentially faced with at least two more weighty problems:

4. If the existence of a Levitical cities system is taken as at least somewhat historically plausible, one must come to grips with the composition of the cities' populations and the functions of the various constituencies. Almost no one believes that the enumerated cities would have accommodated only Levites, but the precise proportions of Levites to non-Levitical inhabitants remains up for debate. Moreover, the usage of pastureland outside the cities—a factor of utopianism, in many accounts—becomes an added concern here.
5. A fifth and final problem is the function of Levitical cultic or judiciary personnel, if they are indeed posited as historical residents of the cities (regardless of whether they are thought to comprise the entire population or only a slim percentage of it). The roles attributed to the Levites by modern scholars have encompassed everything from peripheral cultic specialists, serving in the role of local priests, to judiciary officials.

Often, this problem of function is related to the problem of the cities' relationship vis-à-vis the central authority (i.e., the monarchy, or the established power structures of the day).

In a comprehensive examination of the Levitical Cities Lists, then, one would be forced to deal with these five categories of inquiry: (a) textual differences, (b) utopianism, (c) date of the historical referent (if applicable) and textual composition, (d) constituency, and (e) the constituency's social function and relationship to the sitting central authority. Of these five categories, the first three will comprise the principal areas of comparison between scholars throughout the remainder of this study, with the final two referred to only implicitly.[12] The textual integrity of the Levitical Cities List is introduced briefly in section II; because the utopianism and historical background of the list cannot be adequately disentangled, they are discussed together in section III under the broad rubric "Utopianism, Date, and Historicity of the Lists." In section IV, I discuss significant challenges to the consensus concerning the varying texts of Josh 21 and 1 Chr 6, especially in relation to the utopian and historical qualities of the lists. As noted above, all five categories are inextricably interrelated, and the divisions made below are all somewhat artificial. Nonetheless, the attempt to separate and clarify these points of disagreement among interpreters serves as a useful heuristic enterprise, and proves instructive as patterns of interpretive decisions are observed.

II. Textual Differences

The clear differences in the final forms of Josh 21 and 1 Chr 6 occasioned some discussion in the early years of study on the Levitical cities, although usually the discussion of this category was subordinated to other, putatively more important concerns, if not disregarded altogether. Wellhausen, for example, made no mention of the textual differences between Josh 21 and 1 Chr 6 in his discussion of the Levites' inheritance. Samuel Klein took the two different forms of the list seriously, attributing them to two different recensions.[13] According to Klein's theory, both variants depicted the authentic historical reality in which each was written, although the older of the two recensions should be traced back to the time of David and Solomon.[14] However, Klein's methodological principles were extremely conservative

---

12. For a summary proceeding chronologically, see Götz Schmitt, "Levitenstädte," *ZDPV* 111 (1995): 28–48, esp. 28–32.
13. Samuel Klein, "The Cities of the Priests and the Levites, and the Cities of Refuge" (in Hebrew), *Journal of the Jewish Palestine Exploration Society* (1934–35): 81–107.
14. Ibid., 93–94.

and easily refuted. His attempts to prove the historical verifiability of the list have occasioned much resistance in light of the forced argumentation he employed in order to place Levites in the enumerated cities, no matter how tendentious the report.

As an example of the conservative nature of Klein's interpretation, we might point to his connection of Obed-edom the Gittite (2 Sam 6:10–11 // 1 Chr 13:13–14), who was later considered among the Levites (1 Chr 15:18, 21, 24–25; 16:5, 38; 26:4, 8, 15; 2 Chr 25:24), with the Levitical city Gath-rimmon (Josh 21:24, 25; 1 Chr 6:54; see also 19:45).[15] This correspondence is predicated on two dubious assumptions: First, it posits that the designation of Obed-edom as הגתי in 2 Sam 6:10, 11 and 1 Chr 13:13 indicates his familial origins in Gath-rimmon rather than in Philistine Gath. But use of the same gentilic elsewhere, used both independently (Josh 13:3; 2 Sam 15:18 [הגתים]) and as a gentilic modifying a personal name (2 Sam 15:19–22; 18:2; 21:29 // 1 Chr 20:5), ubiquitously refers to the city Gath of the Pentapolis; David's close association with the Philistines of Gath in Israelite historical memory and tradition would suggest that the shared source of 2 Sam 6:10 and 1 Chr 13:13[16] did not intend to indicate that Obed-edom was from Gath-rimmon.[17]

---

15. Ibid., 86; cf. Schmitt, "Levitenstädte," 29.

16. The relationship between synoptic passages in Samuel–Kings and Chronicles is beyond the scope of the discussion here. The majority of scholars see Samuel–Kings, in some form properly labeled as "Deuteronomistic," as the Chronicler's primary *Vorlage*, though a notable minority of scholars have followed the suggestion of A. Graeme Auld that both Samuel–Kings and Chronicles derive from a common, substantially shorter (and now lost) textual source. See, e.g., Steven McKenzie, *The Chronicler's Use of the Deuteronomistic History* (HSM 33; Atlanta: Scholars Press, 1984); Baruch Halpern, "Sacred History and Ideology: Chronicles' Thematic Structure—Indications of an Earlier Source," in *The Creation of Sacred Literature: Composition and Redaction of the Biblical Text* (ed. Richard Elliott Friedman; University of California Publications: Near Eastern Studies 22; Berkeley and Los Angeles: University of California Press, 1981), 35–54; Baruch Halpern and David S. Vanderhooft, "The Editions of Kings in the 7th–6th Centuries BCE," *HUCA* 62 (1991): 179–244, esp. 237–38; cf. A. Graeme Auld, "Prophets through the Looking Glass: Between Writings and Moses," *JSOT* 27 (1983): 3–23, esp. 7–9, 14–16; further, see idem, *Kings without Privilege: David and Moses in the Story of the Bible's Kings* (Edinburgh: T&T Clark, 1994).

17. An additional objection to linking Obed-edom with Gath-rimmon may be the failure of the text to designate him as גת הרמוני. The second element of compound toponyms (e.g., Gath-hepher, Bethlehem) normally arose as a designation of the kinship group in whose territory the town lay or who comprised a prominent lineage within the settlement. Thus, Gath-hepher is to be reckoned as "Gath of the family Hepher" (for Hepher, see Num 26:32, 33; 27:1; Josh 17:2, 3) and Gath-rimmon as "Gath [i.e., winepress, estate] of the family of Rimmon" (for the PN Rimmon, see 2 Sam 4:2, 5, 9; see Lawrence E. Stager, "The Archaeology of the Family in Ancient Israel," *BASOR* 260 [1985]: 23–24 and sources cited there; as well as Karel van der Toorn, *Family Religion in Babylonia, Syria, and Israel: Continuity and Change in the Forms of Religious Life* [Studies in the History and Culture of the Ancient Near East 7; Leiden/New York: Brill, 1996], 190–91). In cases of such compound

Second, Chronicles' designation of Obed-edom as a Levite is self-evidently a late development accounting for the ark's temporary stationing in his house. Cross-cultural study of genealogical data suggests that manipulation of genealogies is a common practice;[18] in this case the author of Chronicles most likely incorporated Obed-edom into the Levitical genealogical system in order to justify the ark's unplanned and otherwise unexplained stay in the home of someone who was (previously) manifestly of non-Levitical heritage.[19]

In his own work on the Levitical cities, William Foxwell Albright essentially sustained the date of the earlier edition of the list proposed by Klein.[20] However, Albright challenged Klein's assertion that the lists represented two recensions, arguing instead that they could be traced back "to a single origi-

---

names, we normally encounter people's origins described in terms of the town name compounded with the familial unit, not the town name alone (which would have been relatively undiagnostic): hence, בית הלחמי, "the Bethlehemite," in 1 Sam 16:18; 17:58; 2 Sam 21:19.

18. E.g., Robert R. Wilson, *Genealogy and History in the Biblical World* (Yale Near Eastern Researches 7; New Haven: Yale University Press, 1977), esp. 27–36.

19. See, e.g., Ralph W. Klein, *1 Chronicles: A Commentry* (Hermeneia; Minneapolis: Fortress, 2006), 335, 354. Klein points already to Josephus, *Ant.* 7.83, for the conflation of this Obed-edom of 2 Sam 6:10–12 with the Levite of the same name in 1 Chr 15:18, 21, 24. For more general discussions of genealogical adjustment in order to incorporate non-Levites into the Levitical guild, see, e.g., Kurt Möhlenbrink, "Die levitischen Überlieferungen des Alten Testaments," *ZAW* n.F. 11 (1934): 184–231, esp. 191–97; William Foxwell Albright, *Archaeology and the Religion of Israel* (5th ed.; Baltimore: Johns Hopkins Univeristy Press, 1968 [originally published 1942]; repr., OTL; Louisville: Westminster John Knox, 2006), 109–10; Roland de Vaux, *Ancient Israel: Its Life and Institutions* (London: Darton, Longman & Todd, 1961; repr., Biblical Resource Series; Grand Rapids: Eerdmans, 1997), 362, 371; A. H. J. Gunneweg, *Leviten und Priester: Hauptlinien der Traditionsbildung und Geschichte des israelitisch-jüdischen Kultpersonals* (FRLANT 89; Göttingen: Vandenhoeck & Ruprecht, 1965), 32–34; J. Maxwell Miller, "The Korahites of Southern Judah," *CBQ* 32 (1970): 58–68; Robert B. Robinson, "The Levites in the Pre-Monarchic Period," *Studia Biblica et Theologica* 8/2 (1978): 3–24; Menahem Haran, *Temples and Temple-Service in Ancient Israel: An Inquiry into Biblical Cult Phenomena and the Historical Setting of the Priestly School* (Oxford: Clarendon, 1978), 76–83; Norman K. Gottwald, *The Tribes of Yahweh: A Sociology of the Religion of Liberated Israel, 1250–1050 BCE* (Maryknoll, N.Y.: Orbis Books, 1979; repr., Biblical Seminar 66; Sheffield: Sheffield Academic Press, 1999), 320; Timothy Polk, "The Levites in the Davidic-Solomonic Empire," *Studia Biblica et Theologica* 9/1 (1979): 3–22; Stager, "Archaeology of the Family," 27–28.

Similar arguments can be mustered against some of Samuel Klein's other "historical" data. I point here to two cases: (1) Klein's wrangling of Hosea's references to Tabor and Mizpah (which he equated with Ramoth-gilead; Hos 5:1; "Cities," 88–91) and (2) his assumption that Absalom had intended his trip to Hebron to round up not only tribal dignitaries but priests as well (ibid., 92).

20. Albright, "List," esp. 56–58; see previously idem, *Archaeology and the Religion of Israel*, 121–25.

nal and that their divergence is due almost entirely to scribal mistakes."[21] In order to make this argument, Albright compared the two lists in MT Josh 21 and MT 1 Chr 6 with their Greek counterparts in LXX^A (Alexandrinus) and LXX^B (Vaticanus). The argument is convincing, insofar as Albright was able to show that many of the variants could, in fact, be explained as inner-Hebrew corruption. However, several of Albright's arguments raise suspicions.

In a first suspicious line of argumentation, Albright pointed to the importance of Hebron in the premonarchic and early monarchic periods. Inferring from the similar omission of Jerusalem from the list that major "secular capitals" had been intentionally left out, Albright excluded Hebron from the original list along with Shechem.[22] Because each group of cities enumerated from the tribes of Judah and Ephraim (within which Shechem was counted, although cf. Josh 17:2) displayed anomalies that could be accounted for by excising Hebron and Shechem from the original form of the list, this dual omission posed no troubles for Albright's schema: he argued that an author, recognizing the strange omission of two obviously important priestly cities, inserted Hebron and Shechem into an already full forty-eight-city list, secondarily bringing the number of cities to fifty. With the effects of haplographies, however, the list eventually fell back into a form containing forty-eight cities.[23] The coincidental nature of this speculation is striking and would suggest that something more than the fortuitous happenstance of textual corruption is at stake.[24]

Albright did not consider Jerusalem's omission problematic precisely because it was common knowledge that the city had remained "non-Israelite" until the days of David. Since the historical framework of Josh 21 places the system in the period of the conquest, it would have been an obvious anachronism for the author to include Jerusalem.[25] However, in opposition to Albright, this argument could equally have applied to other towns that, according to

---

21. Albright, "List," 50.
22. Ibid., 59 n. 24; Albright was followed tentatively in this emendation by Robert G. Boling ("Levitical Cities: Archaeology and Texts," in *Biblical and Related Studies Presented to Samuel Iwry* [ed. Ann Kort and Scott Morschauser; Winona Lake, Ind.: Eisenbrauns, 1985], 23–32, esp. 24). For Hebron as a political seat, see earlier Möhlenbrink, "Die levitischen Überlieferungen," 195.
23. Albright, "List," 53–54.
24. For this criticism, see already Zecharia Kallai, *Historical Geography of the Bible: The Tribal Territories of Israel* (Jerusalem: Magnes, 1986), 453–54.
25. See already Yehezkel Kaufmann, *The Biblical Account of the Conquest of Palestine* (trans. M. Dagut; Jerusalem: Magnes, 1953); subsequently republished as idem, *The Biblical Account of the Conquest of Canaan* (trans. M. Dagut, with a preface by Moshe Greenberg; Jerusalem: Magnes, 1985), 67 (page numbers are cited according to the republication).

the biblical narrative, came under Israelite control only during the monarchic period, such as Gezer (Josh 16:10; Judg 1:29; but 1 Kgs 9:15–17), Ayalon (Judg 1:35), Taanach (Josh 17:11–12; Judg 1:27; but 1 Kgs 4:12), Rehob (Judg 1:31), and Nahalol (Judg 1:30). More likely, in my opinion, the omission of Jerusalem from this list was designed to differentiate the Levites of all stripes from the Jerusalem-based Zadokites, whose control over the Jerusalem temple—and consequent privileging over non-Zadokite Levites—was an established fact only during the exilic and post-exilic periods (Ezek 44:10–16).[26] The term used in Ezek 44:15 to describe the Zadokites is "Levitical priests" (הכהנים הלוים). Previously, the term had been used in Deuteronomy, seemingly to indicate a much broader lineage group (Deut 17:9, 18; 18:1; 24:8; 27:9). Its use in Ezek 44:15 thus seems to be an explicit attempt to narrow the referent of Deuteronomy's "Levitical priests" retrospectively.[27] In any case, we have here assumed a system that divorces "Levites" from "Zadokites" entirely[28]—whether original

---

26. Similarly, Kaufmann relied on the list's differentiation between the Aaronids and the remaining Levites to explain Jerusalem's omission from the list (*Conquest of Canaan*, 67–68); although cf. Schmitt, "Levitenstädte," 44; and below.

27. Multiple attempts have been made to deal with the varying statuses of the Levites in the diverse biblical sources; for entrants in the debate, see, e.g., Gerhard von Rad, *Studies in Deuteronomy* (SBT 9; London: SCM, 1953), 66–68; G. Ernest Wright, "The Levites in Deuteronomy," *VT* 4 (1954): 325–30; J. A. Emerton, "Priests and Levites in Deuteronomy: An Examination of Dr. G. E. Wright's Theory," *VT* 12 (1962): 129–38, esp. 133–34; Aelred Cody, *A History of Old Testament Priesthood* (AnBib 35; Rome: Pontifical Biblical Institute, 1969), 125–74; Raymond Abba, "Priests and Levites in Deuteronomy," *VT* 27 (1977): 257–67; John R. Spencer, "The Levitical Cities: A Study of the Role and Function of the Levites in the History of Israel" (Ph.D. diss., University of Chicago, 1980), 246–48; Rodney K. Duke, "The Portion of the Levite: Another Reading of Deuteronomy 18:6–8," *JBL* 106 (1987): 193–201; idem, "Punishment or Restoration? Another Look at the Levites of Ezekiel 44.6–16," *JSOT* 40 (1988): 61–81; Stephen L. Cook, "Innerbiblical Interpretation in Ezekiel 44 and the History of Israel's Priesthood," *JBL* 114 (1995): 193–208; Ulrich Dahmen, *Leviten und Priester im Deuteronomium: Literarkritische und redaktionsgeschichtliche Studien* (BBB 110; Bodenheim: Philo, 1996); Risto Nurmela, *The Levites: Their Emergence as a Second-Class Priesthood* (South Florida Studies in the History of Judaism 193; Atlanta: Scholars Press, 1998), esp. 83–163; Gary N. Knoppers, "Hierodules, Priests, or Janitors? The Levites in Chronicles and the History of the Israelite Priesthood," *JBL* 118 (1999): 49–72; Deborah W. Rooke, *Zadok's Heirs: The Role and Development of the High Priesthood in Ancient Israel* (OTM; Oxford: Oxford University Press, 2000), 43–79, esp. 45–47; Joachim Schaper, *Priester und Leviten im achämenidischen Juda: Studien zur Kult- und Sozialgeschichte Israels in persischer Zeit* (FAT 31; Tübingen: Mohr Siebeck, 2000), 79–129. For a solution that fits within the present interpretive framework, see Hutton, "Levitical Diaspora (I)," 229.

28. For the difficulties involved in the genealogical determination of Levites, Zadokites, and Aaronids, see, e.g., John R. Spencer, "Priestly Families (or Factions) in Samuel and Kings," in *The Pitcher Is Broken: Memorial Essays for Gösta W. Ahlström* (ed. Steven W.

to the list or secondarily imposed—and we should not expect to find Jerusalem here. With Albright's argument reliant upon the omission of Jerusalem from the list countermanded, there is no compelling reason to assume that Hebron and Shechem—neither of which could claim Zadokite centrality—were not included in the original list.

Albright attempted to bolster Klein's placement of Levites in some of the enumerated cities in a second methodologically unsound argument. Pointing to the Priestly family Libni (Exod 6:17; Num 3:18, 21; 26:58; 1 Chr 6:2, 5; cf. 1 Chr 6:14), Albright argued that the place of Libnah in the list was validated. The assignment of the Levitical family Jokmeam to the Qohathite lineage—and specifically, of the Hebronite lineage thereof (cf. the name יָקְמְעָם in 1 Chr 23:19; 24:23)—could similarly validate the assignment of Jokmeam to the Qohathite lineage in 1 Chr 6:53 (in the face of the variant קבצים in Josh 21:22): "It stands to reason that an accidental parallel like this—all the stronger because Ephraim [which donated Jokmeam] was attributed in our list of Levitic cities to Kohath—was not invented for the purpose!"[29] Here Albright assumed, of course, that the genealogy had in fact *not* been invented for the purpose of validating the Levitical Cities List contained in 1 Chr 6, and that the list itself displayed no influence from the genealogy of 1 Chr 23. The reasoning is circular: like Klein's case of Obed-edom "the Gittite" discussed above, Albright's argument places far too much trust in the historical reliability of the Chronicler's genealogies. As already noted, more recent sociological and anthropological models have demonstrated the fabricated nature of genealogies.[30] No matter which text may have taken chronological precedence over the other, nothing precludes the supposition that one was not edited with the other in mind.

In light of the preceding discussion, it is clear that any comprehensive study of the Levitical Cities Lists in Josh 21 and 1 Chr 6 must deal adequately with the textual *realia* available in MT and in the versional witnesses (minimally, the LXX and the Dead Sea Scrolls, whose discovery was roughly contemporaneous with Albright's publication). Less obvious, however, is the very real need for sociologically and anthropologically informed approaches to the Chronicler's genealogies. These genealogies are themselves inextricably intertwined with the composition history of the Levitical Cities Lists and must be considered critically as part of the larger project. Textual study alone is methodologically insufficient.

Holloway and Lowell K. Handy; JSOTSup 190; Sheffield: Sheffield Academic Press, 1995), 387–400; see also, e.g., Cody, *History of Old Testament Priesthood*, 146–74; Nurmela, *Levites*, esp. 83–163; Rooke, *Zadok's Heirs*, 43–79.

29. Albright, "List," 55–56; quotation from 56.
30. See nn. 18 and 19 above.

III. Utopianism, Date, and Historicity of the Lists

A. Early Connections of the List to the (Pre-)Conquest and Monarchic Eras

Despite his assertion that "[n]o Palestinian topographer who examines this list can fail to be convinced of its substantial authenticity,"[31] Albright himself recognized the idealism inherent in the list's construction. Because the system was "artificial from the beginning," he declared, the subsequent loss of any towns to non-Israelite population groups disrupted the order, and thus the stability, of the entire system.[32] Moreover, Albright does not seem to have believed that the system had ever been fully established, since he considered it "very unlikely that efforts to settle Levites in the newly conquered Canaanite cities around the periphery of Israel were successful,"[33] although he did presuppose a concerted and sustained attempt on the part of David's royal administration to move Levitical population groups into the enumerated cities.[34] It is clear from the outset of the present discussion that the schematic and artificial nature of the Levitical Cities Lists must be dealt with, both by those who wish to dismiss the lists' historicity and by those who wish to sustain it.

An attempt to hold a similarly early setting for the recognizably idealized and impractical list of Levitical cities was made not long after the appearance of Albright's article by Yehezkel Kaufmann.[35] Kaufmann mobilized a series of arguments to show that the utopian projection represented in Josh 21 had never been implemented as such, but rather comprised a Priestly program that sought to articulate P's ideal situation upon entry into the land of Canaan, before the institution of the monarchy. By positing the staggeringly early premonarchic date, predicated upon the utopian and artificial nature of the list, Kaufmann was able to make several specious connections. First, he viewed Jerusalem's omission from the list (along with other cities that were manifestly Priestly and Levitical cities shortly after the Israelites' entry into the land: "*Shiloh, Nob, Bethel, Gilgal, Mizpah, Dan, Beersheba, Rama*") as an indication that the list had been compiled in anticipation of or shortly after the conquest, since no writer would have forgotten to include these cities.[36] Second, Kaufmann

---

31. Albright, "List," 55.
32. Ibid., 59.
33. Ibid.
34. Albright, *Archaeology and the Religion of Israel*, 123–25; cf. Kaufmann, *Conquest of Canaan*, 67.
35. Kaufmann, *Conquest of Canaan*, 65–71.
36. Ibid., 67 (emphasis Kaufmann's); cf. Kallai, *Historical Geography*, 455; Jan Svensson, *Towns and Toponyms in the Old Testament with Special Emphasis on Joshua 14–21* (ConBOT 38; Stockholm: Almqvist & Wiksell, 1994), 83.

linked the schematic nature of the cities' distribution to the (early) Priestly writer's "utopian *demand*" to maintain a strict differentiation between priests and Levites. The Levitical Cities List, he argued, "carries this division to its *extreme*" by "embody[ing] it in a *territorial* segregation."[37] Third, the division of the land assigning the Levitical cities from Judah, Simeon, and Benjamin to the Aaronids (whom Kaufmann equated with "Priests") and relegating the Levites (i.e., non-priests) to the remainder of cities in the north was unbelievable and confirmed for Kaufmann that the list was "utterly fictitious."[38] Finally, the putatively premonarchic-era idealism of the list is bolstered by the allotment of cities to be apportioned by Dan. Because Dan's donation to the Levites corresponds to its southern possession (Josh 19:40–46, 48), prescribed by lot, rather than with its actual northern location (Josh 19:47; Judg 18), the Levitical Cities List can be nothing other than a utopian, programmatic expression from the time of the conquest.[39]

Like Albright's insistence that the omission of Jerusalem signaled an early date for the Levitical Cities List, so too does the date of the list theorized by Kaufmann flounder upon closer inspection of the list's genealogical assumptions, along with the historical development of the sacred lineages in the Iron Age. Although full discussion of these issues is not possible here, a few short criticisms may be offered. Kaufmann assumed far too static a division between "priests" and "Levites" and thus failed to understand correctly the utopian nature of the Levitical Cities List. In preferring to subsume the list's problematic aspects into issues of "Priestly" over against "Levitical" function, Kaufmann arbitrarily privileged one theoretical construct over another.[40] Moreover, Kaufmann's thesis concerning the "obsolete, literary utopia, a memorial to the aspirations of the Priesthood at the time of the Conquest,"[41] does not adequately consider the possibility that a later writer intentionally cast the list as a conquest-era document in order to provide some verisimilitude with the chronological context of the list in Judges. If the list *is* to be

---

37. Kaufmann, *Conquest of Canaan*, 67–68; quotation from 67 (emphasis Kaufmann's).
38. Ibid., 68.
39. Ibid., 68–69, 71.
40. Aside from the delicacy of genealogical issues (discussed above), the schematic binary opposition between (Mushite) "Levites" over against (Aaronid) "priests," defended, e.g., by Frank Moore Cross (*Canaanite Myth and Hebrew Epic: Essays in the History and Religion of Israel* [Cambridge, Mass.: Harvard University Press, 1973], 195–215), is contested by more anthropologically sensitive studies. For example, Baruch Halpern posits the existence of a variety of competing holy lineages *within* the "Levite" group ("Levitic Participation in the Reform Cult of Jeroboam I," *JBL* 95 [1976]: 31–42; for further discussion, see Hutton, "Levitical Diaspora [I]," 223–34; and idem, "Southern, Northern, and Transjordanian Perspectives," in *Religious Diversity in Ancient Israel and Judah* [ed. Francesca Stavrakopoulou and John Barton; London/New York: T&T Clark International, 2010], 160–61).
41. Kaufmann, *Conquest of Canaan*, 71.

considered utopian and ideal, this would not be because it represents the unfulfilled dreams of a putatively conquest-era Priestly writer.

B. Revised Dating of the List: Alt and Noth

A more plausible understanding of the historical conditions and utopian ideals underlying the Levitical Cities Lists has been under development since the 1920s and 1930s in the work of Albrecht Alt, Martin Noth, and others. This variation of the thesis claiming a fundamentally unrealistic structure of the Levitical Cities Lists continues, like Kaufmann's analysis, to link the structure of the list with its purported historical context. Accordingly, the author's impulse to create the list as such stemmed from a sincere desire to see the list's tacit assertions realized, or at least to organize Israelite or Judahite social life meaningfully. Unlike Kaufmann, however, Alt and his followers have dated the form of the lists themselves to a relatively late period.

In a pair of articles written during the 1920s Alt argued for the legitimate historicity of the boundary descriptions in Josh 13–19.[42] The descriptions themselves, he argued, could be traced back to a very early period in Israel's occupancy of the land in which the historical realities of population settlement were unpredictable and not subject to schematization—thus, they could perhaps be traced even to the premonarchic era.[43] Various remarkable features of the lists, such as the division of Tappuah from its dependent field-lands in Josh 17:8, suggest as much.[44] However, Alt found no compelling reasons to date the texts themselves to such an early date. With the final form of Josh 13–19 uncoupled from the historical memories preserved in its constituent boundary descriptions and the later city lists, the Levitical Cities List in Josh 21 also became unmoored from its putative historical referent. In a third article, published in 1951, Alt compared the historical background of the Levitical Cities List to that of several other Judahite topographical lists contained in the Hebrew Bible.[45] Alt drew attention to the physical distribution of the Levitical cities: they clustered at the borders of the land, with two significant areas bereft of any cities at all. These geographical lacunae could be explained, Alt

---

42. Albrecht Alt, "Judas Gaue unter Josia," *PJ* 21 (1925): 100–116 = idem, *Kleine Schriften zur Geschichte des Volkes Israels* [*KS*] (2 vols.; Munich: Beck, 1953), 2:276–88; idem, "Das System der Stammesgrenzen im Buche Josua," in *Beiträge zur Religionsgeschichte und Archäologie Palästinas: Ernst Sellin zum 60. Geburtstage dargebracht* (ed. William F. Albright; Leipzig: Deichert, 1927), 13–24 = *KS* 1:193–202. All page numbers are given according to republished versions in *KS*.

43. Alt, "System," 1:198–202.

44. Ibid., 200.

45. Albrecht Alt, "Bemerkungen zu einigen judäischen Ortslisten des Alten Testaments," *Beiträge zur biblischen Landes- und Altertumskunde* 68 (1951): 193–210 = *KS* 2:289–305.

argued, through reference to the history of Josiah's reign, and particularly to the account of his religious reforms (2 Kgs 23:4–8, 10–15, 19–20). According to 2 Kgs 23:8a, Judah was nearly emptied of Levitical priests upon Josiah's consolidation of ritual responsibilities in Jerusalem. Conversely, Samaria's priests were all killed at Josiah's command (vv. 19–20).[46] For the most part, the enumerated cities can be found at the southern and western edges of Judah's tribal territory, although a few of the Benjaminite cities were clustered just north of Jerusalem; these cities, Alt argued, were reserved as residences for the Levitical ministrants at the central temple.[47] Alt surmised that the Judahite portion of the Levitical Cities List depicted not an actual state of affairs but rather merely the unfulfilled orders issued by Josiah.[48] Alt's observations provided a plausible set of reasons for the odd distribution of the cities. These reasons both necessitated and justified dating the texts to the late monarchic period.[49]

In one of the first redaction- and source-critical examinations of Josh 21, Noth seized on Alt's separation of the list's historical background from its present form and literary context. Thus enabled, Noth attempted to trace a discernible developmental history in the Levitical Cities List. He asserted the secondariness of the cities of refuge in the list, citing three separate indicators. First, the insertion of Shechem among the cities of Ephraim (Josh 21:21a*) had been performed erroneously. Although the city had presumably been allotted to Manasseh, the tribe from which its eponymous ancestor derived (cf. Josh 17:2), the town was described in Josh 20:7 as being "on Mt. Ephraim (בהר אפרים)." The redactor who inserted the name Shechem in 21:21a* had done so mistakenly, having misinterpreted the topographic notice as designating the city's location in the tribal inheritance of Ephraim, rather than in the topographic region of Mount Ephraim, where both Ephraim and Manasseh dwelled.[50] Second, the cities of refuge are missing in other passages in which other Levitical cities from the same allotment occur. Noth compared the omission of Bezer in Josh 13:18 with 21:36–37, and of Qedesh in 19:35bβ with 21:32. Third, the double appearance of Hebron in Josh 21:11, 13 signaled to Noth the only point of overlap in the two lists, thus providing the redac-

---

46. Ibid., 2:294–300. Tryggve N. D. Mettinger subsequently drew attention to the fact that there is little evidence for Alt's assumption that the Levites had originally been settled more evenly throughout Judah (Mettinger, *Solomonic State Officials: A Study of the Civil Government Officials of the Israelite Monarchy* [ConBOT 5; Lund: Gleerup, 1971], 98).

47. Alt, "Bemerkungen," 299.

48. Ibid., 299–300.

49. Ibid., 300–301; see also idem, "Festungen und Levitenorte im Lande Juda," in idem, *KS* 2:306–15, esp. 310–15. Alt was followed in this dating by, e.g., Gunneweg, *Leviten und Priester*, 64–65.

50. Noth, *Das Buch Josua* (HAT I/7; Tübingen: Mohr, 1938), 97 = *Das Buch Josua* (2nd ed.; HAT I/7; Tübingen: Mohr, 1953), 127. This criticism has been followed by many of the interpreters discussed below (e.g., Schmitt, "Levitenstädte," 33).

tor with sufficient reason to integrate the list of the cities of refuge with the Levitical Cities List.[51] The resultant *irregularity* of the list occasioned for Noth a search for the historical conditions behind the Levitical Cities List. Noth pointed to the limited distribution of the Aaronid Levites, who resided solely within the late-preexilic territory of Judah, and the widespread distribution of the other priestly families in Transjordan and Cisjordan. The latter dispersal, he argued, was a vestige of an earlier state of affairs, the reminiscence of peripheral Levites whose way of life had not been totally eradicated—perhaps not yet even touched—by the centripetal forces of Josiah's reform. Yet the tradition-historical data such as the Priestly document's threefold division of the Levitical tribe into Qohathites, Gershonites, and Merarites, as well as the postexilic era prominence of the Aaronids, points to a post-monarchic date for the list's historical referent, argued Noth.[52]

The work of Alt and Noth made possible a distinct conceptual break between the historical referent(s) of the Levitical Cities List, a relatively early list of these Levitical cities, and the two distinct forms that were eventually taken by that prototype in their respective literary contexts. This tripartite distinction is an important one, as will be seen in the following discussion. Although Noth's sensibilities concerning the distribution of Levitical families are sound—indeed, they are very much in line with the thesis of the present study—his arguments addressing the final form of the Levitical Cities List are easily countered. For example, Noth makes the a priori assumption that the early version of the Levitical Cities List underlies the boundary descriptions in Josh 13–19. Accordingly, the Levitical Cities List was unable to supply the boundary descriptions with the names of the cities of refuge because the Levitical Cities List itself did not have them.[53] The supposition is a hazardous one, not least because the connections made here are tenuous. True, Josh 13:18 and 21:36–37 align nicely, save the omission of Bezer in the former verse:

13:8	ומפעת	וקדמת	ויהצה
21:36–37	ואת־מיפעת ...	את־קדימות ...	את־בצר ... ואת־יהצה ...

The same cannot be said, however, of 19:35bβ and 21:32, where the overlap of toponyms is tenuous at best and conjectural at worst:

---

51. Noth, *Josua*, 97 (2nd ed., 127); Noth was followed in this assessment by Cody, *History of Old Testament Priesthood*, 160.

52. Noth, *Josua*, 100–101 (2nd ed., 131–32).

53. Noth, *Josua*, 97 (2nd ed., 127): "Der sekundäre Charakter dieser Namen ergibt sich einmal daraus, daß an anderen Stellen des Josua-Buches die Namen aus Jos 21 zitiert worden sind, als die Namen der Asylstädte hier noch nicht standen ..." ("The secondary character of these names comes to light immediately, since at other places in the Book of Joshua the names are cited from Josh 21 as though the names of the cities of refuge did not yet stand here ...").

19:35bβ	וכנרת:	וחמת רקת	
21:32	את־קרתן	... את־חמת דאר	את־קדש בגליל ...

Moreover, Noth's assumption neglects the possibility that the Levitical Cities List was fleshed out from the boundary descriptions, a possibility Noth himself posited elsewhere.[54] Finally, the repeated mention of Hebron in Josh 21:11, 13 can certainly be traced to an addition of some sort, but only obliquely suggests that the rest of the cities of refuge were interpolated from the list in Josh 20. Götz Schmitt points out that in every mention of a city of refuge in Josh 21, the city stands first in the tribal allotment (vv. 13, 21, 27, 32, 36, 38). Furthermore, comparison with related texts demonstrates the secondary nature of most of Josh 21:11–13a*. The verb ויתנו in v. 11aα[1]* governs the remainder of the chapter, acting as the fulfillment of Moses' command in Num 35:2 that the Israelites "should give" (ונתנו) cities to the Levites from their own tribal allotments. Otherwise, vv. 11* and 12 stand almost completely outside the otherwise regular structure of vv. 13–40. We must suppose that the datum concerning the delivery of Hebron's fields to Caleb in v. 12 was added secondarily to smooth out the tension with Josh 15:13, where this tribe receives as part of its allotment "Qiryat-arba of the clan of Anak, that is, Hebron" (את־קרית ארבע אבי הענק היא חברון). This locution was also evidently inserted into the Levitical Cities List in front of the name Hebron, which stood originally at the head of the enumerated cities. Finally, because the insertion of vv. 11aα[2]β, 12 had disrupted the tightly composed ordering of the list, the redactor was forced to pick up the list with a *Wiederaufnahme*, inserting v. 13a*.[55] Noth's proposal is thus not necessary; one may ask further, is it *likely*? The raw numerical regularity of Josh 21:13–40 would suggest not.[56]

C. The Schematic Nature of the List in Joshua 21

One of the most prominent points of relative consensus on the nature of the Levitical Cities List is its fundamentally schematic structure (at least in Josh 21) that, with a few exceptions, assigns four cities from each tribe. This applies to Benjamin (Josh 21:17–18; but cf. 1 Chr 6:45[57]); Ephraim (Josh 21:20–22; cf.

---

54. E.g., Noth, *Josua*, 99 (2nd ed., 129). For this criticism, see also Schmitt, "Levitenstädte," 33; and cf. esp. 44–46.

55. Schmitt, "Levitenstädte," 33.

56. See here particularly Kallai, *Historical Geography*, 452; and Schmitt, "Levitenstädte," 33–34.

57. The textual minus in 1 Chr 6:45 (גבעון; cf. Josh 21:17) suggests that the verse has probably suffered haplography through graphic similarity to the immediately following גבע (see, e.g., Kallai, *Historical Geography*, 469). The city עלמון (Josh 21:18) is paralleled by עלמת, which occurs before ענתות in 1 Chr 6:45.

THE LEVITICAL DIASPORA (II) 61

1 Chr 6:51-54[58]); Dan (Josh 21:23-24; cf. 1 Chr 6:54[59]); Manasseh (albeit in two parts: Josh 21:25; cf. 1 Chr 6:55[60] [west-Manasseh]; and Josh 21:27 = 1 Chr 6:56[61] [east-Manasseh]); Issachar (Josh 21:28-29 = 1 Chr 6:57-58[62]); Asher (Josh 21:30-31 = 1 Chr 6:59-60[63]); Zebulun (Josh 21:34-35; cf. 1 Chr 6:62[64]); Reuben (Josh 21:36-37 = 1 Chr 6:63-64[65]); and Gad (Josh 21:38-39 = 1 Chr 6:65-66[66]). The three exceptions are Judah and Simeon, who are listed together and whose collective contribution adds up to nine cities (Josh 21:13-16; cf. 1 Chr 6:[39-41], 42-44[67]), and Naphtali, which donates only three cities (Josh 21:32 = 1 Chr 6:61[68]). The overwhelming regularity of this system, in which most of the tribes donate a fixed number of cities (9 tribes × 4 cities = 36) and the other three a commensurate number between them (9 + 3 = 12 cities, averaging 4 apiece), is

---

58. Again here 1 Chr 6:53-54 has suffered the haplography of the introduction of the Danite donation, and correspondingly omits אלתקא and גבתון (cf. Josh 21:23), and considers אילון and גת־רמון as Ephraim's fifth and sixth donated cities (cf. Josh 21:24). For discussion, see, e.g., Kallai, *Historical Geography*, 465-67.

59. Compare the preceding note.

60. The cities תענך and גת־רמון of Josh 21:25 are replaced by ענר and בלעם in 1 Chr 6:55.

61. A slight graphic variation has occurred between גלון (*ketiv*, but cf. *qere* גולן) and בעשתרה (Josh 21:27) and גלון and עשתרות (1 Chr 6:56); Kallai considered בעשתרה "an abbreviation or a corruption" of בית עשתרות (*Historical Geography*, 471). As Schmitt points out, it is possible that originally both halves of Manasseh donated their cities to the Qohathite Levites; this arrangement would have resulted in a more uniform distribution of cities, with each Levitical lineage receiving twelve cities (assuming the concomitant textual move postulated by Yoram Tsafrir; see Schmitt, "Levitenstädte," 32-33; and n. 68 below).

62. Here, too, a variety of textual variations appear: קשיון (Josh 21:28) // קדש (1 Chr 6:57); ירמות and עין־גנים (Josh 21:29) // ראמות and ענם (1 Chr 6:58).

63. Cf. משאל (Josh 21:30) // משל (1 Chr 6:59); חלקת (Josh 21:31) // חוקק (1 Chr 6:60).

64. As in the cases of Benjamin and Dan, it is likely here that the text of 1 Chr 6:62 has suffered haplography. Moreover, the names of the cities involved do not bear any significant graphic relationship: cf. יקנעם, קרתה, דמנה, and נהלל (Josh 21:34-35) over against רמונו (but cf. דמנה) and תבור (1 Chr 6:62).

65. In a rare move, the editors of *BHS* have reconstructed Josh 21:37-38 entirely on the basis of versional and other manuscript evidence (the verses are missing in Codex Leningradensis). For this reason, no intra-MT[L] graphic variations occur).

66. The variation in these verses is entirely orthographic: cf. רמת בגלעד and יעזר (Josh 21:38, 39) over against ראמות בגלעד and יעזיר (1 Chr 6:65, 66).

67. Compare the following (apparently graphic) variations: חלן (Josh 21:15) vs. חילז (1 Chr 6:43); דבר (Josh 21:15) vs. דביר (1 Chr 6:43); עין (Josh 21:15) vs. עשן (1 Chr 6:43). The town יטה (Josh 21:16) is omitted in 1 Chr 6:44.

68. Cf. חמת דאר (Josh 21:32) vs. חמון (1 Chr 6:61); and קרתן (Josh 21:32) vs. קריתים (1 Chr 6:61). Yoram Tsafrir solved this discrepancy by arguing that Beth-shemesh of Naphtali (Judg 1:33) had been mistakenly transposed to the combined allotments of Judah and Simeon under the influence of Josh 19:40-48, which enumerates Dan's southern tribal allotment, including an עיר־שמש ("The Levitic City of Beth-shemesh: In Judah or in Naphtali?" [in Hebrew], *ErIsr* 12 [1975]: 44-45; Eng. summary, *119).

too obvious to miss. The earliest critical interpreters remained content to concede the utopianism of the list but insisted on the list's foundational historicity, with a historical referent in the premonarchic (Kaufmann) or monarchic periods (Klein, Albright). As described above, Alt and Noth sought fundamentally to uncouple the lists' date and underlying reality from the putative historical context attributed to them, and to treat the actual historical "system" of cities separately from the historical development undergone by the text. As will be seen below, this was a valuable theoretical move, since it allowed scholars to be more precise in their conceptualization of the various attendant problems. Yet the divorce of text and historical background brought with it other difficulties. For example, Noth's attempts to unhitch the historical system of Levitical cities from their literary documentation allowed his concomitant supposition concerning the secondariness of the six cities of refuge. But this hypothesis undid the neat regularity of the system, supposing that originally the list held only forty-three cities (including Hebron, which was common to both lists). The sheer coincidence involved in an irregularly structured list becoming a regular and schematic one through the arbitrary insertion of a set of cities whose number was already fixed defies plausibility.

Obviously, the schematic regularity of the Levitical Cities Lists, as related by the Masoretic Text of Josh 21, should trigger suspicion as to whether the represented system was in fact practicable and, for that matter, whether the biblical report bears any historical credibility whatsoever. This suspicion has typically manifested itself in a number of different ways: we can gather the reaction to the Levitical Cities List's schematic nature—whether actual or only apparent—in two loosely homogenous camps. The first group maintains, more or less, that behind the Levitical Cities List existed a real system of cities, which has been schematized through compositional means. The second group displays less concern with any purported historical reference of the list(s) and concentrates instead on determining the literary relationship of the lists in Josh 21 and 1 Chr 6. Naturally, the two groups utilize many of the same features to make their arguments, and the positions are necessarily interrelated. For heuristic purposes, I maintain this rough division of primary concerns in the following discussion.

D. The Historical-Realist Camp

Interpreters maintaining a realistic historical background for the Levitical Cities List(s) have themselves been divided over the issue of exactly how schematic the lists were. Benjamin Mazar stressed the absolute historicity of the list, downplaying Kaufmann's view of the lists as an unfulfilled ideation.[69] For

---

69. Benjamin Mazar, "The Cities of the Priests and the Levites," in *Congress Volume: Oxford, 1959* (VTSup 7; Leiden: Brill, 1960), 193–205, esp. 195.

Mazar, several clues pointed to a Solomonic date of an actual historical system of Levitical cities. Among these clues was the inclusion of Gezer in the list, a city that was purportedly not a part of Israel's territorial holdings until its delivery into Solomon's hand by his father-in-law, Pharaoh (1 Kgs 9:16).[70] However, more recent historiographical methods than Mazar's have proven to be more skeptical about the veracity of this notice. Klein, Albright, and Kaufmann had all used similar data to justify their own respective datings of the list's historical reference, and, like many of the scholars who preceded him, Mazar seems to have assumed that all the enumerated Levitical cities had to have been in operation as Levitical centers at the same time for the list's background to be considered "historical." All in all, Mazar's analysis was not only cogent but fruitful as well, since it permitted him to counter Alt's and Noth's respective theories with the hypothesis that the Levitical Cities List presented an authentic, historical record of a centrally oriented system of administration imposed on the outlying areas of David and Solomon's newly constituted kingdom or on other border regions in need of subjugation.[71] Yohanan Aharoni followed Mazar in this assessment, although Aharoni dated the system to David's reign rather than Solomon's.[72] All in all, Mazar's proposal converged nicely with 1 Chr 26:29–32, wherein it is stated that David appointed Levites from Hebron as overseers of the Transjordanian tribes.[73] Yet it is not so clear

---

70. Ibid., 201.
71. Ibid., 200, 203–4. Mazar posited Egyptian influence, suggesting that this was a "policy deeply rooted in established custom, i.e. in the administrative and religious practice of the Ancient Near East in general and the Land of Canaan in particular" (ibid., 204; see also Mettinger, *Solomonic State Officials*, 99–101; but cf. Boling, "Levitical Cities," 23, 28; and idem, "Levitical History and the Role of Joshua," in *The Word of the Lord Shall Go Forth: Essays in Honor of David Noel Freedman in Celebration of His Sixtieth Birthday* [ed. Carol L. Meyers and M. O'Connor; Winona Lake, Ind.: Eisenbrauns, 1983], 241–61, esp. 242–43, 250).
72. Yohanan Aharoni, *The Land of the Bible: A Historical Geography* (rev. ed.; Philadelphia: Westminster, 1979), 301–5. See also the work of J. Maxwell Miller, who not only dated the Levitical city system to the united monarchy but also argued that the city list of 2 Chr 11:5–12 was a historical reminiscence that Rehoboam had strengthened certain cities of Judah whose support was not already assumed because of Levitical affiliation ("Rehoboam's Cities of Defense and the Levitical City List," in *Archaeology and Biblical Interpretation: Essays in Memory of D. Glenn Rose* [ed. Leo G. Perdue, Lawrence E. Toombs, Gary L. Johnson; Atlanta: John Knox, 1987], 273–86; cf. earlier Alt, "Festungen und Levitenorte," 306–15). Cf., however, Mettinger, who argued for a Solomonic date, citing Gezer as the definitive indicator (*Solomonic State Officials*, 98–99 and 99 n. 8).
73. See also Roddy L. Braun, *1 Chronicles* (WBC 14; Waco, Tex.: Word Books, 1986), 254; H. G. M. Williamson, *1 and 2 Chronicles* (NCB; Grand Rapids: Eerdmans, 1982), 173; cf. Kallai, *Historical Geography*, 455; Ehud Ben Zvi, "The List of the Levitical Cities," *JSOT* 54 (1992): 77–106, esp. 79–80; Sara Japhet, *1 Chronik* (HThKAT; Freiburg: Herder, 2002), 422; and R. Klein, *1 Chronicles*, 496–97.

that Mazar's assumptions need to be borne out fully for the list to retain some of its historical credibility.

It is immensely difficult to align archaeological records with the system of Levitical cities as portrayed in the Levitical Cities List(s) and as posited by Mazar. The first problem is a textual one—it is not altogether clear that we can arrive at a suitable, consensus-bearing group of cities identified in the two preserved versions of the Levitical Cities List. Yet even when the overlapping cities in the two lists can be identified with precision, a tenth-century B.C.E. date is difficult to sustain for all of them. In his massive dissertation, John L. Peterson published the results of surface surveys he had conducted at each putative "Levitical" city.[74] Peterson's results pointed to an eighth-century date for the system of Levitical cities; it was this century, he argued, in which pottery sherds at nearly all the examined sites provide evidence for the occupation and inhabitation of a contemporaneous system of Levitical cities.[75] In this dating, Peterson came close to supporting the hypothesis put forward by Roland de Vaux, who earlier had suggested dating the historical background of the lists—although not the composition of the lists themselves—to the early schismatic period of the monarchy.[76] Despite Peterson's thorough documentation of his fieldwork and the rigor with which his team sought access to all these sites, this dissertation demonstrates a few of the problems with investigation into the Levitical cities. First of all, not only does Peterson's conclusion follow Mazar (and others) in assuming that the Levitical cities all functioned contemporaneously in a single, centrally controlled system,[77] but it also assumes that Peterson has correctly identified all forty-eight of the cities.[78] By way of example, Peterson identifies the Levitical city Mahanaim as modern day

---

74. John L. Peterson, "A Topographical Surface Survey of the Levitical 'Cities' of Joshua 21 and 1 Chronicles 6: Studies on the Levites in Israelite Life and Religion" (Th.D. diss., Chicago Institute of Advanced Theological Studies and Seabury-Western Theological Seminary, 1977).

75. Ibid., 714–15. Boling supported the results of Peterson's study ("Levitical Cities," 29–31; and idem, *Joshua: A New Translation with Notes and Commentary* [AB 6; Garden City, N.Y.: Doubleday, 1982], 492–97, esp. 494).

76. De Vaux, *Ancient Israel*, 366–67; but cf. idem, *The Early History of Israel* (London: Darton, Longman & Todd, 1978), 530. De Vaux suggested in this later venue that the Levites had been settled in their cities long before the system was committed to memory in the Levitical Cities List.

77. Contrary to the cities' function imagined by Mazar, Peterson suggested that the Levitical cities served as "Yahweh teaching centers," that is, as centers of religious education designed to produce a normative religious presence in the non- or quasi-Israelite ethnic areas. Mazar and Peterson therefore differ on the controlling body of the Levitical city system, even if they agree on the centripetal orientation of the forces governing it (Peterson, "Topographical Surface Survey," 713–20, esp. 717–19; quotation from 718; see also Boling, "Levitical Cities," 27; idem, *Joshua*, 495–97).

78. For the difficulties of correctly identifying the Levitical cites of Reuben (and a few

T. Ḥaǧǧāǧ (2154.1731).⁷⁹ Although this identification of the city continues a tradition inaugurated by luminaries in the field (e.g., Noth and de Vaux), more recent work has demonstrated the plausibility of the city's identification with the nearby T. aḏ-Ḏahab al-Ġarbīya (2149.1771)—an identification with an equally prestigious pedigree (e.g., Dalman and Mazar).⁸⁰ Second, Peterson's study assumes that the results of surface surveys accurately divulge the settlement history of a site. Peterson addresses this latter variable himself in his concluding chapter: "While anyone involved in surface surveying would quickly admit that a century could easily be missed at a few sites, it is more difficult to argue against 30."⁸¹ One may readily concede Peterson's point in theory, but in light of the preceding concern, I would respond that the project of surface surveying to assess a common date in which several cities were occupied is only as solid as the identification of the cities themselves. Moreover, Eveline J. van der Steen has recently summarized the pottery assemblages at both sites proposed as the location of Mahanaim (T. Ḥaǧǧāg and T. aḏ-Ḏahab al-Ġarbīya), reporting numerous exemplars of early Iron Age pottery at each location.⁸² In short, both sites bear evidence of a substantially earlier Iron Age settlement than that claimed by Peterson for T. Ḥaǧǧāg.⁸³

Shortly before the completion of Peterson's dissertation, Aelred Cody published his own discussion of the Levitical cities.⁸⁴ Although the short study

---

divergences from Peterson's identifications), see J. Andrew Dearman, "The Levitical Cities of Reuben and Moabite Toponymy," *BASOR* 276 (1989): 55–66.

79. Peterson, "Topographical Surface Survey," 603–14, 703.

80. For the recent attempts at identification through textual and linguistic investigations, see Alexander Achilles Fischer, *Von Hebron nach Jerusalem: Eine redaktionsgeschichtliche Studie zur Erzählung von König David in II Sam 1–5* (BZAW 335; Berlin: de Gruyter, 2004), 81–84; Jeremy M. Hutton, "Mahanaim, Penuel and Transhumance Routes: Observations on Genesis 32–33 and Judges 8," *JNES* 65 (2006): 161–78; idem, review of Yoel Elitzur, *Ancient Place Names in the Holy Land* (Jerusalem: Magnes; Winona Lake, Ind.: Eisenbrauns, 2004), *Maarav* 14 (2007): 77–97, esp. 84–96; and idem, "Jacob's 'Two Camps' and Transjordanian Geography: Wrestling with Order in Genesis 32," *ZAW* 122 (2010): 20–32.

81. Peterson, "Topographical Surface Survey," 714.

82. E. J. van der Steen, *Tribes and Territories in Transition: The Central East Jordan Valley in the Late Bronze and Early Iron Ages: A Study of the Sources* (OLA 130; Leuven/Dudley, Mass.: Peeters, 2004), 230–31.

83. See also Boling, "Levitical Cities," 30. An added difficulty in assenting to Peterson's conclusion is the fact that the chart provided in his conclusion registers many more sites without eighth-century occupation than Peterson admits in his prose account ("Topographical Surface Survey," 701–3).

84. Aelred Cody, "Levitical Cities and the Israelite Settlement," in *Homenaje a Juan Prado: miscelánea de estudios bíblicos y hebráicos* (ed. L. Alvarez Verdes and E. J. Alonso Hernandez; Madrid: Consejo Superior de Investigaciones Científicas, Instituto Benito Arias Montano de Estudios Henbráicos, Sefardies y Oriente Próximo, 1975), 179–89; in this essay, Cody departed somewhat from what was a much briefer but, in my opinion, a more historically sophisticated discussion in his *History of Old Testament Priesthood*, 160–65, esp. 161.

is extremely conservative in its approach to the biblical text, it does contribute meaningfully to the present discussion in an important way: Cody recognized that the cities of the list may not have formed a full-fledged contemporaneous system.[85] Drawing from the biblical reports of the Levites' occupation of land, and from the lists' representation of Levitical property rights (or lack thereof), Cody emphasized the varying ages of Levitical settlement in each of the cities. Hebron was perhaps the oldest of the Levitical settlements, he claimed, citing the property rights established in that city (and contrasting the situation of the wandering Levite from Bethlehem in Judg 17:7–13). In fact, argued Cody, "An analogous situation perhaps obtained in the other Levitical cities of southwestern Judah, and the Levites may have arrived in the South at the very beginning of permanent Israelite settlement, as one of the groups associated with Moses."[86] Accordingly, other areas were capable of hosting Levitical גרים during the late twelfth and eleventh centuries, but the natively Canaanite urban centers such as Taanach and Ibleam remained unavailable for Levite settlement until they had been claimed by the Davidic monarchy.[87] Cody placed no emphasis at all on the supposed monarchic sponsorship that Mazar and Aharoni had envisioned, but instead posited that the "Levitical cities" were designated as such purely on account of the indigenous inhabitants' willingness to host incoming, landless Levites. This freed Cody from desperately seeking to find a single period in which all the cities somehow aligned to form a "system," but the problems with the theory—both its uncritical reliance on the biblical text as a historical account of the settlement period and its inability to envision a deeper cause for inclusion in the list than mere Levitical occupation—are obvious.

In a much more literarily sensitive study than either Mazar's or Cody's, Menahem Haran argued that the accounts of the Levitical cities in Josh 21 and 1 Chr 6 display *both* idealized, utopian elements *and* realistic, historically plausible traces.[88] Wellhausen had appealed to the Priestly writer's project of promoting priests at the expense of Levites in order to ground his original challenge to the historical plausibility of the Levitical Cities List. For Haran, however, it was inconceivable that, had the late author P composed the account himself, he would not have gathered all the priests into the temple precinct[89]— or at least placed them within the idealized Priestly "land of Israel!"[90] In short,

---

85. See similarly Boling, "Levitical Cities," 31; idem, *Joshua*, 496.
86. Boling, "Levitical Cities," 184.
87. Ibid., 187.
88. Menahem Haran, "Studies in the Account of the Levitical Cities: I. Preliminary Considerations," *JBL* 80 (1961): 45–54; and idem, "Studies in the Account of the Levitical Cities: II. Utopia and Historical Reality," *JBL* 80 (1961): 156–65.
89. Haran, "Studies: II," 159.
90. Ibid., 161; for further discussion of the Priestly view of the land's boundaries, see, e.g., Moshe Weinfeld, "The Extent of the Promised Land: The Status of Transjordan," in *Das*

Haran interpreted the wide distribution of the Levitical cities as a Priestly concession to what could only be understood as a historical reality that was not subject to the Priestly agenda.

Similarly, Zecharia Kallai recognized the schematic nature of the system, arguing, "the *theoretical features* of this system may be a basic characteristic of this institution."[91] In Kallai's model, the text of Joshua's list is essentially complete, containing the schematically mandated forty-eight cities (including the tribal allotment of Reuben reconstructed on the basis of LXX Josh 21 and MT 1 Chr 6), "whereas that of I Chronicles is extant in a frame derived from a version resembling that of Joshua, or even identical with it, but displays several deliberate changes and perhaps also corruptions incurred in the course of transmission."[92] Despite this privileging of the version found in MT Josh 21, Kallai recognized that "both versions suffered corruption in the course of the copying and there is, therefore, room to complete and to correct the versions mutually."[93] The schematic nature of the lists, he argued, may have contributed to the two lists' variants. Recognizing that, in fact, *both lists assumed a forty-eight-city system as their fundamental organizational principle*, Kallai suggested that, in some cases, the schematization of the lists had been maintained at the cost of some historically Levitical cities being excluded from each list: "there is a possibility that more cities were given to the Levites than are noted in one of the lists but that no list deviated from the immutable numerical framework."[94] This admission of a historical facticity masked by a textual utopianism dovetails with the assertions of Haran.

IV. Textual Criticism in Conversation with Historical Concerns

A. Composition-Critical Attempts at Synthesis: A. G. Auld

Text-critical study of the Levitical Cities Lists has constituted an increasingly important facet of recent scholarship, thanks in large part to the efforts of A. Graeme Auld. Auld sought to deal with the respective passages in Josh 21 and 1 Chr 6 as *texts* rather than merely as *lists*.[95] Until 1979, scholars had

---

Land Israel in biblischer Zeit (ed. Georg Strecker; Göttingen: Vandenhoeck & Ruprecht, 1983), 59–75; and David Jobling, "'The Jordan a Boundary': Transjordan in Israel's Ideological Geography," in *The Sense of Biblical Narrative*, vol. 2, *Structural Analyses in the Hebrew Bible* (JSOTSup 39; Sheffield: JSOT Press, 1986), 88–133, 142–47.

91. Kallai, *Historical Geography*, 457 (emphasis added).
92. Ibid., 464.
93. Ibid., 466.
94. Ibid., 468; see also 474.
95. A. Graeme Auld, "The 'Levitical Cities': Texts and History," *ZAW* 91 (1979):

treated Josh 21 as the primary, or better, text of the Levitical Cities List, and 1 Chr 6 as the more corrupted version. Among the textual variants leading to this opinion were 1 Chronicles' omission of several intermediate numerical tallies (e.g., Josh 21:16b, 18b) and incorrect tallies of cities, the latter apparently due to the inadvertent omission of certain cities (e.g., the total of thirteen cities given in 1 Chr 6:45 after having named only eleven in vv. 42–45a). Auld argued, however, that the regularity of the account in Josh 21—which is, after all, a *narrativized* account of the distribution of the Levitical Cities—does not bolster its inherited status as the more historically authoritative of the two lists but rather diminishes it. First Chronicles 6:39–66 "must not be judged on the basis of Joshua 21," Auld argued. Instead, "Its rationale is one of growth and not of structure."[96] That is to say, examined on its own terms, the text of 1 Chr 6 gives the impression of simply having "*just grown.*"[97] Auld envisioned this growth as having occurred in five stages, the first of which comprised the "list of Aaronite cities (so obviously in and from Judah . . . that no comment [as to the tribal allotment from which the donation was made] was required)" (i.e., vv. 42–44).[98] The second stage comprised the addition of the Benjaminite cities donated to the Aaronid family (v. 45a), along with the tribal affiliations of the donations to the remaining Qohathites (v. 46 [until גורל]), the Gershomites (v. 47 [until בבשן]), and the Merarites (v. 48 [until גורל]), along with the somewhat summary note in v. 49. Auld's third stage was the simple addition of the "pedantic note" in v. 50, followed by the addition of the full list of donated cities and their respective tribal affiliations in the fourth stage (vv. 51–66). Finally, in the fifth of Auld's stages, the numerical tallies were added to vv. 47, 48, and 49.[99]

Auld's thesis cut against the grain of a well-established interpretive framework holding the primacy of the list in Josh 21. That text, he argued, showed several interpretive elaborations on the part of the editor who inserted the list into the Deuteronomistic History. Not only was the textual material rearranged and fully integrated into the surrounding Deuteronomistic narrative,

---

194–206; republished in idem, *Joshua Retold: Synoptic Perspectives* (Old Testament Studies; Edinburgh: T&T Clark, 1998), 25–36 (pagination below is given according to the republication). Additionally, Auld cites the dissertation of a near contemporary of his at Edinburgh (J. P. Ross, "The 'Cities of the Levites' in Joshua XXI and I Chronicles VI" [Ph.D. diss., Edinburgh University, 1973]). This latter dissertation was unavailable to me.

96. Auld, "Levitical Cities," 26; see also idem, "Cities of Refuge in Israelite Tradition," *JSOT* 10 (1978): 26–40; republished in idem, *Joshua Retold: Synoptic Perspectives* (Old Testament Studies; Edinburgh: T&T Clark, 1998), 37–48, esp. 43–45 (again, here I cite pagination from the republication).

97. Auld, "Levitical Cities," 27 (emphasis original); see also idem, "Cities of Refuge," 43.

98. Auld, "Levitical Cities," 27.

99. Ibid., 27–28.

argued Auld, but several additions were made in the text of the account as well.[100] To complicate matters, Auld found that the text of LXX Josh 21 (especially LXX^B), which was distinctly shorter than MT Josh 21, was much closer to the text of MT 1 Chr 6.[101] The novelty of Auld's basic thesis occasioned several accompanying (and concomitantly bold) conclusions. First, he claimed that "[f]urther discussion can be freed of the numerical incubus of 48 and also of its close associate, the principle of tribal equality."[102] Moreover, the dating of the texts to the monarchic period—especially in the *early* monarchic period—was rendered impossible, given Joshua's reliance on a fully developed form of 1 Chronicles, which had been composed only in the Persian period. But the purported lateness of the text's composition did not prevent Auld from hazarding a hypothesis concerning the historical background of the texts: after all, "[i]rregularity has a ring of authenticity."[103] Based on the work of Yoram Tsafrir,[104] Auld surmised that the Chronicler's list had, in fact, at one time contained a fully schematic forty-eight names but had been corrupted subsequent to the achievement of regularity, possibly under the reverse influence of Josh 21.[105] The textual histories of 1 Chr 6 and Josh 21, for Auld, were inextricably entangled. Moreover, if they were predicated on some historical system of Levitical Cities in operation, it was a system whose scale was severely reduced, limited to the eight or nine cities of the original Judahite-Simeonite donation, or perhaps thirteen cities, including the Benjaminite allotment as well.

Once he had argued for the primacy of the Chronicles text, Auld made a second interpretive move: he argued that the thirteen cities of the Chronicler's second-stage list (i.e., those of Judah, Simeon, and Benjamin) had at some point *all* been recognized as "cities of refuge" (ערי המקלט; v. 42).[106] The designation of Hebron as an individual "city of refuge" in Josh 21:13 was only secondary and was *not* dependent on Josh 20:7: "if it were, we should expect the first, or more strictly only, mention of Qiryat-Arba to be labelled ʿ*yr mqlṭ hrṣḥ*,

---

100. Ibid., 28–31; see also idem, "Cities of Refuge," 41–45. Unfortunately, a complete accounting of all the emendations that Auld posited is impossible here.

101. Auld, "Levitical Cities," 31–32; see also idem, "Cities of Refuge," esp. 43–44; and idem, "The Cities in Joshua 21: The Contribution of Textual Criticism," *Textus* 15 (1990): 141–52; republished in idem, *Joshua Retold: Synoptic Perspectives* (Old Testament Studies; Edinburgh: T&T Clark, 1998), 49–57 (pagination cited according to the republication).

102. Auld, "Levitical Cities," 35.

103. Ibid., 36.

104. Tsafrir, "Levitic City of Beth-shemesh," 44–45.

105. In particular, Auld cites the double mention of the donation of Hebron to the Levites (Josh 21:11, 13 = 1 Chr 6:40, 42), but of its surrounding agricultural fields and dependent villages (Josh 21:12 = 1 Chr 6:41) to Caleb (cf. Josh 14:13–14; 15:13): the direction of influence could only have been unidirectional, argued Auld. For the argument, see Auld, "Levitical Cities," 30–31, 36; and idem, "Cities of Refuge," 45.

106. Auld, "Cities of Refuge," 46.

like Shechem in v. 21. . . . It would seem," continued Auld, "that the concept of *mqlṭ* and the name *qryt-ʾrbʿ* did not *always* go hand in hand."[107] Rather, the idea of "refuge" was adopted by the editor of Josh 21 on the basis of his source, 1 Chr 6. Afterwards, an editor fleshed out the list of cities of refuge in Josh 20:7 secondarily on the basis of Josh 21:11, 21, 27, 32, 36 [LXX[B]], and 38, and the meaning of the term ערי המקלט was altered somewhat (along with the textual emendation to עיר המקלט), narrowed to describe, for example, Hebron alone of the Judahite-Simeonite allotment.[108] Auld contested, "Each of the six names in Joshua 20 heads the relevant sub-section of the longer list [i.e., Josh 21:11–40]. Indeed, that may be the reason why *these* names were quarried from the longer list by an editor who wanted to report, after Joshua's account of the land-division, that effect had been *given* to the legislation on refuge in Deuteronomy 19." Numbers 35:9–15 was secondary as well.[109]

Auld's argumentation is specious here, and a number of commentators have subsequently responded to his literary privileging of the list in 1 Chr 6. As Auld himself admitted in the latest of his essays specifically dedicated to the Levitical Cities Lists, responses have usually come from at least three primary quarters: the exegetical-textual, the historical-geographical, and the literary-critical.[110] The first two of these camps are discussed briefly in the following section.

B. Historical-Geographical Responses to Auld

Foremost among the early scholarly works responding to Auld from a historical-critical perspective were Zecharia Kallai's English translation of *Historical Geography* and Nadav Naʾaman's *Borders and Districts in Biblical Historiography*.[111] The former has already been discussed above because Auld's thesis is not central to its discussion. Conversely, Naʾaman's chapter on the Levitical

---

107. Ibid., 46.

108. Ibid., 46–48. But cf. Ben Zvi, "List of the Levitical Cities," 88–89: lexical patterns in the names of both lists may indicate that Josh 21 was relying on ch. 20, and not vice versa.

109. Auld, "Cities of Refuge," 46.

110. Auld, "Cities in Joshua 21," 50–52. As exemplars of the exegetical-textual approach, Auld lists, among others, Boling, "Levitical Cities," already cited in brief above. More substantial text-critical responses have been leveled subsequent to 1990 and will be discussed below. In the third category, he lists Magnar Kartveit, *Motive und Schichten der Landtheologie in I Chronik 1–9* (ConBOT 28; Stockholm: Almqvist & Wiksell, 1989), 69–77; Enzo Cortese, *Josua 13–21: Ein priesterschriftlicher Abschnitt im deuteronomistischen Geschichtswerk* (OBO 94; Freiburg: Academic Press; Göttingen: Vandenhoeck & Ruprecht, 1990), esp. 77–85. The second category comprises only the works of Zecharia Kallai and Nadav Naʾaman, the latter discussed in the following section.

111. Nadav Naʾaman, *Borders and Districts in Biblical Historiography: Seven Studies in Geographical Lists* (Jerusalem Biblical Studies: Jerusalem: Simor, 1986), 203–36.

Cities List was composed in direct response to Auld and deserves recognition as a primary respondent.

Over the course of his study of the Levitical Cities List, Na'aman reviewed the secondary literature; most of this review has been replicated to some extent in the present study, and can be safely set to the side. In its essentials, Na'aman's argument reasserted the consensus opinion that the composition of Josh 21, with its perfectly schematic (i.e., *literary*) division of forty-eight cities among the twelve tribes, preceded that of 1 Chr 6,[112] but Na'aman argued against a monarchic date for the list. He asserted, in opposition to Haran, that "the absence of cities like Dan, Bethel, Mizpah, Gilgal, Bethlehem, Beer-sheba, Arad, Nebo and Ataroth . . . is surprising" and could not be accounted for simply by making the artificial distinction between "shrine cities" and "Levitical cities."[113] Rather, he found in this curious omission reason to doubt the early monarchic setting of the list. This removal of a secure, early date for the list allowed Na'aman some flexibility in positing a historical context he felt to be more in line with any indicators of authentic historical reliability that might be found in an otherwise utopian list. Although Na'aman sustained the primacy of the obviously utopian Josh 21, he also judged the principle underlying Auld's privileging of 1 Chr 6 as compelling: "The exceptional allocation of the nine cities to the tribe of Judah (including Simeon) has the ring of authenticity."[114] The author of the Levitical Cities List had utilized two earlier lists of cities (i.e., the boundary descriptions in Josh 13–19 and the cities of refuge in Josh 20) to flesh out a historical situation with which he was familiar: the existence of thirteen putative "Levitical" cities in Judah (including Simeon) and Benjamin.[115] Eight of the nine cities of Judah and Simeon are present in the city list of Judah (Josh 15:21–62).[116] Similarly, two of the four Levitical cities donated by Benjamin are found in that tribe's city list as well (Geba and Gibeon; Josh 18:21–28); the other two, Anathoth and Alemeth, are listed together as sons of Becher in 1 Chr 7:8. Because Na'aman dated the Judahite province list to the late monarchy, following Alt, he thus concluded "that the list of 13 Aaronite cities should also be dated to the time of Josiah, and that the complete system of Levitical

---

112. Ibid., 209–16.
113. Ibid., 207–8.
114. Ibid., 216.
115. Ibid., 216–27.
116. Only Beth-shemesh is absent from that text. However, the city's archaeological remains demonstrate its existence in the late monarchic period, allowing Na'aman to conclude that the city's absence in Josh 15:21–62 poses no problems to his thesis. Cortese did not render judgment on the historical veracity of the list but recognized here cause to consider whether the editor of the list had used an earlier source: the absence of most of Simeon's donated cities from Josh 19:1–9 suggests reliance on at least one other document (*Josue 13–21*, 83).

cities was likewise composed at that time."[117] On the basis of this historical kernel, the author of the Levitical Cities List extrapolated a list of forty-eight names, for the most part dividing them evenly between the remaining tribes. The list is thus an entirely literary concoction.

A significant caveat to Na'aman's appropriation of Auld's synthesis is appropriate here. Were Tsafrir's observation concerning the accidental transposition of Beth-shemesh from Naphtali to Judah to be accepted, Auld suggested, "The transposition of Beth-shemesh must have occurred *after the achievement of* [the list's] *regularity*."[118] However, it will be recalled that Auld had posited that the nine-city system of the Judahite-Simeonite donation to the Aaronid Qohathites was an authentic historical datum *precisely because of its numerical irregularity*. At the same time, for Auld, "the theory, familiar to us from Numbers 35, of a regular distribution may have been sufficient impetus to the achievement of the full list."[119] These assumptions are theoretically inconsistent. If Auld were to be successful in both (a) his positing of an irregularly formed historical kernel onto which the remainder of the Levitical Cities List gradually accreted *and* (b) his admission that a forty-eight city list was once evenly divided among the tribes, he would be caught in a position quite similar to Albright's, described above. The irregularity of Auld's initial stage of the list's formation—posited as historical solely by virtue of the numerical irregularity (i.e., its "ring of authenticity")—would have been alleviated through a redistribution of Beth-shemesh to Naphtali, in order to provide for the perfectly symmetrical division of the final stage's forty-eight cities divided evenly among the tribes. Then, in a second—this time potentially inadvertent—redistribution, Beth-shemesh was reapportioned to the Aaronids dwelling in Judah-Simeon. Any assumption that the "ring of authenticity" is a compelling historical datum is philosophically inconsistent with Tsafrir's observation concerning Beth-shemesh. Auld himself hedged when trying to account for Tsafrir's insight,[120] and Na'aman was forced to reject Tsafrir's hypothesis outright.[121] But this rejection of the hypothesis is grounded precisely in the assumption that the remaining tribal donations of the Levitical City List were composed schematically and artificially on the basis of the boundary descriptions and city lists. As with Albright's posited (and convenient) haplography after the insertion of Hebron and Shechem, it is highly unlikely that Beth-shemesh was doubly transposed from Judah to Naphtali and back to Judah.

---

117. Na'aman, *Borders and Districts*, 229–33; quotation from 229–30; see similarly Svensson, *Towns and Toponyms*, 82–89, esp. 89.

118. Auld, "Levitical Cities," 36 (emphasis added).

119. Ibid.

120. E.g., "What is at stake is Tsafrir's invitation to believe that a transposition occurred in an otherwise regular common [or source] text" (Auld, "Levitical Cities," 36).

121. Na'aman, *Borders and Districts*, 216 n. 20; see above for discussion of Tsafrir, "Levitic City of Beth-shemesh," 44–45.

In an extended section of his chapter on the Levitical cities, Naʾaman reviews the overlap of these lists with the Levitical Cities List of Josh 21, capably showing the high degree of coincidence. In fact, it was these same lists that Naʾaman used to validate eight of the nine cities in the Judahite-Simeonite donation! Yet he grounds the inherence of Beth-shemesh to the Judahite portion of the Levitical Cities solely on the archaeological merits of that city. Naʾaman's hypothesis stumbles on the fact that the only mentions of a city Beth-shemesh in Josh 13–19 occur in the boundary description of Issachar (19:22) and the city list of Naphtali (19:38).[122]

A final geographical-historical position is worthy of note: G. Schmitt argued strenuously against the position espoused by those such as Alt, Noth, and Mazar (among others) that the open spaces of the Levitical cities list were indicative of an authentic historical background underlying the list. Schmitt argued that the topographical lacunae were due simply to the schematic enumeration of the cities: when a tribe as large as Manasseh donates exactly as many cities as a smaller tribe such as Dan or Naphtali, there are bound to be such open areas.[123] Like Haran, Schmitt stressed the confabulatory, artificial nature of the Levitical Cities List in Josh 21, arguing that the present form of the text cannot possibly divulge an authentic historical reality. But Schmitt took this argument a step further: the fact that Josh 21 is clearly utopian does not rule out the possibility that an earlier list had been modified somehow from one or more earlier sources—whether expanded, abbreviated, or a combination of the two is ultimately not entirely recoverable, although the large degree of overlap between Josh 13–19 and 21 suggests that the latter may have been fleshed out with the former in view.[124] In order to bolster this hypothesis, Schmitt analyzed the source-critical argument of Auld, arguing that although 1 Chr 6 does indeed seem to demonstrate a more natural shape, it too bears the hallmarks of an intentional adherence to the artificial forty-eight-city schema embodied by Josh 21, not to mention a variety of markers signaling that it, too, has been secondarily worked into its present literary context.[125] Thus, despite the artificiality of the list in its present form—both in terms of the number of cities supplied by each tribe and the identification of the respective Levitical lineages to which the cities were donated[126]—Schmitt found reason to with-

---

122. See similarly Schmitt, "Levitenstädte," 33.
123. Ibid., 34–35.
124. Ibid., 35–36. Notice that the supposition that Josh 13–19 served as the source-text stands in direct opposition to Noth's hypothesis that Josh 13–19 had been fleshed out on the basis of Josh 21 (before the secondary insertion of the cities of refuge).
125. Schmitt, "Levitenstädte," 36–40. In this regard, Schmitt anticipated the later works of Knoppers and Sparks (see below).
126. Schmitt, "Levitenstädte," 40–44; cf. Cody, who argued that the clustering of Levitical sub-lineages was not an artifical element imposed secondarily by the redactor of the text, but rather a genealogical gerrymandering engineered by the occupant Levites

hold an entirely negative judgment concerning the list's historical background. Although we are unable to penetrate behind the current text, argued Schmitt, the obscurity of the cities chosen from Judah suggests that we might look for the origins of the Levitical Cities List in an authentic traditional memory of cities inhabited entirely or almost entirely by a martial affiliation (*kriegerische Gefolgschaft*) known as "Levites."[127]

In summary, the challenge Auld posed to the historical reliability of the Levitical Cities List has occasioned a few significant geographical-historical responses. Although they do not admit some of Auld's conclusions, both Na'aman and Schmitt would agree with Auld that the list's verisimilitude is called into question because of the list's obviously schematic nature. Nonetheless, the possibility of reconstructing an approximation of the list's historical background does not appear to be in danger of collapsing entirely, according to these hypotheses. Both Na'aman and Schmitt suggest that oddities of the list's present form—for Na'aman the number of cities donated to the Aaronids, and for Schmitt the obscurity of those cities—leads to a restricted view of the historical background of any putative *system* of "Levitical cities." In contradistinction to these geographical-historical interpretations, the most recent attempts to understand the Levitical Cities Lists have been conducted in the text-critical realm, with much less emphasis placed on any underlying reality of the Levitical cities "system." These analyses are, rather, more immediately concerned with the history of the biblical text itself.

C. Textual-Literary Responses to Auld

A few years after Na'aman's late-monarchic dating of the Levitical Cities List's historical core, Ehud Ben Zvi posed a significant challenge to any purported historicity of the list. He pointed out the incongruity of the list's obvious prioritization of the Aaronids with the reconstructed historical context of the various competing Levitical groups.[128] Further, Ben Zvi reminded his interlocutors of a simple principle: although the lists purported to describe the period of the

---

themselves in an attempt to express their newfound "regional solidarity" (Cody, *History of Old Testament Priesthood*, 161).

127. Schmitt, "Levitenstädte," 46–47; quotation from 46.

128. Ben Zvi, "List of the Levitical Cities," 81–83, 86; see earlier Noth, *Josua*, 100 (2nd ed., 131); Cody, *History of Old Testament Priesthood*, 159–61; although cf. Haran, who had agued that the lists placed the Aaronids and non-Aaronid Levites on equal footing ("Studies: II," 161–63). The authentic historical context, according to scholars such as Frank Moore Cross and Baruch Halpern, most likely featured a much more fluid and ambivalent relationship between the Aaronid (or Zadokite?) priests and the (Mushite?) Levites than the static picture emerging from the Levitical Cities List in either Josh 21 or 1 Chr 6 (Cross, *Canaanite Myth and Hebrew Epic*, 195–215; Baruch Halpern, "Sectionalism and the Schism," *JBL* 93 [1974]: 519–32; idem, "Levitic Participation," 31–42; see more recently

united monarchy, they were not necessarily written in that period; rather, the lists, like the surrounding textual material, show evidence of composition in the late- or post-monarchic period.[129] Numerically, the schematization of the Levitical Cities List suggests an artificial attempt to regularize an otherwise anomalous distribution of cities, so Ben Zvi concluded "that the mentioned irregularities in the pattern were brought about by a list of nine cities that reflects an early source."[130] More important for Ben Zvi's argument, however, was the redactional history of the pentateuchal and Deuteronomistic texts dealing specifically with the Levitical cities (Num 35:9–34; Deut 4:41–43; 19:1–13; Josh 20:1–9). In contrast to Auld's analysis (see above), Ben Zvi found two traditions concerning the original mandate for the cities of refuge: in the first (Deut 19:1–7), only three cities are included in the system. In the second tradition, the system comprises six cities, three on each side of the Jordan River (Num 35:9–15; compare Josh 20). In neither text are the cities identified by name. Subsequently, an editor or editors sought to harmonize the two traditions through the insertion of Deut 19:8–9 (and possibly 4:41–43, although the interpretation of the latter passage is ambivalent, and *could* be read as the anticipatory fulfillment of Deut 19:1–7).[131] This secondary extension of the system of the cities of refuge into the eastern Israelite tribal allotments is an ideological attempt to maintain parity between those living in Cisjordan and those in Transjordan and can only be dated to the post-monarchic period, argued Ben Zvi.[132] The ideational function of the list is further evident in the gathering of the Aaronid priests precisely in the Judah-Benjamin region, essentially removing the city of Hebron from its Qohathite (but non-Aaronid) inheritance (e.g., Exod 6:18; Num 3:19; 1 Chr 5:28; 6:23; 15:9; 23:12, 19; but cf. 1 Chr 26:23), and supplanting other Levitical lineages (e.g., Libni and Korah) from their own "rightful" (and perhaps more historical) endowments in southern Judah.[133]

Hutton, "Levitical Diaspora [I]," 223–34; and idem, "Southern, Northern, and Transjordanian Perspectives," 160–61).

129. Ben Zvi, "List of the Levitical Cities," 84–85; see there for additional bibliography. Contemporaneously, John R. Spencer found the lists' most likely date of composition to be the postexilic period ("Levitical Cities," *ABD* 4:310–11).

130. Ben Zvi, "List of the Levitical Cities," 87; cf. p. 101, where Ben Zvi admits that the list may initially have included the four cities of Benjamin as well, bringing the total to thirteen.

131. Ibid., 91–96. For a more recent discussion of the relevant passages, see Ludwig Schmidt, "Leviten- und Asylstädte in Num. xxxv und Jos. xx; xxi 1-42," *VT* 52 (2002): 103–21.

132. Ben Zvi, "List of the Levitical Cities," 99–100.

133. The issue of Levitical lineages is an important one, but unfortunately cannot be handled in this venue. For fuller discussion, see ibid., 101–5.

With the historical background of the Levitical Cities List called entirely into question in this perspective, two responses in particular are worthy of note. Working independently, Gary N. Knoppers and James T. Sparks have arrived at remarkably similar conclusions concerning the validity of many of Auld's premises and assertions.[134] Knoppers's well-organized discussion of the textual data takes seriously Auld's valid contention that the textual variants are indeed important to our understanding of the relationship between Josh 21 and 1 Chr 6. But Knoppers adduces a significant weakness in Auld's hypothesis, namely, that Auld had assumed that most of the textual variants—ordering of sections, addition or substitution of phrases, and the like—were intentional: "[Auld's] theory devotes little attention to the accidents of textual transmission that produce variants."[135] Knoppers's detailed analysis of the two passages' respective literary contexts and lexical elements deals a devastating blow to the theory that would hold the primacy of 1 Chr 6. Repeatedly, Knoppers demonstrates that the common elements of the two lists fit better in the Priestly traditions' narrative arc (e.g., the repeated use of the collocation נתנו להם את עיר/ערים/GN to describe the donation of the cities, consonant with the narrative context of Josh 21, but completely out of place in 1 Chr 1–9[136]); that 1 Chr 6 demonstrates lexical dependence on Josh 21 out of character with the Chronicler's lexical choices elsewhere; and that the toponyms known from Josh 21 simply do not appear frequently enough in 1 Chronicles to warrant viewing the latter book as their origin. Knoppers argues cogently and persuasively that it was the Chronicler, not the editor of Josh 21, who adapted the work of a predecessor toward his own literary and ideological ends: "the new sequence [in 1 Chr 6] highlights the assignments given to the sons of Aaron, contextualized within the Qohathite phratry, and honors the distinction that the Chronicler observes between the tribe of Levi and those specific members (Aaronides) of this tribe, who serve as priests."[137] Far from demonstrating the reliance of Josh 21 on 1 Chr 6, however, Knoppers argues forcefully that both MT Josh 21 and 1 Chr 6 demonstrate reliance on an *Urtext* much closer to the somewhat shorter LXX Josh 21, which "bears witness to a stage in the development of this work that is earlier, or at least different, from MT Joshua."[138] Knoppers proposes two viable models through which we might better understand the textual variants between MT Josh 21 and 1 Chr 6:

---

134. Gary N. Knoppers, "Projected Age Comparisons of the Levitic Townlists: Divergent Theories and Their Significance," *Textus* 22 (2005): 21–63; James T. Sparks, *The Chronicler's Genealogies: Towards an Understanding of 1 Chronicles 1–9* (Academia Biblica 28; Atlanta: Society of Biblical Literature, 2008), 125–62.

135. Knoppers, "Projected Age Comparisons," 28.

136. For this observation, see already Ben Zvi, "List of the Levitical Cities," 77–78 n. 1.

137. Knoppers, "Projected Age Comparisons," 49.

138. Ibid., 51–63; quotation from 62; see also Japhet, *1 Chronik*, 179; and R. Klein, *1 Chronicles*, 183–85, 213.

> The text of Joshua may have continued to grow (and change) after the Chronicler used it in the Persian period. In this explanation, the pluses appearing in LXX and MT Joshua are basically a post-Chronistic phenomenon. Alternatively, there may have been multiple editions of Joshua already in existence, when the author of Chronicles began his work. In this case, the Chronicler happened to employ an edition of Joshua that was somewhat different from and briefer than the editions of the work that were to make their appearance in the LXX and MT.[139]

In a complementary study, published three years after Knoppers's essay (although its author was apparently unaware of its predecessor), J. T. Sparks examines the validity of Auld's larger premises that: (a) the shorter of two synoptic texts is the more original; (b) the more disordered of two texts is the more "natural," and therefore original; and (c) there was necessarily a unilinear development from 1 Chr 6 → LXX Josh 21 → MT Josh 21.[140] First, like Knoppers, Sparks points out that Auld's hypothesis leaves little room for accidental omissions, and that the Chronicler's modus operandi involves rearrangement of his sources more frequently than Auld admitted; shorter is not necessarily more primary.[141] Second, Sparks challenges Auld's premise that a more disorderly text necessarily demonstrates greater antiquity than an orderly one.[142] Although the data Sparks adduces suggest that his criticism is correct, I find Knoppers's argument on this datum much more pointed: Auld assumed not only that disorder signals antiquity but that 1 Chr 6 is, in fact, disordered! Knoppers argues persuasively that the Chronicler's rearrangement of the Levitical Cities List may be *different from* but *no less intentionally organized than* the list's original state in Josh 21: the derivative version in 1 Chr 6 simply sets the Aaronid priests apart from the remainder of the Levites—a project clearly in line with the Chronicler's purposes in the genealogy of Levi. The Aaronids appear in 1 Chr 5:27–41 separately, whereas the full set of three Levitical genealogies is held in abeyance until 6:1–38 (which again culminates in the Aaronid branch of the Qohathites; vv. 35–38); Auld's contestation of the primacy of 1 Chr 6 on the basis of its purported disorderliness is impeachable on at least two counts.[143] Finally, Sparks dedicates an extended discussion predicated on

---

139. Knoppers, "Projected Age Comparisons," 63.
140. Sparks, *Chronicler's Genealogies*, 131.
141. Ibid., 132–34. I am less persuaded by Sparks's critique that Auld's "presupposition fails because it does not allow for the harmonizing influence of versions upon one another which would allow an older text to be influenced by a newer" (ibid., 134). I do not disagree with Sparks's statement, but rather with its application: Auld admitted in a number of different places (e.g., "Levitical Cities," 36) that a newer text could influence an older one; the flaw in his argument was simply that he applied this principle belatedly (i.e., *after* he had already privileged 1 Chr 6).
142. Sparks, *Chronicler's Genealogies*, 135–40.
143. Knoppers, "Projected Age Comparisons," 45–51, esp. 49–50; see earlier Kartveit, *Motive und Schichten*, 72–73.

the text-critical data to various models of the lists' development. He concludes, similarly to Knoppers, that MT Josh 21 and 1 Chr 6 were each more developed, divergent forms of an earlier common text (Joshua 21 [revised]), itself a somewhat developed form of *Ur* Joshua 21.[144]

V. A Way Forward: Anthropological Investigation

Despite the confusion occasioned by so many interlocking attempts at revision, harmonization, and standardization, a few generalizations may be made. Previous commentators have typically understood the lists as literary units underlying the present framework of their respective contexts. Each framework was, to some extent, erected around this underlying list, using certain presuppositions about the list's nature, and each list was adapted to its literary context. In most cases, scholars studying the lists themselves have not understood the enumerations of cities as contextually bound to the various frameworks they inhabit. The lists—comprising groups of cities and fixedly corresponding to kinship groups, both the Israelite tribal benefactors and the Levitical sub-tribe recipients—are therefore often separated from the surrounding material and analyzed as independent constructions. Some scholars have understood these constructions as historical reconstructions, harking back to an authentic situation theoretically verifiable through archaeological or textual examination. Others have understood them as purely confabulated constructs, established as a utopian ideal and never actually instituted. Representatives of both positions have made compelling arguments. In this final section, I briefly sketch a way forward through the impasse occasioned by these sometimes mutually exclusive positions.

In 1982, Chris Hauer proposed that an anthropologically sensitive investigation of the Levites could prove instructive.[145] "Since the Levites were a priestly tribe," he argued, "a national plan of Levitical settlement suggests the establishment of a national ecclesiastical cult. This is turn suggests a state level organization holding sway from Dan to Beersheba, and on both sides of the Jordan."[146] These criteria formed the framework of Hauer's attempts to date the Levitical cities system, which he, like many before him, placed during the Davidic reign of the united monarchy. Accordingly, the list named only

---

144. Sparks, *Chronicler's Genealogies*, 140–50. Sparks diverges from Knoppers in tracing the origins of LXX Josh 21 to *Ur* Joshua (so that it was a sister tradition of Joshua [revised] rather than a sister of MT Josh 21). The depth of detail needed to arbitrate this distinction is impossible to probe in the present venue and must await further investigation elsewhere.

145. Chris Hauer, Jr., "David and the Levites," *JSOT* 23 (1982): 33–54.

146. Ibid., 39.

those cities institutionalized by David as members of the system, although the Levites were spread more thoroughly across the land.[147]

Hauer's adoption of the developmental schema proposed by A. F. C. Wallace—in which cultic organizations progressed from "individual" through "shamanistic" and "communal" to culminate in the "ecclesiastical" arrangement[148]—necessarily strikes the contemporary reader as somewhat misguided, such evolutionary theories having long since been outdated.[149] Likewise, the foundational assumption that David indeed ruled over a full-blown state (rather than, say, a tribal chiefdom or some less cohesive form of social organization) has been challenged and currently remains the subject of an increasingly entrenched debate.[150] Finally, Hauer's piece was published shortly after those of Auld, and likely had not yet had time to take account of the severe difficulties the ensuing argument posed for the overly idealized historical status of the Levitical cities "system." Nonetheless, Hauer recognized that the social worlds surrounding the Levitical Cities Lists—that is, both those in which the lists were produced and those that they purport to record—form an invaluable frame of reference for any researcher who would study these texts. Like many before him, Hauer recognized that a historical background of the lists could not stop simply at a geographical reconstruction of the various locales mentioned by the Levitical Cities List but instead must integrate the sociological roles occupied by the Levites during the transmission history of the biblical text.

Various literary and textual caveats have been adduced to account for the striking numerical schema of the Levitical Cities List(s) and the odd geographical distribution of the cities named there. Historically, there seems to be little reason at all to consider them a system per se in which all of them served simultaneously to fulfill any single role or even a limited number of roles (e.g., governmental administrative centers, sites of religious education or ritual specialization, residences of ritual personnel, and so on). Likewise, there is no impetus to consider the forty-eight cities of the list—no matter which textual version of the list—a definitive list of the forty-eight cities occupied entirely

---

147. Ibid., 48.

148. Anthony F. C. Wallace, *Religion: An Anthropological View* (New York: Random House, 1966).

149. For a considerably less restrained evaluation of Wallace's book, see Clifford Geertz, review of Anthony F. C. Wallace, *Religion: An Anthropological View*, *American Anthropologist* 70 (1968): 394–96.

150. Among a host of discussions, see, e.g., Daniel Master, "State Formation Theory and the Kingdom of Ancient Israel," *JNES* 60 (2001): 117–31; Robert D. Miller II, *Chieftains of the Highland Clans: A History of Israel in the 12th and 11th Centuries B.C.* (Bible in Its World; Grand Rapids: Eerdmans, 2005); and Emanuel Pfoh, *The Emergence of Israel in Ancient Palestine: Historical and Anthropological Perspectives* (Copenhagen International Seminar; London: Equinox, 2009).

or in part by Levitical cultic specialists. Furthermore, we are chastened again and again to be wary of the putative genealogical relations obtaining between the various Levitical lineages: "Aaron, Levi and Zadok all represent different priestly factions which held sway at different times and . . . the association of the three, as priests descended from the same family, was a later, literary and historical fabrication."[151] In short, the conclusion that *these lists as they stand are fabrications designed in part to legitimize the Aaronid Priests of the Persian Period* is inescapable; the lists in their current form are substantially products of a Judahite author's imagination and served to organize Israelite tribal life in a distantly remembered past while at the same time providing a blueprint for social and religious organization in the postexilic period.

Nonetheless, in these lists and in narratives featuring Levitical figures, we occasionally catch glimpses of an apparently authentic historical reality. For some, the irregular number of cities granted to the Aaronid priests signals a conceivable toehold in reality. For others it is the lack of explanation for the otherwise mundane and relatively unknown localities named as Levitical cities that triggers the suspicion that these lists are more than mere confabulation. In my opinion, an underlying reality behind these lists is signaled by the cities' distribution along tribal boundaries—precisely that quality cited by some as demonstrating the list's purely speculative and unreliable origins, based on other texts. I have proposed elsewhere, and can suggest here only in brief, that an anthropological parallel to the Levites may be found in the Ahansal tribe of the Moroccan Atlas Mountains.[152] Undoubtedly, this conclusion will not (and should not!) satisfy the curious intellect: the present essay comprises only the initial sounding of a planned monograph, in which I intend to argue that the Levitical Cities Lists preserve an authentic historical memory of a sociological system, constrained by topography and ecology, wherein early Levitical social function(s) determined the location of such "Levitical cities" (whatever that designation encompasses) precisely at tribal boundaries. These locales were, in some cases, the seats of respected intertribal mediators, and in other cases, the residences of defunct religious personnel. Some were probably, in Boling's locution, "rival sanctuary towns."[153] The degree to which any of these towns were occupied by Levites—active or laicized—is most likely unrecoverable and was maximally probably slight. Nonetheless, the cross-cultural parallel adduced here suggests that such lineages, engaged in a struggle for recognition and the attendant subsistence provided by such recognition, tend

---

151. Spencer, "Priestly Families (or Factions)," 398.

152. Hutton, "Levitical Diaspora (I)," 223–34; see also idem, "All the King's Men: The Families of the Priests in Cross-Cultural Perspective," in Seitenblicke: Literarische und historische Studien zu Nebenfiguren im zweiten Samuelbuch (ed. Walter Dietrich; OBO 249; Fribourg: Academic Press; Göttingen: Vandenhoeck & Ruprecht, 2011), 121–51.

153. Boling, "Levitical History," 247.

to settle precisely along tribal boundaries. Accordingly, I would suggest, it was the observed overlap between the historically remembered Levitical system and the tribal boundaries described in Josh 13–19 that occasioned the author's fleshing out of the list with cities from the boundary descriptions in a kind of "pious fiction." And, like the Levitical enclaves and lineages about which so much is narrated in the biblical text, the parallel Ahansal exemplars do not form any sort of officially recognized or established "system," since they operate ostensibly as *franchises*. Nonetheless, they may at times be co-opted by central authorities, their resources and social stature subordinated to the demands of an especially powerful central government.

The accuracy of this parallel remains for the time being indeterminate; more study is necessary, as is the construction of a fuller argument for points of tangency. Yet the commonalities that I allude to here and have pointed out more explicitly elsewhere suggest that a plurality of emerging methodologies can help us to understand better the lists of the Levitical cities. Not only must we rely on the traditional modes of source, redaction, and textual criticism to isolate the earliest stages of passages concerning Levites. We must also attend to social-scientific analyses of the Levites' place in Israelite religion; only through a concerted combination of methodologies will we be able to arrive at a more developed understanding of, as both Martin Noth and Lawrence Stager have described it, the "Levitical Diaspora."

The Social Status of Priestly and Levite Women

Sarah Shectman

In his book *Rites and Rank*, Saul Olyan posits that "[d]istinctions in status, whether significant or minor, are the building blocks of hierarchy."[1] Such distinctions can be identified in various oppositions operating within the text, for example, in binary oppositions such as priest/non-priest.[2] In ancient Israel, where "non-priest" and "Israelite" are synonymous, this is evident in the opposition priest/Israelite, which in turn leads to the triadic construction priest/Levite/Israelite. These in turn may give way to secondary binary oppositions such as priest/high priest, in which one element of the original grouping is split. These oppositions privilege one element over the other(s), the vehicle through which hierarchies of status emerge. The opposition holy/common in particular has a major bearing on status in biblical Israel. Gradations of holiness affect an individual's status in regard to distance from the holy, resulting in a hierarchy: high priest > priest > Levite > common (lay) Israelite.[3] In this

---

In this paper I will use the terms "priestly women" and "Levite women" to denote women who are affiliated with priests or Levites (that is, with men of the tribe of Levi), primarily through birth or marriage and occasionally also through purchase. Although "priests" and "Levites" are two different groups of men and women in the Priestly and related material, they are the same group—the Levitical priests—in the Deuteronomistic History (DtrH). To use Olyan's term, these women's "primary male bond" is with a priest or a Levite (Saul M. Olyan, *Rites and Rank: Hierarchy in Biblical Representations of Cult* [Princeton: Princeton University Press, 2000], 31). I will also refer to women with *priestly* or *Levitical status*, by which I mean that they have a status particular to membership (by birth or by marriage) in these groups, albeit not one that is the same as the status of men in these groups.

My thanks go to Jeffrey Stackert and Annette Schellenberg for their feedback on earlier versions of this paper. I am particularly indebted to Saul Olyan for his thoughtful and thorough comments. Thanks also to Jeremy Hutton and Mark Leuchter for inviting me to participate in the Levites and Priests in History and Tradition Consultation at the 2010 annual meeting of the Society of Biblical Literature and to the audience members who commented on and responded to my paper.

1. Olyan, *Rites and Rank*, 115.
2. Ibid., 7.
3. Ibid., 36. This is particular to the view of the Priestly material of the Pentateuch (P and H); Ezekiel does not recognize a high priest. Although in P/H the Levite is technically

schema, those of higher status, namely, priests, are those with greater access to the holy who therefore face greater restrictions, particularly on purity, than do lay Israelites.[4]

Scholars have long applied such models to gender in the Hebrew Bible, identifying a binary opposition between men and women or a triadic construction of priests/Israelite men/Israelite women.[5] I propose extending Olyan's analysis by examining the particular status of women as it intersects with the binary opposition holy/common; specifically, I will examine the status of women in the families of priests and Levites, those who stand at the top of the Israelite ritual hierarchy. This will expose a triadic opposition between female members of priestly, Levitical, and lay Israelite families and perhaps even an opposition between priestly women and lay Israelites, both male and female. Such increasingly complex oppositions suggest that issues of women's status in the Hebrew Bible are more nuanced than previous studies have argued.

As Olyan notes, status generally may be birth-ascribed or non–birth-ascribed,[6] with male priestly status in the Hebrew Bible being birth-ascribed. A male priest can convey his own birth-ascribed status secondarily to depen-

---

a layperson, as we will see, the Levites' access to the tithe indicates that they have an intermediate status between priest and non-Levite layperson. Ezra–Nehemiah and Chronicles reflect the structure found in the Priestly material. In DtrH and Jeremiah, the distinction between priest and Levite is unknown, although D recognizes the high priest, as do Haggai and Zechariah. For an overview, see Risto Nurmela, *The Levites: Their Emergence as a Second-Class Priesthood* (South Florida Studies in the History of Judaism 193; Atlanta: Scholars Press, 1998); Joachim Schaper, *Priester und Leviten im achämenidischen Juda: Studien zur Kult- und Sozialgeschichte Israels in persischer Zeit* (FAT 31; Tubingen: Mohr Siebeck, 2000).

4. "The more access to the holy the fewer the instances of sanctioned defilement" (Olyan, *Rites and Rank*, 60–61).

5. See, e.g., the chapter subhead "Israelite: Laymen, Priests, and Women," in Jacob Milgrom, *Leviticus: A New Translation with Introduction and Commentary* (3 vols.; AB 3, 3A, 3B; New York: Doubleday, 1991–2000), 2:1409; and Rachel Havrelock, who extends the priest/Israelite and male/female oppositions to a metaphor whereby the priests are the male and all Israel is the female ("Outside the Lines: The Status of Women in Priestly Nationalism," in *Embroidered Garments: Priests and Gender in Biblical Israel* [ed. Deborah W. Rooke; HBM 25; Sheffield: Sheffield Phoenix Press, 2009], 89–101).

Whereas oppositions such as holy/common and pure/impure are explicit in the text (see, e.g., Lev 10:10; 11:47; 20:25; Ezek 22:26; 44:23), the oppositions male/female or man/woman are somewhat more implicit, though no less operative in the text. Indeed, at some level the two are seen as complementary elements (see, e.g., Gen 1:27; 2:23–24), but the very fact of the differences between men and women in the text indicates that this implicit opposition is at work.

6. Olyan, *Rites and Rank*, 8–9. The Hebrew Bible tends to focus on birth-ascribed status. See also Claudia Camp (*Wise, Strange and Holy: The Strange Woman and the Making of the Bible* [JSOTSup 320; Gender, Culture, Theory 9; Sheffield: Sheffield Academic Press, 2000], 193), who cites Howard Eilberg-Schwartz and Mary Douglas as similarly noting that ascribed status and hierarchies result in greater restrictions on individual autonomy.

dents within his household, including women and houseborn slaves, which grants those dependents access, for example, to holy food.[7] Those dependents then have a kind of secondary, non–birth-ascribed status, although it may be largely symbolic and is easily lost through separation from the household.[8] For this discussion, however, I wish to borrow from and extend Olyan's terms with slight distinctions, adding categories of birth-ascribed and non–birth-ascribed status for women as well, thus differentiating between women born into priestly or Levitical households and those women who marry into such families. The difference between men and women in this case is that a woman's priestly status is always secondary, in that it is always derived from her relationship to priestly men, whether by birth or marriage. Thus, a priest's daughter would have (always secondary) birth-ascribed status, whereas a priest's wife would have (secondary) non–birth-ascribed priestly status if she did not come from a priest's family.[9] Adding this distinction is important because, as we will see, there are situations in which a woman's status through either birth or marriage into a priestly family can be lost and situations in which it is not lost despite a change in the woman's relationship to a priestly male.

We discover very little in the biblical text about specific women of the tribe of Levi. Jochebed (Exod 6:20; Num 26:59), Miriam (Exod 15:20–21; Num 12:1–15; 20:1; 26:59; Deut 24:9; Mic 6:4), Zipporah (Exod 2:21; 4:25; 18:2), and the Levite's concubine, also called his wife (Judg 19:1), are the primary examples, but the text gives us little practical information about what status might have accrued to them as a result of their affiliation. In the cases of Zipporah and

---

7. Olyan, *Rites and Rank*, 32. Olyan calls this status "secondary and contingent," based on the recipient's "primary bond of dependency to the priest who heads their household." Olyan terms this a "privilege" that can be lost upon departure, for example, through marriage to an outsider. Note, though, that marriage does not break the bond between a priest and his daughter where mourning is concerned (see below).

8. Olyan, personal communication.

9. Birth-ascribed status, whether primary or secondary, male or female, can be lost. For women, for example, it may be lost upon divorce or widowhood: a woman who is not of priestly lineage and who marries a priest would lose her status within the priestly family if she were divorced or widowed. As with other divorced or widowed women—especially if she did not have sons—she would (when possible) return to her father's house, where she would resume her status with him as her primary male bond. See Gen 38:11; Lev 22:13; Ruth 1:6–8. Ezekiel 44:22, which states that a priest may marry only a virgin Israelite or the widow of another priest, may indicate that wives of priests were perceived as retaining some aspect of their priestly status after their widowhood, or it may indicate that the possibility of pollution from a woman who had been with another man was considered less if that other man had also been a priest and therefore of holy status. This might also be an indication that Ezekiel is particularly concerned with the genealogical purity of the priestly line. On this distinction, see Christine Hayes, *Gentile Impurities and Jewish Identities: Intermarriage and Conversion from the Bible to the Talmud* (Oxford: Oxford University Press, 2002), 27.

the Levite's concubine, this affiliation is secondary.[10] Some textual vestiges of an earlier, important role for Miriam seem scattered through the pentateuchal text, but none of these really seem to have much to do with her position in the tribe of Levi, if this was even a factor in the early form of the traditions about her.[11] It is also important to keep in mind that many of these texts do not recognize a distinction between priest and Levite; their authors would therefore not be concerned with differences in status between different members of the tribe of Levi. And as none of these are Priestly legislative texts, the authors are likely not concerned with the types of issues to be discussed below, which derive not only from the texts' Priestly authorship but also from their legislative cultic genre.

The bulk of available information about the wives, sisters, and daughters of Levites and priests appears in the pentateuchal instructions concerning various family rites such as marriage, mourning, and access to sacred meals and donations. There is some related material in the book of Ezekiel as well, but for the purposes of this essay I will be concerned with the pentateuchal sources only and will leave mention of Ezekiel to the footnotes. I have chosen to focus on the Priestly[12] material from the Pentateuch because it offers some particularly enticing details, but I will also include some comparisons with Deuteronomy. This will primarily be an exploration of textual ideology, making some observations and drawing some conclusions about what these laws might mean for the status of women as it is perceived in these biblical legal collections. The question of whether the pentateuchal laws, especially the Priestly ones, represent an ideal never put to use or are reflective of real legal practice is difficult to resolve. The laws may all be theoretical, without practical implementation, but if so, the same is true for all the biblical laws, and so distinctions between rules governing men and women—and their implications—remain.

---

10. Although, as Olyan reminded me (personal communication), Zipporah is in fact the daughter of a priest—a Midianite one.

11. Susan Ackerman, "Why Is Miriam Also among the Prophets? (And Is Zipporah among the Priests?)," *JBL* 121 (2002): 47–80; Rita J. Burns, *Has the Lord Indeed Spoken Only through Moses? A Study of the Biblical Portrait of Miriam* (SBLDS 84; Atlanta: Scholars Press, 1987).

12. I will treat both the P and the H material together because the two largely agree with one another on the divisions of the tribe of Levi. Most of the priestly material discussed here, however, stems from H rather than P. That H includes more material about family practices fits with H's tendency to include women more broadly in order to illustrate its ideology; see Sarah Shectman, "Women in the Priestly Narrative," in *The Strata of the Priestly Writings: Contemporary Debate and Future Directions* (ed. Sarah Shectman and Joel S. Baden; AThANT 95; Zurich: Theologischer Verlag, 2009), 184. Although the material in the Holiness Code (Lev 17–26) has little to say about Levites, it does presuppose their separate role from the priests, and H material outside of Lev 17–26 does make the difference explicit. See Baruch A. Levine, *Numbers 1–20: A New Translation with Introduction and Commentary* (AB 4; New York: Doubleday, 1993), 104–5.

I. Rules about Sex and Marriage

Leviticus 21:7–8, 13–14 contain a small number of legal stipulations about whom priests may marry.[13] These rules follow directly on prohibitions concerning mourning rites and, like them, focus on familial relations.[14] Some rules pertain to all Aaronide priests and some to the high priest only. They do not extend to the general category of Levites since, as Lev 21:8 makes clear, the stipulations are related to the priests' role in offering sacrifices.[15] The list of women whom an Aaronide priest may marry excludes prostitutes, "defiled" women, and divorced women. The high priest is also forbidden from marrying a widow. The issue here seems to be impurity that could be transmitted to the husband and the children through the woman (see esp. v. 15).[16] That a

---

13. See also Philip Peter Jenson, *Graded Holiness: A Key to the Priestly Conception of the World* (JSOTSup 106; Sheffield: JSOT Press, 1992), 128–30.

14. On Lev 21:5–6 pertaining to mourning, see Milgrom, *Leviticus*, 2:1801.

15. However, on the possibility that this layer of H does not recognize a distinction between priests and Levites, see Levine, *Numbers 1–20*, 105.

The Hebrew phrase לחם אלהים, which appears only once outside of Lev 21–22, includes both holy and most-holy food portions, as indicated by Lev 21:22. The similar construction אשי יהוה appears more often in P than in H texts and is especially used in reference to portions of offerings that are considered most holy. However, Lev 21:6 explicitly equates the two. Milgrom suggests that אשי is a shortened form of לחם אשי; see Milgrom, *Leviticus*, 1:162.

16. The precise nature of this impurity is a matter of some confusion and contention, however. Biblical impurity can be ritual, moral, or genealogical in nature (see Hayes, *Gentile Impurities*; Jonathan Klawans, *Impurity and Sin in Ancient Judaism* [Oxford: Oxford University Press, 2000]). Hayes interprets this text as referring to genealogical impurity (*Gentile Impurities*, 27). At issue is the terminology, especially the meaning of the root חלל. Although חלל can have a meaning of "profane" as distinct from "defile" (usually represented by טמא; *HALOT* 1:319, 2:376), in the Holiness material the two may be used interchangeably (see Milgrom, *Leviticus*, 2:1327). Hilary Lipka notes that חלל indicates "sexual acts which result in religious defilement" (*Sexual Transgression in the Hebrew Bible* [HBM 7; Sheffield: Sheffield Phoenix Press, 2006], 140 n. 58; see also 250). Eve Levavi Feinstein says that the חללה is "somewhere between the divorcée and the prostitute" ("Sexual Pollution in the Hebrew Bible" [Ph.D. diss., Harvard University, 2010], 214). Feinstein also argues that the behavior is "disgracing," rather than defiling, to the father (p. 216); she suggests that חלל "refers to the reduction in status that results from the contamination" (p. 70). Hayes notes that in a later period זנה, "harlot," means any disallowed woman and "marriage with a zonah affects the holy seed of the priestly line" (*Gentile Impurities*, 72). Klawans argues that sexual defilement of a woman is a matter of moral impurity, which is why the defiled woman is then excluded from marrying a priest (*Impurity and Sin*, 29). However, this argument seems to hinge on terms such as טמא, תועבה, and חנף, which do not actually appear in this passage. Milgrom's claim that חללה refers to a woman who has been raped (*Leviticus*, 2:1807) is unfounded. For our purposes, however, the nature of the impurity is less important than its result in restricting the types of women a priest may marry and, thereby, the behavior of women born or married into priestly families.

divorced woman is prohibited but a widow is not for any but the high priest may be an indication, as Jacob Milgrom argues, that a negative stigma was associated with divorce.[17] However, since divorce is not elsewhere negatively stigmatized in the Hebrew Bible,[18] an explanation along the lines of affiliation—the primary defining factor in these rules about women—offers a more plausible solution. If the husband is still alive, despite the divorce the woman's primary male bond remains slightly muddled. If the husband is dead, then issues of affiliation no longer exist. This is adequate for Aaronide priests generally, but not for the high priest, who, presumably because of his increased sanctity, must marry a woman whose primary male bond has only been to her father.[19]

The high priest is required to marry a virgin[20] מעמיו, "of his own kin." The precise meaning of מעמיו is not clear in this context; elsewhere עם can have a broad, pan-Israelite meaning, and indeed, according to Exod 6:23, Aaron marries a Judahite woman, Elisheba.[21] In the context of Lev 21, however, some have argued that מעמיו means a woman only from another priestly family.[22] The use

---

17. Milgrom, *Leviticus,* 2:1808; see also Feinstein, "Sexual Pollution," 217. That the issue of divorce is related to status and is therefore seen as worse than widowhood makes sense, but it is not entirely satisfying as an explanation. As Feinstein notes, men leave some kind of "essence" on their female sexual partners; this is inherently problematic because common essences cannot mix with holy ones. "Women are viewed as primarily affected by the seed of their past partners" (p. 220).

18. Deuteronomy 24:1–4, an interpretational conundrum, indicates only that remarriage after the second divorce may be an ethical problem; see Robert W. Wall, "Divorce," *ABD* 2:217–18; Jeffrey Tigay notes that the issue seems to be the similarity to adultery (*Deuteronomy* דברים: *The Traditional Hebrew Text with the New JPS Translation* [JPS Torah Commentary; Philadelphia: Jewish Publication Society, 1996], 220). In Ezra 10, divorcing foreign wives is seen as a positive act.

19. Note that in Ezek 44:22, all priests are forbidden from marrying divorced women, but they may marry the widow of another priest. Even if the issue in Lev 21 is one of moral rather than ritual or genealogical impurity (in that moral impurity is not contagious to people, although it does pollute the land; see Klawans, *Impurity and Sin,* 26–27), the high priest must presumably also be above reproach in moral concerns; hence the increased restriction.

20. See Lipka, *Sexual Transgression,* 79–80, 95, 204.

21. The other women named in this Priestly genealogy are Jochebed (v. 20), a Levite but, as she is Aaron's mother, not an Aaronide, and the daughter of Putiel (v. 25), whose tribal affiliation is not given.

22. Milgrom, *Leviticus,* 2:1820; Hayes, *Gentile Impurities,* 27. However, Hayes argues that "lay Israelites are not holy in the Priestly strand" (ibid., 27) and therefore they are not required to maintain this degree of genealogical purity. But this particular text derives from H, which does extend a concept of holiness to all of Israel (as Hayes herself observes), despite maintaining distinctions between priests and lay Israelites. Thus, this claim that the legislator here means that the high priest may only marry a member of another priestly family is difficult to substantiate.

of the term in vv. 1, 4, and 15 in the context of family members for whom a priest may mourn suggests that indeed this degree of closeness is indicated,[23] although it could be intended in a broader sense to mean that the priests may not mourn for just any Israelite. In other words, the high priest must marry a woman who has birth-ascribed priestly status. A regular priest's wife, unless her father was also a priest, attains priestly status only through marriage. The law therefore imposes further restrictions on the priests and their families, particularly the high priest. This opposition between high priest, priest, and non-priest conveys higher status to the priests, implicitly indicating higher status for women of the priests' families.[24] According to these regulations, we might conclude that a priest's daughter would have been less likely to marry outside of her close kin group, and her virginity would have been more closely guarded. Another restriction on these women's sexual freedom appears in Lev 21:9, which states that a priest's daughter who becomes a prostitute is subject to death by burning.

Two additional texts bear on the issues of sex and marriage in families of the tribe of Levi. In the first, Lev 21:12, the high priest is forbidden from leaving the sanctuary. If this applies at all times, then we must wonder just what sort of family arrangement the high priest would have had. The impracticality of such a prohibition suggests that it is related to the preceding laws concerning mourning and applies only to a time when a close family member of the high priest has died.[25] However, the following law, which requires the high priest to marry a virgin, does depart from the context of mourning and so allows the possibility that this verse does as well. It is also possible that, as noted above, these laws describe an idealized set of principles, in this case about the high priest's exclusive position, that were never really put into practice.[26] In any case, the law reinforces the exclusive sanctity of the high priest even where his immediate family is concerned.

The second text—or group of texts—concerns the encampment of the tribe of Levi around the tabernacle, as outlined in Num 3–4. The tribal muster, as is the case with the other tribes, includes only males, who are the cultic officiants. The Priestly material is inconsistent about the age at which the men of the tribe

---

23. See Feinstein, *Sexual Pollution*, 217–18.

24. This dichotomy is implicit insofar as this status is not formally categorized and explicated in the text, although the restrictions may be explicit indicators of this status. If the ability to marry a priest, especially a high priest, was a privilege available only to certain women, then the ability itself would have been an indicator of status.

25. Milgrom, *Leviticus*, 2:1816–17. Milgrom argues that it is a specific prohibition that he should not leave to follow the funeral procession, citing a parallel scenario in Lev 10:6–7, which suggests that otherwise he could have left.

26. Ezekiel 45:4 claims that the priestly abodes adjoin the sanctuary; possibly this was also the case with the sanctuary here, although such a conclusion is only theoretical.

start their service, but in any case it does not begin until adulthood.[27] Numbers 3:15, however, enrolls males from a month old. Surely where there are infants, there are nursing mothers very close by, and yet no women, no other children, and no men beyond the age of service are mentioned here. Perhaps the presence of the families is simply assumed; perhaps they are encamped beyond the close ring of the tribe of Levi just outside the tabernacle; or perhaps only the adult men of all the tribes are included and all of the affiliated family members are camped outside of the array described in these chapters. Indeed, the description seems to be based on a military model, and so again we may be in the realm of the ideal, not daily social reality.[28] Nevertheless, as before, the text reinforces the maleness of the cultic servant class and the general distance of women (among others) from things sacred.[29]

The indication in all of these texts is that greater restrictions are placed on women who are affiliated with the tribe of Levi.[30] These restrictions especially relate to how the women's behavior, especially their sexual history, affects the sanctity of the priests through marriage. Such restrictions are unsurprising. There are no commensurate restrictions on whom male Levites may marry; the description of the camp does not mention women and might exclude them from proximity to the tabernacle, although this is inconclusive. The access of priestly or Levitical women to sacred persons and to sacred food donations,[31] to be discussed below, offers clearer parallels between the roles of women in priestly and Levitical families. Thus, while these women faced greater restrictions, they also had an increased social status, reflected in their access to the sacred. Furthermore, although males with primary, birth-ascribed priestly status can lose this status through certain actions,[32] priestly women are in a precarious position in that their status, whether through birth or through marriage, may be lost through divorce (or widowhood) from a priest or through marriage to a non-priest. Thus, their social position, because it is dependent

---

27. Numbers 4:3 cites thirty years as the age at which Levitical service begins; according to Num 8:24, service begins at twenty-five. These chapters do distinguish the duties of the Aaronide line from the rest of the Levites, although much of the material applies to all members of the tribe, both priest and Levite.

28. See Levine, who notes that there is no mention of families or family terminology; the camp consists of fighting men (*Numbers 1–20*, 125, 143).

29. Again, Ezekiel offers an alternative, placing the Levites' cities close to the temple (45:5) and thus explicitly allowing the priests' and Levites' families increased access to the holy members of their families.

30. See Jenson, *Graded Holiness*, 123.

31. Although the tithe, the sacred portion given to the Levites, is in fact desanctified, it still retains some kind of special status; therefore I have included it in the category of "sacred donations." See the discussion below.

32. Leviticus 21–22 enumerates various ways in which priests might be excluded, either temporarily or permanently, from service; in some cases they might still have access to sacred foods (see Lev 21:22), but in others they would be cut off completely (e.g., 22:3).

on the primary male bond, is both more restricted and more precarious than that of other Israelites.

II. Mourning

The women of priestly families are among those for whom a priest could mourn in a visible and therefore public way, drawing attention to the woman's place in the priestly family. According to Lev 21:1–4, a priest is allowed to perform mourning rites for mother, father, son, daughter, brother, and virgin (unmarried) sister. The high priest is excluded from mourning rites even for parents, an effect of his superior sacred status (Lev 21:11).[33] The exclusion of the wife from the list of family members for whom a regular priest may mourn indicates that the concern here is people who are in the priest's direct blood line—who can be thought of as sharing the same blood as the priest and as having birth-ascribed priestly status.[34] The same woman may be mourned by her son, who shares her blood and who is also a priest. In this instance, then, the mother has birth-ascribed priestly status with respect to her son[35] but

---

33. Contrast Ezek 44:25, where priests (Ezekiel does not distinguish between priest and high priest) can mourn for parents, brother, and unmarried sister. According to Olyan, mourning reinforces social bonds (*Biblical Mourning: Ritual and Social Dimensions* [Oxford: Oxford University Press, 2004], 51) but also makes the mourner like the dead in some ways (pp. 40–44). Mourning rites also "function to separate the mourner ritually from society and the cult" (p. 35), and mourning therefore poses a "serious threat to the sanctuary and other holy space" through corpse contamination (p. 38). The restrictions placed on the priests thus make sense in light of their sacred status. Olyan also suggests that there may be mourning rituals other than corpse contact, shaving, and laceration that were permissible for priests (including even the high priest; pp. 119–20), but the text is not explicit in this regard.

34. Milgrom notes that the priest may engage in certain mourning rites, just not those that are conceived of as defiling (*Leviticus*, 2:1798). He also notes that the phrase הקרובה אליו, "nearest to him" (v. 3) refers to close kinship, namely, those having the same mother and father, rather than being spatial (p. 1799).

35. This may be no more than an indication that the relationship between mother and child was close and important enough (in general) to constitute an exception for regular priests. But even if this is the case, it nevertheless points to the importance of the mother. If parallels to other maternal relationships are any indication, then we might point to the role of the king's mother and the higher status that she seemed to attain (at least in certain cases). Being the mother of an individual with higher status, then, might convey higher status on the mother as well. On the queen mother and/or גבירה, see Susan Ackerman, "The Queen Mother and the Cult in Ancient Israel," *JBL* 112 (1993): 385–401; Nancy R. Bowen, "The Quest for the Historical Gĕbîrâ," *CBQ* 54 (2001): 597–618; Zafrira Ben-Barak, "The Status and Right of the Gĕbîrâ," *JBL* 110 (1991): 23–34. Ben-Barak argues that the queen mother attained higher status and influence only in certain very limited circumstances. Bowen argues that the queen mother and the גבירה are two different appellations that might apply to the same woman but did not necessarily do so. Ackerman, in contrast,

non–birth-ascribed priestly status where her husband is concerned, and this in addition to the fact that she might also be a priest's daughter whose father could mourn for her.[36]

A sister is included only when she is a member of the priest's household; once she has married and her primary male bond is to another man, regardless of his status, the priest may no longer observe mourning rites for her.[37] It is striking that no such restrictions pertain to the daughter, despite a similar rule for married daughters partaking of priestly food portions. Like the bond between mother and son, the connection of the daughter in a line of direct descent from the priest is strong enough to override the fact that her affiliation may have changed. Again, though, these relational terms may apply variously to the same woman, and so one priestly man may be able to mourn for a woman as his daughter while his son may not mourn for her as his sister; that is, she may have birth-ascribed status with respect to some men and non–birth-ascribed status with respect to others. It seems, then, that mourning is restricted to relationships in which the mourner and the deceased share a relationship of birth-ascribed priestly status: mother and son, father and daughter, but not husband and wife or brother and married sister. The bond seems to move vertically between generations but not laterally within a single generation once the woman has left the household.[38] These laws thus reveal a complicated series of individual relationships at work and a precariousness in the status of women in relation to priestly men, in contrast to non-priestly families, in which any member could mourn for any other member.

---

sees the queen mother as a royal figure with an important cultic role. All agree that, at least in certain cases, women in the royal court, especially the mother of the king, might achieve a high degree of influence and, therefore, of status in comparison to other women. It is therefore plausible that the mother of a priest, especially as she is, after all, singled out as someone for whom the priest may mourn, has a higher status than other women by virtue of her relationship to her son(s).

36. The text does not address what happens if the mother is divorced or if she then remarries. It may be that the text's ideology does not permit this possibility at all; however, if the issue is indeed direct descent—vertical rather than horizontal relationships (as discussed below)—then neither divorce nor remarriage would preclude a priest's mourning for his mother.

37. The absolute nature of the law indicates that this applies even if she is married to a priest. The fact that a divorced or widowed daughter of a priest—who is likely in many cases also a priest's sister—can return to her father's house and resume her right to eat sacred food, as will be discussed below, confirms that family affinity can change despite blood ties. Camp notes that the sister occupies a unique position, in that she is, "by birth, of the 'right' lineage and yet, by gender, not-Us" (*Wise, Strange and Holy*, 191).

38. This would seem to me to go against Camp's argument that women are other enough that they have ultimately to be excluded from the priestly lineage (*Wise, Strange and Holy*, 197). The evidence here suggests that this might be the case for certain relationships in which the blood bond was not seen as strong enough, but that in others it is not the case.

III. Priestly Food Portions

The priests are entitled to certain portions of the offerings of the Israelites. In addition to the tithe of the tithe,[39] they also receive parts of many sacrifices, offerings of firstfruits, firstlings, and the like. According to the Priestly system, many of these offerings are considered קדש קדשים, "most holy," and are restricted to consumption only in a holy place and only by the male priests (Aaron and his sons).[40] Other sacred donations, however, are considered simply קדש, "holy," and may be consumed by the priest's family—all who "are clean in [his] house." This appears to mean that these may be eaten in the priests' homes, rather than only in the sanctuary.[41] Leviticus 22 clarifies who is meant by this: anyone born into the priest's household; the slave, but not the hired laborer; and the unmarried daughter or the divorced or widowed daughter who has no children.[42] The wife is not mentioned, although she would surely be included, as she is a member of the household.[43] The status of the daughter here echoes the status of the sister (but not the daughter!) where mourning is concerned: once her primary male bond is no longer with the priest—her birth-ascribed priestly status is lost—she is not treated as a member of the priest's family and she can no longer partake of the sacred food.[44]

---

39. Or possibly, according to Lev 27, the entire tithe; see below.

40. Variously throughout the sacrificial laws in Leviticus, but see esp. Lev 7:6. Interestingly, the phrase כל-זכר בכהנים יאכלנו (Lev 7:6) suggests that there are some "of the priests" who are not male. This may be an acknowledgment of the closeness of women in these families or of their rights of access to other food portions. Otherwise, the construction is merely redundant. Leviticus 6:22 and 2 Chr 31:19 use the same phrase. Confusingly, the breast and thigh portions that are restricted to the sons in Lev 7:34 are permitted for both sons and daughters in Lev 10:14. According to Lev 22 and Num 18, though, any foods that may be consumed by members of the priests' families who are not in the male priestly line may be consumed by slaves and other family members as well. Possibly this means that there are some offerings that are extended to the priests' daughters but not to anyone else, but Num 18:11 suggests that "sons and daughters" may simply be another way of saying "your [entire] household."

41. Milgrom, *Leviticus*, 2:1847; according to Milgrom, this is the reason behind Lev 22:3, which states that the person consuming a sacred donation must be ritually pure. The laws related to the שלמים in Lev 7:11–18, as well as Hag 2:12, indicate that holy portions of offerings could indeed leave the sanctuary precinct.

42. Jenson notes: "Although the priesthood was exclusively male, the entire extended family of priests was affected by priestly status" (*Graded Holiness*, 123), yet it seems that really it is the nuclear rather than the extended family that is affected. The qualification that the daughter have no children is yet another indication that mother–child blood relations override other relationships, as reflected in the fact that a priest may mourn for his mother or daughter but not for his married sister.

43. This is the conclusion of Olyan, *Rites and Rank*, 31. The wife is not specifically excluded in this case, as she is in the list of people for whom the priest can mourn.

44. She may, of course, be married to another priest, in which case she would be enti-

Interestingly, these laws indicate that a woman of a priestly family had access to sacred foods to which even a male Levite did not have access. Although the שלמים rule indicates that the layperson (and presumably the Levite) can also partake of sacred food in certain limited situations, this is the only sacred food (קדש) that a non-priest is allowed to eat.[45] If access to sacred foods is indeed an indicator of status, then a woman in the family of a priest would have had a higher status than a male Levite, according to the Priestly system.[46] Indeed, a slave within the priest's household would also have had access to such sacred food and so in this limited circumstance can be said to have a higher status vis-à-vis access to the sacred as well. It is probably going too far to say that this extends to every aspect of social status; surely a slave, of whatever station, would have had limited status by virtue of being a slave. Thus, a priestly woman, too, should not necessarily be seen as having higher status than a Levite male, except perhaps in a certain limited, cultic sense. Hierarchies of female and slave status no doubt still applied. Nevertheless, these rules indicate that status is a complex matter and that the status of women and of slaves within priestly households would have been, by virtue of the women's or slaves' relationship to the priest and their access to sacred foods, higher than the status of women and slaves, respectively, in Levite or lay households. We might speak, then, of *constellations* of privilege and status,[47] where multiple factors play a part, with an ebb and flow between elements and among groups of people. Overall, a male Levite would have higher status than, say, the slave of a priest, but this is a result of numerous elements coming together to determine that status; in regard to access to holy foods alone, however, the members of the priest's household would have a status higher than that of a male Levite.

Deuteronomy 18:1–8 also gives a portion of various offerings to the priests.[48] However, Deuteronomy says nothing about where these are eaten or

---

tled to the portions taken home by her husband and/or son(s). But the law is concerned only with a single priest's family at a time.

45. There is some tension here, with the שלמים being called holy alongside H's stipulation that no layperson may eat holy foods. Leviticus 19:5–8 indicates that H does consider the שלמים to be holy and allows the Israelite to eat it. Either the שלמים is an exception or Lev 22 refers only to the sacred portions given to priests, which are considered to have a status different from the שלמים (this seems to be the reading of Milgrom [*Leviticus*, 2:1861]).

46. Olyan notes that Levites do not have access to the holy portions available to the priests and the priests' dependents, including women (*Rites and Rank*, 30–31). The households of priests do not seem to be strictly limited to this food, however; that is, they are never explicitly forbidden from eating other, nonsacred foods, and therefore it seems unlikely that the food restrictions are intended to maintain the holiness of those in proximity to the priests.

47. This idea of "constellations" was suggested to me by Saul Olyan (personal communication) and strikes me as an apt metaphor for the complex system of social dynamics.

48. In theory, all male Levites are (potentially) priests according to Deuteronomy;

about whether the priest's family members may share them. As with the tithe, the Deuteronomic legislation about the priests is remarkably silent about the priests' families, never mentioning them at all. Nevertheless, Deut 18:1 refers to the "whole tribe of Levi," which would presumably have been understood to include women, as did the other tribes.

IV. Tithes (Levites)

As with the priests, the Levites receive certain offerings in the Priestly legislation as well. Complicating the issue of the status of Levitical (in contrast to priestly) women is the fact that the status of the Levites in the Priestly material is not entirely clear.[49] The Levites are not holy as are the priests, but neither are they fully laity, despite the fact that their access to holy foods, for example, is the same as the laity's.[50] According to the pentateuchal legislation, the Levites receive the tithe as compensation for their work.[51] The clearest statement of the tithe rule appears in Num 18:21–31, which states that the Levites are entitled to the tithe, of which they must in turn tithe a portion ("a tithe of the tithe") to the priests. This process desanctifies the main portion of the tithe and allows the Levites and their households (that is, their families, their slaves

---

however, the centralization of the sanctuary in Jerusalem effectively meant that only those Levites serving in Jerusalem would in practice be priests. Levites from outside Jerusalem were eligible to come to the temple to serve, but in practice not all did so, or realistically would have been able to do so. The result would have been a distinction between those priests actively in service and those not, the latter often referred to as "rural" or "provincial" Levites. Although the priestly material also assumes a centralized cult, it is very specific about the roles of both priests and Levites in relation only to the central sanctuary and thus does not reflect the same issues of redundant rural priests that are a part of the Deuteronomic system. See Menahem Haran, *Temples and Temple-Service in Ancient Israel: An Inquiry into the Character of Cult Phenomena and the Historical Setting of the Priestly School* (Oxford: Clarendon, 1978), 61–62. On the role of the rural Levites, see recently Mark Leuchter, "'The Levite in Your Gates': The Deuteronomic Redefinition of Levitical Authority," *JBL* 126 (2007): 417–36.

49. See Jeffrey Stackert, *Rewriting the Torah: Literary Revision in Deuteronomy and the Holiness Legislation* (FAT 52; Tübingen: Mohr Siebeck, 2007), 185, esp. n. 45; Camp, *Wise, Strange and Holy*, 200–206; Olyan, *Rites and Rank*, 28–30. As Olyan notes, Chronicles seems to solve this by making the Levites holy and the priests most holy, thus clarifying the hierarchical structure (*Rites and Rank*, 28). Milgrom notes that the Priestly author avoids using the root קדש in reference to the Levites (*Leviticus*, 3:2428). In Num 17:5, Korah and all the non-Aaronides (that is, Levites), are called זר, "stranger."

50. Although the Levites receive the tithe, it is desanctified in order for this to happen; thus, it is common, as is the food of the laity. However, the restrictions on its consumption indicate that it is not of the same quality as laypeople's food.

51. Milgrom, for example, notes the nature of the tithe as the Levites' sole source of income (*Leviticus*, 3:2422–23).

and servants, and likely their non-Levite dinner guests as well) to eat it anywhere they choose.[52]

According to Lev 27:30–33, however, the tithe is a holy donation that belongs to Yhwh, that is, to the priests rather than to the Levites. This passage is considerably less detailed and informative than the one in Num 18; on the surface, it seems to contradict Num 18. It could refer to the status of the Levites' tithe before the priests' portion is separated from it,[53] or it could be a variant law from another priestly strain.[54] If Lev 27 indeed represents a separate law indicating that the tithe belongs entirely to the priests, then it would fall into the category of the priestly food portions, discussed above.[55] In any case, as it does not specifically mention priests or Levites and is mostly concerned with contents rather than distribution, it may be left out of consideration here.

The result of the Priestly laws is that the tithe, despite ultimately being desanctified, nevertheless has a special kind of status; it is not that the tithe can be returned to the layperson once it is desanctified, after all. The tithe is the special perquisite of the Levites and its limited nature conveys some element of restricted access and therefore increased status, despite the fact that

---

52. Stackert, *Rewriting the Torah*, 186; Levine, *Numbers 1–20*, 452; Milgrom, *Leviticus*, 3:2427–28.

53. Milgrom notes that the tithe is referred to as קדש also in Num 18:32 (*Leviticus*, 3:2427); Milgrom takes this as a reference to the status of the tithe before the priests' portion is separated from it. A similar situation may apply in Deut 26:13, which also calls the tithe holy, to be treated carefully and not brought into contact with anything unclean. However, it is also given not only to the Levite but to the resident alien, the widow, and the orphan. Because the Levite is synonymous with the priest in Deuteronomy, the tithe's being sacred is at one level less problematic, although the fact that the tithe is here given to laypeople as well is more problematic. This may also refer to the status of the tithe before it is given to the Levites, or it may be an indication that there were a small number of holy foods, like the שלמים, that could be eaten by certain laity. Ian Wilson solves certain of these difficulties by proposing that the third-year tithe was in fact offered in Jerusalem and that the widow and orphan have access to it because of Deuteronomy's particular theology where those groups are concerned; see "Central Sanctuary or Local Settlement? The Location of the Triennial Tithe Declaration (Dtn 26:13–15)," *ZAW* 120 (2008): 323–40.

54. According to Milgrom, Lev 27 is H, whereas Num 18 is P (Milgrom, *Leviticus*, 3:2397). He sees a historical progression from H to P to D, where the tithe originally went to the sanctuary, then became the perquisite of the Levite, and ultimately reverted to the owner (p. 2425). Not only does this require reading an H text as earlier than P, but Milgrom then goes on to detail how the lack of Levites in the Second Temple period resulted in the tithe reverting to the priests, which would suggest, contra Milgrom's own argument, that his H tithe law is better situated at the end of this historical progression, in the postexilic period. It is better to read Num 18 as H and Lev 27 as stemming from another layer of H, following Stackert, *Rewriting the Torah*, 197.

55. That the tithe in Lev 27 is called "holy," not "most holy," means that in this case it would be included with those sacred portions that can be shared with clean members of the priests' households, excluding hired workers.

it is technically no more sacred than any other common food.⁵⁶ The tithe's availability to the families (or households; ביתכם) of the Levites suggests that Levitical women would likewise have shared in some measure in the increased status conveyed by the right of access to the tithe.

In Deuteronomy as well, the Levites receive a portion of the tithe as a means of support, to compensate for their lack of territory. Although there is no division between Levites and priests in Deuteronomy, the centralization of worship resulted in a distinction between those Levites serving in the central sanctuary and those who remained outside of Jerusalem and were thus not actively officiating at the temple.⁵⁷ The Deuteronomic tithe law seems to have this latter group in mind in particular, as its members would not have had access to the priestly sacrificial portions being offered at the central altar.⁵⁸ Instead, the Levites who receive the tithe in Deuteronomy are one of a group of several types of social unfortunates who have a right to it.

Deuteronomy legislates a two-tiered system: for two years, the tithe is shared by the owners with the Levites (Deut 12:17–19; 14:22–26), and in the third year, the tithe is given to the Levite, the orphan, the widow, and the resident alien (Deut 14:27–29). The two-year tithes may be eaten only in the sanctuary—indicating sacred status—whereas the third-year tithe is akin to profane slaughter and is stored locally for the needy to come and partake of it at will. According to Deut 12:18, the Levite is included among the group of pilgrims who go to the central sanctuary to enjoy the two-year tithe, thus ensuring that the rural Levites, who lack access to the priestly sacrificial portions, are taken care of in all years.⁵⁹ Notably, Deuteronomy says nothing about gender or age among Levites here, despite the fact that the list in which the Levites appear includes the Israelites' sons, daughters, and male and female slaves.⁶⁰ Surely the Levites had families, though, who would likewise have had access to this food.⁶¹

---

56. As Stackert notes, the law "serve[s] to equate the Levites with lay Israelites, but ... actually fail[s] to do so fully" (*Rewriting the Torah*, 186).

57. See n. 48 above.

58. For a contrary view, however, which sees the tithe as being offered at the central sanctuary in conjunction with a pilgrimage, see Wilson, "Central Sanctuary or Local Settlement."

59. See Milgrom, who notes that the inclusion of the Levite and not the resident alien, widow, and orphan, in the first two years is a "consequence of Deuteronomy's guilt for having deprived the Levites of their prior rights to the tithe" (*Leviticus*, 3:2433). See also Richard D. Nelson, *Deuteronomy: A Commentary* (OTL; Louisville: Westminster John Knox, 2002), 186.

60. Deuteronomy 12:18; see also Deut 5:14; 12:12; 16:11, 14.

61. Possibly this is an indicator that the Levites were an occupational group who did not have families—that their parents and siblings would have been members of other tribes or social groups and that they did not marry or have children. However, this latter in particular seems unlikely, and it is difficult to imagine how their wives and children thus would

The nature of the tithe as a kind of charity or social welfare system is especially pronounced in Deuteronomy. Although the tithe may impart some temporary special status to all who consume it as a festival meal, it is not restricted to any particular group of people. The third-year tithe is no more than alms given to the poor. The Levite does have access to the tithe in all three years, it is true, and Levites are mentioned specifically despite the fact that there were undoubtedly other poor families in Israel. This is likely an acknowledgment of the Levites' status above other recipients of the third-year tithe, but on the whole Deuteronomy's law—making the tithe widely available to a number of groups—only highlights the Levites' marginal social status. This contrasts with the Priestly legislation, in which access to the tithe is far more restricted. Nevertheless, the Priestly source's tithe is similarly connected to the fact that the Levites have no tribal allotment of their own and thus no land on which to grow their own crops for food. The tithe is an integral part of a welfare system that helps to support the landless cultic class. At the same time, though, the tithe is a special, semi-sacred donation that is restricted to a certain time and place for consumption. This semi-sacredness imparts a special status to those who are allowed to eat it. As a result, women of Levitical families, according to the Priestly laws, would have had access to restricted food and a commensurately higher social status; in the Deuteronomic laws, in contrast, the Levites and their unmentioned families, despite being technically of the same cultic class as the officiating priests in the temple, seem to have a lower social status, although one nevertheless worth singling out as distinct from other marginal groups.

V. Conclusions

Olyan observes that "[d]enial of access to cultic and quasi-cultic settings not only establishes boundaries around the sanctuary and its analogues but contributes to the shaping of status differences between individuals and groups."[62] The Priestly legislation concerning marriage, mourning, and access to the tithe and other sacred foods shows that women in priestly and Levitical families were subject to unique social standards and restrictions while also having rights of access to restricted people and foods. These rules indicate a high degree of social stratification between women of priestly, Levite, and lay groups within the biblical social structure. Although the rules may be idealized literary constructions, they nevertheless indicate a certain set of hierarchical principles on the part of their authors. As Olyan also notes, "High-status persons draw upon economic, political, legal, and theological resources that allow them to

---

have fared if they were not also permitted to share the tithe. As is often the case, this seems to be one in which the biblical author is not overly concerned with certain details.

62. Olyan, *Rites and Rank*, 115.

wield significant power."[63] We can imagine, then, that the wife or the mother of a priest, and especially of a high priest, could have enjoyed a status well above that of other women and perhaps even of certain men. In this regard, she might have had much in common with the queen mother, or גבירה, who seems to have enjoyed heightened status as a result of her affiliation with royal men.[64] Although priestly women would not have had more access to sacred locations, their symbolic access to the sacred could have applied outside the sanctuary. The status of these women varies according to relationship (birth-ascribed or non–birth-ascribed) and is also very precarious, in that it depends on the primary male bond and can be lost: through marriage to a non-priest for those with birth-ascribed status or through divorce for those with non–birth-ascribed status.

Whereas the Priestly legislation presents a reality of economic dependence as one of privilege and prerogative, Deuteronomy's cultic classifications, especially regarding the rural Levites, seem generally to denote a lower status and a more marginal social and economic position. The Levites here are mentioned without any reference to their family members, female or male. Although the majority of Levites, and their families, were likely in a dependent social position, some vestige of their special status remains in the ways in which they are singled out. At the same time, the Levitical priests at Deuteronomy's central sanctuary, and their families, would have enjoyed a commensurately high social status, reflecting stratification within the cultic class, as in the Priestly material. Thus, a picture emerges in which, according especially to Priestly ideology, we can discern complex and fragile constellations of status among different groups of women in the biblical social structure.

---

63. Ibid., 117.
64. See n. 35 above.

Part II
Priests and Levites in Scriptural Context

The Violent Origins of the Levites: Text and Tradition

Joel S. Baden

The various texts of the Hebrew Bible that deal with the Levites are in agreement that the Levites are considered a group apart, separate from the other Israelite tribes or the rest of Israelite society.[1] While any authentic historical reconstruction of the place of the Levites in ancient Israel, or the development of their role in society, is perhaps inaccessible with any degree of certainty, the traditional explanations for their separate status are present in a number of literary manifestations, particularly in the Pentateuch. The Priestly source attributes the separation of the Levites to a divine decree handed down at Sinai (Num 1–4), as it does for so many other phenomena, without any explanation for the choice of the Levites in particular.[2] The focus of this paper, however, will be on four other pentateuchal descriptions of the origins of the Levites' special status. Despite being spread across the books of the Pentateuch, and despite comprising both prose and poetry, all four of these texts—Gen 34, Exod 32, Gen 49, and Deut 33—hold in common the tradition that the Levites were chosen for special treatment as a result of an act of violence. The specific nature of this act, however, as well as its location both in time and space, differs among these passages. This paper will examine these four texts on their own and in relationship to one another, with an eye toward making some preliminary suggestions as to the literary and traditional relationships between them.

Poetry

In the tribal poem of Gen 49, the second set of sayings deals with Simeon and Levi together (vv. 5–7). They are described as angry and wrathful (v. 7), and violent (v. 5)—whatever we make of the word מכרתיהם.[3] They kill, they

---

1. Cf. Exod 38:21; Lev 25:32–33; Num 1–4; 8; 18; 31:30; 35:1–8; Deut 10:8–9; 12:12, 19; 14:27, 29; 16:11, 14; 18:1–8; 21:5; 26:11–13; 31:9, 25; Jos 13:14, 33; 14:3, 4; 18:7; 21:1–41; Judg 17; 19:1; 1 Kgs 12:31; Isa 66:21; Jer 33:21–22; Ezek 45:5; 48:13; Mal 2:4; 1 Chr 6; 15; 23:25–32; 24; 2 Chr 8:14; 11:14; 19:8; 23:6, 18; 29; 31:2, 4; 35:3–6; Ezra 3:8; 6:18; 7:24; Neh 10:28; 12:47; 13:30.
2. See George Buchanan Gray, *A Critical and Exegetical Commentary on Numbers* (ICC; Edinburgh: T&T Clark, 1903), 25.
3. For a summary of the various proposals, see Raymond de Hoop, *Genesis 49 in Its*

maim (v. 6), and as a result they are disinherited, divided, and scattered among the tribes of Israel (vv. 6–7). Unlike in the saying of Reuben (vv. 3–4), which explicitly mentions the specific crime for which Jacob's firstborn is punished— "he mounted his father's bed"—no details are provided in these verses to justify the attribution of violence to the two brothers. Though it is usual to draw a direct line between Gen 49:5–7 and Gen 34—and this connection will be discussed below—it is worth stating at the outset that there is nothing in the poem that makes any direct or even indirect reference to the events involving Dinah and Shechem in Gen 34; not a single word, beyond the two names, has any resonance with the earlier narrative.[4] All we can say with certainty is that this passage represents a tradition in which Simeon and Levi are rendered landless because they are violent—apparently by nature.

The tribal poem of Gen 49 is usually and correctly understood as an originally independent piece, almost certainly part of a larger tradition of collections of sayings about the various Israelite tribes (cf. Deut 33; Judg 5).[5] It is, however, embedded in the larger narrative of Jacob's life, both by placement and by introductory and concluding transitions.[6] Scholars have long recognized that the source in which this poem has been preserved, as Jacob's last words, is J.[7] While the author of J is not the author of the poem, the poem

---

Literary and Historical Context (OTS 29; Leiden: Brill, 1999), 101–9. The centrality of violence in this passage is emphasized by Hans-Jürgen Zobel, *Stammesspruch und Geschichte: Die Angaben der Stammessprüche von Gen 49, Dtn 33 und Jdc 5 über die politischen und kultischen Zustände in damaligen "Israel"* (BZAW 95; Berlin: Töpelmann, 1965), 7.

4. See John Skinner, *A Critical and Exegetical Commentary on Genesis* (2nd ed.; ICC; Edinburgh: T&T Clark, 1930), 516: "the terms of the oracle are perfectly general and in part unsuited to the supposed circumstances [i.e., the story of Gen 34]; and it seems to me to be the habitual character of the tribes which is denounced, and not any particular action." See also n. 33 below.

5. On the nature and age of the poem, see Frank Moore Cross and David Noel Freedman, *Studies in Ancient Yahwistic Poetry* (1950; new ed.; Biblical Resource Series; Grand Rapids: Eerdmans, 1997), 46–47.

6. The introduction, v. 1b, projects the sayings, originally understood as describing the present state of the tribes, into the future, as this is the only way the poem can fit into its narrative context; the conclusion, v. 28abα[1] (to אביהם), describes the poem explicitly as the final words of Jacob, that is, as part of the overarching patriarchal narrative.

7. See Julius Wellhausen, *Die Composition des Hexateuchs* (4th ed.; Berlin: de Gruyter, 1963), 60; Benjamin W. Bacon, *The Genesis of Genesis* (Hartford: Student Publishing Co., 1893), 220; August Dillmann, *Genesis Critically and Exegetically Expounded* (trans. William B. Stevenson; 2 vols.; Edinburgh: T&T Clark, 1897), 2:450; J. Estin Carpenter and G. Harford-Battersby, *The Hexateuch According to the Revised Edition* (2 vols.; London: Longmans, Green & Co., 1900), 2:76; S. R. Driver, *The Book of Genesis* (12th ed.; WC; London: Methuen, 1926), 381; Hermann Gunkel, *Genesis* (trans. Mark E. Biddle; Mercer Library of Biblical Studies; Macon, Ga.: Mercer University Press, 1997; German original 1901), 453; Skinner, *Genesis*, 512; Richard Elliott Friedman, *The Bible with Sources Revealed: A New View into the Five Books of Moses* (San Francisco: HarperSanFrancisco, 2003), 114.

belongs to the source J, just as in a novel in which a character sings a well-known song: the author of the novel is not the author of the song, but the song belongs to the novel.

While Gen 49:5–7 treats Simeon and Levi as a pair, the tribal poem of Deut 33 deals with the Levites independently—indeed, Simeon goes unmentioned entirely—and at some length (vv. 8–11). While Gen 49:5–7 seems to separate out the Levites as a result of their inherently violent nature, Deut 33:8–11 describes, albeit obliquely, a particular historical event: the testing of the Levites at Massah and Meribah—whatever form that testing may have taken—and their successful passing of the test, in the course of which they disregarded their kinship ties for the sake of upholding Yahweh's commandments (vv. 8–9). The separation of the Levites in this case is not viewed negatively, but in exceedingly positive terms: far from being punished, they are rewarded with the role of cultic administrator (v. 10), they are blessed, and their enemies are to be smitten (v. 11).

The sense of violence is muted in this passage. The disregarding of family in favor of Yahweh, however, suggests that there must have been some act by which the Levites publicly and decisively made this choice. In addition, the conclusion to the saying about Levi has obvious violent connotations, the likes of which are not evident, at least not as explicitly, in the other sayings in this poem.[8] We may say without hesitation, however, that this poem preserves a positive construction of the Levites, in which their action, whether or not we can tentatively call it violent, results in their being marked off as specially devoted to Yahweh, both in attitude and in practice.

As with Gen 49, Deut 33 is an originally independent collection of tribal sayings, and its composition should not be attributed to any of the four pentateuchal sources. At the same time, it is, like Gen 49, part of one of the pentateuchal documents. The question, however, is which one. We may begin with a process of elimination. Deuteronomy 33 is assuredly not P, which has no interest in poetry. It is also not E; to E belongs the poem in the preceding chapter, Deut 32, which has been introduced in the E portion of Deut 31 (vv. 16–22, 30).[9] It also makes little sense in D, where it has no place either rhetorically or

---

8. In addition to the phrase "smite the loins," the word חילו, commonly taken as "substance," has military connotations. The exception in Deut 33 may be the saying regarding Joseph, whose "horns" "gore the peoples, the ends of the earth altogether" (v. 17). The obscurity of this statement, however, renders it difficult to draw too much meaning from it.

9. See Otto Eissfeldt, *The Old Testament: An Introduction* (trans. Peter R. Ackroyd; New York: Harper & Row, 1965), 226–27; more recently and extensively Menahem Haran, *The Biblical Collection: Its Consolidation to the End of the Second Temple Times and Changes of Form to the End of the Middle Ages* (in Hebrew; 3 vols.; Jerusalem: Magnes, 1996–2008), 2:71–80, though I cannot agree with Haran's view that this E passage was included by a Deuteronomic editor, or that there is any secondary D introduction to Deut 32; D knows

structurally.¹⁰ That leaves only J.¹¹ There are also positive reasons to think that this poem made up part of the J document. First, we know that the author of J included other extended poems in his work, Gen 49 and Exod 15.¹² Second, we already have the structurally similar use of another collection of tribal sayings at the end of Jacob's life: Deut 33 represents the final words of Moses, just as Gen 49 represents the final words of Jacob.¹³ Third, and perhaps most important, Deut 33 fits very well between the preceding and following pieces of J. The last time we encountered J, the Israelites had just reached the top of Pisgah in Moab, in Num 21:16–20.¹⁴ They were, in other words, at the very border with Canaan, at a spot that was traditionally understood to be the last stop before crossing into the promised land.¹⁵ The next piece from J is the notice of Moses' death in Deut 34:5.¹⁶ The poem of Deut 33 fits nicely between these two: the Israelites arrive at the place of Moses' death, he delivers his farewell speech, and then he dies; the parallel with Gen 49 is evident.

If Deut 33 is indeed from J, then we have to reckon with two conflicting views regarding the Levites in the two J poems: one in which they are judged negatively and one in which they are judged positively. This ostensible contradiction evaporates when it is remembered that the author of J is not the author of either of the poems. He uses them for the farewell speeches of his two great

---

nothing of this song (or Deut 33), and its inclusion here is due entirely to the pentateuchal compiler.

10. In the preceding D section (32:45–47), Moses tells Israel to take the words of the Torah (i.e., the laws of D) to heart; these words are a fitting conclusion to Moses' great speech to the Israelites, and their power would be strangely undercut by the poem of Deut 33.

11. See Benjamin W. Bacon, *The Triple Tradition of the Exodus* (Hartford: Student Publishing Co., 1894), 269–73; Menahem Haran, *Temples and Temple-Service in Ancient Israel: An Inquiry into Biblical Cult Phenomena and the Historical Setting of the Priestly School* (1978; repr., Winona Lake, Ind.: Eisenbrauns, 1985), 67.

12. On the attribution of the hymn in Exod 15 to J, see S. R. Driver, *The Book of Exodus* (Cambridge Bible for Schools and Colleges; Cambridge: Cambridge University Press, 1918), 132–40; Frank Moore Cross, *Canaanite Myth and Hebrew Epic: Essays in the History of the Religion of Israel* (Cambridge, Mass.: Harvard University Press, 1973), 123–24; Friedman, *Sources Revealed*, 144–46.

13. Jacob's burial instructions to his sons in 49:29–32 belong to P.

14. See Joel S. Baden, *J, E, and the Redaction of the Pentateuch* (FAT 68; Tübingen: Mohr Siebeck, 2009), 135–37.

15. See the similar tradition regarding the top of Pisgah in Deut 3:27; 34:1.

16. The words "Moses died" in this verse must have been held in common by at least three sources: J, E, and P. J may have contained only these words, given the parallel of Gen 49:33; E would have read "Moses the servant of Yahweh died in the land of Moab," as this designation for Moses is a feature of E alone and this is how E refers to his burial place (in Deut 34:6); and P would have had "Moses died there at the command of Yahweh," as this phrase is unique to the Priestly source (cf. Exod 17:1; Lev 24:12; Num 3:16, 39, 51; 4:37, 41, 45, 49; 9:18, 20, 23; 10:13; 13:3; 33:2, 38; 36:5). It is unlikely, against most commentators, that D is present in this chapter.

protagonists, Jacob and Moses. As overviews of the community of Israel on the verge of its transitions from individuals to tribes and from tribes to territories, they serve his rhetorical purposes at these key moments. The precise contents of these poems were, to a certain extent, beyond the author's control, and therefore also the conflicting views therein regarding the Levites.[17] Yet the author of J did choose these poems, perhaps out of many, and we can see his design in choosing which poem to insert at which place, especially when looking through the lens of the treatment of the Levites. The poem of Gen 49:5–7 talks about the Levites by reference to their ancestor Levi, who is, in the context of the narrative in which the poem is situated, still alive. The poem of Deut 33:8–11 describes the Levites as a tribe acting in unison, as makes sense given the situation in the overarching narrative, when the tribes as defined groups are about to take possession of their various land-holdings.

Prose

It has long been recognized that the narrative of Dinah and Shechem in Gen 34 is composite, though the wide variety of reconstructions testifies to the difficulty of separating the passage into its constituent sources.[18] The complete anal-

---

17. We may take under consideration the possibility that J altered the beginning of Gen 49 to elevate Judah to the highest position among the sons of Jacob; see David Carr, *Reading the Fractures of Genesis: Historical and Literary Approaches* (Louisville: Westminster John Knox, 1996), 251. Yet the evidence suggests that these three tribes are disenfranchised not merely to serve the rhetorical purpose for a Judean author of elevating Judah, but because they historically had disappeared, or nearly so, as independent landed tribal groups within Israel. Thus it is quite possible that Gen 49 reflects this historical situation as well as that of the political rise of Judah, and that the verses about Reuben and Simeon and Levi are original.

18. See the variant proposals of, e.g., Wellhausen, *Composition*, 45–47; Abraham Kuenen, *An Historico-Critical Inquiry into the Origin and Composition of the Hexateuch (Pentateuch and Book of Joshua)* (trans. Philip H. Wicksteed; London: Macmillan, 1886), 326; W. E. Addis, *The Documents of the Hexateuch* (2 vols.; London: David Nutt, 1892), 1:68–69; Dillmann, *Genesis*, 2:293–301; Carpenter and Harford-Battersby, *Hexateuch*, 2:52–54; Edgar S. Brightman, *The Sources of the Hexateuch: J, E, and P in the Text of the American Standard Edition* (New York: Abingdon, 1918), 62–63; Bacon, *Genesis*, 177–80; Driver, *Genesis*, 302–8; Gunkel, *Genesis*, 356–65; Skinner, *Genesis*, 417–22; Claus Westermann, *Genesis 12–36* (trans. John J. Scullion; CC; Minneapolis: Fortress, 1985), 535–45. A summary and critique of older scholarly opinions may be found in Albert de Pury, "Genèse xxxiv et l'histoire," *RB* 76 (1969): 5–49, esp. 5–9. Many scholars see P in this chapter, usually on the basis of the theme of circumcision and the use of the root טמא, yet this is unnecessary. The practice of circumcision was known to all the pentateuchal authors, and the word טמא does not have here the specific notion of ritual defilement that it takes on in P. There are also those who argue for the essential unity of the chapter, with or without a few secondary insertions: see, e.g., E. A. Speiser, *Genesis: Introduction, Translation, and Notes* (AB 1; Garden City, N.Y.: Doubleday, 1964), 266–67; Erhard Blum, *Die Komposition der Vaterge-*

ysis of this passage is beyond the scope of this paper, but it will suffice to say that there appear to be two distinct versions of the event in the text.[19] In one, Shechem sees and falls in love with Dinah, and goes through what would seem to be the standard procedure in cases of courtship between two foreign parties: the sending of a relative as a go-between, the tantalizing description of communal property, and the offer of a bride-price. In response to these advances, the sons of Jacob, speaking collectively, engage in the trickery involving circumcision and take advantage of the temporary disablement of the Shechemites to slaughter and plunder the entire town; Jacob is no more than a bystander, as his sons do all the dealing with Hamor and Shechem. In this story, Dinah is never violated; in fact, she is never even taken from Jacob's home.

In the other story in Gen 34, Dinah is indeed taken and kept in Shechem's house. Jacob hears about this first, because his sons are working in the field, but he waits for their return to say or do anything. Shechem's actions constitute an obvious violation of ethical, communal, and perhaps religious standards, and Jacob's sons, upon hearing the news, are rightly angered. Two of them—identified in marked terms as "two of Jacob's sons, the brothers of Dinah"—take it upon themselves to arm themselves and remove Dinah from Shechem's house by force. They do so, killing Shechem and Hamor along the way, and Jacob is unhappy. He is concerned that their hasty actions have put the entire family in danger from the surrounding peoples, but the brothers, Simeon and Levi, defend their actions as necessary for maintaining their sister's—and by extension the family's—honor. In this story, Jacob plays a larger role, albeit one mostly defined by absence of action; Dinah is in fact violated; and only Hamor and Shechem, not the entire town, are killed. There is no trickery here, merely the straightforward response of Simeon and Levi, alone among the brothers, to the actions of Shechem. Their response, however, is distinctively violent, at least insofar as they are contrasted in their action with the other brothers (and Jacob), who are inactive; Jacob's response further highlights the unusual nature of Simeon and Levi's action, although the author does leave them with the last word.

The first story, in which Dinah stays at home and the brothers all act in tandem, is to be ascribed to E. The trickery employed by the brothers is reminiscent of the despoiling of the Egyptians (Exod 3:21–22; 11:2–3; 12:35–36), and the depiction of Jacob and his sons as fearsome connects with what follows in E in Gen 35:5, in which the surrounding peoples are afraid of Jacob's family as they leave Shechem.[20] The second, in which Simeon and Levi are the main actors, belongs to J. The motif of being in the field is recurrent in the J

---

schichte (WMANT 57; Neukirchen-Vluyn: Neukirchener Verlag, 1984), 213–16; Friedman, *Sources Revealed*, 88–89.

19. I owe the basis of the following analysis to Dr. Baruch Schwartz.
20. There may be a connection also to the story in Judg 9, which has also been attrib-

VIOLENT ORIGINS OF THE LEVITES   109

patriarchal narratives (Gen 24:63-65; 27:27; 30:14-16; 37:7), and the view of circumcision in Gen 34, as a national custom necessary for belonging to the Israelite group, does not comport well with the magical sense of circumcision found elsewhere in J (Exod 4:24-26). Thus, to J belongs yet another tradition, this one presented in prose, of the Levites, or at least their ancestor Levi, acting in a distinctively violent fashion.

In Exod 32:26-29, the Levites answer the call of Moses, defining themselves, against the rest of the Israelites, as "for Yahweh" (v. 26).[21] They are commanded to kill a number of their fellow Israelites, and they do so without comment (vv. 27-28). For this they are rewarded with blessing from Yahweh and the right to dedicate themselves to Yahweh (v. 29). As has long been noted, in the otherwise coherent and continuous E story of the golden calf in Exod 32 this episode stands apart. Not only does this passage contain no clear reference to the context of the golden calf; it is narratively problematic. It appears to be a punishment for the people's sin, but the people are punished elsewhere in the story by being made to drink the water made from the calf in v. 20 and by a plague from Yahweh in v. 35—both of which passages do, in fact, have explicit connections to the surrounding narrative. Moses' request in vv. 30-33 that the people be forgiven makes no sense after the sinners have ostensibly been punished in vv. 26-29. Because the verses about the Levites seem not to belong to E,[22] and stand in contradiction to P (in which the Levites are invested in Num 1-4)[23] and D (in which the Levites are set apart after the giving of the second set of tablets; Deut 10:8-9)[24]—both of which set the investiture of the Levites at the time and place of the revelation in the wilderness—these verses can be attributed only to J.[25]

Yet these verses are equally out of place in the J Sinai narrative. In their current location, they come between the ascension of Sinai by Moses, Aaron,

---

uted to E by Menahem Haran, "*Pirqê šᵊkem*," in *Miqrā' wᵊ'ôlamô* (Jerusalem: Magnes, 2009), 360-89 (at 385 n. 57).

21. Exodus 32:25 is more properly the conclusion to the preceding section, vv. 21-24.

22. There is also no mention of this episode in D's recounting of the events at Horeb, which follows the E narrative of Exod 19-24; 32-34, thus strongly suggesting that this passage was not part of E. On D's dependence on E, see Baden, *Redaction*, 99-195, esp. 153-72.

23. Thus, these verses cannot be due to a priestly author or interpolator, as suggested by Addis, *Documents*, 152; Yehezkel Kaufmann, *The Religion of Israel: From Its Beginnings to the Babylonian Exile* (trans. and abridg. Moshe Greenberg; Chicago: University of Chicago Press, 1960), 195.

24. Thus, these verses cannot be due to a Deuteronomic author or interpolator, as suggested by Kuenen, *Hexateuch*, 247.

25. See Bacon, *Triple Tradition*, 137-38; Carpenter and Harford-Battersby, *Hexateuch*, 2:131-32; Driver, *Exodus*, 354-55; A. H. McNeile, *The Book of Exodus* (2nd ed.; WC; London: Methuen, 1917), 207-9; John Van Seters, *The Life of Moses: The Yahwist as Historian in Exodus-Numbers* (Louisville: Westminster John Knox, 1994), 316-17; Haran, *Temples*, 66-67 n. 11.

Nadab, Abihu, and the seventy elders in Exod 24:1-2, 9-11bα and Yahweh's speech to Moses in Exod 33:1-5. The narrative of the Levites assumes that Moses is back in the camp (32:26), while both of the surrounding passages locate him on the mountain (and there is no notice of his descent or re-ascent). More important, there is no notice in J's narrative of any sin by the people that would justify the Levites' massacre: as far as we are aware, the people are waiting patiently at the foot of the mountain. In light of Deut 33:8-11, however, we may consider relocating Exod 32:26-29 to the end of J's narrative of the episode at Massah and Meribah, in Exod 17:1bβ-7.[26]

Such a move is not purely speculative. First, there are verbal connections between Exod 32 and Deut 33, especially in the instruction by Moses to the Levites to kill "brother, neighbor, and kin" (v. 27) and his statement that the Levites had each been "against his son and brother" (v. 29); both utterances resonate directly with Deut 33:9.[27] Both passages also conclude with blessing (Exod 32:29; Deut 33:11). Second, the idea of Yahweh punishing the people after they have complained—and even after Yahweh has acted in response to their complaint—is attested elsewhere in J, in the similarly constructed narrative in Num 11.[28] There the Israelites complain about a lack of meat (Num 11:4-6), while in Exod 17 they complain about a lack of water (vv. 2-3); Moses, exasperated, turns to Yahweh in despair (Num 11:13), just as he does at Massah and Meribah (Exod 17:4); Yahweh provides the meat to satisfy the people (Num 11:18-23, 31-32), as he does with the water (Exod 17:5-6); and immediately thereafter he strikes the people with a plague (Num 11:33). This final element is ostensibly missing from the narrative in Exod 17; the story of the Levites in Exod 32 would fit nicely there. And, of course, the narrative of Exod 17 and the poem of Deut 33 would thereby be brought more closely into line; if the story of the Levites does not belong with Exod 17, then we are left to wonder what the author of Deut 33 imagined had happened at Massah and Meribah that involved the Levites, as well as what the author of J thought the Levites were responding to in Exod 32.

---

26. The connection between Exod 32:26-29 and 17:1bβ-7 was drawn by Karl Budde, *Der Segen Moses: Deut. 33* (Tübingen: Mohr, 1922), 25; Samuel E. Loewenstamm, "The Investiture of Levi," in idem, *From Babylon to Canaan: Studies in the Bible and Its Oriental Background* (Publication of the Perry Foundation for Biblical Research in the Hebrew University of Jerusalem; Jerusalem: Magnes, 1992), 55-65. Yet Loewenstamm discussed only the tradition, attempting to explain how the tradition of the investiture of the Levites moved from Massah and Meribah to the golden calf episode, and thus his conclusions belong to the preliterary stage. As I am describing this as a literary process—and a post-authorial one at that—my views are somewhat different. Similarly, Van Seters (*Life of Moses*, 316-17) argues that both Exod 17:1bβ-7 and 32:26-29 have a common origin in Deut 33. On the assignment of Exod 17:1bβ-7 to J, see Baden, *Redaction*, 174-77.

27. See Van Seters, *Life of Moses*, 317.

28. On the source division of Num 11, see Baden, *Redaction*, 108-10.

We are still left, then, with the question of why the pentateuchal compiler would have moved these verses from the end of Exod 17:1bβ–7 to their current location in Exod 32. The most compelling reason would have been the historical claim implicit in the J narrative (and Deut 33:8–11): that the investiture of the Levites took place before the revelation in the wilderness. This claim, as we have already seen, contradicts the testimonies of P and D, both of which locate the event at the mountain. The compiler would have seen that this was an event that could hardly happen twice—at least not at two different times in two different places—and would therefore have looked for an appropriate place for it in the Sinai/Horeb narrative. Since the passage involves a major punishment for a communal Israelite sin, there could hardly be any other choice than precisely where these verses are currently located.

It thus seems likely that the narrative of Exod 32:26–29 belongs to J, and belongs more properly with J's narrative of Massah and Meribah in Exod 17:1bβ–7. The Levites are blessed and granted the right to serve Yahweh because they alone observed Yahweh's commands, and the proof of their devotion was the slaughter of their fellow Israelites, disregarding all kinship ties. As with Deut 33:8–11, the picture of the Levites here is undoubtedly positive, despite the fact that—indeed, precisely because—they commit a savage act of violence against their own people.

Complementary Traditions

It seems, then, that J preserves two traditions regarding the Levites, each represented in both poetry and prose. These two traditions have in common the notion that the Levites are separated from the rest of the Israelites as the result of an act of violence.[29] Yet there the similarities end. The first group, Gen 49:5–7 and Gen 34, focuses on the actions of the eponymous tribal ancestor, Levi. He is described in both texts, in conjunction with his brother Simeon, as violent by nature, more so at least than the rest of Jacob's sons. His violent act is directed against non-Israelites, and the reaction to this act, if not from the author himself then certainly from his character Jacob, is negative. This tradition, furthermore, has no apparent connection with the priestly role of the Levites. It is, rather, entirely focused on the rationale for the ancestor's—and by extension the tribe's—land disenfranchisement.

The second tradition, in Deut 33:1–8 and Exod 32:26–29, is, by contrast, entirely about the manner in which the Levites acquired their priestly role in Israelite society. In both texts the Levites are treated as a tribe, as is only fitting given the historical context in which the poem and story are set. In this

---

29. See A. H. J. Gunneweg, *Leviten und Priester: Hauptlinen der Traditionsbildung und Geschichte des israelitisch-jüdischen Kultpersonals* (FRLANT 89; Göttingen: Vandenhoeck & Ruprecht, 1965), 46.

tradition the tribe as a whole answers the call to dedicate itself to Yahweh and is rewarded with the service of the deity. The Levites' violent act is directed against Israelites, against their own kin, as both texts emphasize, and the reaction to this act is entirely positive, even resulting in blessing. If the first tradition has no connection with priestly service, it is equally true that the second tradition has no connection with land disenfranchisement.[30]

Thus the two traditions preserved by J are complementary. In the combination of the two, the author of J has produced a complete picture of the Levites: landless and engaged in the service of Yahweh. (Note that these two aspects of the status of the Levites are combined by P in Num 1–4.[31]) Though one portrayal is negative and one positive, they are separated in the narrative by generations, and are not contradictory. We may see the earlier disenfranchisement of Levi as a necessary precursor to the later special status of the Levites. We may also take the raising of the Levites to the status of temple servant in the second group of texts as a conscious reversal of their previously lowly status. This reading is appealing because it takes into account the difference between the reaction to Simeon and Levi's actions in Gen 34 according to Jacob and according to the author of J: Jacob is distressed and disinherits the brothers, but the author of J, by giving them the last word in Gen 34:31, seems to view their action positively. This sets up a sense that Jacob has perhaps wronged Levi in Gen 49:5–7, and that their positive status in the subsequent texts stands not only as a correction but as a justification of their behavior.[32] A sequence of prioritizing can be seen in the traditions of the Levites adopted by J: they value kin over custom (Gen 34:31), and YHWH over kin (Exod 32:26–29//Deut 33:1–8).

---

30. Whether this distinction is a result of the earlier-versus-later dating of the two traditions, as has been frequently proposed, is beyond the scope of this paper. Suffice it to say that the simple linear progression of traditions seems, at least in my opinion, highly unlikely, and there is no obvious reason why two contemporaneous lines of tradition could not emphasize different aspects of a single group. Genesis 34 and 49 present a "secular" tribe of Levi because according to none of the sources has a professional priesthood arisen in Israel in the patriarchal period—indeed, there is not as yet such a thing as Israel. Too often the narrative context is disregarded in tradition-critical reconstruction.

31. Again, the combination of traditions in P does not necessitate a later dating of P relative to the other texts under consideration here. It simply means that P has taken the two traditions also known to J and combined them in his own manner, with his own historical assumptions, theological ideas, and literary style.

32. Kaufmann takes Exod 32:26–29 as evidence that the Levites redirected their violent nature to the service of protecting the portable tent and Moses (*History*, 238).

Between Poetry and Prose

If the poems of Gen 49 and Deut 33 are indeed earlier collections of tribal sayings incorporated into the J narrative, then it must be asked whether the J prose passages in Gen 34 and Exod 32:26-29 are to be understood as based on their poetic counterparts.[33] The answer is, most likely, yes and no. Genesis 49:5-7 preserves the tradition that Levi was violent, but makes no clear reference to any historical situation in which that violence manifested itself.[34] Conversely, Gen 34 does not clearly articulate the disenfranchisement of Levi as part of its narrative. Yet J's version of the events in Gen 34 does seem to be to some extent dependent on the assessment of Levi in Gen 49:5-7. The two narratives in Gen 34, E and J, have in common the idea that there was some relationship between Dinah and Shechem, and that Jacob's sons responded to this relationship with an attack on Shechem. If this was the traditional base on which both E and J wrote their versions of the story, then we have to account for the particulars of J's narrative: why are Simeon and Levi the ones singled out for the act of vengeance? We can see how the author of J came to this conclusion: he had before him an old tradition in which Simeon and Levi were particularly violent—so much so that Jacob saw fit to disinherit them—but the tradition, at least in the poetic version the author of J had to hand, contained no specifics. And he had before him a tradition in which Jacob's sons acted violently, in the story of Dinah and Shechem. The combination of the two traditions would have made easy sense. Indeed, the story of Dinah and Shechem may have been the only one for which J could have adopted the allusion in Gen 49; there is no other story in which Jacob's sons act violently (at least not that

---

33. This question is usually put the other way—are the poetic passages based on the narratives, or at least on the traditions behind the narratives?—as if the prose traditions must be earlier, though it is unclear why this should be the case. In fact, if we accept the suggestion that the author of J took the older poem and inserted it into his newly created narrative, the question must be whether the narrative—not the underlying tradition, but the literary product itself—is based on the poetry; or, at least, how is the narrative related to the various older traditions, including the poetry, available to the author?

34. See Skinner, *Genesis*, 516 (quoted above in n. 4); Westermann, *Genesis 37-50*, 226; de Pury, "Genèse xxxiv," 30-33; James L. Kugel, *The Idea of Biblical Poetry: Parallelism and Its History* (Baltimore: Johns Hopkins University Press, 1981), 32-33 n. 83. Contra Driver, *Genesis*, 307, 383; Gunkel, *Genesis*, 359; Martin Noth, *A History of Pentateuchal Traditions* (trans. Bernhard W. Anderson; Englewood Cliffs, N.J.: Prentice-Hall, 1972; repr., Chico, Calif.: Scholars Press, 1981), 86; Gerhard von Rad, *Genesis* (trans. John H. Marks; OTL; Philadelphia: Westminster, 1972), 423; de Hoop, *Genesis 49*, 98-101. It is hard to imagine how one could, without having Gen 34 already in mind, reconstruct even a shred of the narrative of Dinah and Shechem from Gen 49:5-7. As a parallel case we might take the song of Lemech in Gen 4:23-24 (also from J, and strikingly similar; cf. Kugel, *Idea*, 32-33 n. 83), the story behind which, if a story is indeed assumed, is impossible to reconstruct.

Jacob is aware of such that he might respond; he is never enlightened as to the circumstances surrounding the attempted murder and sale of Joseph).

The author of J constructed his version of this story in accordance with the judgment of Gen 49:5-7, emphasizing two key features: the singling out of Simeon and Levi as the protagonists, and Jacob's negative response to their action.[35] The actual disinheritance was not included in Gen 34 because this took place only on Jacob's deathbed, in his farewell speech. But the historical event that justified the disinheritance could be described, at its proper time. We can draw a direct analogy with J's treatment of Reuben.[36] Again, Gen 49 preserves a disinheritance, this time of the eldest brother, on the basis of an obscure reference, "mounting his father's bed" (v. 4). The author of J provides in the note in Gen 35:22a the historical referent for this allusion—but no more, except to make the necessary statement that Jacob found out about Reuben's actions—so that when the reader or listener comes to the poem in Gen 49:3-4, Jacob's disinheritance of Reuben does not come out of the blue.[37]

It is important to remember that the J story in Gen 34 was not composed entirely on the basis of Gen 49. The author of J knew the tradition of Dinah and Shechem and would have written it anyway, we may assume, even if he did not know Gen 49 and plan to include it in his work, just as E did. Yet the particular shape that he gave to the story in writing it was dependent on Gen 49:5-7, at least in part. Similarly, we should keep in mind at least the possibility

---

35. This analysis is similar to that of Sigo Lehming, "Zur Überlieferungsgeschichte von Gen 34," *ZAW* 70 (1958): 228-50. Lehming, however, does not hold to the same source analysis, and therefore his conclusions differ somewhat. Whereas he sees the inclusion of Simeon and Levi as a late stage in the literary composition of the story, my claim is that it is a J variant of the tradition contemporaneous with that of E. We agree insofar as the inclusion of Simeon and Levi is in any case not a basic part of the oldest tradition, but is rather a development that is rooted in the description of the two brothers in Gen 49:5-7. Blum argues for the dependence of Gen 34 on Gen 49:5-7 but believes Gen 34 to be for the most part a unified composition (*Komposition*, 216-21); so too Eduard Nielsen, who argues that the Levites were added secondarily to the narrative of Gen 34 (*Shechem: A Traditio-Historical Investigation* [Copenhagen: G. E. C. Gad, 1955], 281-83). Ulrike Schorn argues that the beginning of Gen 49 (vv. 3-8) was edited by the same person who wrote Gen 34:30 and redacted the chapter as a whole (*Ruben und das System der zwölf Stämme Israels: Redactionsgeschichtliche Untersuchungen zur Bedeutung des Erstbegorenen Jakobs* [BZAW 248; Berlin: de Gruyter, 1997], 258-59).

36. See Blum, *Komposition*, 218.

37. Although it may be assumed that the tradition on which J based the note in Gen 35:22a contained some version of Jacob's disinheritance of Reuben, we should not therefore assume that the author of J preserved this continuation in his narrative. Indeed, the fact that the disinheritance comes later, in Gen 49, speaks strongly against this possibility; had the author of J included it here, it would have been redundant later. The same is, of course, true of the disinheritance of Simeon and Levi, which J has presented in the narrative as mere approbation—the disinheritance proper is yet to come.

that the oblique reference in Gen 49:5-7 is in fact to the tradition of Dinah and Shechem, if not to its literary manifestation in Gen 34; in other words, it is possible that Simeon and Levi were known to a strand of Israelite tradition as the brothers who acted violently in defense of their sister, and that both Gen 49:5-7 and Gen 34 are reflexes of this tradition.[38] Yet the lack of any reference to the story of Dinah and Shechem in Gen 49 speaks against this possibility.

As for the second tradition, that of Deut 33:8-11 and Exod 32:26-29, a similar situation obtains. The author of J did not invent the story of getting water from a rock in order to provide a historical background for the description of the Levites in Deut 33:8-11. The tradition of Moses getting water from the rock was evidently a common one, as the P version in Num 20:2-13 attests, and the dual name Massah and Meribah is also part of a defined strand of tradition.[39] Again, however, the particular shape that J's version of this event takes is due in part to the presentation of Deut 33:8-11.[40] We may suppose that both the author of the older poem and the author of J knew a tradition in which the Levites were invested at the site where Moses drew water from the rock (and that this took place before Sinai rather than after, as in P), in which case this element was drawn not from Deut 33, but rather from the common tradition underlying both texts. Yet we might also note that J seems to have little interest in the priesthood in general,[41] and this instance of special recognition for the Levites is somewhat out of character. If so, then it is possible that the author of J did in fact base the inclusion and actions of the Levites on Deut 33—perhaps in lieu of a divine plague, as in Num 11. Certainly some of J's wording derives from the poetic description, most distinctively in the kinship language, and perhaps also in the element of blessing.

In both narratives, J relates a common Israelite tradition, whether of Dinah and Shechem or water from a rock, and also particularizes it in light of the description and assessment of the Levites in the older poetry. The prose passages are therefore not dependent on the poetry in the absolute sense—the stories would presumably have been included in J's narrative in any case, as they are in the other pentateuchal sources—but J's unique versions of these

---

38. See Noth, *Pentateuchal Traditions*, 86-87; Gunneweg, *Leviten*, 50-51.

39. It appears in Exod 17:1bβ-7; Deut 33:8; and Ps 95:8, where its presence seems to confirm that the combination of these names is part of a tradition, rather than the invention of either the author of J or the author of Deut 33.

40. See Bruno Baentsch, *Exodus-Leviticus-Numeri übersetzt und erklärt* (HKAT I/2; Göttingen: Vandenhoeck & Ruprecht, 1903), 272-73; Van Seters, *Life of Moses*, 316-17. Stefan Beyerle takes the opposite approach and sees the elements of Deut 33:8-11 that are most strongly parallel to Exod 32:26-29 as redactional and explicitly based on Exod 32 (*Der Mosesegen im Deuteronomium: Eine text-, kompositions-, und formkritische Studie zu Deuteronomium 33* [BZAW 250; Berlin: de Gruyter, 1997], 133-34).

41. Haran, *Temples*, 65.

stories do betray a knowledge of the poetic traditions as well as a reshaping on the basis of them.

The Violence of the Levites

We may finally consider the commonality underlying all four texts: the violence of the Levites as a determining factor in their tribal and social status. Despite the different manifestations of this violence, and the opposing evaluations of it, it is hard to overlook the fact that this quality is in the forefront of both traditions. The basis for the association of the Levites and violence, however, is not obvious. We might look to the narrative of Pinehas in Num 25:6–13 as an example of priestly violence against fellow Israelites on behalf of Yahweh's laws (v. 8),[42] and also to the story of 2 Chr 23, in which the Levites are given the task of guarding the young king Joash and slaying anyone who enters the temple, where he was being kept (v. 7). If these stories add depth to the portrayal of the Levites as zealously violent on behalf of the laws, the temple, and the divinely ordained king, however, they can be related to only one of the two pentateuchal traditions, that in Deut 33:8–11 and Exod 32:26–29. We are still left to wonder how this violence took on a negative aspect when retrojected back onto the tribal ancestor Levi. Furthermore, the story in Num 25 belongs to P, and does not refer to Levites but rather to the line of Aaron in particular, that is, the high priesthood, while the story of 2 Chr 23 depicts the Levites as only one group of many engaged in the defense of the king (or more properly the temple), and then only under orders. Even if we suppose that these passages are manifestations of the same tradition of levitical violence as Deut 33 and Exod 32, they do not help much in understanding the underlying tradition itself.

The evidence does not allow us to make any conclusive statements as to the origin of the connection of Levites and violence. Yet the connection is undeniably present, and the variant reflexes of it in the J source attest to its age and flexibility in the service of describing the salient features of the status of the Levites in Israelite society.

---

42. This connection is alluded to by Michael Fishbane, *Biblical Interpretation in Ancient Israel* (Oxford: Clarendon, 1985), 398.

Between Shadow and Substance: The Historical Relationship of Tabernacle and Temple in Light of Architecture and Iconography

Cory D. Crawford

Central to the understanding of the provenance of the Priestly source (P) of the Pentateuch is the question of the relationship between the wilderness tabernacle and the Jerusalem temple. The similarities between the two structures have hardly been lost on anyone, though the nature of this relationship remains unclear. By now the historical impossibility of a newly nomadic group procuring materials for the production of a lavish tent sanctuary is so well rehearsed as to need little comment, though the corresponding problem of the *Sitz im Leben* of the group responsible for the tabernacle texts remains a point of controversy.[1] At issue, of course, is not simply the source or inspiration of

---

In preparing this paper I have profited from the expert advice and productive conversations with many colleagues. Thanks are due particularly to Baruch Schwartz, Joel Baden, Irene Winter, Jon Levenson, Jeffrey Stackert, and Lawrence Stager. Errors remain my own.

1. The following two statements from differing ideological camps serve to illustrate the point: "Very strange is the contrast between this splendid structure [i.e., the tabernacle], on which the costliest material is lavished and wrought in the most advanced style of Oriental art, and the soil on which it rises, in the wilderness amongst the native Hebrew nomad tribes, who are represented as having got it ready offhand, and without external help. The incompatibility has long been noticed, and gave rise to doubts as early as the time of Voltaire" (Julius Wellhausen, *Prolegomena to the History of Israel, with a reprint of the article Israel from the Encyclopedia Britannica* [foreword by Douglas A. Knight; Scholars Press Reprints and Translations; Atlanta: Scholars Press, 1994], 39; repr. of *Prolegomena to the History of Israel* [trans. J. Sutherland Black and Allan Menzies; Edinburgh: A&C Black, 1885]; trans. of *Prolegomena zur Geschichte Israels* [2nd ed.; Berlin: G. Reimer, 1883]). Cf. the similar comment of Menahem Haran, who proposes a Priestly *Sitz im Leben* entirely different from that proposed by Wellhausen: "It is evident that as depicted in P the tabernacle is largely imaginary and never existed in Israel. Anyone who believes that the semi-nomadic tribes who made their way from Egypt to Canaan were capable of erecting such a magnificent edifice in their midst violates the laws of historical reality, and it is up to him to substantiate his argument" (*Temples and Temple-Service in Ancient Israel: An Inquiry into Biblical Cult Phenomena and the Historical Setting of the Priestly School* [1978; repr., Winona Lake, Ind.: Eisenbrauns, 1985], 189). See also the lengthier discussion of this specific prob-

the tabernacle construction narratives in Exod 25–30; 35–40 but also the historical location the author(s) of the narratives and the light it casts on the history of Israelite institutions and religion in the first millennium B.C.E. The purpose of this paper is to reexamine the relationship between tabernacle and temple—and thereby a slice of Israelite religious history—via, first, a survey of the problems in current stances toward the issue and, second, a discussion of two overlooked points related to the architecture and iconography of each that help to elucidate the historical relationships involved.

I. Temple and Tabernacle in Recent Research

It is customary to begin with the work of Julius Wellhausen, since the position he voiced has come to dominate the conversation, either in commanding assent or in engendering protest. For our purposes, especially in a volume dedicated to priests, it is worthwhile to reproduce a passage that lays out the implications of the relationship between tabernacle and temple for understanding the priesthood:

> To bring the sons of Aaron into comparison with the sons of Zadok, as a proof of their higher antiquity, is just as reasonable as to bring the tabernacle into comparison with the temple of Jerusalem for a similar purpose. The former are priests of the tabernacle, the latter of the temple; but as in point of fact the only distinction to be drawn between the Mosaic and the actual central sanctuary is that between shadow and substance, so neither can any other be made between the Mosaic and the actual central priesthood. In the Priestly Code the ancient name is introduced instead of the historical one, simply in order to maintain the semblance of the Mosaic time.[2]

Unmistakable here is the language of the book of Hebrews, wherein the tabernacle is also relegated to the status of a shadow (σκιά, Heb 8:5) and compared with the substance, that is, for Hebrews, Christ.[3] It is precisely this assertion of the immateriality of the tabernacle to which much scholarly attention has been turned, and therefore the bases and assumptions that led Wellhausen to this view are worth reviewing briefly. Wellhausen argued for a historical understanding based on a careful comparison of the sources of the Pentateuch and other texts, finding that P assumed a centralized cult,

---

lem in Mark K. George, *Israel's Tabernacle as Social Space* (SBLAIL 2; Atlanta: Society of Biblical Literature, 2009), 3–5.

2. Wellhausen, *Prolegomena*, 125.

3. In German the allusion is stronger, with shadow opposed explicitly to body: "Jene nämlich sind die Priester der Stiftshütte, diese die des Tempels; wie aber faktisch kein anderer Unterschied zwischen dem mosaischen und dem wirklichen Centralheiligtum besteht, als der zwischen Körper und Schatten, so auch kein anderer zwischen der mosaischen und der wirklichen Centralpriesterschaft" (Wellhausen, *Prolegomena zur Geschichte Israels*, 129).

whereas D had been forced to argue for it. Applying the same logic to Ezekiel, he found that assumptions made by P had to be asserted by the exilic prophet, and therefore P must have postdated both D and Ezekiel.[4] A second point is Wellhausen's Hegelian framework leading to the view that the cultic legislation at the core of P is the result of a long process of ossification or denaturalization of a once vibrant, spontaneous religion, and (in yet another assumption) since the sources represent stages in Israel's "national" story, they can be arranged to follow that development, with P occupying the final position.

Few today would admit to an agreement with the teleology implicit in the latter, but arguments based on the relative dating of the sources continue to the present. In a most recent treatment of the tabernacle, Mark George understands the social setting of the Priestly authors to be precisely exilic, in which priests are attempting to make sense of the loss of both temple and sovereign, and thus advance the idea of a social structure based on the memory of the Jerusalem temple, knowledge of ancient Near Eastern tent sanctuaries, and the JE document.[5] Occupying a more extreme position, William Propp, in his 2006 commentary on Exodus, agrees with Terence Fretheim's view that, since P "knows" no monarchy, it must have been an anti-monarchic and, more properly, anti-temple protest, "advocating worship in a tent [without a king] as in days of yore."[6] This position, for which Propp can only find "implicit" evidence, exemplifies the perpetuation of Wellhausen's assumptions that P's narrative behaves like the other sources. If D shows itself concerned with monarchy and centralization, and P does not, it must be because by the time P wrote these were no longer important political issues.[7] In order to make this case, other comparative issues must be ignored. The fact that P deliberately attempts to avoid anachronism, such as in its pre-Mosaic lack of the divine name and of sacrifice, urges caution in comparison to the author of Deuteronomy especially, who is unabashed when it comes to placing contemporary

---

4. "The distinction between priest and levite which Ezekiel introduces and justifies as an innovation, according to the Priestly Code has always existed; what in the former appears as a beginning, in the latter has been in force ever since Moses, —an original datum, not a thing that has become or been made. That the prophet should know nothing about a priestly law with whose tendencies he is in thorough sympathy admits of only one explanation, —that it did not then exist" (Wellhausen, *Prolegomena*, 124).

5. George, *Israel's Tabernacle as Social Space*; see esp. the discussion on pp. 10–11.

6. William H. C. Propp, *Exodus 19–40: A New Translation with Introduction and Commentary* (AB 2A; New York: Doubleday, 2006), 732; cf. Terence E. Fretheim, "The Priestly Document: Anti-Temple?" *VT* 18 (1968): 313–29.

7. Propp, *Exodus 19–40*, 732; of course, Wellhausen was not the first nor the only to make these assumptions. Since, however, he most rigorously associated the sources and the development of Israelite religion, becoming a figure with whom scholars continue to grapple and whose views are among the most widely known in academic circles, I engage his work in order to draw out commonly held assumptions and arguments.

concerns in the mouth of Moses. It also ignores, or at least undertheorizes, the contradiction in the position that posits, on the one hand, that the muting of royal power in the narrative was evidence of a historical (exilic or postexilic) period but, on the other, that the elaborate descriptions of the tabernacle are the opposite, a fiction.

Recent studies in source criticism have driven home the point not only that one cannot assume these points about the sources, but that such assumptions directly contradict the evidence at hand. Joel Baden argues that in the original stratum of P one detects no trace of a parenetic rupture in the fourth wall, such as is found in D and even in P's successor, the Holiness Code (H).[8] Thus, the absence of obvious royal concerns, at least at the narrative level, may be the result of nothing more than P's more particularly attuned sense of history, in which even the sacrificial system has its chronological limits. Even without this observation, one is confronted still with the assumption of the extent to which P behaves like D or H. Must priests (at Jerusalem or otherwise) develop a sweeping narrative that actively and positively eliminates other cult sites from consideration? Must it propose a plan by which these competing sanctuaries will be eliminated, or is to ignore them enough? Once these old assumptions are recognized as unwarranted and P is cut loose from its conceptual moorings to J, E, and especially D, a different picture can take its place, one that might have P as the articulation, by priests and, with Menahem Haran, *for* priests, of the basis for a contemporary cult in the history of Israel.[9]

As George and Propp show, at the heart of conclusions made about the historical setting of the priests lie these assumptions regarding the literary character of pentateuchal sources, especially as they relate to one another. For Wellhausen as for many others since, the main pentateuchal sources could not have been coeval in origin and therefore must have been composed in series, not in parallel.[10] Outgrowths of these ideas include Martin Noth's view that P looked back and revised the earlier JE traditions and Frank Moore Cross's influential argument that P was not a narrative source but rather a redactional layer.[11] These hypotheses have been strongly refuted in recent source-critical

---

8. Joel S. Baden, "Identifying the Original Stratum of P: Theoretical and Practical Considerations," in *The Strata of the Priestly Writings: Contemporary Debate and Future Directions* (ed. Sarah Shectman and Joel S. Baden; AThANT 95; Zurich: TVZ, 2009), 13–29.

9. Haran, *Temples and Temple-Service*, 142–48; idem, "Behind the Scenes of History: Determining the Date of the Priestly Source," *JBL* 100 (1981): 321–33.

10. See Baden's treatment of the development of the relative dating of the sources, especially of "JE": *J, E, and the Redaction of the Pentateuch* (FAT 68; Tübingen: Mohr Siebeck, 2009), 1–98, as well as his excursus on the relationship of P to J and E (ibid., 197–207).

11. Martin Noth, *Pentateuchal Traditions* (trans. Bernhard W. Anderson; Englewood Cliffs, N.J.: Prentice Hall, 1972), 234; Frank Moore Cross, *Canaanite Myth and Hebrew Epic: Essays in the History of the Religion of Israel* (Cambridge, Mass.: Harvard University Press, 1973), 293–325. For others who view P as a redactional layer, see, e.g., John Van Seters, *The*

scholarship: Klaus Koch and Baruch Schwartz have mounted serious challenges to the view of P as a redactional stratum, and Baden has recently built on these studies, demonstrating that no separate JE redaction existed prior to the full composition of the Pentateuch and that there is no basis for understanding P as a response to J, E, or D.[12] The only sources to be clearly dependent on the others are D, who apparently knows J and E (though separately), and H, who probably revised the literary legal corpora of E and D.[13]

If P, then, is not only *not* the redactor but is not derivative of these sources, the date of P cannot be correlated with the other sources in the way that European and North American scholars have argued.[14] The basis for the exilic or postexilic composition of P is thus seriously undermined, and the major obstacles for a preexilic P are removed. What remains, for our purposes, is the problem of the historical relationship of P to the monarchy and cult, and one of the crucial hinges on which this question turns is still whether and how the Jerusalem temple and the tabernacle are related—indeed, given the relatively few clear indications of datable political concerns, this nexus is vital to the inquiry.

That they are indeed related can be visually established by a glance at any of the ubiquitous reconstructions of the tabernacle (Exod 25–30; 35–40) and the temple of Solomon (1 Kgs 6–7). Both are rectangular, long-axis type constructions similarly divided and apportioned. Both have outer courtyards possessed of an altar and a laver. Both show an interior space itself divided in two: an antecella with golden lampstands, golden incense altar, and golden table, and an inner sanctum in which golden cherubim directly mark the presence of the deity. In addition, the bronze altars of the temple and tabernacle

---

Life of Moses: The Yahwist as Historian in Exodus–Numbers (Louisville: Westminster John Knox, 1993); Rolf Rendtorff, *The Problem of the Process of Transmission in the Pentateuch* (trans. John J. Scullion; JSOTSup 89; Sheffield: JSOT Press, 1977); Erhard Blum, *Studien zur Komposition des Pentateuch* (BZAW 189; Berlin: de Gruyter, 1990).

12. Klaus Koch, "P — Kein Redaktor! Erinnerung an zwei Eckdaten der Quellenscheidung," *VT* 37 (1987): 446–67; Baruch J. Schwartz, "The Priestly Account of the Theophany and Lawgiving at Sinai," in *Texts, Temples, and Traditions: A Tribute to Menahem Haran* (ed. Michael V. Fox et al.; Winona Lake, Ind.: Eisenbrauns, 1996), 103–34; Baden, *Redaction*.

13. On the revision of H, see Jeffrey Stackert, *Rewriting the Torah: Literary Revision in Deuteronomy and the Holiness Legislation* (FAT 52; Tübingen: Mohr Siebeck, 2007).

14. Arguments for preexilic P have, on the contrary, been advanced especially by Israeli biblical scholars, since the latter half of the twentieth century. See Yehezkel Kaufmann, *The Religion of Israel: From Its Beginnings to the Babylonian Exile* (trans. and abridg. Moshe Greenberg; Chicago: University of Chicago Press, 1960); Haran, *Temples and Temple-Service*; Israel Knohl, *The Sanctuary of Silence: The Priestly Torah and the Holiness School* (Minneapolis: Fortress, 1995); see also the similar position of Richard E. Friedman, "Torah (Pentateuch)," *ABD* 6: 614. For a summary of other studies pointing to a preexilic origin of P, see Ziony Zevit, "Converging Lines of Evidence Bearing on the Date of P," *ZAW* 94 (1982): 481–511.

courtyard are the only two bronze altars mentioned anywhere in the Hebrew Bible.[15] Haran shows that the homologies go even deeper, as a careful look at both demonstrates a distinct material gradation that marks the spaces as increasingly holy from the outer court to the inner sanctum.[16]

These similarities notwithstanding, and notwithstanding the aforementioned historical problems associated with a nomadic wilderness group's access to resources and means of production, many treatments of the tabernacle in the past sixty years have emphasized the differences between tent and temple, adducing historical analogues that have complicated the issue of the origin of the tabernacle considerably, resulting in a more complex (if less certain) picture of the historical origin of the tabernacle construction narratives. Haran himself noted that "however clear the connection is between P's tabernacle and Solomon's temple there is actually no reason to suppose that P's description is *altogether* a late retrojection. It also has a certain substratum of ancient and quite authentic tradition."[17] He goes on to argue that, since P never even mentions Jerusalem and never gives the slightest hint that the tabernacle should be superseded by Solomon's temple, we should understand the basis of the tradition to be found in the sanctuary at Shiloh, which was overlaid with Solomonic details after Shiloh was destroyed.[18]

To this one would add the proliferation of attempts to explain the tent shrine on the basis of ancient Near Eastern archaeological, iconographic, and textual data in an effort to argue that the view of the tabernacle as a straightforward retrojection of the Jerusalem temple into the wilderness wandering traditions is no longer tenable. Cross's 1947 article in the *Biblical Archaeologist* was one of the broadest attempts since Wellhausen to set the tabernacle structure on a historical footing, making use of philology, archaeology, and ethnoarchaeology even while locating the composition of P in the exile. Since then, the search for the basis of the tabernacle narratives has proceeded largely independent of source-critical argumentation. Ancient analogues have been adduced with the more famous candidates including the tent of El known from Ugarit, the "battle tent" of Ramesses II, the Timna valley shrine, and analogous structures mentioned in Mari texts.[19] These studies show what is already

---

15. The bronze altar is not described in the temple construction narrative of 1 Kgs 6–7, but it is mentioned explicitly in 1 Kgs 8:64; 2 Kgs 16:14. See discussion in Haran, *Temples and Temple-Service*, 191.

16. Ibid., 158–65, 189–94.

17. Ibid., 195 (emphasis mine).

18. Ibid., 194–204.

19. Frank Moore Cross, "The Priestly Tabernacle and the Temple of Solomon," in *From Epic to Canon: History and Literature in Ancient Israel* (Baltimore: Johns Hopkins University Press, 1998), 84–95; Kenneth A. Kitchen, "The Tabernacle—A Bronze Age Artifact," *ErIsr* 24 (1993): 119*–29*; Michael M. Homan, *To Your Tents, O Israel!: The Terminology, Function, Form, and Symbolism of Tents in the Hebrew Bible and the Ancient Near

apparent in the Hebrew Bible itself: for all their similarities, tabernacle and temple differ sharply from each other in many respects. The very dimensions of the tent and of the main temple building, for example, are not equivalent, and efforts to discover the equation relating the measurements have largely failed. Thus, the frequent refrain of studies of this type is one that emphasizes the differences between the two: "Thus the tabernacle has many connections with second millennium BC tent shrines and cannot be understood as a later creation artificially designed to (pretend to) anticipate the temple,"[20] or, more succinctly put, "if P modeled the Tabernacle on the Temple, why did he do such a poor job of copying?"[21]

Thus, one finds, on the one hand, source-critical studies about the tabernacle narratives that are less concerned with the historical realities of P and, on the other, studies concerned with the historical reconstruction of the tabernacle that tend to ignore the implications for P and the Jerusalem temple. The dearth of rigorous historical studies of P in the thirty years since Haran's work has coincided almost perfectly with the unraveling of the consensus not just on the literary background of pentateuchal texts but also on the ability even to call them discrete sources.[22] Tacit proof of this might be found in the steady stream of studies on the tabernacle that almost totally eschew the historical question in favor of other methodologies and interests.[23] Nevertheless, both

---

East (CHANE 12; Leiden: Brill, 2002), 89–128; Daniel E. Fleming, "Mari's Large Public Tent and the Priestly Tent Sanctuary," *VT* 50 (2000): 484–98; Richard S. Hess, *Israelite Religions: An Archaeological and Biblical Survey* (Grand Rapids: Baker Academic, 2007), 202–3.

20. Hess, *Israelite Religions*, 205; see also Cross, "Priestly Tabernacle and the Temple of Solomon," 84–85 and passim. Note that this is the conclusion reached already by Haran on purely literary grounds.

21. Homan, *To Your Tents*, 124; cf. the nearly identical question raised by Jonathan S. Greer: "If such descriptions were merely a retrojection of an idealized Jerusalem temple, should we not expect to find more congruence?" ("An Israelite *Mizrāq* at Tel Dan?" *BASOR* 358 [2010]: 28 n. 3).

22. On this see Baden, *Redaction*, 1–10.

23. For quite recent studies of the tabernacle that avoid or entirely omit the historical problem in favor of other questions, in addition to George, *Israel's Tabernacle*, see Michael B. Hundley, *Keeping Heaven on Earth: Guarding the Divine Presence in the Priestly Tabernacle* (FAT 2/50; Tübingen: Mohr Siebeck, 2011); Amy Cooper Robertson, "'He Kept the Measurements in His Memory as a Treasure': The Role of the Tabernacle Text in Religious Experience" (Ph.D. Diss., Emory University, 2010); Myung Soo Suh, *The Tabernacle in the Narrative History of Israel from the Exodus to the Conquest* (Studies in Biblical Literature 50; New York: Peter Lang, 2003). Homan, for his part, is clearly keen to elucidate the historicity of the tabernacle itself, but understandably leaves off situating the implications of his study within the work of P as a whole (see the comparatively brief summary in *To Your Tents*, 129–37). One detects hints of the implications of recent source-critical studies in, for example, the work of George, whose self-designated "agnostic position" represents a middle way between the emerging analyses, though it is not without its challenges. He sees the tabernacle as the production of a group of exilic priests who, as mentioned above, drew on

the realignment of historical focus away from the Jerusalem temple and the important reevaluation of pentateuchal sources might productively be recombined and the fruits of each applied to the question of the historical *Sitz im Leben* of the tabernacle narratives and, by extension, of the Priestly source.

II. Architecture and Iconography in Temple and Tabernacle

To bring the conclusions of source criticism and material culture to bear on the understanding of the horizon of the tabernacle texts, it is useful to add two points of comparison that, it will be concluded, help to clarify the picture of the Priestly school.

The first concerns an apparent divergence of dimensions. One expects that the invention of one structure on the basis of the other would show a relatively clear coherence in dimensions, since so much attention is given to the measure of sacred space in the Hebrew Bible. The dimensions of the tent itself, to which most want to compare temple dimensions, are never clearly given; instead the width of its constituent frames (קרשים) is given (1.5 cubits), as well as the number of frames (Exod 26:15–35; 36:20–30). Besides the question of exactly how these frames are assembled, one must also decide how the corners relate to the sides, whether one is to understand six frames across the back or eight.[24] Uncertainty over how the frames structuring the tent are related to each other has resulted in varying interpretations: since antiquity a 10 × 30 (cubit) structure has been favored, though, as Homan notes, this has been largely motivated by a desired measure (i.e., one proportional to the temple of Solomon) rather than by a careful reading of the text.[25] Others, such as Richard

---

a variety of sources that may have included memories and oral traditions as well as textual materials. This allows him to maintain the exilic composition of the text while accounting for the preexilic analogues, and, what is more, to argue for a priestly promulgation of a utopian social structure—one that had no hope of a reconstitution of any temple—cloaked in the garb of a fictive, composite shrine (*Israel's Tabernacle*, 12–13). While this may be seen as a way of bringing archaeology into conversation with source criticism, the advances in the latter described above suggest that the situation may not be so neatly parsed, since George's assumption of an exilic setting on the basis of lack of attention to monarchy and temple is, as discussed above, not the best explanation for the narrative contours of the document. In the end, however, as with the other studies, for George the historical question is clearly secondary to the application of critical space theory, which nevertheless, as will be shown below, draws important conclusions about the tabernacle as a structuring agent for P's ideal society.

24. See Propp, *Exodus 19–40*, 503–4.

25. Homan, *To Your Tents*, 166–67 (see also the preceding discussion on 142–65). Homan points out that even were the 10 × 30 footprint meant to evoke one-half the dimensions of the temple, one is still left with a (10-cubit) height that would exist in a different proportion to given temple dimensions, since the temple measured 30 cubits in height.

Friedman, posit a 6- or 8-cubit wide × 20 cubit long footprint on the basis of overlapping קרשים, or a 12 × 30 cubit enclosure on the assumption that the frames were abutted.²⁶ Homan proposes yet another understanding: 31.15 × 10.9 cubits.²⁷ The fact that still no clear consensus exists on the dimensions of the tent stands in stark contrast to the dimensions of the court enclosure and even of its gate, which are explicitly and plainly noted: 100 cubits × 50 cubits the court (Exod 27:9–13; 38:9–13), 20 cubits the gate (Exod 27:16; 38:18).

At first glance, there is no apparent congruence with the dimensions of the temple; rather it seems that a situation obtains opposite to that of the tabernacle dimensions: there are no courtyard dimensions given for the temple; only interior dimensions of the building itself are listed. They are given in 1 Kgs 6:2–4 as 30 cubits high × 60 cubits long × 20 cubits wide. Thus, by comparison, a 12 × 30 cubit tabernacle would constitute roughly half of the interior space of the main hall of the temple, whereas a 6 × 20 cubit version puts one in the range of the interior dimensions of the holy of holies, as Friedman famously argued.²⁸ Neither of these solutions fits a known temple dimension precisely, and thus, without careful consideration of 1 Kgs 6, it would appear that this aspect of the comparison would be evidence of the use of divergent source material in the composition of the tabernacle texts.

The temple dimensions, however, are misleading indicators of overall size when taken by themselves, since the measurements constitute *interior* dimensions. They do not include the dimensions of the three-tiered יציע surrounding the main hall on three sides, nor do they explicitly account for the thickness of the walls. This is most apparent in the increasing width of the three tiers of the surrounding structure, described in 1 Kgs 6:5–6 as widening from the bottom story (5 cubits) to the top (7 cubits) as they go up so as to account for the greater thickness of the walls at the bottom, thus constricting the *interior* space where the walls are thickest.²⁹ This width is clearly not intended to be

---

This assumes, though, that the 30-cubit measure is of a piece with the horizontal (interior) dimensions. One expects otherwise, since the holy of holies was said to be 20 cubits high, fitting the same proportions as would a 10 × 30 cubit tent. I do agree with Homan generally, however, in his analysis of the other difficulties in proposing a 10 × 30 cubit tent.

26. Yohanan Aharoni, "Arad: Its Inscriptions and Temple," *BA* 31 (1968): 25; Richard Elliot Friedman, *The Exile and Biblical Narrative: The Formation of the Deuteronomistic and Priestly Works* (HSM 22; Chico, Calif.: Scholars Press, 1981), 50–51; Propp, *Exodus 19–40*, 505.

27. Homan, *To Your Tents*, 180. Though Homan's argument is carefully reasoned from textual, archaeological, and botanical evidence, I doubt his conclusions, since nowhere else do we find dimensions given in such fractional units. See discussion of temple measurements below.

28. Richard Elliot Friedman, *Who Wrote the Bible?* (New York: Summit, 1987), 181–87; see discussion in Homan, *To Your Tents*, 167–77.

29. The dimensions in LXX differ from those in the MT: 25 cubits high × 40 cubits long × 20 cubits wide. These are most likely corruptions caused initially by a misunder-

included in the 20-cubit width of the house. In order to assess accurately the width of the entire temple building, then, one must take into account, at the very least, twice (once for each side) the thickness of the walls of the *bayît*, twice the interior width of the surrounding structure, and twice the thickness of the outer walls of the surrounding structure. Although the thickness of the walls is not given in 1 Kings, Ezekiel accounts for wall thicknesses of between 5 and 6 cubits (e.g., Ezek 41:2, 5, 12).

Adding everything together, we are confronted with a building whose full exterior width is most likely 50 cubits, which is the width proposed also by, for example, Th. Busink and Michael Chyutin.[30] By similar reasoning, the total length of the building approaches 100 cubits, although we know less about the axial dimensions of the building, especially in the way the vestibule relates to a likely staircase and platform like those mentioned in Ezek 40:49; 41:8. A 100-cubit length is supported also by the fact that other monumental buildings in Israelite tradition are explicitly given these dimensions: the royal "House of the Forest of Lebanon," whose 50-cubit width and 30-cubit height would also correspond to the Solomonic temple (1 Kgs 7:2; note its 50-cubit width and 30-cubit height) as well as to the temple of Ezekiel's vision (Ezek 41:15). These are not surprising data since, as R. B. Y. Scott notes, ancient Near Eastern building traditions in general demonstrate a textual and material affinity for round numbers.[31] Thus, one should not look to the tent itself to replicate temple dimensions, but rather to the courtyard dimensions and temple footprint.

In sum, while efforts to correlate the main hall of the temple with the tent sanctuary itself yield no apparent congruency, one does find the strong possibility of correlation in the overall exterior dimensions of the temple building and the tabernacle court, as well as in the tabernacle entrance screen with the 20-cubit width of the temple vestibule and main hall. If this obtains, one might entertain the possibility that the core spaces of the temple and tabernacle were

---

standing of the construction of the interior shrine in MT 6:16 and by an attempt to make sense of the five-cubit "storied structure" (יציע; 6:10 [*qere*]), which D. W. Gooding thinks the LXX understands as a loft above the interior ceiling. See his intricate discussion in "Temple Specifications: A Dispute in Logical Arrangement between the MT and the LXX," *VT* 17 (1967): 168–72. On the dimensions as interior measurements, see ibid., 156–57; Mordechai Cogan, *1 Kings: A New Translation with Introduction and Commentary* (AB 10; New York: Doubleday, 2000), 237.

30. Twenty cubits (interior hall) + 10 cubits (north and south hall walls) + 10 cubits (north and south widths of bottom story "stepped structure") + 10 cubits (north and south exterior walls). Th. Busink, *Der Tempel von Jerusalem von Salomo bis Herodes: Eine archäologisch-historische Studie unter Berücksichtigung des westsemitischen Tempelbaus* (2 vols.; Studia Francisci Scholten memoriae dicata 3; Leiden: Brill, 1970, 1980), 1:165–66; Michael Chyutin, *Architecture and Utopia in the Temple Era* (trans. Richard Flantz; Library of Second Temple Studies 58; New York/London: T&T Clark, 2006), 62.

31. R. B. Y. Scott, "The Hebrew Cubit," *JBL* 77 (1958): 205–14; idem, "Postscript on the Cubit," *JBL* 79 (1960): 368.

similarly buffered on all sides: in the case of the tabernacle, the courtyard surrounds the main sanctuary while the stepped structure and the vestibule of the temple similarly surround the main hall and cella. Of course, the homology proposed here cuts across the relationship of the outer courts, lavers, and bronze altars in each structure, but flexibility is one of the advantages of analogy, which requires only enough correspondence to draw the connection. It is possible, then, that the courtyard measurements were another way the link between tabernacle and temple was strengthened, and the observation thus would reinforce the idea that the one had the other in mind, if not in view.

The second point to be made concerns the shared visual repertoire of temple and tabernacle. The temple of Solomon is described in 1 Kgs 6–7 as having been adorned with a variety of images and patterns. The courtyard boasted a huge bronze sea, cast like a lotus cup (כוס פרח שושן; 7:26), under which were installed twelve bovine (בקר), three facing each cardinal direction (7:25). Also in the courtyard of the temple, the ten wheeled stands (מכנות) that supported basins had frames (שלבים) decorated with lions, bulls, cherubim, and possibly palmettes (7:29).[32] The pillars Jachin and Boaz, on the portico, had lotus capitals that were also adorned with hundreds of pomegranates and geometric patterns (שבכה; 7:17–20). Wooden doors leading into the antecella and cella, as well as the walls enclosing each of these spaces, bore carved and gilded cherubim (6:32–33), palmettes (תמרת; 6:29), and rosettes (פטורי צצים; 6:29). The aforementioned lampstands were, as is well known, described with floral imagery (7:29).

The visual elements of the tabernacle, for its part, also included floral iconography of the type discussed above. The lampstand is described in vegetal terms (cf. Exod 25:31–35), and if one admits priestly vestments, we find pomegranates (Exod 28:33–34; 39:24–26) and at least one rosette (ציץ; Exod 28:36; 39:30) as part of the repertoire. The singular figural images in the tabernacle, described at various points, were the cherubim, depicted on portals and in the holy of holies (cf. Exod 25:18; 26:1, 31). Thus, all of the main imagery of the tabernacle is also indicated in the temple of Solomon, but the opposite is not true, at least not when looking only at the record in 1 Kgs 6–7.

What to my mind is most interesting about temple iconography, however, and is never discussed in treatments of the relationship between temple and tabernacle, is that the preexilic temple iconography changed over time in not insignificant ways. Though several Judean monarchs were said to have manipulated, refurbished, or remodeled the temple, the one that is most clearly relevant to the original temple appearance seems to be that of Ahaz in the eighth

---

32. The note about the cherub–palmette pair in 7:36 may in fact be attributed to a secondary source that was influenced by the imagery of the house interior (in 1 Kgs 6:29), and may even have wished to avoid the bovine imagery of 7:25, 29. See Cogan, *1 Kings*, 272, and John Gray, *I & II Kings: A Commentary* (2nd ed.; OTL; London: SCM, 1970), 191–92.

century. Most commentators understandably do not designate this a reform, especially since it involved the incorporation of an apparently Assyrian altar, but the effects of the change on the items described in such detail in 1 Kgs 6–7 should not be overlooked. One of the major transformations he effected, besides the import of the altar most infamous for the Deuteronomistic Historian, involved the removal of the twelve bronze bulls from underneath the sea as well as a removal of the frames of the basin stands, which were decorated with lions and bulls, and the basins themselves (2 Kgs 16:17), leaving the bronze sea and ten wheeled stands with no figural imagery and no basins. This is most often either summarized by scholars as political or economic necessity generated by Assyrian imperial expansion—which it certainly appears to have been, though scholars treat it mostly as culturally insignificant—or assumed, with the usual assessment of the Deuteronomistic Historian, to be further evidence of Ahaz's lack of concern for Israelite religious tradition. Since he is not marked as a reformer bringing a straying populace in line with some normative ideal, the change must have been undesired by all but the royal elite. A careful reading, however, reveals that no such criticism of this particular move is present in 2 Kgs 16. Indeed, when put in the context of the Deuteronomistic Historian's crusade to impugn especially this monarch, the silence speaks strongly. One might even go so far as to read between the lines a tacit acceptance of this act, which can be explained by reference to other known influences in the Israelite dialogue with images.

Elsewhere in the Hebrew Bible the removal or manipulation of imagery is framed in overtly iconoclastic terms. The stories of Aaron and the gold calf (Exod 32), Jeroboam and the calves (1 Kgs 12), Hezekiah and the bronze serpent (2 Kgs 18), and Josiah and Asherah and the chariots of the sun (2 Kgs 23) all explain the addition or removal of imagery in terms of adherence to or deviation from orthodox religious practice. With these episodes in mind, one wonders why no clear explanation is given for the targeting of these particular items, especially when certain items were apparently left by Ahaz, namely, the wheeled stands (now basically unadorned). Perhaps the robbery of the temple imagery, like that of Hezekiah and Josiah, was not an undesired development, especially when one considers the problem presented by bovine imagery elsewhere in the Deuteronomistic History, but the generally negative portrayal of Ahaz had to be maintained. Whatever the case, it is important to recognize that, while this removal can be understood as a desperate economic measure targeted at available bronze, it was nevertheless a carefully selective removal that produced significant changes in the iconographic system of the temple. Removing the bulls and the frames meant that all faunal imagery, save cherubim, was now absent not just from the courtyard but also from the temple itself. One is forced to ask, then, which constraints forced or allowed Ahaz to remove these particular items and not others.

I would argue that the particular selection of the faunal imagery, coupled with the relative paucity of demonstrable references to these items, suggests that the conceptual need for the imagery was declining, if not outright reversed.³³ It is possible that, given the origin of this imagery in an Iron Age artistic *koine*, significant cultural attachment to it never fully developed or had, as noted above, become explicitly problematic.³⁴ It is even more likely that the imagery, particularly the lions and bulls, became problematic in the context of an increasingly fraught battle over political identity that played itself out in the arena of visual representation.³⁵ Whatever the case, Ahaz's changes brought the temple into accordance with a particular understanding of the "second" commandment. Exodus 20:4–5 forbids the Israelites from making "a sculpted image (פסל) or any likeness (תמונה) of what is in the skies above or in the earth below or in the waters under the earth," and not to worship them. Deuteronomy 4:15–19 interprets this injunction as including not just anything that one might find in the skies, on the earth, or in the oceans, but also particularly figural imagery: "the representation of a man or woman, any beast on earth, the representation of any winged bird that flies in the sky or of anything that crawls on the ground, or of any fish in the waters under the earth." As Brian Schmidt points out in reference to these verses, not explicitly forbidden are "images derivative of the inanimate world, floral forms, and *Mischwesen* (composite forms comprising theriomorphic and anthropomorphic elements)."³⁶

---

33. One is tempted to add here the intriguing possibility that the decline of figural imagery coincides somehow with the apex of Assyrian reluctance to represent deities anthropomorphically, a trajectory outlined in Tallay Ornan, *The Triumph of the Symbol: Pictorial Representations of Deities in Mesopotamia and the Biblical Image Ban* (OBO 213; Göttingen: Vandenhoeck & Ruprecht, 2005).

34. On the artistic *koine* that gave rise to Iron Age forms, see, e.g., Marian H. Feldman, *Diplomacy by Design: Luxury Arts and an 'International Style' in the Ancient Near East, 1400–1200 BCE* (Chicago: University of Chicago Press, 2006). On the use of foreign artistic forms in the temple of Solomon, one finds statements frequently made in histories of ancient Israel, such as: "the temple plan, decorations, and furnishings were fairly typical of the Iron Age, and eclectic. This is what one would expect, of course, for a sacred precinct constructed and decorated by Phoenician craftsmen" (J. Maxwell Miller and John H. Hayes, *A History of Ancient Israel and Judah* [2nd ed.; Louisville: Westminster John Knox, 2006], 217). For a more explicit discussion of the imagery in the context of ancient Near Eastern forms, see Philip J. King and Lawrence E. Stager, *Life in Biblical Israel* (Library of Ancient Israel; Louisville: Westminster John Knox, 2001), 330–38.

35. See, e.g., Nathaniel Levtow, *Images of Others: Iconic Politics in Ancient Israel* (Biblical and Judaic Studies from the University of California, San Diego 11; Winona Lake, Ind.: Eisenbrauns, 2008).

36. Brian Schmidt, "The Aniconic Tradition: On Reading Images and Viewing Texts," in *The Triumph of Elohim: From Yahwisms to Judaisms* (ed. Diana Edelman; Kampen: Kok Pharos, 1995), 82.

Here Schmidt unintentionally describes the categories of temple imagery operative *after* the removal of the lions and bulls: namely, inanimate objects, flora, and composite creatures. Surely it is no coincidence that the prohibition of certain types of images permitted the configuration of imagery (known independently) of the temple in the wake of Ahaz's changes. Thus, this evidence, too, suggests that, by his specific targeting of the figural imagery, Ahaz was either acting in response to or actively participating in the reshaping of cultural norms concerning representation in the Israelite religious milieu. Either the paradigm described by Schmidt was a rubric allowing (or even necessitating) the removal of those particular images, or the removal of the images helped to engender such a classificatory schema.[37] Either way, Ahaz's actions constitute an important statement in the conversation about visual representation in Judah, one that, in my view, had important consequences for the textual representation of the tabernacle.

It is striking that the collective visual repertoire of the tabernacle closely matches not as much that of the temple as described in 1 Kgs 6–7, but rather the version understood to have existed after Ahaz's remodeling: there was no figural imagery besides cherubim, only one water vessel stood in the courtyard—on a stand with no apparent adornment, no less. This observation, together with that concerning the temple dimensions discussed above, adds weight to the argument that the description of the tabernacle was shaped in reference to knowledge of the first Jerusalem temple. The implications of this observation merit further comment.

First, if the points about Ahaz are to be admitted, the iconographic correlation suggests that if the tabernacle texts were indeed crafted with the temple in mind, they were done so after Ahaz. While for most scholars this would constitute a point so basic as to be nearly irrelevant, it also leads to another observation, namely, that the shaping of these texts was not the result of literary analysis on the part of a Priestly author. That is, the authors of the tabernacle descriptions did not rely on a text like 1 Kgs 6–7 in projecting their temple-like construction into the corporate past, since a copy of 1 Kgs 6–7 would have yielded proportions of 20 × 30 × 60 cubits and faunal imagery in the courtyard. Rather, I hold the final tabernacle narrative to be a result of converging streams of tradition that included the physical experience—not the literary copy—of the post-Ahaz temple of Jerusalem. A purely literary exercise

---

37. One notes here too that, if one understands the bronze serpent to have been erected in the temple courtyard, Hezekiah may have been contributing to the same conversation by his removal of Nehushtan (2 Kgs 18:4). It would have fallen under the category of *Mischwesen*, therefore permissible as an image, but it was the particular behavior before the image, not the inherent qualities of the image itself, that became problematic. Thus, according to 2 Kgs 18:4, it was a different prohibition under which Nehushtan became a target, viz., that which forbade Israelites from bowing down to or serving an image.

would have looked much more like the convergence of temple and tabernacle in the Chronicler's work. This evidence, then, would not detract from Haran's view of the origin of the Priestly source in Hezekiah's reign.

If this is correct, it not only suggests something about the possible experiential source of the correlation between tabernacle and temple, but it also reveals something about P's audience. If the author indeed intended his audience to connect temple and tabernacle, he did not lead them through a point-by-point textual comparison, but rather the comparison turned on the hinges of a shared experience of the Jerusalem temple. This is also in favor of Haran's view that, at least initially, P was a document that circulated in Priestly circles long before it was made public under Ezra in the era after the exile. It also militates against the views of Fretheim and Propp that the purpose of P was to undermine the Jerusalem priesthood by turning Solomon's temple into a wandering shrine.

Finally, these observations are most interesting, in my view, for the way they force one to ask what was gained in bringing the two structures together. In answering this question, it is important to move beyond the simple concerns about historicity that are the usual extent of the discussion. If Haran and others have correctly characterized P in calling it the promulgation of a utopian view carefully devoid of parenetic instructions for ostensibly future generations, what did it accomplish? At a most basic level, legitimation appears to be an operative force in the combination of the two structures, especially in light of the unease over the construction of a permanent place of Yahweh's dwelling expressed in opposing schools of thought (cf. 2 Sam 7). It placed tent and temple traditions on the same trajectory, locating the temple in the central events of Israel's collective memory and providing a visual reference for and material verification of the tabernacle traditions in the wake of the dismantling of the tent shrines at Shiloh and Jerusalem. To the politically informed, this congruence may have had the effect of bridging the gap between Shilonite traditions and those initiated by Solomon in effort to minimize the influence of the earlier, tribal institutions, and to mitigate the deposing of Abiathar and the Shilonite priesthood. It brings the northern priests into the picture at the same time that it subordinates them and their traditions to the current concerns of the Jerusalem temple hierarchy, resolving the discord undoubtedly created by the influx of disenfranchised cultic functionaries in the aftermath of the Assyrian destruction of the north and the abolishment of competing shrines under Hezekiah.[38]

The visual-spatial argument made by casting the tabernacle in the mold of the temple thus had political and social ramifications for *both* temple and tabernacle. It was a move that can be seen as participating in the (re-)invention of both traditions, in the sense articulated by Eric Hobsbawm. He characterizes

---

38. See discussion and notes in Stephen L. Cook's essay in the present volume.

invented traditions as "responses to novel situations which take the form of reference to old situations," and as "a process of formalization and ritualization, characterized by reference to the past, if only by imposing repetition."[39] This is most prevalently done "when a rapid transformation of society weakens or destroys the social patterns for which 'old' traditions had been designed" and for the purpose of "establishing or symbolizing social cohesion or the membership of groups, real or artificial communities."[40] The narrative that frames the lawgiving at Sinai in P, of which the tabernacle is arguably the centerpiece, co-opts the Shiloh traditions and reforms the hierarchy with the Levitical priests operating in a role subordinate to the Aaronids. Contra Wellhausen, this is not something that P needs to argue for; it is simply asserted as if it had always been the case, but not because it had already happened. The utopian picture, as pointed out by Haran, was directed initially at priests, possibly including those that now found their status diminished in the south.[41] If this is the case, one finds George's recent analysis of the graded tabernacle space as not *reflective of* but *defined by* social hierarchy particularly important, even if one disagrees with his historical placement of the tabernacle.[42] Viewed in this way, the alignment of the temple and tabernacle in the Priestly source is not the result of historical ignorance or accidence. It is the careful manipulation of history that actively seeks to construct the present.

P thus looks toward past and present simultaneously: in one motion it establishes the historical legitimacy of the temple via its identification with older wilderness traditions at the same time that it actively memorializes the tabernacle in the contemporary edifice on Mount Zion. This Janus view allows P's "utopian" world to be reified in the present while speaking ostensibly about a collective past. It materially relates contemporary structures and practice, such as Sabbath and royal institutions, to creation and theophany.[43] It is here that its character as foundation myth comes most clearly into view, not as "aggressive towards the present,"[44] as one finds in D, but instead as a document whose pur-

---

39. Eric J. Hobsbawm, "Introduction: Inventing Traditions," in *The Invention of Tradition* (ed. Eric J. Hobsbawm and Terence Ranger; Cambridge: Cambridge University Press, 1983), 1-14, here 2 and 4, respectively. Although Hobsbawm and the volume's other contributors seem mostly concerned with the complete invention of tradition—that is, from scratch—I consider the invention of tradition here to be an overhaul of previous texts and concepts that is, effectively, invention.

40. Ibid., 4, 9.

41. See Haran, "Behind the Scenes of History."

42. George, *Israel's Tabernacle*, 17-44.

43. See Moshe Weinfeld, "Sabbath, Temple and the Enthronement of the Lord—The Problem of the Sitz im Leben of Genesis 1:1–2:3," in *Mélanges bibliques et orientaux en l'honneur de M. Henri Cazelles* (ed. A. Caquot and M. Delcor; AOAT 212; Kevelaer: Butzon & Bercker, 1981), 501-12.

44. Haran, *Temples and Temple-Service*, 146.

pose might be seen as directed toward the production of space, or of a reality constructed through spatial means. To the cultically informed observer in the First Temple period, the edifice thus came to constitute a visual testimony to earlier traditions, much the way the menorah and the bronze serpent housed the cultural memories of desert theophany and the wilderness wanderings. In this connection, if we can be relatively certain of the congruence between the sacrificial system of P and the cultic service of the Jerusalem temple, the framing of these activities in a space so strongly associated with earlier traditions would have made sacrificial performance in the Jerusalem temple a regular act of social memorializing in addition to its many other functions.[45] If the Chronicler's attempts to weave these two (by then literary) traditions together more explicitly are any indication, P was ultimately successful.

---

45. On other functions and meanings, see, e.g., David Janzen, *The Social Meanings of Sacrifice in the Hebrew Bible: A Study of Four Writings* (BZAW 344; Berlin: de Gruyter, 2004), esp. 110-19. On temple sacrifice and its relation to cosmology, see Jonathan Klawans, *Purity, Sacrifice, and the Temple: Symbolism and Supersessionism in the Study of Ancient Judaism* (Oxford: Oxford University Press, 2006), esp. 104-6.

What Do the "Levites in Your Gates" Have to Do with the "Levitical Priests"? An Attempt at European–North American Dialogue on the Levites in the Deuteronomic Law Corpus

Peter Altmann

Wellhausen's *Prolegomena* marks the foundation for both recent European and recent North American scholarship on the Levites and therefore forms the beginning point for tracing the trajectories of the two divergent conversations in current scholarship. He makes the centralization of worship and the attending effects of this "reform" on the priesthood a central category for tracing the religious-historical and thereby the composition-historical progression of the literature of the Old Testament/Hebrew Bible. He states,

> The turning-point in the history of the sacrificial system was the reformation of Josiah; what we find in the Priestly Code is the matured result of that event. It is precisely in the distinctions that are characteristic of the sacrificial law as compared with the ancient sacrificial praxis that we have evidence of the fact that, if not all exactly occasioned by the centralisation of the worship, they were almost all somehow at least connected with that change.[1]

Thanks to Annette Schellenberg, Safwat Marzouk, and Gary Knoppers for their interaction with earlier drafts of this essay. All translations from German-language secondary literature are my own, except where otherwise noted.

1. Julius Wellhausen, *Prolegomena to the History of Israel: With a Reprint of the Article Israel from the "Encyclopaedia Britannica"* (trans. J. Sutherland Black and A. Menzies; with preface by W. Robertson Smith; Edinburgh: Adam & Charles Black, 1885), 76. Note also the recent statement by Jeffrey Stackert: "In fact, Wellhausen arranges the various biblical presentations of the Levites on a chronological continuum with virtually no overlap and identifies Ezek 44:6–16 as an Archimedean point for understanding Levitical history and their relationship to the priesthood. To his mind, it is this text that introduces the cultic distinction between priests and Levites: it differentiates between the Zadokites (בני צדוק) and Levites and reserves the priesthood for the Zadokites. The Levites are thus demoted from their previous place as altar priests and are not simply returned to an original subordinate position vis-à-vis the priests. . . . In order to justify this innovation, Ezekiel polemically argues that Levitical service at the high places was sinful, and that they must bear their own guilt by serving as Temple guards and slaughterers. The Levites can thus be identified with

Deuteronomy—along with Ezekiel—stands as the hinge between the earlier JE decentralized worship and the Priestly material, along with Chronicles, which takes centralization and the demotion of the Levites to minor clerics to be a more or less foregone conclusion. With regard to the Levites, Wellhausen concluded that this change to one central place of worship led to their relegation to second-class cultic personnel in the exilic and later periods, while earlier—as seen in the texts such as Judg 17–18, Deut 33, 1 Kgs 12 (if Jeroboam's priests also included some Levites), and 2 Kgs 23[2]—they served at sanctuaries throughout the Israelite and Judahite territories.

If both scholarly communities assume the same Wellhausian point of departure, then why are the current discussions so different in European and North American scholarship with regard to Levites and priests? In order to address this question I will narrow the investigation to the divergent approaches to the relationship between the "Levites in your gates" and the "Levitical priests"[3] more closely tied to the central sanctuary in Deut 12–26. My goal is to create a forum for the development of a mutually agreed-upon point of departure and dialogue for future studies. To state the particular problems for the Levites in Deuteronomy: (1) What is the relationship between the two distinct groups of Levites in the Deuteronomic text? and (2) How do these Levite texts compare to other treatments of/silence on Levites in biblical texts?

I will begin by briefly examining the entries concerning "Levi, Levites" or "Priests and Levites" by Robert Kugler in the most recent English encyclopedia (*NIDB*, 2007) and by Reinhard Achenbach in the most recent German work (*RGG*, 4th ed., 2002)[4] as examples of the various approaches with regard to:

'the priests of the high places' (כהני הבמות) who, according to the Deuteronomistic historian, did not approach the altar at the Jerusalem Temple (2 Kgs 23:8–9)" (Jeffrey Stackert, *Rewriting the Torah: Literary Revision in Deuteronomy and the Holiness Legislation* [FAT 52: Tübingen: Mohr Siebeck, 2007], 199).

2. This position can even be found in the often more skeptical European discussion: Hermann Spieckermann, *Juda unter Assur in der Sargonidenzeit* (FRLANT 129; Göttingen: Vandenhoeck & Ruprecht, 1982); more recently Joachim Schaper, *Priester und Leviten im achämenidischen Juda: Studien zur Kult- und Sozialgeschichte Israels in persischer Zeit* (FAT 31; Tübingen: Mohr Siebeck, 2000).

3. The phrase "Levitical priests" is, of course, only one translation offered for הכהנים הלויים, which appears in Deut 17:9, 18; 18:1; 24:8; 27:9. The phrase "the priests, the sons of Levi" occurs in 21:5; 31:9. Other mentions of "Levitical priests" are Josh 3:3; 8:33; Jer 33:18; Ezek 43:19; 44:15; 2 Chr 5:5; 23:18; 30:27.

4. Robert Kugler, "Levi, Levites," *NIDB* 3:642–43; idem, "Priests and Levites," *NIDB* 4:596–613; Reinhard Achenbach, "Levi/Leviten," *RGG* 5:293–95. Eckart Otto's entry in *RGG* maintains that the family or local priests in Judg 17–18, the Elides in 1 Sam 2–4, and the Zadokites in 1 Kgs 1–2 all depict a preexilic, pre-Josianic situation ("Priestertum. II. Religionsgeschichtlich. 1. Alter Orient und Altes Testament," *RGG* 6:1646–49). He accepts here a connection between landless Levitical priests in local and private sanctuaries with the Levites in Deut 14:27–29. Otto elsewhere denies this connection between the reform

(1) pre-Deuteronomic traditions, (2) comparative analysis, (3) connections with historical events, and (4) redaction-critical methodology.[5] While one can argue about whether these represent the "most important" or "cutting-edge" positions, I think they provide a fairly accessible and broad starting point.[6] After comparing the two approaches and their potential for overlap I will then turn to one specific text, Deut 18:1–8.

I. A Brief Comparison of Approaches to the Levites in Deuteronomy

A. North America

Kugler's entries on the "Levites" and "Priests and Levites" in *NIDB* do not reflect mainstream North American positions on all issues pertaining to the developments of the Levites;[7] however, they nonetheless lay out basic tenets of North American scholarship that provide a helpful contrast to the European

---

actions of Josiah in 2 Kgs 23 affecting the local priests and the Levites in Deut 14 ("Die post-deuteronomistische Levitisierung des Deuteronomiums: Zu einem Buch von Ulrich Dahmen," *ZABR* 5 [1999]: 277–84).

5. A fifth category suggested by Gary N. Knoppers (personal communication) that could have been included is the considerable attention given to text-critical matters in the North American discussion as a means to answer some of the riddles, such as Zadok's genealogy: for example, Frank Moore Cross, *Canaanite Myth and Hebrew Epic: Essays in the History of the Religion of Israel* (Cambridge, Mass.: Harvard University Press, 1973), 212–14.

6. Other recent treatments include Mark Leuchter, "'Levites in Your Gates': The Deuteronomic Redefinition of Levitical Authority," *JBL* 126 (2007): 417–36; Ulrich Dahmen, *Leviten und Priester im Deuteronomium: Literarkritische und redaktionsgeschichtliche Studien* (BBB 110; Bodenheim: Philo, 1996); Mark A. Christian, "Priestly Power that Empowers: Michel Foucault, Middle-Tier Levites, and the Sociology of 'Popular Religious Groups' in Israel," *JHS* 9 (2009): art. 1 (cited June 22, 2010): http://www.arts.ualberta.ca/JHS/Articles/article_103.pdf; Schaper, *Priester und Leviten*; Reinhard Achenbach, "Levitische Priester und Leviten im Deuteronomium: Überlegungen zur sog. 'Levitisierung' des Priestertums," *ZABR* 5 (1999): 285–309; and Nadav Na'aman, "Sojourners and Levites in the Kingdom of Judah in the Seventh Century BCE," *ZABR* 14 (2008): 237–79.

7. Kugler rejects Cross's analysis of the origins of the Zadokite priesthood, which claims that Zadok was an Aaronid associated with the Hebron sanctuary (*Canaanite Myth and Hebrew Epic*, 207–15), opting instead for a Jebusite/Jerusalemite origin as often found in European scholarship; for a recent reformulation, see Othmar Keel, *Die Geschichte Jerusalems und die Entstehung des Monotheismus* (Orte und Landschaften der Bible 4/1; Göttingen: Vandenhoeck & Ruprecht, 2007). Cf. Saul Olyan, "Zadok's Origins and the Tribal Politics of David," *JBL* 101 (1982): 177–93, and J. J. M. Roberts, "The Davidic Origin of the Zion Tradition," in idem, *The Bible and the Ancient Near East: Collected Essays* (Winona Lake, Ind.: Eisenbrauns, 2002), 313–30, for critique of the Jebusite hypothesis. The general critique against Cross is not the impossibility of his suggestion, but simply that there is little positive evidence for it. However, this critique is also justified for the Jebusite hypothesis.

approach found in Achenbach's work in *RGG*. The following summary highlights important points of Kugler's position for comparison with Achenbach's. For *one thing*, Kugler includes a discussion of the priests and Levites *before the monarchy* in which he concludes—mostly on the basis of Deut 33:8–11 and Judg 17–18—that "already the three basic tasks priests performed across the ancient world are in evidence: . . . sacrifice, . . . divination, . . . And . . . teaching."[8] While perhaps distant from the earlier attempts by W. F. Albright and by Cross and Freedman to anchor the early date of such texts as Deut 33:8–11 on the basis of linguistic dating and similarities with Ugaritic and other epigraphic materials,[9] Kugler nonetheless may be influenced by this North American tradition in that he does not display the same hesitancy that emerges in the mainstream European conversation toward positing Levitical beginnings.[10] With regard to Deuteronomy and the Deuteronomistic History, he concludes that "Deuteronomic tradition" (as he terms it) incorporated a number of earlier references (Josh 3:3; 8:33; Judg 17–18; 19–21). These earlier texts were supplemented with those concerning the Levites in Deuteronomic

---

8. Kugler, "Priests and Levites," 601; see also 600: "However, Deut 33:8–11 and Judg 17–18, two texts with *genuine claims to antiquity far greater than the source in which they appear* [the Deuteronomic Collection], provide reason to accept the model as having some basis in actual practice" (emphasis mine).

9. Frank Moore Cross and David Noel Freedman suggest that only v. 11 was part of the original text of Deut 33:8–11 (on the basis of prose markers in vv. 8–10), and this verse may in fact have belonged to Gen 49 ("The Blessing of Moses," *JBL* 67 [1948]: 203–4). Their conclusion would indicate the secular origins of the tribe of Levi, matching Gen 49. Jeffrey H. Tigay argues, "Verse 8 seems to reflect a different tradition than 10:8 concerning when the Levites were awarded the priesthood, and verse 11's assumption of Levitical wealth does not square with Deuteronomy's picture of them as needy. In addition, the priestly duties that verses 8–10 mention differ partly from those listed in 10:8 and 21:5; those passages include carrying the Ark and blessing in God's name and omit the Urim and Thummim, probably because Deuteronomy sees God's will as communicated exclusively through prophecy. Verse 8 also disagrees with 6:16, and the rest of the Torah, about what happened at Massah and Meribah" (*Deuteronomy* דברים: *The Traditional Hebrew Text with the New JPS Translation* [JPS Torah Commentary; Philadelphia: Jewish Publication Society, 1996], 521). Richard D. Nelson argues: "The shift from the singular language of vv. 8–9a to the plural of vv. 9b–10 suggests a different origin for these respective sections, as does the unexpectedly 'secular' direction taken in v. 11. Verse 11 represents an older materialistic and militaristic blessing, later augmented by vv. 8–9a and then vv. 9b–10 as priestly oriented supplements" (*Deuteronomy: A Commentary* [OTL; Louisville: Westminster John Knox, 2002], 389–90).

10. His approach does not take into consideration the views of those following Yehezkel Kaufmann, who emphasize the preexilic traditions—if not texts—within P, resulting in the contesting of the historical development outlined by Wellhausen, and also allowing for much earlier cultic tasks for the Levites than the current European conversation would entertain. Given my interest in reaching a basic understanding between scholarly contexts, I will not engage in this discussion here.

tradition as "an all-inclusive term for the priests of Israel."[11] In quite traditional North American fashion, Kugler only narrows the time period for this "Deuteronomic tradition" to the "late 7th and early 6th century."[12]

A *second* important category nearly always featured in the North American discussion and important in both this citation and occupying significant space in Kugler's article is the comparison with other ancient or non-modern cultures.[13] This approach investigates the Levite texts with sociological, political, and archaeological data and methodology in order to provide a richer understanding of the implications of the biblical texts. Here one might note Lawrence Stager's classic article "The Archaeology of the Family in Ancient Israel,"[14] which relates the entrance of many European younger sons into monastic orders during the Middle Ages to the Levitical situation, postulating a similar outcome for the identical demographic (i.e., younger sons) in the early monarchic period in Israel. While I will not deal with this theme any further here, it is important for the question of Levitical origins and the question of "Levites" as a designation for a tribe or for a functional group.[15]

Third, Kugler (following Rainer Albertz) argues that 2 Kgs 23:9, along with Deut 18:1–8, "expresses the ideal the Deuteronomic tradition hoped to

---

11. Kugler, "Levi, Levites," 643.
12. Ibid., 642–43.
13. See, for example, the recent work by Jeremy M. Hutton, "The Levitical Diaspora (I): A Sociological Comparison with Morocco's Ahansal," in *Exploring the* Longue Durée: *Essays in Honor of Lawrence E. Stager* (ed. J. D. Schloen; Winona Lake, Ind.: Eisenbrauns, 2009), 228: "This function of the Ahansal may be compared to the Levites' various functions as scholars and teachers of the law . . . ; judges in the gates who provide a local presence of the monarchic juridical procedure . . . ; intertribal mediators and administrators of the Israelite confederation (Joshua 22; Judges 19–20; . . .); and cultic personnel at peripheral altars."
14. Lawrence E. Stager, "The Archaeology of the Family in Ancient Israel," *BASOR* 260 (1985): 1–35, here 27: "The priesthood, I would suggest, provided another institution, which helped 'absorb' a surplus of young males, especially for those who were not firstborns and, as the frontier was closing, stood little chance of inheriting much of the patrimony or of pioneering new land. It is in this social milieu that we should look for the source of some of the Levites, who were added to this sacred 'tribe.' . . . In this patron–client relationship the Levite was, as the root *lwy* denotes, 'attached to' someone else. Samuel was a 'youth' preparing for the priesthood at Shiloh."
15. Kugler, "Priests and Levites," 607–8: "Yet our discussion of the origin of Levitical claims for the priesthood in the Deuteronomic Collection above indicates that at its beginning such rhetoric was only rhetoric, and that, certainly before the exile, the priesthood in fact was a mix of the descendants of 'functional Levites,' who had settled into local sanctuaries, and Zadokites, who had no grounds (or reason) for making claims on Levitical lineage." Whether "Levite" was originally a functional term has been under debate for quite some time. For an earlier discussion against a functional definition, see Aelred Cody, *A History of Old Testament Priesthood* (AnBib 35; Rome: Pontifical Biblical Institute, 1969), 7, 29–38. He draws his primary support of an originally secular tribe from the appearance of related personal names.

achieve, that the vast number of now underemployed priests created by Josiah's centralization efforts would be cared for as *gērîm* (גֵּרִים), figures not unlike the 'functionally Levitical' Levites of the tribal period."[16] This mode of argumentation assumes that the Levites, by which Kugler means at least "functional" Levites, can be equated *at a minimum* with the non-Jerusalemite priests of 2 Kgs 23:9, a common equation in North American scholarship, and that the Deuteronomic tradition was attempting to unify the priesthood in Jerusalem (à la Wellhausen) under the umbrella of what one might refer to as a "functional Levitical-ism." Furthermore, Kugler here views 2 Kgs 22–24 as possessing a modicum of historicity with regard to Josiah's centralization attempt and its failure with regard to the priesthood as on display in the reports of the subsequent kings (esp. 23:32, 37; 24:9; and Ezek 8; 22:26; Jer 28).

Finally, Kugler seems to assume that at least some of the situation reflected in Deut 12–26 emerges from the preexilic period. This last point becomes important not only for its contrast to both the almost century-old position taken by Gustav Hölscher and the more recent views of Reinhard G. Kratz, Juha Pakkala, and Ernst Axel Knauf, all of whom locate *Urdeuteronomium* in the exilic period.[17] I see a more fundamental methodological sensitivity at work here (*my fourth category*): with specific regard for Deut 12–26 or even chs. 5 (or 4:45)–28, North American scholarship seeks a more synchronic reading of Deuteronomy and the texts concerning the Levites in Deuteronomy

---

16. Kugler, "Priests and Levites," 604. See also Rainer Albertz, *Religionsgeschichte Israels in alttestamentlicher Zeit*, vol. 1, *Von den Anfängen bis zum Ende der Königszeit* (GAT 8.1; Göttingen: Vandenhoeck & Ruprecht, 1992). Mentioning Albertz does, of course, serve to break down the heuristic dichotomy of European versus North American, highlighting how the two conversations continue to interact with each other.

17. Gustav Hölscher, "Komposition und Ursprung des Deuteronomiums," *ZAW* 40 (1922): 227–30; Ernst Axel Knauf, "Observations on Judah's Social and Economic History and the Dating of the Laws in Deuteronomy," *JHS* 9 (2009): art. 18 (cited July 26, 2010): http://www.arts.ualberta.ca/JHS/Articles/article_120.pdf; Reinhard G. Kratz, *The Composition of the Narrative Books of the Old Testament* (London: T&T Clark, 2005), 131–32; trans. by John Bowden of *Die Komposition der erzählenden Bücher des Alten Testaments: Grundwissen der Bibelkritik* (Göttingen: Vandenhoeck & Ruprecht, 2000); most recently Juha Pakkala, "The Date of the Oldest Edition of Deuteronomy," *ZAW* 121 (2009): 388–401. The block model of Norbert Lohfink and Georg Braulik also views Deut 16:18–18:22 as receiving its primary shaping in the exilic period—especially 18:6–8 because it was not taken into consideration in 2 Kgs 23:9, yet it was outdated by the time of the Levite-Zadokite compromise (Norbert Lohfink, "Distribution of the Functions of Power: The Laws Concerning Public Offices in Deuteronomy 16:18–18:22," in *A Song of Power and the Power of Song: Essays on the Book of Deuteronomy* [ed. Duane L. Christensen; SBTS 3; Winona Lake, Ind.: Eisenbrauns, 1993], 345–46). Jan C. Gertz does not include any portion of 18:1–8 in what he thinks must have originally belonged to the original inventory of the preexilic Deuteronomic law ("Tora und Vordere Propheten," in *Grundinformation Altes Testament* [3rd ed.; ed. J. C. Gertz; Uni-Taschenbücher 2745; Göttingen: Vandenhoeck & Ruprecht, 2009], 255).

based in the late preexilic period.¹⁸ The point to be made here is the willingness in the North American discussion either to synthesize or to overlook internal tensions in the texts within a singular textual layer. Furthermore, a general skepticism reigns regarding modern scholarly attempts at precise textual stratification.¹⁹

B. European Scholarship

Turning to the European discussion, several differences become clear before even turning to my categories: (1) European scholarship tends to address the problems far more from a redaction-critical methodology, and (2) tends to see texts as emerging from significantly later contexts. A further and related difference is (3) the reliance on *text-internal* markers for dating.²⁰

---

18. My statement here does not necessarily imply that North American scholars employ a more synchronic approach on the whole (at least those who use historical-critical methods). With regard to the study of the Levites as a whole, the North American approach may in fact be more diachronic, since its conclusions date texts between the eleventh century B.C.E. and the fifth century B.C.E., while many European scholars date texts between the seventh/sixth centuries B.C.E. and the third century B.C.E.

19. David M. Carr points out, for example, the likelihood that different traditions colored one another even *before* they were combined, creating significant difficulties for attempts at precise ordering of the layers in texts ("Scribal Processes of Coordination/Harmonization and the Formation of the First Hexateuch(s)," in *The Pentateuch: International Perspectives on Current Research* [ed. T. B. Dozeman, K. Schmid, and B. J. Schwartz; FAT 78; Tübingen: Mohr Siebeck, 2011], 63–83). This point also provides an explanation for some diversity within individual textual layers.

20. Programmatic statements to this effect can be found in the recent monograph by Christoph Koch, *Vertrag, Treueid, und Bund: Studien zur Rezeption des altorientalischen Vertragsrecht im Deuteronomium und zur Ausbildung der Bundestheologie im Alten Testament* (BZAW 383; Berlin: de Gruyter, 2008); and the essay by Reinhard G. Kratz: "Any analysis of the Pentateuch (as well as of the other narrative books) should start at the text-immanent level. This leads to a relative chronology of the literary stages of the formation of the Pentateuch. Only after this is done should one approach the question of where exactly in the history of Israel the individual stages of the Pentateuch can be placed meaningfully" ("The Pentateuch in Current Research: Consensus and Debate," in Dozeman et al., *The Pentateuch: International Perspectives*, 59). Joel S. Baden praises David Wright for taking a similarly text-internal approach in a recent monograph (review of D. P. Wright, *Inventing God's Law: How the Covenant Code of the Bible Used and Revised the Laws of Hammurabi* [Oxford: Oxford University Press, 2009], *RBL* 7 [2010]: cited September 13, 2010 www.bookreviews.org /pdf/7232_7874.pdf). While I see a necessary correction here to assuming that every text has an *identifiable* social-historical context that modern scholars can still discover (note the critique of Benjamin Sommer, "Dating Pentateuchal Texts and the Perils of Pseudo-Historicism," in Schmid et al., *The Pentateuch*), I still find it important to link texts with particular situations. Otherwise texts risk becoming ideal constructs rather than actual immanent creations on the part of the interaction between a particular text/author and (implied) reader at a particular place in time.

Turning to my proposed categories, while Achenbach's entry in *RGG* is significantly shorter than Kugler's corresponding one in *NIDB*, his outline is helpful and provides the necessary data for categorization.[21] First, with regard to pre-Deuteronomic material, he approaches the preexilic, not to mention the premonarchic, period with far more hesitancy. Achenbach's stance is similar to the one found in the most recent (though already fifteen years old!) full-length German monograph about the Levites in Deuteronomy. There, Ulrich Dahmen argues, "Insofar as an old tradition underlies Judg 17f.—which is not impossible, but is all but certain—then we would have at hand at least one case in which certain functions were not necessarily (cf. Judg 17:5), but preferentially (cf. 17:13), assigned to Levites."[22] Achenbach does not see Deut 33, or any other text for that matter, as providing secure information on the Levites before their appearance as *personae miserae* in the pre-Dtr Deuteronomic texts found in chs. 12, 14, and 16. He follows Schmid's conclusion that Deut 33 plays a redactional role corresponding to Gen 49 constructed by the Pentateuch redactor, though he also detects some old motifs of various origins in the former.[23]

---

21. It can also be supplemented by his article, "Levitische Priester und Leviten" (see n. 6 above).

22. Dahmen, *Leviten und Priester*, 373 ("Sofern in Ri 17f. tatsächlich eine alte Tradition vorliegen sollte—was nicht unmöglich, aber alles andere als sicher ist—, läge damit zumindest ein Fall vor, an dem erkennbar wäre, dass bestimmte Funktionen nicht notwendig [vgl. Ri 17,5], aber bevorzugt [vgl. 17,13] Leviten übertragen wurden."). See his similar conclusion concerning Deut 33:8–11: "At the same time, it must be said that the confirmation provided by the lot-oracle was not necessarily reserved for the priests since the earliest period—for which we have no examples—but rather it is only texts reflecting the (at earliest) postexilic relationships (Exod 28:30; Lev 8:8; Num 27:21; Ezra 2:63; Neh 7:65) which draw it [i.e., the lot-oracle] together with the priest/high priest" ("Dazu ist zu sagen, daß die Bestätigung des Losorakels nicht notwendig seit frühester Zeit—für die uns die Belege fehlen—den Priestern vorbehalten gewesen sein muß, sondern nur die erst nachexilische Verhältnisse widerspiegelnden Stellen Ex 28,30; Lev 8,8; Num 27,21; Esra 2,63; Neh 7,65 es mit dem Priester/Hohepriester in Verbindung bringen") (p. 198).

Dahmen does not address the possible appearance of *bāʾûrîm* in 1 Sam 28:6 and *ʾûrîm* in various versions of 1 Sam 14:41 (according to Kittel in *BHK* in a number of Greek and Latin versions [G L L(lg) V]). Especially the reference in 1 Sam 28 seems to be a quite idiosyncratic use of the oracular implement and for this reason a likely candidate for a relatively more ancient text. Of course, it does not occur in relation to the Levites here, however. There is a dissertation addressing the Levites in Deuteronomy currently in progress by Harald Samuel at Göttingen.

23. Achenbach, "Levitische Priester und Leviten," 286–87 n. 7 and 308: "Die Pentateuchredaktion entwirft im Mosesege über Levi Dtn 33,8-11 ein ‚P' und ‚D'-Überlieferung integrierendes Gesamtbild: dem Fluch des Vaters Gen 49 wird der Segen des Mose entgegengestellt." See also idem, "Levi/Levites," 295; and Konrad Schmid, *Erzväter und Exodus: Untersuchungen zur doppelten Begründung der Ursprünge Israels innerhalb der Geschichts-*

The development of this skepticism is on display also in the two most recent standard encyclopedias of religion in German: *RGG* (2002) and *TRE*. Horst Seebass still assumes that Deut 33:8–11 is—without needing any supporting argument—to be understood as a pre-Deuteronomic text,[24] so the trend toward seeing Deut 33 as a later text is quite recent. Achenbach later states that Judg 17–18 and 19–20 do seem like possible preexilic sources,[25] yet he claims, "Involvement of the Levites in the state cults of the northern kingdom is explicitly excluded in 1 Kgs 12:31."[26] I find it quite interesting that, with regard to the preexilic period, Achenbach generally just points the reader to Dahmen's work.[27]

In terms of my *second* category, Achenbach spends almost no time discussing possible sociological parallels that could illuminate the development of the Levites as either tribe or functional group.[28] Instead, Achenbach focuses the

---

bücher des Alten Testaments (WMANT 81; Neukirchen-Vluyn: Neukirchener Verlag, 1999), 94–95.

24. Horst Seebaß, "Levi/Leviten," *TRE* 21:36-40 (published 1991).

25. Achenbach classifies the mention of Levite terminology in Judg 17–21 as Dtr–late Dtr ("Levitische Priester und Leviten," 286 n. 4). His position on the earliest layer of Deuteronomy is similar to that of Dahmen, who states, "The Deuteronomic *Grundschicht* reflects the Levite (*hallewî*) primarily as a social entity, and indeed both as a member of the 'extended family' in the list of cultic participants and also as a member of the series of *personae miserabiles*. He is mentioned exclusively in the singular, with which a typological indicator (appellative) is intended, the concrete function of which in the state, society, or religion of preexilic Judah is no longer to be ascertained in detail" ("Die dtn Grundschicht kennt zunächst den Leviten [*hallewî*] als soziale Größe, und zwar sowohl als Mitglied der 'extended family' in der Kultteilnehmerliste als auch als Glied der personae-miserabiles-Reihe; er wird ausschließlich sing. erwähnt, womit eine Typenbezeichnung angedeutet ist [Appellativum], deren konkrete Funktion in Staat, Gesellschaft oder Religion des vorexilischen Juda nicht mehr im einzelnen zu erheben ist") (*Leviten und Priester*, 394).

26. Achenbach, "Levi/Leviten," 294: "The participation of the L[evites]in the state cult of the northern kingdom is explicitly ruled out in 1 Kgs 12:31" ("Eine Mitwirkung der L. in den Reichskulten des Nordreiches wird in 1 Kön 12,31 explizit ausgeschlossen"). This claim has been disputed by Risto Nurmela, *The Levites: Their Emergence as a Second-Class Priesthood* (South Florida Studies in the History of Judaism 193; Atlanta: Scholars Press, 1998), 39: "To summarize: Judges 17–18 and Exodus 32 indicate that the official priests of the Northern Kingdom were Levites whose participation in the cult was condemned by the southern tradition. The tension between Abiathar and David and the open conflict between Abiathar and Solomon make it very likely that the Levitical priests belonged to the clan of Abiathar. Other contributing factors were Abiathar's northern origin and the role played by the Shilonite prophet Ahijah in the account of the dissolution of the united monarchy." Karel van der Toorn defends a similar reading (*Family Religion in Babylonia, Syria, and Israel: Continuity and Change in the Forms of Religious Life* [Studies in the History and Culture of the Ancient Near East 7; Leiden: Brill, 1996], 305–6).

27. Achenbach, "Levitische Priester und Leviten," 287 n. 11.

28. Achenbach, "Levi/Leviten," 293

greatest portion of his dictionary entry on the exilic and postexilic periods.[29] Two remarks are pertinent here: (1) Origins appear to be of little importance; and (2) almost half of Achenbach's article focuses on Ezek 40–48 and its formulation of the relationship between the Levites and the priesthood.

Turning to category *three*, connection to historical events, Achenbach, following Dahmen and in agreement with Otto, considers the "Levitisierung" of the priesthood to have taken place in the fifth century in the combination of P^g and the non-P Sinai tradition, and the Levites only later became a "tribe." One of the most significant conclusions that Achenbach accepts, then, is that the Levites play no role in the report of Josiah's reform in 2 Kgs 23, thereby separating any connection between this historical event and the concern for Levites not found at the central sanctuary in Deut 18:6–8.[30] Rather, it is only in the wake of the events of 597/587 that saw the leading priestly families deported that circumstances could have led, "quite possibly to the Levites still living in the land to concentrate their actions in the central sanctuary)."[31] He sees no identifiable Levite involvement in the southern cult or any relation to the priests in Jerusalem before the exile. The focus for the historical background for the Levites texts is instead placed in the exilic and postexilic periods.[32]

Turning to category *four*, methodology, the differentiation of redactional layers plays a key role in the European discussion. Achenbach resolves the tension between the centralized and powerful priests of Deut 18:3 (also 17:12; 18:17; 20:2; 26:3–4) and the sojourning *personae miserae* of 18:6–8 by separating the centralized priests from those texts through the identification of redactional strata—or, more often, of short redactional plusses that ascribe these priests to a Levitical group. Although Kugler certainly allows for compositional development over the centuries, he also incorporates comparative data from ancient Near Eastern cultures, thereby seeking to reduce the tensions between the central and peripheral Levites in the Deuteronomic laws by way of complex sociological analogy.

I want to sum up my analysis to this point: When it comes to pre-Deuteronomic traditions, Kugler's understanding runs into problems when he tries to reconcile the secular and sacred origins of the Levites because he views Deut 33:8–11 as generally representing very ancient tradition. Conversely,

---

29. See also Achenbach, "Levitische Priester und Leviten."
30. Achenbach, "Levi/Leviten," 294; idem, "Levitische Priester und Leviten," 285 n. 3. Otto argues, "The major contribution of this monograph is to have finally uncoupled the 'Levitical' theme of Deuteronomy from the report of the reform of Josiah in 2 Kgs 23" ("Es ist das große Verdienst dieser Monographie, endgültig die Levitenthematik des Deuteronomiums von dem Reformbericht der Josia-Reform in 2 Kön 23 gelöst zu haben") ("Die post-deuteronomistische Levitisierung des Deuteronomiums," 284).
31. Achenbach, "Levitische Priester und Leviten," 287–88 [translation mine].
32. See comments below on the importance of Ezra for Achenbach's interpretation.

Achenbach seems to have some difficulty squaring his agnosticism about pre-Deuteronomic traditions of the Levites with the old memories of Levitical cultic action in local shrines in Judges. Judges 17–20 do seem to point to pre-Deuteronomic traditions, meaning that the Levites were not *merely* poor outsiders before or at the time of the *Urdeuteronomium*.

The European methodology focuses on the text-immanent, maximizing tensions and interpreting them as different redactional layers by way of *Tendenzkritik*,[33] leading to precise definition of the layers within Deuteronomy (Dahmen sees seven).[34] Furthermore, European scholarship simply tends to find more tensions in the texts than its North American counterpart. In fact, in Achenbach's article, he criticizes an approach similar to Kugler's for highlighting thematic overlap between texts without differentiating compositional layers in the individual texts.[35]

II. Textual Analysis of Deut 18:1–8

This second section will undertake a brief investigation of Deut 18:1–8, where both the Levitical priests and the scattered "Levites" appear. The intention of this investigation is to provide an example of how the different streams of scholarship approach a specific text. I will also include evaluation at various points from my own perspective. Na'aman brings the primary question—the Levites' relationship to the priesthood—to a head concisely in the following statement: "A crucial question in discussing the status of Levites in the Book of Deuteronomy is dating the phrase 'the Levitical priests.'"[36] Na'aman himself concludes that three appearances of "Levitical priests" belong to the seventh century (17:8–13; 24:8; and 18:1).[37] If Na'aman is correct, then Achenbach's position that the connection between the Levites and priesthood is significantly later must be rejected, though this does not mean that his methodology need be at fault. In this paper I

---

33. Thomas B. Dozeman provides a helpful definition while addressing Joshua that can also be applied more broadly: "The presupposition of redaction criticism is that the identification of the *Tendenz*, the horizon, or the contextual profile of late literary strands will indicate the relationship of Joshua to the Pentateuch and/or the Former Prophets and thus provide some control for the interpretation of its overall history of composition and its function within the larger literary context" ("The Book of Joshua as an Intertext in the MT and the LXX Canons," in *Pentateuch, Hexateuch, or Enneateuch?* [ed. T. B. Dozeman and K. Schmid; SBLAIL; Atlanta: Society of Biblical Literature, forthcoming]).

34. Dahmen, *Leviten und Priester*, 388–91.

35. Achenbach, "Levitische Priester und Leviten," 297 n. 47. In this case, Achenbach argues against the analysis by Stephen L. Cook, "Innerbiblical Interpretation in Ezekiel 44 and the History of Israel's Priesthood," *JBL* 114 (1995): 193–208.

36. Na'aman, "Sojourners and Levites," 262.

37. These occurrences "reflect the idea that the priests suitable for serve [*sic*] in the central temple were of Levitical origin (and by inference, that non-Levitical priests could not carry these duties)" (ibid., 264).

will address only one of Na'aman's suggested preexilic appearances of "the Levitical priests" (18:1) in detail.

The passage Deut 18:1–8 clearly begins a new section in v. 1, which turns the focus to priests. In v. 9 the discussion turns to others matters, giving the section a clear ending. Whether v. 1 is original to Deuteronomy or rather a later addition can be disputed. A possible alternative beginning would be v. 3, וזה יהיה משפט הכהנים, which could be compared to Deut 15:2; 19:4 (both begin וזה דבר).[38] In these verses the statement does not stand as the absolute introduction to a section, so claiming that v. 3 was the original introduction to the Deuteronomic law of the priest requires several hypothetical and questionable steps. There are some signs of pre-Deuteronomic character in v. 3: the identification of the הזבח זבחי, is unusual for Deuteronomy, which generally avoids the use of the זבח offering (12:6, 11, 27 are the only other appearances in the Deuteronomic Code, none of which is typically viewed as part of *Urdeuteronomium*).[39] A similar argument with regard to terminology can be made for הזרע והלחיים והקבה. Debate exists concerning the fact that the priests in v. 3 are not called "Levites." Achenbach could possibly claim this as clear evidence for his position. Yet this is not the case if v. 3 consists of pre-Deuteronomic material, as he also accepts.[40]

Viewing v. 1—in some form—as the Deuteronomic beginning of this text requires, then, that the rule of the priestly provision begin with a negative statement of some sort, but this need not present a problem: 12:13 also begins with a prohibition. Within this verse itself, however, a clear doublet occurs in the renaming of the Levitical priests as "the whole tribe of Levi."[41] I would

---

38. Dahmen finds that the closest parallel to beginning with v. 3 is 1 Sam 8:11 (זה יהיה משפט המלך)—without *wāw* (*Leviten und Priester*, 276).

39. Alexander Rofé represents a minority position that views Deut 11:31–12:7 and 12:8–12 as the earliest layers ("The Strata of the Law about the Centralization of Worship in Deuteronomy and the History of the Deuteronomic Movement," in *Deuteronomy: Issues and Interpretation* [London: T&T Clark, 2002], 97–101). Most scholars find the original layer located in 12:13–27, usually within vv. 13–19 (though not necessarily everything in these verses).

40. Achenbach ("Levitische Priester und Leviten," 290) concludes, "The [earliest] literary kernel of the text has always been assumed—and as is now newly proved by Dahmen—to lie in v. 1* (without, ונחלתו, הלוים כל שבט לוי), 3–4" ("Der literarische Kern des Textes wird seit jeher und jetzt erneut durch Dahmen bestätigt in v. 1* [ohne הלוים, ונחלתו כל שבט לוי]. 3–4 angenommen"). He sees v. 3 as pre-Deuteronomic and v. 4 as "new Deuteronomic" material (ibid.).

41. As for the matter of the נחלתו, neither what it refers to nor whether it is redactional will be addressed here since it does not pertain directly to relationship between the Levites and Levitical priests. Udo Rüterswörden convincingly argues for the redactional nature of נחלתו because of its dependence on כל שבט לוי (*Von der politischen Gemeinschaft zur Gemeinde: Studien zu Dt 16,18–18,22* [BBB 65; Frankfurt a. M.: Athenäum, 1987], 70). Interpreters from both continents see v. 2 as redactional (e.g., Nelson, *Deuteronomy*, 229;

argue on this basis that כל־שבט לוי should be viewed as a secondary insertion, made with the notion of Deut 10:8–9 in mind.⁴²

Achenbach goes a step further and argues that *Levitical* for the priests as a whole in v. 1 is inescapably connected with the backwards reference from v. 2,⁴³ which alludes to Deut 10:8–9.⁴⁴ For him, the historical origins of this Levitical tariff are found in connection not with centralization but with the postexilic *Fortschreibung* that was composed with the intention of motivating Levites to return to the land with Ezra (cf. Ezra 8:15–20). It should be noted that Achenbach also finds support in the fact that Ezra does not make any explicit note of the establishment of a decidedly "Levitical" priesthood.⁴⁵ Yet one should notice here that Achenbach has simply dropped one posited historical context (Josiah's idealized centralization, according to Kugler, or Sennacherib's destruction of Judah, according to Na'aman) for another (Ezra's return to the land). I would suggest that Achenbach makes this step because there is no *text-internal* indication for adducing "Levitical" as an addition.

Alfred Bertholet, *Deuteronomium* [KHAT 5; Freiburg: J. C. B. Mohr, 1899], 57; Gottfried Seitz, *Redaktionsgeschichtliche Studien zum Deuteronomium* [BWANT 93; Stuttgart: Kohlhammer, 1971], 90).

42. Similarly, see Na'aman, who separates the identification of a Levitical tribe—which he dates to the Second Temple period—from the association of the Levites with priestly duties—which he places in the preexilic period ("Sojourners and Levites," 263; earlier also Bertholet, *Deuteronomium*, 57; and Seitz, *Redaktionsgeschichtliche Studien*, 205). Rodney K. Duke notes the redundancy but, instead of suggesting that one phrase is a later insertion, suggests that "the whole tribe of Levi" is instead an "explanatory apposition that expands on the first element, [so] we conclude that the author, motivated by a concern for their socioeconomic situation, wanted to effect legislation in behalf of the Levitical priests—indeed, in behalf of the larger group, the whole tribe of Levi" ("The Portion of the Levite: Another Reading of Deuteronomy 18:6–8," *JBL* 106 [1987]: 198). Kugler does not, however, differentiate layers in Deut 18 ("Levi, Levites," 643).

43. Achenbach "Levitische Priester und Leviten," 292. The entire German statement is as follows: "The introduction of the epithet 'Levitical' for the priests of the central sanctuary in Deut 18:1 inescapably involves, in connection with the introduction of a tariff regulation for the non-priestly Levites, the (largely literal!) reference to this verse (v. 1 *kl šbṭ lwj*, v. 2)" ("Die Einführung des Epitetons 'levitisch' für die Priester des Zentralheiligtums in Dtn 18,1 hat in Verbindung mit der Einführung einer Tarifregelung für die nicht-priesterlichen Leviten zwangsläufig den [weitgehend wörtlichen!] Rückverweis auf diesen Text zur Folge [V.1 *kl šbṭ lwj*, V.2]"). Seitz also dates הלוים in 18:1 later (to an exilic layer), but he still understands 18:6–8 and the phrase הכהנים הלוים in 17:9 as preexilic (*Redaktionsgeschichtliche Studien*, 89–90).

44. In Deut 10:8–9 the Levites are separated after Aaron's death and Eliezer's rise to priesthood, at Yatebatah. This could be an addition to the context, or if nothing else, it is an aside. Why does it crop up at this point? There seems no purpose for it, other than that the focus turned (1) to the priesthood (v. 6: death of Aaron) and (2) to the ark (v. 5: as receptacle for the two tablets).

45. Achenbach, "Levitische Priester und Leviten," 306.

Each commentator's conclusion remains in line with the underlying methodology described above in my third category.

One might argue that the appearance of the priests in other parts of the Deuteronomic Code *without* the descriptor "Levitical" supports the contention that a non-Levitical priesthood had existed previously. Support could be found in Deut 20:2–4, where the mention of a priest appears without the modifier "Levitical." However, as Dahmen notes, Deut 20:1–9 is often viewed as a later insertion as a whole, making its relevance here limited.[46]

The case of Deut 21 is more complicated: here the priests are called, in v. 5, בני לוי כי בם בחר יהוה אלהיך לשרתו ולברך בשם יהוה על־פיהם יהיה כל־ריב וכל־נגע ("the sons of Levi, whom Yhwh your God chose to serve him and to bless the name of Yhwh and according to whose word every dispute and punishment shall be"). It has often been asked whether this verse is actually part of the earliest Deuteronomic layer.[47] Dahmen contends that a redactor inserted v. 5 to take the cultic and ritual action out of the hands of the laity, here meaning the elders.[48] So Deut 21:5 (MT) calls the priests "sons of Levi," a term that otherwise appears in Deuteronomy only in 31:9, itself a text displaying many differences from Deut 12–26.[49]

I would suggest that the burden of proof lies with those who want to view "Levitical" as later, given that the text-internal reasons (e.g., consideration of the term as a doublet) to view it as an addition are insufficient to warrant this conclusion.

Assuming that "Levitical" belongs to *Urdeuteronomium*, then there does not seem to be a logical reason for a *second* mention of "Levitical" in v. 3, which was likely taken over from a pre-Deuteronomic tradition, as argued above. The Levitical nature of the priests has just been mentioned, so this need not be restated with such an insertion into this pre-Deuteronomic text. I would judge v. 4 as Deuteronomic as well, given both its similarity to Deuteronomic lists of produce elsewhere and its significant difference from P's provisions for the priest.[50] Neither Kugler nor Achenbach discusses vv. 3–4, which should be expected, given that these verses are easily included in either theory of *Urdeuteronomium*.

---

46. Dahmen, *Leviten und Priester*, 345.
47. For a brief overview of the history of scholarship, see ibid., 321–25.
48. Ibid., 325.
49. The OG (LXX) of Deut 21:5 instead renders οἱ ἱερεῖς οἱ Λευῖται; otherwise, the phrase "the sons of Levi" is found in Deut 31:9 (MT and OG), Josh 21:10; 1 Kgs 13:31; and Ezek 40:46.
50. Bertholet notes Exod 29:27; Lev 7:31–34; 10:14; Num 6:20; 18:18 (*Deuteronomium*, 57); for the Deuteronomic nature of v. 4, see also Gerhard von Rad, *Das fünfte Buch Mose: Deuteronomium* (4th ed.; ATD 8; Göttingen: Vandenhoeck & Ruprecht, 1983), 87; and Martin Rose, *5. Moses: Teilband 1: 5. Mose 12–25: Einführung und Gesetze* (ZBK; Zurich: TVZ, 1994), 86–87.

Numerous similarities with 10:8–9; 21:5; and 31:9 point to the possibility—or likelihood—that 18:5 is a later insertion, so claims for the originally Levitical affiliation of the priesthood in Deuteronomy cannot be supported from this verse.[51] Such a conclusion could fit with either theory, though Kugler's narrative of the functional group growing into a tribe fits well with the contention that 18:5 and related statements are later additions.[52]

This brings me to the end of the first half of the section. To summarize, I will propose a minimum text for *Urdeuteronomium*. My methodology follows that of Achenbach in providing detailed redaction-historical analysis—though only with regard to the earliest Deuteronomic layer. My interest in this early layer and the inclusion of the modifier "Levitical" in this layer for priests, however, matches the North American discussion more precisely. I am not, however, assigning an absolute date here. Perhaps this analysis assumes more dissonance in this layer than Achenbach's methodology would allow (category four), given that I also assume that some phrases concerning "the Levites in your gates" in chs. 12, 14, and 16 belong to this stratum. Furthermore, I have avoided cross-cultural analysis so far. Here is my proposed text for this section of *Urdeuteronomium* (vv. 1*, 3–4; in the English translation, the bold font matches the Hebrew, the normal font represents my hypothesized later additions):

לא יהיה לכהנים הלוים חלק ונחלה עם ישראל אשי יהוה יאכלון
וזה יהיה משפט הכהנים מאת העם מאת זבחי זבח אם שור אם שה
ונתן לכהן הזרע הלחיים והקבה ראשית דגנך תירשך ויצהרך
וראשית גז צאנך תתן לו

The Levitical priests, the whole tribe of Levi, **shall have no allotment or inheritance within Israel. They may eat the *'iššēh*[53] of the Lord** and his portion, ² but he shall have no inheritance among his brothers. The Lord, he is their inheritance, just as he promised them. ³ **This shall be the priests' due from the people, from those offering a sacrifice, whether an ox or a sheep: they shall give to the priest the shoulder, the two jowls, and the stomach.** ⁴ **The first fruits of your grain, your wine, and your oil, as well as the first of the fleece of your sheep, you shall give him.** ⁵ For the Lord your God has chosen him from all your tribes, to stand and minister in the name of the Lord, him and his sons for all time.

---

51. See Nelson, who notes the interest in the whole tribe in 10:8–9, "serve" and "stand before" in 10:8 (*Deuteronomy*, 229). Rüderswörden, however, sees only מכל־שבטיך as added (*Von der politischen Gemeinschaft zur Gemeinde*, 71).

52. Kugler, however, sets all of this action of "leviticizing the priesthood" still in the late preexilic period ("Priests and Levites," 604).

53. The meaning of this word is notoriously difficult. Achenbach provides a helpful introduction, suggesting mostly from the Priestly material that it is the portion of an offering brought directly before the deity and consumed there representatively by the high priest as the most holy portion ("Levitische Priester und Leviten," 294–95).

I turn now to the second section, about which interpretations are even more divergent: Deut 18:6–8. Interpretation of this section is hampered by (1) whether the duties that the Levites could perform in the sanctuary were priestly, (2) whether the ordinance was for all Levites, and (3) what sort of sociohistorical context this section fits best.

If one glances first at the terminology present, the section begins with the mention of "the Levite from one of your gates from all Israel where he sojourns" (הלוי מאחד שעריך מכל־ישראל אשר־הוא גר שם), which has definite links to, but is different from, the description "the Levite who is in your gates" (הלוי אשר בשעריך; see Deut 14:27, 29; 16:11, 14). The description of this Levite as one who resides in any town of all Israel distinguishes him from the priests at the central sanctuary; however, the chosen place is not mentioned earlier in this section (it does show up as the destination of the Levite in v. 6b) and can therefore be seen as only *implicitly* present. This distinction is quite important, of course, because if one follows my identification of the Levitical priesthood in v. 1 as original, this verse would firmly ground the identification of two groups of Levites. The first group would comprise those Levites directly connected to the central sanctuary, either as altar priests as in 18:3 or as judges as in 17:9.[54] The second group would be those Levites whose connection to or privileges at the central sanctuary must be confirmed here. Furthermore, this "Levite" is mentioned in the singular, and not as one of the group of "Levitical priests." Inclusion of both groups requires a sociological-historical explanation with greater complexity, akin to the North American solutions.

Verse 6 as a whole contains significant overlapping terminology with the earliest section of Deut 12, vv. 13–18/19: the mention of desire (בכל־אות נפשו; cf. 12:15);[55] of one of the locations (אחד; 12:14, although this connection is weakened by the lack of closer terminological links); the use of the second person masculine singular suffix; and, of course, the mention of the place YHWH

---

54. There is, of course, disagreement about whether "Levitical" is original to 17:9. Bernard M. Levinson argues in favor of the word's originality (*Deuteronomy and the Hermeneutics of Legal Innovation* [New York: Oxford University Press, 1997], 98–137), while Jan C. Gertz argues against: "An initial indication that הלוים is secondary in v. 9a is to be found in 19:17. The verse refers back to 17:9, but does not mention that it deals with Levites when speaking about priests. In addition, the designation of the priests as 'Levites' fits well with additional supplements to 17:8–13, which reveal themselves as secondary on other grounds" ("Ein erster Hinweis darauf, daß הלוים in V.9a sekundär ist, findet sich in 19,17. Der Vers greift auf 17,9 zurück, erwähnt aber nicht, dass er sich bei den Priestern um Leviten handelt. Es kommt hinzu, daß die Bezeichnung der Priester als Leviten gut zu weiteren Nachträgen in 17,8-13 paßt, die sich auch aus anderen Gründen als sekundär erweisen") (*Die Gerichtsorganisation Israels im deuteronomischen Gesetz* [FRLANT 165; Göttingen: Vandenhoeck & Ruprecht, 1994], 67).

55. Nelson suggests that this phrase is used "perhaps intending to discourage casual claims" (*Deuteronomy*, 227), yet this seems to run counter to the usage in 12:15.

has chosen (short form, which in my mind means that it could come from any layer, unlike the long formula with שׁם, which points to later layers).⁵⁶

Rodney Duke, following an earlier debate by G. E. Wright and J. A. Emerton that is also continued in a new form in Hutton's anthropological comparison, asks the important question whether all Levites could function as priests. This inquiry finds its solution in the syntax of vv. 6–8.⁵⁷ Contra Wellhausen, Duke argues that these verses address an occasional situation, rather than the right of all Levites. This contention separates the situation narrated in 2 Kgs 23:8–9 from Deut 18, similarly to the schema proposed by Achenbach.⁵⁸ Nelson interprets the force of these verses to lie in the equality of payment for services rendered, "equal work for equal pay," rather than in asserting the rights of all Levites to serve as altar priests at the central sanctuary.⁵⁹ Depending on how many Levites there might have been, the possibility of *all* Levites serving as altar priests quickly becomes impracticable (however, this impossibility is not necessarily problematic within the idealizing picture often presented in

---

56. Peter Altmann, "Deuteronomy's Festive Meals: The Interplay of Politics and Religion in Their Ancient Near Eastern Context" (Ph.D. diss., Princeton Theological Seminary, 2010), 90–93.

57. Duke, "Portion of the Levite," 195–201. Nelson accepts Duke's analysis (*Deuteronomy*, 227–32). G. Ernest Wright questions Wellhausen's dominant position ("The Levites in Deuteronomy," VT 4 [1954]: 325–30). J. A. Emerton provides what in my mind are compelling rebuttals of Wright's assertions ("Priests and Levites in Deuteronomy: An Examination of Dr. G. E. Wright's Theory," VT 12 [1962]: esp. the syntactical analysis on 132–33). Carl Steuernagel translated "die levitischen Priester," stating that the distinction was between priests from this tribe and from others, or from foreign priests. He denies that "the whole tribe of Levi" can be in apposition to "Levitical priests" arguing that Deuteronomy knows of Levites who are not priests, "although they have priestly privileges" ("obwohl sie Priesterrecht haben"). But while he considers both expressions to be later additions, he opts for "the whole tribe of Levi" as earlier (*Das Deuteronomium* [HKAT 3.1; Göttingen: Vandenhoeck & Ruprecht, 1898], 67).

58. As Wright argued, if not all Levites were, or could be, priests, then the differences between P and D are not necessarily that dramatic in this regard ("Levites in Deuteronomy," 330). The connection between Deut 18 and 2 Kgs 23 was assumed in earlier commentaries such as Bertholet, *Deuteronomium*, 57–58; Steuernagel, *Deuteronomium*, 68; and von Rad, *5. Mose*, 87.

59. Nelson, *Deuteronomy*, 227; J. Gordon McConville, *Law and Theology in Deuteronomy* (JSOTSup 33; Sheffield: JSOT Press, 1984), 146–47. He states, "Such relocation is not described as a universal phenomenon, however, nor is the acceptance of such hopeful job seekers mandated or necessarily automatic" (ibid., 229). Given the strong Priestly connotations of the terms "stand before" and "serve the name of YHWH," I do not find Raymond Abba's distinction ("Priests and Levites in Deuteronomy," VT 27 [1977]: 257–67; also Duke, "Portion of the Levite," 199) convincing, in light of the emphasis in 10:8–9 and especially given the connection of 18:1–5 and v. 7 between these duties and the priesthood (see already Steuernagel, *Deuteronomium*, 68). At a minimum, the redactor inserting v. 5 (if redactional) interpreted altar priesthood this way.

Deuteronomy). Yet interpretations such as these that deny the identity of the "brother Levites" in 18:7 with the Levitical priests in the earlier verses must turn to evidence outside the passage itself to reach this conclusion, though the terminological connection to the "Levitical priests" is certainly weak.[60]

Yet again, one might wonder why the incumbent Jerusalemite priests would be willing to share their turf—their offerings—with the outsider "Levite in your gates." However, given the implied addressees of Deuteronomy (the heads of household, the "you"), perhaps the opinions of the central priests did not need to be represented.[61] Therefore, in the end, I would suggest that Deuteronomy does not necessarily have all these power dynamics in view. Such an interpretation unduly limits the possibilities for the construction of a "literary reality" that may or may not speak to a particular historically placed question.

Perhaps more central for Deut 18 and the Deuteronomic law as a whole is the concern to provide for all legitimate "Israelites," defining this term idealistically to include all southerners and northerners who might choose to rally to the banner of Deuteronomic religion.[62] In the case of Deut 18:6-8 the group of concern are those functioning as religious personnel (there seems little reason to assume that "Levite" was a noncultic designation at this point: Gen 34 and 49:5-8, which are related in their approach, are the only texts that do not fit this profile).[63] They are to be cared for in accordance with *their* desire,

---

60. Contra Wright ("Levites in Deuteronomy," 329), even if the Levites did not all serve at the altar, there does not seem to be any way that Deut 18:6-8 designates this Levite who travels to the sanctuary as *anything other than* an altar priest, regardless of whether he also performed other duties. Compare the analysis of Emerton, who does not, however, pick up on the redactional nature of "the whole tribe of Levi" in v. 1 ("Priests and Levites in Deuteronomy," 136). That locution may imply that "Levites" had been a functional designation of a group but not of a tribe. Nelson's statement is the most judicious: "Properly translated, 18:6-8 takes for granted that some Levites would assume priestly office, but does not require that every single Levite be permitted to do so" (*Deuteronomy*, 232). Yet by being so cautious (esp. using the term "require") the definition is less than fulfilling: there is much that Deuteronomy encourages and promotes without necessarily requiring it. McConville admits, even while arguing against the interpretation that all Levites could serve as altar priests according to Deut 18, "It is true that there does not appear to be much difference between 'priests' and 'Levites' in 18.1-8" (*Law and Theology in Deuteronomy*, 143). He must move outside this passage, especially to 27:9-14 and 31:9, 25 to make the argument that D knows of the P differentiation between priests and the Levites as *clerus menor*.

61. Bertholet, for example, calls Deuteronomy *Volksgesetz* (*Deuteronomium*, 56).

62. By including northerners I am arguing against Na'aman's proposal that sees only southern Levite refugees from Sennacherib's invasion as the target of these ordinances ("Sojourners and Levites," 239). That northerners could not be viewed as possible members of "all Israel," is a key plank for his argument, but I do not see why this must be the case: they speak the same language, they worship the same deity, and many biblical texts view the two divided kingdoms under one banner.

63. McConville, *Law and Theology in Deuteronomy*, 144. Cody argues for an originally secular tribe as presented in the biblical narrative, citing Gen 29:31-30:24; 35:16-26;

implying (to my mind) that somehow—realistic or not—what was provided by the consortium of Yhwh, their "Israelite" community, and their "Levitical priest" brothers (see Deut 18:7) would be plenty. In fact, if the apodosis of vv. 6–7 begins in v. 8 (with the change from *yiqtol* + *weqatal* + *weqatal* to *yiqtol*), then the passage takes for granted that the scattered Levites had the right to serve at the central sanctuary.[64]

Indeed, there is a considerable connection between the beginning and end of 18:1–8: both the first and the last verses bring up the payment (חלק, אשי יהוה) and "eating" (יאכלו), thus beginning and ending with priestly tariffs, which ties the section as a whole together.[65] This terminological affinity might support the contention that vv. 6–8 are part of the earliest layer, though a redactor could have constructed this congruence as well.[66]

III. Summary

As a conclusion, I suggest that we understand "the Levites in your gates" to be those who could no longer serve as local priests because of centralization or because of the loss of their sanctuaries. Perhaps this came as a result of Sennacherib's destruction of Judah but not Jerusalem, or the earlier destruction of the northern kingdom. I presume that both events would have included the foreign destruction of Israelite and Judahite sanctuaries and could therefore be taken as bringing about *de facto* centralization. However, simply because it would make sense does not constitute a strong argument for the dating of a text! Such centralization was certainly not seen as theologically mandated by all groups of Israelites or Judahites (if it was even known to them), as empirically supported by the Elephantine writings and the tradition of Deut 27. Unfortunately, these cannot be much more than suggestions on the basis of text-internal data. This is, then, where analyses of the text and

---

48:8–25; 49; Exod 1:2ff.; Deut 27:12–13; 33; Ezek 48:31–35; and 1 Chr 2:1–2 (*History of Old Testament Priesthood*, 34). Of these texts, only Gen 29–30; 49 warrant consideration. Generally speaking, Cody's analysis is backwards in light of the genealogies used in Ezra 2:40 + 61–63; cf. Neh 7:43 ("In fact, in P, after the Exile, the term 'Levite' had already had its sense altered from that of a tribal name to that of a name of a functional class" [p. 34 n. 116]). He notes Hölscher's earlier argument that Gen 34 and 49 are an etiological saga, commenting that this does not mean that there was not an originally secular tribe (Cody, 37). Given the current lack of credibility for a nomadic group of early Israelites, it makes more sense to me for a story of origins to be a story used by the later religious personnel to concretize their sense of belonging. Genesis 34 is generally seen as a Priestly text, and views on Gen 49 range from premonarchic to post-Priestly (see the essay by Joel Baden in the present volume).

64. McConville, *Law and Theology in Deuteronomy*, 146, 151; Nelson, *Deuteronomy*, 227.

65. Seitz, *Redaktionsgeschichtliche Studien*, 90; Nelson, *Deuteronomy*, 229.

66. As noted above, Lohfink finds reason to see vv. 6–8 as exilic ("Distribution of the Functions of Power," 356).

religious-historical background in ancient Israel leave their foundations and become more speculative, and where sociological parallels more typical of the North American context (my category *two*), such as the one offered by Jeremy Hutton, prove most helpful, though of course also somewhat exotic as well.[67] The fundamental connection and distinction between the "Levite in your gates" and the "Levitical priests" does not emerge from the Deuteronomic text itself. This conclusion borders on the banal, yet its restatement fosters a renewed perception with regard to the variation of scholarly discourses. The observation that the text itself provides too little data has led Kugler and North American scholars to both (1) propose sociological comparisons that fit best with these scholars' tendency to date texts earlier, and (2) allow more dissonance within any particular textual stratum. The same situation has led Achenbach and European scholars to make a separation between centralized priests (18:1, 3–4) and the sojourning Levites whose claim to priestly status is made in vv. 1, 6–8. Both discourses turn to a biblically inscribed historical event: North Americans are more amenable to viewing the fall of the northern kingdom, Sennacherib's invasion of Judah, or Josiah's reform as the precipitating event; Achenbach instead imagines the call for Levite participation in the return from exile in Ezra 8 as a decisive chronological marker.

Both discussions allow for the pre-Deuteronomic status of the priestly tariff in Deut 18:3, but the question of pre-Deuteronomic material concerning the Levites remains contentious. Further agreement is found on the insertion of "the whole tribe of Levi" in v. 1, which members of both geographic discourses view as a later step in the redactional process. I do not see textual grounds to move beyond the Wright–Emerton impasse concerning whether *all* Levites were originally considered priests by the Deuteronomic layer, although this assertion was subsequently made explicit through this insertion in v. 1 and its related material in 10:8–9.

Perhaps what can be learned on the side of the North American discussion is that there are good *textual* reasons for Achenbach's applications of redaction criticism. He does well to pick up on the tensions in the text. On the flip side, European scholars may benefit by taking note of the various ways that comparative cultures live with such structural tensions: these need not belong to historically separate societies (though this may be the case). Finally, both groups may help toward establishing a shared dialogue between scholarly cultures and languages by admitting and clearly stating the biblical-historical (e.g., 2 Kgs 23 or Ezra 8) backgrounds they are using as the context for their readings.

---

67. Hutton, "The Levitical Diaspora (I): A Sociological Comparison with Morocco's Ahansal," 229.

THOSE STUBBORN LEVITES:
OVERCOMING LEVITICAL DISENFRANCHISEMENT

Stephen L. Cook

Through much of Israel's monarchic period, at least until the seventh-century reforms of King Josiah, the Levitical priesthood experienced varying degrees of disenfranchisement from the establishment cults of the northern and southern kingdoms. I aim in this essay to unearth evidence that this peripheral status of the Levites finally began to change by Josiah's time. The group's tenacious insistence on maintaining their traditional priestly prerogatives finally paid off. However, their comeback came relatively late for them—toward the end of Judah's history as a state. The development of Judah and Israel as complex, centralized social systems worked entirely against the orientation and values of the Levitical priestly line, which was rooted in the decentralized, lineage-based culture of premonarchic Israel.

To appreciate the history of the Levites' position in ancient Israelite society, it is crucial to recognize that preexilic Israel developed as a monarchic state out of an earlier acephalous, segmentary tribal organization. Due to a combination of factors, including population growth, technological advancement, and external military pressure, Israelite society underwent consolidation as a state-based political entity. It moved away from decentralized, kinship-based social structures toward a more complex, stratified organization with a variety of supra-tribal capacities. Israel's new centralized societal system could never completely replace the earlier village system, however, and the two societal organizations coexisted in tension and conflict side by side for centuries. The Levites had their social roots within the earlier "tribal" system. They understood themselves to be bound together as a family line, descending from their eponymous ancestor Levi. They maintained many traditional values and assumptions, and fought to preserve them in the face of many new challenges that confronted them.[1]

---

1. On the emergence of Israelite monarchy out of an earlier, lineage-based organization of society, see Jeremy Hutton, "All the King's Men: The Families of the Priests in Cross-Cultural Perspective," in *Seitenblicke: Literarische und historische Studien zu Nebenfiguren im zweiten Samuelbuch* (ed. Walter Dietrich; OBO 249; Fribourg: Academic Press; Göttingen: Vandenhoeck & Ruprecht, 2011), 124, 141–42, 144–45; Robert D. Miller, *Chieftains of the Highland Clans: A History of Israel in the 12th and 11th Centuries B.C.* (Grand Rapids:

The growth of the Israelite monarchy could not immediately dissipate the traditional prestige and authority of rural priestly Levitical family lines. In their old, village-based organization, these tribal lines identified with, ministered to, and interpenetrated the whole of society, independent of geographic, political, and economic borders and strictures. The Levites' traditional self-understanding of their role as a priestly sodality and "social glue" within the tribes of old Israel is particularly visible in Ps 16.[2] There, to help voice a prayer song of trust, the psalmist makes metaphorical use of specific language pertaining directly and literally to the lifestyle of a traditional Levite.

While other tribes possessed tenure on inalienable, patrimonial land, the Levites of village Israel had Yahweh alone as their special "portion" (חלק, Ps 16:5; cf. Deut 10:9). God and God's sacred offerings were their sole "heritage" (נחלה, Ps 16:6; cf. Josh 13:14). This arrangement buttressed their role as religious and social mediators among the tribes of Israel. It gave them genealogical independence from the competing, rival tribes around them, and it dispersed them geographically among these segments.

As Israelite society regrouped and entrenched itself as a centralized monarchy, the Levites strove to preserve their society-wide, village-oriented roles performing the Lord's ritual service, arbitrating judicial matters, and fostering societal harmony. In the era of the divided kingdoms, however, the Levites were forced to perdure in the face of an ever-stronger, centralized organization of society that increasingly rendered older assumptions and institutions

---

Eerdmans, 2005); Stephen L. Cook, *The Social Roots of Biblical Yahwism* (SBLStBL 8; Leiden: Brill; Atlanta: Society of Biblical Literature, 2004), 143–94; Steven L. McKenzie, *King David: A Biography* (Oxford/New York: Oxford University Press, 2000), 138–45; Frank S. Frick, *The Formation of the State in Ancient Israel: A Survey of Models and Theories* (SWBA 4; Sheffield/Decatur, Ga.: Almond, 1985). As Hutton notes, the Israelites at first experienced only a developing or nascent state-based organization, in which kinship structures still had a role to play ("All the King's Men," 138–39). The perduring role of kinship sensibilities as state formation progressed in Israel is recognized in the relatively recent characterization of the united monarchy as a "patrimonial state." This characterization is based on a model derived from the social-scientific typologies of Max Weber. See Lawrence E. Stager, "The Patrimonial Kingdom of Solomon," in *Symbiosis, Symbolism, and the Power of the Past: Canaan, Ancient Israel, and their Neighbors from the Late Bronze Age through Roman Palaestina. Proceedings of the Centennial Symposium, W. F. Albright Institute of Archaeological Research and American Schools of Oriental Research, Jerusalem, May 29/31, 2000* (ed. William G. Dever and Seymour Gitin; Winona Lake, Ind.: Eisenbrauns, 2003), 63–74; J. David Schloen, *The House of the Father as Fact and Symbol: Patrimonialism in Ugarit and the Ancient Near East* (SAHL 2; Winona Lake, Ind: Eisenbrauns, 2001); Daniel Master, "State Formation Theory and the Kingdom of Ancient Israel," *JNES* 60 (2001): 117–31.

2. For discussion, see Cook, *Social Roots*, 265–66; Norman K. Gottwald, *The Tribes of Yahweh: A Sociology of the Religion of Liberated Israel, 1250–1050 B.C.E.* (Maryknoll, N.Y.: Orbis Books, 1979), 320, 333; Hans-Joachim Kraus, *Psalms 1–59: A Commentary* (trans. Hilton C. Oswald; Minneapolis: Augsburg, 1988), 235–41.

peripheral, impractical, or irrelevant. As Jeremy Hutton aptly puts it, in this cultural milieu traditional priestly arbiters of political and judicial affairs are "a dying breed . . . their traditional loci of power threatened by new administrative systems."[3] In my view, their actions and words surface in monarchic-era biblical texts—in the book of Deuteronomy, for example—as evidence of activist traditionalists working to turn back the clock, defending old ideas and values with new vigor and imagination.

The Levites' concern to check centralized monarchic powers and protect the interests of the periphery is clear in the book of Deuteronomy, where Levitical interests are always prominent.[4] In a recent lengthy article on the Levites, Mark Christian describes Deuteronomy's remarkable challenge to contemporary centrist ideologies, especially that of the Assyrian monarchs. In Assyria, Christian notes, "the sovereign retains exclusive control over the production and maintenance of law."[5] By contrast, Deuteronomy advocates nurturing Israel as an integrated assembly of human beings in mutual interrelationship (a קהל, Deut 5:22), an assembly constituted not by coercion but by a covenant with Yahweh.[6]

---

3. Hutton, "All the King's Men," 145. Hutton notes how, as the "variety of [the Levites'] social roles was increasingly restricted in the face of the Israelite and Judean monarchies, these groups were relegated to progressively more specialized tasks" (p. 124). For discussion of how the monarchy's new state systems of liturgical and sacrificial practice began to erode traditional worship systems, see Cook, *Social Roots,* 181–85.

4. It was Gerhard von Rad's classic, breakthrough arguments that impressed on the scholarly world the key role of the Levites as bearers of the values and traditions that crystalized in Deuteronomy (for a good, recent review, see Peter T. Vogt, *Deuteronomic Theology and the Significance of Torah: A Reappraisal* [Winona Lake, Ind.: Eisenbrauns, 2006], 36–37). See also Cook, *Social Roots,* 62 n. 39 and the bibliography cited there; Robert G. Boling, "Levitical History and the Role of Joshua," in *The Word of the Lord Shall Go Forth: Essays in Honor of David Noel Freedman in Celebration of His Sixtieth Birthday* (ed. Carol L. Meyers and M. O'Connor; Winona Lake, Ind.: Eisenbrauns, 1983), 242–44; Richard Elliott Friedman, *Who Wrote the Bible?* (1987; San Francisco: Harper & Row, 1997), 120–24. For an up-to-date annotated bibliography of scholarship on Deuteronomy, see Stephen L. Cook, "Deuteronomy," in Oxford Bibliographies Online (published online September 2010), accessible at: http://www.oxfordbibliographiesonline.com/browse (DOI: 10.1093/obo/9780195393361-0029).

5. Mark A. Christian, "Priestly Power that Empowers: Michel Foucault, Middle-Tier Levites, and the Sociology of 'Popular Religious Groups' in Israel," *JHS* 9 (2009): art. 1, 52.

6. See, e.g., Eckart Otto, *Das Deuteronomium im Pentateuch und Hexateuch: Studien zur Literaturgeschichte von Pentateuch und Hexateuch im Lichte des Deuteronomiumrahmens* (FAT 30; Tübingen: Mohr Siebeck, 2000), 124. A powerful current trend in biblical scholarship envisions Deuteronomy emerging in dialogue with the imperialistic and monopolistic claims of Assyria of the eighth and seventh centuries B.C.E. Challenging these claims, the political theology of Deuteronomy advocated inclusivism over against domination; it spoke up for the weak over against the tyranny of the strong. Deuteronomy's critique took aim not just at Assyria but at Judah's own monarchic society. On the Assyrian setting

Moses introduces the covenant in Deut 5:1 by summoning everyone to gather together as one assembly, as "all Israel." His command to them, "Hear," is an imperative in the singular, addressing them as a singular "Thou." The covenant confronts Israel as a singular body, a collective whole oriented around God's presence. It pushes all individuals, even monarchs, to leave the quest for personal power and privilege behind and partake of a larger, shared, and integrated life. Israel's king is to be a covenantal "brother" (אח, Deut 17:15). By diligently observing the covenant, he is to learn "to fear the LORD his God," never "exalting himself above other members of the community [אחיו, 'his brothers']" (Deut 17:19–20).

In a world where the elite of Assyria arrogated imperial authority to themselves, Deuteronomy's political vision of an integrated society characterized by human mutuality and a tempered and checked monarchy is downright astonishing. Deuteronomy 17:8–13 describes the final arbiters of law and order in Israel as the Levitical priests, not the king. If a legal case proves too difficult to adjudicate at the local level, then one must "go up to the place that the LORD your God will choose, where you shall consult with *the levitical priests*" (vv. 8–9; see also 19:17). The final decision on such cases reposes in the senior cleric (v. 12).

The Levites, not the monarch and his state bureaucrats, are those qualified to render final judgment based on their vocational expertise in covenantal instruction and interpretation (v. 10; cf. 17:18; 31:9, 25–26; 33:10; 2 Kgs 17:27–28). The king's basic task according to Deut 17:18–20 is to continuously study his copy of the law, carefully certified by the Levites as true and correct (cf. Deut 31:9). He has no judicial responsibilities, a pointed contrast to the assumptions of other biblical traditions such as those of Ps 72:1–4; 1 Sam 8:5–6; 1 Kgs 3:9; Isa 9:7; 11:2–5.[7]

---

of Deuteronomy's politics, see further Moshe Weinfeld, *Deuteronomy and the Deuteronomic School* (Oxford: Clarendon, 1972); Hans Ulrich Steymans, *Deuteronomium 28 und die adê zur Thronfolgeregelung Asarhaddons: Segen und Fluch im Alten Orient und in Israel* (OBO 145; Fribourg: Academic Press; Göttingen: Vandenhoeck & Ruprecht, 1995); Bernard M. Levinson, *Deuteronomy and the Hermeneutics of Legal Innovation* (New York: Oxford University Press, 1997); J. G. McConville, *God and Earthly Power: An Old Testament Political Theology. Genesis-Kings* (LHBOTS 454; London/New York: T&T Clark, 2006), 28–29.

7. On the eclipse of royal judicial authority in Deut 17:14–20, see Norbert Lohfink, "Distribution of the Functions of Power: The Laws Concerning Public Offices in Deuteronomy 16:18—18:22," in *A Song of Power and the Power of Song: Essays on the Book of Deuteronomy* (ed. Duane L. Christensen; SBTS 3; Winona Lake, Ind.: Eisenbrauns, 1993), 336–52; Levinson, *Hermeneutics*, 138–43; Cook, *Social Roots*, 42–44; J. G. McConville, *Deuteronomy* (Apollos Old Testament Commentary 5; Leicester: Apollos; Downers Grove, Ill.: IVP Academic, 2002), 284, 293–96, 305–6. Levinson aptly describes the sole duty of Deuteronomy's hamstrung monarch: "while sitting demurely on his throne to 'read each day of his life' from the very Torah that delimits his powers (vv. 18–20)" (*Hermeneutics*, 141). Both

The Levites' prerogative of final judicial decision making in the book of Deuteronomy partially restores the traditional influence, responsibility, and prestige accorded to them in old, village-era Israel. Their reempowerment moves to restrain the royal center, insisting that kings share powers and privileges with remnants of an older, pre-state locus of authority.[8] The Levitical lineage should maintain its traditional neutrality, independent from the monarchy, in order to represent the values and interests of all Israel's kin groups and lineages resident throughout the land. The concern is to keep "all the people" (Deut 17:13), the whole of "Israel" (17:12), a holy community purged of evil at all levels (17:7).

The Levitical judges of Deut 17 remain resident out in the land of Judah, among the people whose interests they represent in Jerusalem. Maintaining their independence from the interests of the royal capital, they offer only periodic service there. Verse 9 with its language of being "on duty at that time" (NLT) assumes a rotation system that brings Levites from peripheral locales into Jerusalem for fixed periods. Their presence at the monarchic center exerts covenantal leverage against all temptations of the monarchy to pursue domination and tyranny.

Deuteronomy's proposal to reenfranchise country Levites and have the monarchy share power with them would have appeared starkly anachronistic when King Josiah first enforced the Deuteronomic Code. Judah's development as a hierarchical and bureaucratic monarchy had occurred precisely at the expense of older, lineage-based modes of societal polity in which the Levites had their social roots.[9] The Levites' older modes of operation can be helpfully

---

the text's arrangement and its contents in this section of Deuteronomy work to "divest the king of his judicial authority," reassigning it to the newly envisioned cultus (ibid., 143). For the view that vv. 18–19 are a Deuteronomistic addition to the text from after Judah's exile, see A. D. H. Mayes, *Deuteronomy* (NCB; London: Oliphants; Grand Rapids: Eerdmans, 1981), 273; Udo Rütersworden, *Von der politischen Gemeinschaft zur Gemeinde: Studien zu Dt 16,18–18,22* (BBB 65; Frankfurt am Main: Athenäum, 1987), 89–90.

8. Deuteronomy's program represents what Mark Christian describes as a vision of the royal state sharing power with peripheral agents and even non-agents of the monarchy ("Middle-Tier Levites," 61 n. 216). Such a vision harks back to the situation at the monarchy's rise, where, as Hutton puts it, priestly lineages "perceived themselves to operate somewhat independently from the monarchy, and still within the framework common to kinship-based society" ("All the King's Men," 142).

9. Yet the older system of polity was stubbornly persistent. It remained strong in the early monarchic era, when the biblical texts clarify that King David ruled by consent of a lineage-based segmental system. Note how in 2 Sam 2:4a; 5:1–3 David's rule is based on the consent of tribal representatives (see Hutton, "All the King's Men," 144). The same system reasserted itself at key junctures in monarchic history, when crises of dynastic succession provoked the intervention of the countryside and its tribal representatives (e.g., 2 Kgs 11:13–18; 21:23–24; 23:1–3; Mic 5:1–5) (see Cook, *Social Roots*, 45–49, 52–53, 61, 211–14).

illuminated through cross-cultural comparison with the activities of priestly families in the acephalous, segmentary societies studied by ethnographers.[10]

Priestly functionaries within non-centralized, lineage-based societies, such as old Israel, often wield significant mediatory and judicial power as well as surprising leverage over political leaders. Thus, tribal priests intervene in conflicts between societal segments to help them avoid violence. As "professional neutrals" they help maintain peace and justice within the precarious, genealogically based balance of their societies. Traditional clan heads, field commanders, and chiefs depend on their sacral support and ritual collaboration for effectiveness. In many lineage-based societies, priests are the primary chief-makers and the ones who control the effectiveness of chiefs.[11]

The Levites are being stubborn indeed in insisting on repristinating these vestigial norms that would necessarily lie very uneasily alongside monarchic power in the new centralized, bureaucratized configuration of the Judean state.[12] Such stubbornness put them at risk. King Josiah, the texts report, could

---

10. Hutton has recently drawn extraordinarily fruitful comparisons between the Levites of ancient Israelite society and the Ahansal tribe of priestly "saints" living among companion Berber tribes in the High Atlas Mountains of Morocco. Despite some significant discontinuities between the two groups, Hutton argues that "there are sufficiently numerous and inherent sociological, political, and economic similarities between them to allow fruitful cross-cultural comparison" ("All the King's Men," 123). See also Cook, *Social Roots*, 165, 180, 186–90, 235–36, 246, 259, 283. The remarkable correlations between the Levites and the Ahansal were first noticed by Lawrence E. Stager, "The Archaeology of the Family in Ancient Israel," *BASOR* 260 (1985): 27. The authoritative ethnographic treatment of the group is Ernest Gellner, *The Saints of the Atlas* (London: Weidenfeld & Nicolson, 1969). Additional studies by Gellner are listed by Hutton ("All the King's Men," 147).

11. See Cook, *Social Roots*, 189–90, 235–36, 259. Hutton summarizes the several social roles of the Ahansali "saints" (Berber *igurramen*). These include arbitrating disputes (such as land claims) both within Berber groups and between them, administering the collective oaths of lineage groups, providing sanctuary for those involved in blood-feuds and serving as referees and guarantors in the election of tribal chiefs ("All the King's Men," 126–27). The *igurramen* understand themselves to appoint the tribes' new chieftains, and members of the lay tribes often agree with this assessment. Their appointments put a "divine imprimatur" on the selection proceedings and render them socially binding (ibid., 128–29, 145). The same pre-state prerogative of priestly lineages in chief-making and in controlling the effectiveness of chiefs is visible in the biblical texts, e.g., in 1 Sam 10:17–27; 15:27–28; 2 Sam 19:11–15; 1 Kgs 1:19, 25; 11:29–31. On the power of the priestly lineages to command respect independent of the authority of the crown, see, e.g., 1 Sam 22:17; 1 Kgs 2:26.

12. As Frank Moore Cross aptly puts it, "States, designed to centralize power, and to impose hierarchical rule, do not generate rules based on kinship. They do not legislate egalitarian laws, nor devise segmentary genealogies. On the contrary, the survival of the league and covenantal institutions in Israel placed limits on the evolution of kingship and the arbitrary powers ordinarily exercised by the monarchical city state" ("Kinship and Covenant in Ancient Israel," in idem, *From Epic to Canon: History and Literature in Ancient Israel* [Baltimore: Johns Hopkins University Press, 1998], 17).

be quite intolerant of the claims of country priests (see 2 Kgs 23:5, 19–20; 2 Chr 34:5).[13]

The traditional Levites advocating a reenfranchisement along the lines of Deuteronomy were sticking their necks out in more ways than one. On the one hand, of course, there was great risk inherent in testing the limits of the monarchy's capacity for tolerance and capitulation. On the other hand, however, the Levites' stubbornness had the potential to distance them from their traditional support base. A reenfranchisement into power and privilege risked compromising their traditional neutrality and critical edge.

Not everyone among the Levites' traditional community of support on society's periphery would rejoice in a new Levitical alliance with the center of state society. Should Deuteronomy's vision of Levitical reenfranchisement actually come about, how could anyone ensure that the Levites would retain their independence and integrity? What would prevent the monarchy from coopting them completely for its own ends once their priestly roles were fully federalized?

In a recently published study, Dean McBride outlines compelling evidence from the book of Jeremiah that precisely these tensions did in fact arise and fracture the Levitical community in the wake of King Josiah's Deuteronomy-like reforms.[14] The book betrays clear signs of conflict between two groups of Levites: those who insisted on priests maintaining their critical leverage over against the crown and others, reenfranchised as part of King Josiah's reforms, who appeared to the former group to have sold out to very dangerous, complacent thinking in Jerusalem.[15]

Jeremiah, presented by his editors as the quintessential prophet-like-Moses of Deut 18:15–19, represents the former group. His enemies, whom we encounter in the poetic confessions and explanatory prose of his book, represent the latter. As a key Mosaic prophet, Jeremiah was subject to the resistance and violence often aimed at those in this role (cf. Num 12:1–2 [E source]; 1 Kgs 19:10, 14; Hos 6:9).

Unique language and cross-referencing in Jeremiah, McBride argues, sounds the alarm against the pragmatism and complacency that often

---

13. Although the NRSV in 2 Kgs 23:5 states that Josiah "deposed" idolatrous priests, the Hebrew verb שבת used there can also mean "exterminate" (see BDB 991 *Hiph.* 2, where 2 Kgs 23:5 is listed. Note the translation of the NJB; cf. NET n.).

14. S. Dean McBride Jr., "Jeremiah and the Levitical Priests of Anathoth," in *Thus Says the Lord: Essays on the Former and Latter Prophets in Honor of Robert R. Wilson* (ed. Stephen L. Cook and John J. Ahn; LHBOTS 502; New York/London: T&T Clark, 2009), 179–96.

15. McBride argues cogently that disenfranchised country Levites, especially a group of Abiathar's descendants at Anathoth, were brought back into the ranks of Jerusalem's scribal officials and clergy at the time of Hezekiah's and Josiah's Deuteronomic reforms (see "Jeremiah and the Levitical Priests," 188–89).

accompany political empowerment. The referencing intentionally recalls how the Levites, when in power, tended to incur divine wrath. When in charge at Shiloh in the premonarchic era, the Levites succumbed to devastating failures, which eventuated in a series of tragedies. These culminated in the dismissal from Jerusalem's temple of Abiathar, David's chief Levite, in fulfillment of God's decree of judgment against Shiloh's Levitical personnel (1 Kgs 2:27).[16]

The banishment of their forebear Abiathar to Anathoth represented an awful divine judgment against the Levites' family line for neglect of the covenant (1 Kgs 2:27; cf. 1 Sam 2:27–36; 3:10–14). The verbal allusions of Jeremiah invite the reader to recall this momentous judgment, and to consider the events of the prophet's book to be yet another chapter in the complex saga of the line. Favored of God (Jer 33:17–22) and now back in power after Josiah's reforms, as they were both under David and at Shiloh, the Levites must be vigilant lest history repeat itself. Intertextual resonances between Jer 19:3 and 1 Sam 3:11 underscore the very real possibility that the Levites' history of judgment might come back to haunt them.[17]

McBride's evidence is strong that Jeremiah's book indeed cross-references the story of Solomon's banishment of Abiathar to Anathoth in the territory of Benjamin (1 Kgs 2:26). The first verse of Jeremiah declares the prophet one of the priests who lived at Anathoth. Later in the book the prophet buys the field of a Levitical relative in Anathoth, having the right of redemption to buy it. Echoes of the mention of Abiathar's "field" in 1 Kgs 2:26 are hard to miss, especially since Jer 32 mentions Anathoth three times (vv. 7–9).

The Levitical tradents of Deuteronomy aimed at a new incorporation not only into Judah's centralized judicial system but also into the central cult of the Jerusalem temple. They wished to bring the long exile from temple service of Abiathar's kin to an end. Deuteronomy 18:1–8 insists that the whole tribe of Levi constitutes Judah's priesthood. Outlying Levites, should they desire, are allowed to perform sacrifices at the temple in Jerusalem. Verse 5 reads, "The LORD your God has chosen Levi out of all your tribes, to stand and minister in the name of the LORD, him and his sons for all time." According to v. 7, any Levite passionate about altar service in Jerusalem may certainly minister there, "like all his fellow-Levites who stand to minister there before the LORD."

---

16. It is difficult to establish firmly the historicity of Abiathar's membership in the Levitical house of Shiloh, especially his descent from Eli (for discussion, see Hutton, "All the King's Men," 133–35). Nevertheless, despite scholars' legitimate questions, the texts of Jeremiah and of the Court History/Succession Narrative do affirm Abiathar as a Shiloh Levite (see esp. 1 Sam 22:18–21; 1 Kgs 2:27). Whatever Abiathar's exact genealogy, I find no reason for skepticism that after Shiloh's destruction he likely accompanied the remnant of the Elides in a migration to Nob (1 Sam 22:18–20). As Hutton admits, "the model presented by the Ahansal (and indeed by North African *shurfa* in general) permits the migration of priestly families" ("All the King's Men," 133).

17. I am grateful to Jeremy Hutton for bringing these resonances to my attention.

We can only imagine the tenacity of the Levites of Deuteronomy's time in believing that they could leverage a centralized cult-system to their group's advantage. They believed themselves capable of repristinating an older, lineage-based organization of society in an era when new state-based military, economic, and judicial power had long been eroding all the systems of this earlier way of life.

From its very start, Deut 18 breathes the air of old tribal Israel. The first verse of the chapter reiterates lineage-based understandings of the tenure of kinship units on permanently allotted landed patrimonies. These understandings had persisted as a social substratum for centuries, while societal centralization in Judah and Israel proceeded as an extended process. According to Deut 18:1–2, all Israel's tribes have an allotment and inheritance within Israel's territory except for the Levites, who have only the Lord as their inheritance. The inherited patrimony is the means of livelihood bestowed by God, and in the Levites' case this means of sustenance was to be the offerings and parts of sacrifices of worshipers. Traditionally, they depended on a share of such revenues of Israelite worship for their very lives. Now, after many assorted disruptions of this income in the course of the monarchic era, they would be allowed to receive it again at the central temple.[18]

Did the seventh-century Deuteronomic reforms of King Josiah actually implement the ideal of Deut 18? Did some of the Levitical priests of the countryside, such as the ones resident at Anathoth, find reenfranchisement in Jerusalem's sacrificial cult, reversing the exile of their ancestor Abiathar? In a highly influential argument, Julius Wellhausen said no.[19] He interpreted Deut 18's vision as an ideal doomed to fail. He argued that 2 Kgs 23 directly attests to this failure and that Ezek 44 provides a moral rationale for what happened. It was out of the de facto collapse of this piece of Deuteronomic legislation,

---

18. A degradation of the Levites' traditional privilege of receiving offerings and sacrifices traces back to the destruction of their base at Shiloh (Ps 78:60–61), to Saul's attack at Nob (1 Sam 22:6–23), and to the (at least partial) expulsions of Levitical cult personnel by both Solomon (1 Kgs 2:27) and Jeroboam (1 Kgs 12:31; 13:33; 2 Chr 11:13–17; 13:9). Later, Hezekiah decommissioned high places, where some Levites continued to serve (2 Kgs 18:4, 22); Assyria devastated still more places of service in 701 B.C.E.; and Manasseh may well have made some of the high places he reestablished into shrines of monarchic clerics, not of Levites (2 Kgs 21:3; 23:5). The provisions of Deut 18 would thus have been highly welcomed by the group. They are in keeping with Deuteronomy's calls for special care of the Levites (Deut 12:19; 14:27, 29; 16:11, 14; 26:11–13).

19. Julius Wellhausen, *Prolegomena to the History of Ancient Israel, with a Reprint of the Article Israel from the Encyclopedia Britannica* (trans. J. Sutherland Black and Allan Menzies; New York: Meridian, 1957; 1st German ed. 1878), 121–67. For one good summary and critique of Wellhausen's position, see Stephen L. Cook, "Innerbiblical Interpretation in Ezekiel 44 and the History of Israel's Priesthood," *JBL* 114 (1995): 193–208.

according to Wellhausen, that the present scriptural distinction between sacrificing priests and non-sacrificing Levites arose.

Contrary to Wellhausen's view, a close reading of 2 Kgs 23:9 and its literary context suggests that Deut 18's vision did not in fact immediately fail. Modern English translations of the verse misunderstand the sense of the Hebrew when they offer renderings that deny that any Levites ascended to Jerusalem (cf. the NRSV: "The priests of the high places, however, did not come up to the altar of the LORD in Jerusalem, but ate unleavened bread among their kindred"). In a recent article on the Levites, Mark Leuchter renders 2 Kgs 23:9 in a manner almost opposite to that of the NRSV: "The priests of the high places did not go up [to the altar of the LORD in Jerusalem] until they ate unleavened bread among their brethren [= fellow Israelites]."[20] This rendering highly commends itself.

Leuchter's translation is true to the Hebrew syntax of the verse, where a כי אם clause follows a negative statement expressed with an imperfect verb. This syntax signals an expression leaning on an "unless/until" clause. In such a case, the initial negative statement does not express a general fact but, as Bill T. Arnold and John H. Choi explain, a situation that is *reversed* after something specific happens.[21] In short, in 2 Kgs 23:9 the Levites *do* eventually serve at the Lord's altar in Jerusalem, but only after fulfilling a certain condition. This condition, which I will discuss momentarily, involved the ceremonial consumption of unleavened bread in the presence of fellow Israelites.

As Leuchter argues, his improved reading of 2 Kgs 23:9 fits the rhetoric of the Deuteronomistic account of Josiah's reform of the nation far better than Wellhausen's understanding. The Deuteronomists tend to gloss over Josiah's failures and would scarcely have voiced a negative evaluation of his work enfranchising the Levites.[22] Further strengthening Leuchter's interpretation is the fact that the Hebrew Bible appears to preserve the names of two close rela-

---

20. Mark Leuchter, "'The Levite in Your Gates': The Deuteronomic Redefinition of Levitical Authority," *JBL* 126 (2007): 429. For earlier, extensive arguments for this new reading, see W. Boyd Barrick, *The King and the Cemeteries: Toward a New Understanding of Josiah's Reform* (VTSup 88; Leiden/Boston/Cologne: Brill, 2002), 189-93; cf. Gösta W. Ahlström, *Royal Administration and National Religion in Ancient Palestine* (SHANE 1; Leiden: Brill, 1982), 68-69.

21. Bill T. Arnold and John H. Choi, *A Guide to Biblical Hebrew Syntax* (Cambridge/New York: Cambridge University Press, 2003), 155 sec. 4.3.4 (m); see also John C. Beckman, *Williams' Hebrew Syntax* (3rd ed.; Toronto: University of Toronto Press, 2007), 197 sec. 556; Paul Joüon, *A Grammar of Biblical Hebrew* (trans. T. Muraoka; 2nd ed.; Subsidia Biblica 27; Rome: Pontifical Biblical Institute, 2006), 603 sec. 173b; *IBHS* 642-43 sec. 38.6.

22. Leuchter, "Levite in Your Gates," 428 and n. 43; cf. Baruch Halpern, "Why Manasseh Is Blamed for the Babylonian Exile: The Evolution of a Biblical Tradition," *VT* 48 (1988): 501-3. What is more, as Barrick observes, there is precious little logic in the commonplace scholarly argument that Deut 18:1-8 was foiled by the resistance of the resident Jerusalem priesthood. Jerusalem's chief priest Hilkiah and his associates were among the

tives (cousins) of Jeremiah from the Levites of Anathoth who in fact did join ranks with the priests of Jerusalem under Josiah's rule in conformity with the vision of Deut 18. The texts picture the priests Maaseiah (Jer 35:4) and Zephaniah (Jer 21:1; 29:25–26, 29; 37:3) ensconced within central-temple circles in the era after Josiah's reforms. They were apparently the son and grandson of Jeremiah's uncle Shallum (Jer 32:7).[23]

The matter is clinched when one turns to the puzzling reference in 2 Kgs 23:9 about eating *unleavened* bread. The cryptic clause begins to make real sense once the verse is read as a positive statement that some Levites *were* reenfranchised at Josiah's time.

Deuteronomy has specific interest in the festival of Unleavened Bread, combining it with Passover to create a major new covenantal assembly of all of Judah's families (Deut 16:1–8).[24] Josiah implemented the new Deuteronomic vision of the Passover holiday, co-opting it as a means of solidifying his political innovations and the support of the nation. Fascinatingly, the king appears to have been extremely interested in the role of the Levites in the celebration of the feast and in their sharing in the unleavened bread.

According to 2 Kgs 23, Josiah crowned his Deuteronomic reforms with a Passover of a kind not seen since the days of the judges (v. 22). According to Chronicles, it was at this Passover that the king organized the Levites for service in Jerusalem (2 Chr 35:2–4). All this followed the precedent of Hezekiah, who himself had held a great Passover in Jerusalem as a centerpiece of his reform and had given the Levites his patronage after they demonstrated great skill in temple service there (2 Chr 30:22; 31:2).

According to Chronicles, to opt out of the new centralized Passover was essentially to reject the covenant (2 Chr 30:8). To join in the Passover festival, by contrast, was to celebrate one's inclusion in the covenantal assembly. Josiah's thinking must have followed these very lines, and he moved to restrict Levitical enfranchisement to those rural priests willing to join with their fellow Israelites around the observance of eating unleavened bread at Passover time.

With the litmus test of unleavened bread in place, Josiah had the means to ensure the loyalty of the Levites, about whom he doubtless had real concerns. He was surely well aware of their independent basis of power rooted in old, village-era Israel. Moving to contain any possible threat from their side, he insisted that all Levites desiring inclusion in the ranks of his federalized clergy adopt the rites of his new Passover feast. In this manner they were to

---

central architects of the Deuteronomic reforms. Would Hilkiah's own subordinate priests really have defeated his efforts? (*King and the Cemeteries*, 188–89).

23. For discussion, see Robert R. Wilson, *Prophecy and Society in Ancient Israel* (Philadelphia: Fortress, 1980), 234, 246; McBride, "Jeremiah and the Levitical Priests," 192–94.

24. See Levinson, *Hermeneutics*, 95.

demonstrate their embrace of the crown's particular vision for implementing Deuteronomy's covenant. They were to bow to Josiah's new, uniform polity.

That Josiah had his own interpretation of Deuteronomy seems certain. His version of the ideal monarch, evident in his management of his reform program, appears far more aggressive and authoritarian than what the law of the king in Deut 17:14–20 would appear to intend.[25] Indeed, his entanglement in the cult and his heavy-handed supervision of the Passover (cf. 2 Kgs 23:21) is strikingly non-Deuteronomic. Adopting a brazen revisionism, he harmonizes Deuteronomic law and the interests of the crown.

The wording of 2 Kgs 23:9 appears to reflect Josiah's boldness in claiming the right to interpret Deuteronomy in his own way in order to bring the Levites under royal control. A literal reading of Deut 16 would suggest that the gathered assembly of all Israel should break up after Passover to allow for a reverse pilgrimage out of Jerusalem. The people were apparently supposed to return home to the outlying towns for local celebrations of the festival of Unleavened Bread (see Deut 16:7).[26] In contrast to this literal reading, Josiah appears to have insisted that the covenant community, and especially the Levites, remain in Jerusalem and celebrate the second festival there.

In Josiah's interpretation of Deuteronomy, everyone was to remain in the capital for both Passover and the subsequent pilgrimage feast (see 2 Chr 35:17). This would have cut against traditional Levitical practice. The Levites were accustomed to presiding over local celebrations of an Unleavened Bread festival (Exod 13:6).[27] By eating "unleavened bread" in Jerusalem they were buying into Josiah's program.

Josiah apparently demanded that all Levites wishing for his patronage observe things his way. They had to prove their loyalty to the crown by staying in Jerusalem and eating "unleavened bread among their kindred." The phrase "among their kindred" in 2 Kgs 23:9 probably refers to the assembly still gath-

---

25. See Dale Launderville, *Piety and Politics: The Dynamics of Royal Authority in Homeric Greece, Biblical Israel, and Old Babylonian Mesopotamia* (Grand Rapids: Eerdmans, 2003), 322; Gary N. Knoppers, *Two Nations under God: The Deuteronomistic History of Solomon and the Dual Monarchies*, vol. 2, *The Reign of Jeroboam, the Fall of Israel, and the Reign of Josiah* (HSM 53; Atlanta: Scholars Press, 1994), 124, 166, 173–74, 215, 223–25; Levinson, *Hermeneutics*, 95–96.

26. On the interpretation of Deut 16:7, see Levinson, *Hermeneutics*, 89.

27. The idea that the Levites had to adhere to Josiah's specific form of the Unleavened Bread festival as a test of their loyalty to the crown was suggested to me by Susan Ackerman (Dartmouth College) at the Brown University Moskow Symposium: "Social Theory and the Study of Israelite Religion: Retrospect and Prospect" (Providence, R.I., February 27–March 1, 2010). Cf. Leuchter's description of Josiah's condition placed on the Levites as a possible "pledge of allegiance" ("Levite in Your Gates," 429) and Barrick's notion of an "unleavened bread test" (*King and the Cemeteries*, 193). Barrick envisions a "court putsch" aimed at "placing [the priesthood] more firmly under the control of the faction now in power" (ibid.).

ered at Jerusalem for Passover. The term אחים in the phrase is standard Deuteronomic diction signaling members of the covenant community (cf. Deut 1:16; 3:20; 10:9; 15:7; 17:15).[28] We saw it used above in Deut 17:15, 19–20, a passage insisting that Israel's king must remain a covenantal "brother."

Second Kings 23:8–9 supposes Deuteronomy to intend that a great many former priests of the high places should come up to help officiate at sacrifices. Jerusalem would not accommodate a permanent presence of Levites in such numbers, so I suggest that a system of rotating Levites is likely in view.[29] We have seen a similar rota system embraced in Deut 17:9. Thus, a Levite would "ordinarily" be resident "anywhere in Israel," but might "visit" the Jerusalem temple periodically to perform altar service (Deut 18:6 NAB).

Evidence from the texts of Jeremiah's so-called confessions appears to confirm the existence of a Levitical rota system in the era after Josiah's reform. The system allowed for some of Jerusalem's cult officiants to maintain their primary residence in outlying towns. In the confessions we catch glimpses of newly federalized partisans of the temple establishment resident out in Jeremiah's village town of Anathoth.

Specifically, close study of the confessions and related texts shows that Jeremiah's challenges to the official cult first provoked death threats in his home village of Anathoth (Jer 11:21, 23; 12:6).[30] The prophet's first opponents were his own townsfolk, indeed his very own kin. Jeremiah 12:6 describes the foes specifically as the relatives of Jeremiah, "your brothers and your father's house" (cf. 20:10). The partisans of Jerusalem's temple out in Jeremiah's town are not sons of Aaron, as one might at first suppose. (Anathoth is one of four towns in southern Benjamin assigned to Aaronide families according to Josh 21:17–18; 1 Chr 6:45 [NRSV: v. 60].) They are Jeremiah's fellow Levitical priests, descendants and relations of Abiathar.[31]

---

28. Leuchter, "Levite in Your Gates," 429.

29. Deuteronomy 18:6–8 depicts two sets of priests, some stationed in Jerusalem and some resident in the countryside. If v. 8b envisions some Levites permanently disposing of their affairs in their hometowns, then Deuteronomy may imagine that some rural priests had the desire to relocate in Jerusalem (see Aelred Cody, *A History of Old Testament Priesthood* [AnBib 35; Rome: Pontifical Biblical Institute, 1969], 128). Relocation would not be practicable on a large scale, however, and the evidence of Jeremiah is that not all newly federalized Levites took up permanent residence in the capital.

30. As William L. Holladay notes, even if the telltale verses represent secondary clarifications, they likely provide useful historical information. They have a specificity alien to what a redactor would create on his own (e.g., consider the incidental words of the kinfolk in Jer 11:21 and 12:6). Further, it is unlikely that a later editor would invent a scenario of familial strife in contradiction to traditions elsewhere in Jeremiah about the prophet enjoying good family relations (32:6–15; 37:12). See Holladay, *Jeremiah 1: A Commentary on the Book of the Prophet Jeremiah Chapters 1–25* (Hermeneia; Minneapolis: Fortress, 1986), 371, 375.

31. See McBride, "Jeremiah and the Levitical Priests," 190.

Apparently the long exile from temple service of Abiathar's kin had now come to an end. The Anathothite defenders of Jerusalem were likely resident priests not currently on duty at the temple. Language about them in the first confession in Jer 11:23 parallels that directed against temple personnel committing wickedness in God's house in Jer 23:11–12. What is more, elsewhere in the book of Jeremiah, the type of death threats the prophet received in Anathoth are specifically associated with his prophetic attacks on the temple and God's chosen city (see Jer 26:6–9, 11, 21; 36:5; 38:3–4). It is out in Judah that Jeremiah first faces the ire of those invested in Zion's sacral protection. His Levite neighbors are surprisingly wrapped up in Jerusalem's central cult.[32]

The Anathothite defenders of the Jerusalem temple appear to have been particularly offended by prophecies against Zion "in the name of the LORD" (Jer 11:21). The same phraseology resounds in the hostile response to Jeremiah's temple sermon: "How dare you claim the LORD's authority to prophesy such things!" (Jer 26:9 NET).[33] Jeremiah's temple sermon would have provoked the particular ire of his fellow Anathothites, given the salt that it threw into their wounds about the destruction of Shiloh, their former home base (Jer 7:12–14; 26:6).[34]

Jeremiah's Levitical kin took his threats against the central cult very personally. In the confessions, Jeremiah quotes their language of taking "revenge" on him (Jer 20:10). Such enmity makes sense when we recall that local shrines were now decommissioned, and the Levites likely clung to their recent reintegration at Jerusalem. Just when they had finally come back into power as in the old days at Shiloh, their own relative was undermining the new federalized system that sanctioned their priesthood and granted them patronage.

The evidence about Levitical history that can be gleaned from Jeremiah is buttressed by a brief look at Ps 78's layers of composition. Just as in the book of Jeremiah, traditional Levitical understandings come into tension with newer Zion-oriented perspectives in the present, composite form of the psalm, a psalm of Asaph. The internal evidence of Ps 78 attests to the potential for a clash in allegiances among the Levites—the very potential that we see actualized in Jeremiah's saga.

---

32. For discussion, see McBride, "Jeremiah and the Levitical Priests," 190 n. 32, 191–92; Wilson, *Prophecy and Society*, 244–46; cf. Walter Brueggemann, *A Commentary on Jeremiah: Exile and Homecoming* (Grand Rapids: Eerdmans, 1998), 117.

33. See Holladay, *Jeremiah 1*, 370. Also see Jer 26:20; the "sinister parallel" between Jeremiah's situation in his village and the earlier threat against Uriah ben Shemaiah from the side of the Jerusalem establishment has now been noted by Leslie C. Allen (*Jeremiah* [OTL; Louisville/London: Westminster John Knox, 2008], 147).

34. As McBride writes, the "consternation of temple personnel, reminded of Shiloh's loss of divine election, is all the more understandable if among them were 'Anathothites' who, like Jeremiah himself, claimed descent from the Elide priesthood" ("Jeremiah and the Levitical Priests," 192).

The original Asaphite authors of Ps 78 were northern Levites who saturated their liturgical poetry with proto-Deuteronomic language and thinking, including the conviction that God could abandon even a central shrine like Shiloh (Ps 78:60).[35] Jerusalem-oriented redaction in vv. 9, 67–69 of the psalm, however, shows evidence of the Levitical tradents of the psalm compromising with perspectives at home among Jerusalem's central priests. Such compromises likely arose within a setting of Levitical reenfranchisement, perhaps a reincorporation into service at Jerusalem during the reforms of Kings Hezekiah and Josiah (cf. the mention of Asaph in the context of Hezekiah's reforms in 2 Chr 29:30).

Psalm 78 in its present layered form embodies a struggle between the Deuteronomic emphasis on God's freedom to abandon any specific central shrine (vv. 59–61) and alternate, competing claims about Zion's eternal foundation (vv. 67–69). In his temple sermon, the prophet Jeremiah engaged these very tensions and their potential to clash. He knew that his Anathothite brethren in the audience were torn between the two poles of the psalm, the pole of Deuteronomy, on the one hand, and the pole of Zion, on the other. He worked to stress the current overriding relevance of the Deuteronomic pole, of vv. 60–61 and the witness of these verses to the catastrophic fate of Shiloh, God's onetime chosen shrine (Jer 7:12, 14; 26:6).

Additional texts could be examined and further arguments made, but perhaps enough has been said to establish the tenacity of the Levites about their reempowerment and about the pitfalls they encountered when their wishes became reality. Let me sum up my observations in this essay. In keeping with its probable ties to Levitical tradents, Deuteronomy appears to have mounted a multipronged plan for overcoming Levitical disenfranchisement. Contrary to Wellhausen's influential reconstruction, the program appears to have actually been temporarily implemented on the ground. It included rotating country Levites into the capital to serve as interpreters of the covenant at the palace, to hear legal cases within appeals courts, and to serve as altar priests at the temple.

The aim of Deuteronomy and its Levitical tradents was to temper centralized monarchic power and ensure justice and holiness throughout the entire land, especially in the vast rural sphere. By pursuing an alliance with the central powers of society, however, the Levites risked losing their critical edge over against monarchic authority. They risked harmonizing their Deuteronomic traditions with the very different theology of Zion held by many of Jerusalem's rulers and priests.

King Josiah's particular implementation of Deuteronomic reforms does in fact appear to have brought about some of the perils to which the reforming

---

35. For discussion of the proto-Deuteronomic theology of the Asaphite Psalms, see Cook, *Social Roots*, 17–19, 24–25, 53–57.

Levites were exposing themselves. His reforms appear to have compromised the critical independence of at least some Levites. Jeremiah and other Deuteronomic purists ended up judging some of Josiah's new federalized Levites as having sold out to the interests of Jerusalem's establishment. The prophet holds that divine judgment now awaits these opponents, likely in a form comparable to what their ancestors experienced centuries earlier at the destruction of Shiloh.

Part III

Priests and Levites in Exegetical Context

MIDDLE-TIER LEVITES AND
THE PLENARY RECEPTION OF REVELATION

Mark A. Christian

I. INTRODUCTION

In this paper, I set out to continue my research into the various diachronically and geographically determined roles of Levites in what I call the Plenary Reception of Revelation (hereafter PRR). The PRR occurs in events described already in pentateuchal texts in which YHWH discloses law directly to the entire, thus *plenary*, assembly. In view of its theological weightiness, the fact that the tradition survives only fragmentarily (e.g., Exod 20:18–22; 33:1–4; Deut 4:10–12, 33–37; 5:4, 22)[1] suggests that it does not belong among the traditions of the "official" religion[2] in which Mosaic mediation of legal revelation

---

I wish to thank the editors for the invitation to participate on the inaugural panel of the "Levites in History and Tradition" program unit at the annual meeting of the Society of Biblical Literature in 2009 in New Orleans, Louisiana. The present study constitutes a significantly reworked version of the original lecture and incorporates further developed views expressed in an unpublished paper, "Integrating the Alien," presented at the SBL annual meeting in San Diego in 2007. A longer version of the present paper will appear as ch. 6 of my forthcoming Vanderbilt dissertation, "Levites and the Plenary Reception of Revelation."

1. Space constraints preclude detailed analysis of these passages and their place in the developmental history of the Pentateuch. I devote chs. 2–3 of my dissertation to the *Forschungsgeschichte* and exegetical analysis of these and similar passages in Exodus and Deuteronomy, respectively. Connecting themes and traditions across the entire canon are noted and brought to bear in that discussion.

2. The descriptives "official," "urban," "national," and "book" religion, on the one hand, and "popular," "folk," even "domestic" and "household" religion (cf. German *häuslichen Kult/Religion*), on the other hand, all have their problems. For a general discussion of the problem, see Mark A. Christian, "Priestly Power That Empowers: Michel Foucault, Middle-Tier Levites, and the Sociology of 'Popular Religious Groups' in Israel," in *JHS* 9 (2009): art. 1, 1–81, esp. 9–13, 18–19, and 26–28; for more detailed engagement, see Francesca Stavrakopoulou, "'Popular' Religion and 'Official' Religion: Practice, Perception, Portrayal," in *Religious Diversity in Ancient Israel and Judah* (ed. Francesca Stavrakopoulou and John Barton; London: T&T Clark, 2010), 37–58; on p. 50 the author suggests that traditions of *un*written "revelation" are the preserve of less official religion.

dominates.[3] I believe levitical[4] cult prophets and their supporters among lay leadership, on the one hand, and elite priests sympathetic to their cause, on the other, comprise the primary purveyors of the PRR. The qualifier *middle-tier* designates non-elite priests[5] whose ministry is normally located outside of urban centers—that is, in villages and residential towns in which the great majority of Israelites live and worship. A text such as Jer 11:13 suggests that such towns may have had multiple cultic sites. Indeed, Ziony Zevit's important 2001 monograph emphasizes the variance among "shrines and wayside chapels" common in the Syro-Palestinian countryside and "found in both Israel and Judah during the Iron Age."[6] Saul Olyan lists regional sanctuaries

---

3. In the Pentateuch, the dominance of the figure of Moses was helped along significantly by the Pentateuchal Redaction (PentRed) accomplished by upper-tier priests (Zadok-Levites or Aaronide-Levites) and datable to the fifth century.

4. I prefer to use the lower case spelling of the adjectival form of "Levite," thus "levitical," because of Semitic *lwy*'s non-tribal origins. For further disputation of the Levites' putative "tribal" affiliations, see Johannes Lindblom, *Erwägungen zur Herkunft der Josianischen Tempelurkunde* (Lund: Gleerup, 1971), 28, 32 and n. 30; Reinhard Achenbach, "Levitische Priester und Leviten im Deuterononium: Überlegungen zur sog. 'Levitisierung' des Priestertums," *ZABR* 5 (1999): 285–309; idem, "Die Tora und die Propheten im 5. und 4. Jh. v. Chr.," in *Tora in der Hebräischen Bibel: Studien zur Redaktionsgeschichte und synchronen Logik diachroner Transformationen* (ed. Reinhard Achenbach et al.; BZABR 7; Wiesbaden: Harrassowitz, 2007), 26–71, 31; Ulrich Dahmen, *Leviten und Priester im Deuteronomium. Literarkritische und redaktionsgeschichtliche Studien* (BBB 110; Bodenheim: Philo, 1996).

5. For middle-tier prophets in the ancient Near East, see Jonathan Stökl, "Female Prophets in the Ancient Near East," in *Prophecy and Prophets in Ancient Israel: Proceedings of the Oxford Old Testament Seminar* (ed. John Day; LHBOTS 531; New York: T&T Clark, 2010), 47–61; the author argues that whereas Old Babylonian Akkadian *āpiltu* and Neo-Assyrian *raggintu* denote professional female prophets, Old Babylonian *muḫḫūtum* ("raver" who also prophesies) and Neo-Assyrian *maḫḫūtum* "are neither professional prophets nor lay prophets, but they occupy something of a middle ground" (ibid., 47–48, 51); for female lay prophets at Mari, see ibid., 50–54.

6. Ziony Zevit, *The Religions of Ancient Israel: A Synthesis of Parallactic Approaches* (London: Continuum, 2001), 340. Such sites "were mostly conceived as auspicious places where a deity dwelt, or resided regularly or occasionally, or where a deity could be called to presence and immanence. They were not merely places where one could call out to a deity who may have been far away" (ibid.). Nonetheless, in a careful study, Rüdiger Schmitt finds significant evidence of cultic activity in residential areas in Iron I–IIc (1200–586 B.C.E.) Israel ("Kultinventare aus Wohnhäusern als materielle Elemente familiärer Religion im Alten Israel," in *Berührungspunkte: Studien zur Sozial- und Religionsgeschichte Israels und seiner Umwelt: Festschrift für Rainer Albertz zu seinem 65. Geburtstag* [ed. Ingo Kottsieper, Rüdiger Schmitt, and Jakob Wöhrle; AOAT 350; Münster: Ugarit-Verlag, 2008], 441–77). The variance among objects *likely* used in cultic praxis is great. As a rule, homes of the early and/or proto-Israelite settlements have a delimited inventory of ceramic and objects. Apart from Tell Jawa in Jordan, Iron Age Israel has little certain archaeological evidence for regular domestic cult practice on top of the upper floor. Ritual rites take place mainly on the first floor, and usually in the kitchen. The findings from the immediate domain of the

according to their most probable period of activity: the "Bull Site" and Shiloh in Iron I; Dan, Meggido 338 and 2081, Beersheba, and Arad during Iron II.[7]

Daily worship in rural sanctuaries would have required cooperation between priest and laity. In contrast, elite priests stationed in urban centers would have had less contact with the general population; they would accordingly concern themselves with securing and maintaining relations in elitist environments. For example, by upholding the tenets of "official" (cf. urban) religion[8] they would further the interests of institutions centered in larger cities.[9] Though the priorities of elite religious or civil leadership tended to conflict with those of non-elites, individuals among the former group at times became disillusioned with their own regnant party's ideology. Elites wishing to support a popular movement[10] would need to do so cautiously, however, usually behind the scenes. Accordingly, we would not expect to see much evidence of this phenomenon in ancient literature. Instead, such support tends to be expressed in a reticent, often rhetorical manner. To the extent that it does find a place in the literature, it is usually "voiced" by, or cryptically attributed to, a level of leadership situated between the highest and lowest strata in society. In some cases, for example, in Neh 8 and the *office laws* of Deuteronomy (16:18–18:22),

---

preparation of foodstuffs point to the important function of women in ritual rites in families (ibid., 455–56; cf. Carol Meyers, "Household Religion," in Stavrakopoulou and Barton, *Religious Diversity in Ancient Israel and Judah*, 118–34, 121–24). William G. Dever considers various explanations for both the lack of mention of specific cult objects and confused reports about them (e.g., the אשרה, אשתרת, and אֲשֵׁתוֹרֶת), concluding that biblical writers "deliberately avoided mentioning them because they sought to suppress popular cults that in their view were heterodox" ("Folk Religion in Ancient Israel: The Disconnect between Text and Artifact," in Kottsieper et al., *Berührungspunkte*, 425–39, here 435).

7. Saul M. Olyan, "Family Religion in First Millennium Israel," in *Household and Family Religion in Antiquity* (ed. John Bodel and Saul M. Olyan; Malden, Mass./Oxford: Blackwell, 2008), 113–26, 115 and nn. 14–15.

8. Philip R. Davies ("Urban Religion and Rural Religion," in Stavrakopoulou and Barton, *Religious Diversity in Ancient Israel and Judah*, 104–17, here 108) has a maximalist view of "urban" religion: "There was an urban religion of the home, the street, the gate and the market as well as the more public religion of the temples." The urbanizing of "rural religion" occurs as the "city" brings into close juxtaposition "the different cultic spheres of its inhabitants—the court, merchants, soldiers, farmers, artisans, and other foreign residents." The regular contact of urban and rural religion, moreover, produces numerous smaller shrines and "everyday rites" in addition to city temples and official rites. "We know of city shrines, for example, at gates and crossroads, as well as altars within households."

9. For the fourfold categorization of Iron II cities in Israel into residential, administrative, royal, and capital, respectively, I follow Douglas A. Knight, *Law, Power, and Justice in Ancient Israel* (Library of Ancient Israel; Louisville: Westminster John Knox, 2011), 161–73; cf. Davies, "Urban Religion," 107.

10. To be sure, elites align themselves with the ideas and movements deriving from lower classes and their local representatives for a variety of reasons and based on a plethora of motivations.

the attribution is reasonably clear. In others, such as the Holiness Code (Lev 17–26; H), the attribution is so faint as to require more nuanced reconstruction. Thankfully, analogous (con)texts in other parts of the Hebrew Bible offer some guidance.

In addition to performing a close reading of key passages in Leviticus with recourse to lateral, "holy community" traditions in other texts,[11] I will employ rhetorical strategies in order to bring reticent aspects of the author/audience discourse into view. This methodological approach helps bring to the fore the radical nature of H's ideas regarding the holy *fraternité*'s qualifications for priestly service.

A. Where and What Are the Levites, Really?

One searches in vain for a consistent picture of the Levites, even within the Pentateuch alone.[12] Moreover, scholars have typically taken insufficient account of the non-urban population's more fluid view of priests, cult, and, perhaps most importantly, the priests' own role in cultic activities in village contexts. However, assumptions about priests in the Hebrew Bible often depend more on the history of the Western Christian priesthood of the last two millennia than on an unbiased reading of texts pertaining to priests and the communities they served. Modern preconceptions tend to obscure further the already faint impressions and allusions that might steer readers—and probably did steer ancient audiences—in a different conceptual and interpretative direction.

In Num 8:14 (cf. 16:9) Moses distinguishes between Levites and the people:[13] "Thus you shall separate the Levites from among the other Israelites,[14] and the Levites shall be mine." The words *liminal* and *marginal* prove useful in this connection, as the surrounding context indicates that the Levites are experiencing simultaneous demotion (Num 8:19–20, 26) and promotion—the latter in that they are wholly dedicated to Yhwh (vv. 14, 16, 18) for special service. Yhwh has become their virtual inheritance. Though this theological conferral is apparently an honor and most certainly a distinction, the upshot of it for the Levites is instability; their simultaneously liminal and marginal position in society would have remained blatantly indeterminate.[15]

---

11. These readings will usually concentrate synchronically on the proto-canon (e.g., post-Pg and post-Dtr redactions and traditions; e.g., Exod 19:6; Deut 7:6; 14:2; cf. Isa 61:6a; 62:12a).

12. But cf. Thomas B. Dozeman, *Commentary on Exodus* (Eerdmans Critical Commentary; Grand Rapids: Eerdmans, 2009), 710.

13. See Karl Elliger, *Leviticus* (HAT 4; Tübingen: Mohr Siebeck, 1956), 277 n. 25.

14. "Separation" here (בדל *hip'il*) has both ritual and spatial aspects.

15. See Christian, "Priestly Power That Empowers," 3–5 and n. 8; and Mark Leuchter, *The Polemics of Exile in Jeremiah 26–45* (Cambridge: Cambridge University Press, 2008), 167.

As for the question of the Levites' spatial location, in his consideration of the literary situation (*literarische Ort*) of Josh 15 and its function with chs. 13–21, Jacobus Cornelis de Vos turns up two significant phases in the treatment of Levites in the book of Joshua, with links to Numbers.[16] In both phases the land becomes increasingly ritualized and the land-division texts become increasingly assimilated and/or harmonized with one another and with other texts in the Hebrew Bible. The first phase aggrandizes the Aaronide Eleazar at the Levites' expense. A central goal of this phase is to "clericalize" the land.[17] In a further systematizing phase connections are made with Num 26. Form-critical analysis of key terms (e.g., גבול, מטל with the exclusive meaning of "boundary," נחלה, למשפחתם[ו]) reveals connotations of a divine order (*Ordnung*) established by boundaries and numbers.[18] Joshua 18:1–10* is key for this phase: this text resides in the center of the land-division texts both structurally and conceptually, with Shiloh representing the tabernacle (18:1, 8, 9, 10),[19] which the Levites are to guard and protect.[20] In this conception complete rest becomes possible only after the Levites obtain their cities (21:44). The area of the land-division complex (*Landverteilungskomplex*) reveals a topographical gradation in nearness to the deity: The tent of meeting and Yhwh's presence reside in the center of the land surrounded by the Levites, with the other tribes located in successive concentric rings beginning with Judah and Joseph.[21]

This diachronic development illustrates the Levites' status fluctuation in a positive direction in terms of honor and religious authority. At the same time, their positioning between Yhwh and the tribes of Israel, especially in view of their Aaronide-Levite competitors,[22] seems tentative, as if it were a momentary victory barely won on the literary and theological plane. If one wishes to gain a consistent picture of the Levites, the analogy of gaming pieces used in discussions of priestly prerogative and proximity to the divine may capture some of its essence. Belonging to an ancient tribe does not assure one's belonging in a tribal society. Knowing this all too well, the Levites may have

---

16. Jacobus Cornelis de Vos, *Das Los Judas: Über Entstehung und Ziele der Landbeschreibung in Josua 15* (VTSup 95; Leiden: Brill, 2003).

17. Ibid., 535: "Hier gilt das Interesse dem Aaroniten Eleasar. Vermutlich, waren es darum Aaroniten, die die Landverteilung 'klerikalisieren' wollten."

18. Ibid.: "Diese Ordnung is durch Grenzen und Zahlen genau festgelegt."

19. Ibid., 536.

20. This is made clear because of other remarks about the special belongingness (*Zugehörigkeit*) of the Levites to God as their inheritance (13:14, 33; 14:4b; 21:1–41) as well as the indirect allusion to Levites as keepers of the tabernacle in 18:1 (ibid., 536).

21. Ibid., 537–38, and the elucidative diagram on p. 539.

22. The contrast between the pro-Levite stage and the earlier pro-Aaronide stage points to conflict of interest between circles of Aaronide-Levites and Levites (ibid., 536-37).

sought a sense of belonging on a different socioreligious plane, in a conceptually experimental sodality[23] with its own budding charter.

B. Structure of the Present Study

The present study takes as its points of departure three main texts: Neh 8, Lev 17–26 (receiving the most extensive treatment), and several texts in Deuteronomy, particularly the office laws in Deut 16:18–18:22. For a literary-critical basis I employ aspects of the analyses of Eckart Otto, Reinhard Achenbach, and Christophe Nihan regarding post-Pg and post-Dtr texts. For the treatment of key texts in H elucidating relations between office and community, I have looked to the work of Klaus Grünwaldt, Jacob Milgrom, and, to a lesser extent, Israel Knohl. For rhetorical strategies, I am especially indebted to Jan Joosten's recent work on H,[24] which has assisted the extrapolation of aspects of the proclamation and reception of revealed law.

II. Scenario One: Nehemiah 8

A. Cultically Competent Community:
A Levite-Led National Assembly

Geographically, Ezra's reading of *tôrâ* in Neh 8—a postexilic text reflecting the Levites' recently increased status—reflects an urban setting with Levites interpreting the Hebrew text into the common language of the people, probably Aramaic.[25] Chronologically, I accept 445 B.C.E. and 398 B.C.E. as the onsets of the respective missions of Nehemiah and Ezra.[26] Together, these two eras witnessed the literary activity that produced the post-Dtr and post-

---

23. See José E. Ramírez Kidd, *Alterity and Identity in Israel: The* גר *in the Old Testament* (BZAW 283: Berlin: de Gruyter, 1999), 62.

24. Jan Joosten, "La persuasion coopérative dans le discurs sur la loi: pour une analyse de la rhétorique du Code de Sainté," in *Congress Volume: Ljubljana, 2007* (ed. Amdré Lemaire; VTSup 133; Leiden: Brill, 2010), 381–98; idem, "Moïse, l'assemblée et les fils d'Israël: La structuration du pouvoir dans le Code de Sainteté," forthcoming in a volume edited by A. Wénin.

25. See Ezra 4:17–18 (King Artaxerxes' letter to Rehum and Shimshi); William Schniedewind, "Aramaic, the Death of Written Hebrew, and Language Shift," in *Margins of Writing, Origins of Cultures* (ed. Seth L. Sanders; Oriental Institute Seminars 2; Chicago: Oriental Institute of the University of Chicago, 2006), 137–47, 139.

26. For this dating, see Christophe L. Nihan, "Ethnicity and Identity in Isaiah 56–66," in *Judah and the Judeans in the Achaemenid Period: Negotiating Identity in an International Context* (ed. Oded Lipschits, Gary N. Knoppers, and Manfred Oeming; Winona Lake, Ind.: Eisenbrauns, 2011), 67–104, esp. 72 and passim. See also Juha Pakkala, *Ezra the Scribe: The Development of Ezra 7–10 and Nehemia 8* (BZAW 347; Berlin/New York: de Gruyter, 2004), 79–80 and n. 199.

P Hexateuch redaction (HexRed)[27] and Pentateuch redactions (PentRed),[28] respectively.

Though Neh 8 lacks reference to the holiness of the community, the emphasis on hallowing the day (three times in vv. 9–11) prohibits blood-kin responsibilities that defile, such as mourning (אבל *hitpa'el*), weeping (בכה *qal*), and grieving (עצב *nip'al*). Verse 9 announces the sacralization of the occasion, "the day is holy to the Lord . . . [therefore] do not mourn or weep." Grieving arguably poses more difficulties for priests than for laypersons (cf. Lev 10:6); this is made clear in H (Lev 21:1–6; see below). The notorious stress on ethnic homogeneity elsewhere in Ezra-Nehemiah (Ezra 9–10; Neh 13:23–28), along with the Levites purifying themselves (טהר *hitpa'el*; Neh 13:22) for the task of guarding against unlawful trespass on the Sabbath (13:15–22; note that vv. 23–28 deal with the problem of intermarriage), indicates a marked concern for maintaining the sanctity of the community and consecrating their religious assemblies, practices (cf. Neh 9:14[29]; 10:31; Ezra 8:28; 9:2), and the days on which they fall (Neh 8:9–11; cf. 9:14; 10:31; 13:22). Nehemiah 11:1, 18 contain two of the four references to Jerusalem as "the holy city" (עיר הקדש) in the Hebrew Bible.[30] One may conclude from this that Neh 8 promotes the notion that the community can and should be holy, an expectation that becomes eminently more pronounced in H and parts of Ezekiel.

The expectation of the Levite-led assembly in Neh 8 (cf. 9:4–5) to both prepare for and observe Sukkot is quite high (vv. 13–18; cf. Neh 13:3!). Much is required of them: considerable knowledge, coordinated physical labor, mental discipline, and a willingness to participate in days of *tôrôt* immersion (v. 18a; cf. Josh 1:8). While the initial *tôrâ* event in Neh 8:1–8 could have occurred as described, the account most likely condenses numerous proclamatory events.[31] Alexander Rofé thinks it unlikely that a leading, national figure such as Ezra would have presided over such occasions of proclamation. Rather, it seems more likely that the ceremonies would have been led by regional functionaries

---

27. Reinhard Achenbach, *Die Vollendung der Tora: Studien zur Redaktionsgeschichte des Numeribuches im Kontext von Hexateuch und Pentateuch* (BZABR 3; Wiesbaden: Harrasowitz, 2003).

28. Eckart Otto, *Das Deuteronomium im Pentateuch und Hexateuch: Studien zur Literaturgeschichte von Pentateuch und Hexateuch im Lichte des Deuteronomiumrahmens* (FAT 30; Tübingen: Mohr Siebeck, 2000).

29. The collocation קדש + שבת + (שבתון) "holy sabbath" appears only in Exod 16:23; 35:2; Neh 9:14.

30. See also Isa 48:2; 52:1; Dan 9:24 has "your holy city."

31. There may have been a lengthy (thirteen years?) delay between the time Ezra arrived in Jerusalem and the time he leads the public assembly, fulfilling his commission. Such a delay would be hard to explain to Persian authorities. It may then be best to view the major event (Neh 8) as either a climax or a condensation of many earlier events officiated by Levites commissioned by Ezra (Ezra 7:25–26) to promulgate the law.

such as the Levites, who in Neh 8 receive explicit authorization to supervise.[32] Nehemiah 9:1–5 lend support to this proposal. Here the laity begin the service (vv. 1–3), with the lay leaders themselves reading the law in v. 3 (cf. 13:1[33]). As described, this activity likely ensued with the assistance of Levites, much like what would have occurred as a matter of course in non-urban sanctuaries.[34] Verse 4 includes the Levites and has them lead the service, whereupon they inject prophetic-liturgical direction in v. 5aβ: "stand up and bless the Lord your God forever and ever." This is followed by the lay-Levite cooperative taking charge of the sacral event—without the involvement of Ezra. One would expect the Levites' inspired introduction in v. 5 to be followed by a sermon, and that is precisely what we find in 9:6–10:1 [Eng. 9:6–38]. The fact that the Hebrew text of v. 6 does not mention Ezra at all, in conjunction with Ezra's prior transferral of *tôrâ* ownership to the community and concomitant designation of Levites as its capable handlers in matters of translation, interpretation, and inculcation (8:13), argues against crediting Ezra with the magnificent prayer of ch. 9. Lena-Sofia Tiemeyer finds the ideology in this prayer "distinct from the prevailing ideology of Ezra and Nehemiah as a whole" and attributes the prayer to northern Levites who "lived out the exilic years in Judah."[35] She also argues that Jer 41:4–5 lends support for a northern origin for the prayer. Verse 5, for example, recounts eighty men returning from Shechem, Shiloh, and Samaria and worshiping at God's house at Mizpah.[36]

---

32. E.g., Alexander Rofé, "The Scribal Concern for the Torah as Evidenced by the Textual Witnesses of the Hebrew Bible," in *Mishneh Todah: Studies in Deuteronomy and Its Cultural Environment in Honor of Jeffrey H. Tigay* (ed. Nili Sacher Fox, David A. Glatt-Gilad, and Michael J. Williams; Winona Lake, Ind.: Eisenbrauns, 2009), 230.

33. The reader of the law in v. 1a is left unspecified.

34. See Jacob Wright, "A New Model for the Composition of Ezra-Nehemiah," in *Judah and the Judeans in the Fourth Century B.C.E.* (ed. Oded Lipschits, Gary N. Knoppers, and Rainer Albertz; Winona Lake, Ind.: Eisenbrauns, 2007), 333–48. Wright posits that Neh 8–10 contains the latest layers of the book, building upon traditions in Ezra 2 and Neh 7 and showing "unmistakable parallels with Ezra 3" (p. 345; cf. 346). "Whereas Ezra 3 presents the people as gathering to erect the altar and reinitiate the sacrificial cult, Nehemiah 8–10 presents the people as gathering in a plaza far away from the temple in order to hear the Torah read" (p. 345).

35. Lena-Sofia Tiemeyer, "Abraham: A Judahite Prerogative," *ZAW* 120 (2008): 49–66, 61–63.

36. Whereas Mizpah functioned as an administrative center, nearby Bethel served as a cultic center (Tiemeyer, "Abraham," 63, citing Joseph Blenkinsopp regarding Mizpah and Bethel); see Blenkinsopp, "Bethel in the Neo-Babylonian Period," in *Judah and the Judeans in the Neo-Babylonian Period* (ed. Joseph Blenkinsopp and Oded Lipschits; Winona Lake, Ind.: Eisenbrauns, 2003), 93–107; and idem, "The Judean Priesthood during the Neo-Babylonian and Achaemenid Periods: A Hypothetical Reconstruction," *CBQ* 60 (1998): 25–43.

Like Neh 8 (cf. 13:1–3), the septennial readings of the law in Deut 31:10–13 suggest a royal or capital city as the place of proclamation.[37] Admittedly, on first blush neither text suggests a residential town or village as the venue. (The same holds true for the accounts of the PRR occurring at Sinai and Horeb, respectively, although in these cases an urban setting is not in view.) In light of the complex challenges facing rural villagers attending national events at a single urban center, an unembellished reading of such accounts does not commend itself. Smaller-scale gatherings at local sites would comprise more practical and pedagogically effective contexts for proclamation, preaching, and teaching.

B. Condensing and Urbanizing Revelatory Events

In his recent article, Wolfgang Zwickel turns up little archaeological evidence for a sizable population living in Jerusalem during Nehemiah's time. Excavators have found a piece of a wall and a door that can be assigned to the Achaemenid period, with additional wall fragments plausibly assigned to this time. Zwickel's analysis of certain broken stones leads him to posit significant architectural planning, perhaps in connection with the city wall of Nehemiah (Neh 2:8, 17; 4:1; 6:1; 7:1; 12:27 and passim). *Yehud* stamps are also documented, though not in abundance. In general, the evidence for residential development in Nehemian-period Jerusalem is lacking. Moreover, the number of settlements in Jerusalem's environs drops from 142 in Iron II to 13 in the Persian Period.[38]

As far as can be deduced from archaeological remains, the primary population consisted of elites directly associated with matters of the state, including its religion. Thus, external evidence does not support the idea of a large population participating in the kind of religious events described in Neh 8–9 during the Persian period. While the possibility of people occasionally coming to Jerusalem from villages in the greater region exists, it is more likely that underlying the event described are numerous local events that have been condensed and urbanized. Deuteronomistic texts suggest that fertility cults thrived in the countryside (2 Kgs 16:4; Deut 12:2), and one goal of urbanizing these events was to remove elements of rural unorthodoxy. Also, portraying

---

37. In Deut 31:11, the site is the "place that Yhwh will choose."
38. Wolfgang Zwickel, "Jerusalem und Samaria zur Zeit Nehemias: Ein Vergleich," *BZ* 52 (2008): 201–22, esp. 206–7; cf. Diana Edelman, "Cultic Sites and Complexes beyond the Jerusalem Temple," in Stavrakopoulou and Barton, *Religious Diversity in Ancient Israel and Judah*, 82–103, here 99; cf. Davies, "Urban Religion," 107: "at the end of Hezekiah's reign Judah consisted of little more than Jerusalem and its immediate environs"; Wright (" New Model," 346–47) sees the "major [archaeological] expansions" in Jerusalem occurring not in the fourth century "as commonly thought" but rather in the third century.

the event as Yahwistic and Jerusalemite advanced the agenda of monotheism and centralization, respectively.[39]

Local events were in general of a much smaller scale, occurring at various sanctuaries (or at home—a substitute for the temple[40]) facilitated by spiritually endowed laity—including women[41]—and religious functionaries such as cult prophets. Presiding over the teaching, worship, and inquiries of the deity would have been not elites but rather mid-level religious personnel such as the Levites.[42] In local contexts one would also expect to see increased involvement of local laity and elders, especially perhaps those benefiting from modest education (cf. Neh 9:4).[43] Though our reading of Neh 8 (cf. 13:1–3) remains hypothetical, it is certainly plausible, and it establishes a conceptual and interpretive framework that will prove useful as we proceed through this study.

III. Scenario Two: Leviticus 17–26 (H)

A. Compositional Considerations

In our second scenario, that of Lev 17–26 (H), the participation of the laity within the sphere of the cult is more apparent than in Neh 8, and yet much of it either is presented in understated fashion or must be inferred. Before we proceed to a discussion of H's vision of the ideal distribution of religio-cultic

---

39. Davies, "Urban Religion," 111; cf. Edelman, "Cultic Sites," 85. Davies also speaks of the urbanization of religious festivals and the "imposition of urban onto rural culture" (p. 112). For delineations of urban and rural religion in Phoenicia, see Mark A. Christian, "Mediterranean Grottos and Maritime Ministry in Phoenician-Punic Religion," in *Mélanges Josette Elayi: Phéniciens d'Orient et d'Occident* (ed. André Lemaire; Suppléments à Transeuphratène; Paris: Gabalda, forthcoming).

40. "Temple praxis may, to a certain extent, be family praxis writ large" (Meyers, "Household Religion," 122 n. 19); cf. Stanley K. Stowers, "Theorizing Ancient Household Religion," in Bodel and Olyan, *Household and Family Religion in Antiquity*, 5–19, esp. 12.

41. Various spiritually endowed women are mentioned in biblical texts describing the late monarchic, exilic, Persian, and Greco-Roman periods: for example, Deborah, a "woman prophetess" (אשה נביאה; Judg 4–5), Huldah (2 Kgs 22//2 Chr 34), "the daughters of Ezekiel's people" (Ezek 13:17–23), Noadiah (Neh 6:14), Anna the prophetess (Acts 2:36–38), and Jezebel (Rev 2:20). See now H. G. M. Williamson, "Prophetesses in the Hebrew Bible," in Day, *Prophecy and Prophets in Ancient Israel*, 65–80. Williamson notes that Deborah and Huldah are the last named prophets in the Deuteronomistic History (p. 70). These high-profile personages constitute the tip of the iceberg of gifted women active in local religious contexts that, as a result of their gender and obscurity, go unrecognized in the official literature. P. D. Miller relates that female oracular speakers and intermediaries at Mari and Emar show affinities to Israelite exemplars of these and earlier periods (*The Religion of Ancient Israel* [Library of Ancient Israel; Louisville: Westminster John Knox, 2000], 174–78).

42. See, e.g., Deut 18:6; and Lindblom, *Erwägungen*, 26–30.

43. Christian, "Priestly Power That Empowers," 21–23.

responsibility among Judah's various constituencies, an examination of its composition history is warranted.

The text of H most likely postdates the time of Nehemiah and should therefore be reckoned as both post-P and post-Dtr. H betrays considerable dependence not only on P but also on D.[44] It shares this dual dependence with the post-P and post-Dtr formulation of both the Hexateuch and the Pentateuch,[45] lessening the likelihood that H once existed as an independent code.[46] This view militates against the thesis that much of the code's current formulation took shape prior to the Babylonian exile.

As for its genre, the proposal that H is a vassal treaty faces the difficulty of the conditional promises that fill its final chapter.[47] Consideration of H as law code likewise runs into problems. It employs the formula עולם + חקת + לדרת + possessive suffix to make exclusivistic claims about its legislation vis-à-vis other laws—but 40 percent of this collocation's occurrences are outside of H in Leviticus (3:17; 6:18; 7:36 10:9), as well as in slightly different formulations in Exodus and Numbers (Exod 12:14, 17; 27:21; Num 10:8; 15:15; 18:23). Jeffery Stackert concludes that "this absolute claim eliminates the possibility . . . that H and its pentateuchal competitors can be understood within a scheme of legal development."[48] On thematic grounds as well, its experimental (and rambling) treatment of ethical-ritual and legal topics is

---

44. Jeffrey Stackert emphasizes H's concern to preserve P above all other codes ("The Holiness Legislation and Its Pentateuchal Sources: Revision, Supplementation, and Replacement," in *The Strata of the Priestly Writings: Contemporary Debate and Future Directions* [ed. Sarah Shectman and Joel S. Baden; AThANT 95; Zurich: TVZ, 2009], 201); see also Alfred Cholewínski, *Heiligkeitsgesetz und Deuteronomium: Eine vergleichende Studie* (AnBib 66; Rome: Pontifical Biblical Institute, 1976); cf. Christophe L. Nihan, "The Holiness Code between D and P: Some Comments on the Function and Significance of Leviticus 17–26 in the Composition of the Torah," in *Das Deuteronomium zwischen Pentateuch und Deuteronomistischem Geschichtswerk* (ed. Eckart Otto and Reinhard Achenbach; FRLANT 206; Göttingen: Vandenhoeck & Ruprecht, 2004), 81–122.

45. Otto, "Holiness Code," 139; cf. Reinhard Achenbach, "Das Heiligkeitsgesetz und die sakralen Ordnungen des Numeribuches," in *The Books of Leviticus and Numbers* (ed. Thomas Römer; BETL 215; Leuven: Peeters, 2008), 145–77.

46. Otto, "Holiness Code," 139; Klaus Grünwaldt, "Amt und Gemeinde im Heiligkeitsgesetz," in *Textarbeit: Studien zu Texten und ihrer Rezeption aus dem Alten Testament und der Umwelt Israels. Festschrift für Peter Weimar zur Vollendung seines 60. Lebensjahres* (ed. Klaus Kiesow and Thomas Meurer; AOAT 294; Münster: Ugarit-Verlag, 2003), 227–44, 228–29.

47. Grünwaldt, "Amt," 229; see also Joosten, who contrasts the "stipulations" of the biblical covenant with those of a vassal treaty, which "are aimed specifically at assuring the vassal's allegiance, whereas the substance of the biblical codes is law (including ethical and cultic prescriptions)" (*People and Land in the Holiness Code: An Exegetical Study of the Ideational Framework of the Law in Leviticus 17–26* [VTSup 67; Leiden: Brill, 1996], 20–22; quotation from 22).

48. Stackert, "Holiness Legislation," 196.

not suggestive of a law code.[49] It does, however, share an affinity with sacerdotal legal texts in the way it proposes a compilation of regulations and previously existing customs.[50] One thing is certain: the past is very present in this work.

In actuality, the authors of H perpetuated a different kind of code, which is arranged in complex and often obscure genre modes. Laid out in Lev 17–26 is a parenetic collection designed as an alternative to the organizational and *inhaltlich* schemas typical of elitist formulations that target fellow elites. Such formulations prove less appealing to an audience more apt to respond to kinship- and community-oriented rhetoric. The Holiness Code's deft use of kinship and relational terms in legal sociopolitical contexts facilitates this technique of rhetoric (אחים in Lev 21:10; 25:14 [cf. 39:46]; cf. אזרח "citizen," "native born" in 19:34; 23:42; 24:16, 22). In this regard, the code's producers appear to have taken seriously the task of speaking for and to multiple levels of society. The corpus's inclusion in the book of Leviticus, intricately inlaid into the Priestly Code[51]—and thematically cogent within the larger frame of the Sinai pericope—provides H's parenetic constellation with literary-historical and theological continuity and "structure." As with the Deuteronomic Code's contextualized emplacement within Deuteronomy (D = chs. 12–27*), this helped ensure the assemblage's survival in the form that has come down to us.

In a manner similar to that of Deuteronomy, H "exploits the dialectic relationship between law and account."[52] In this respect it reveals expertise in the "preaching of the law" method that advances its rhetorical intentions and for which Levites have been long and rightfully credited.[53] The ethical-ritual rhetoric in H provokes a *cooperative response*: on one level it provokes the audience to fill in the thematic and discursive lacunae (what might be described today as "active listening"); on another, more observable level, it commands or outlaws various actions in hopes of maintaining the integrity of both the people and the mission to which they are called.[54] H seems acutely aware that the greater community will not embrace a program

---

49. Grünwaldt, "Amt," 229; cf. Joosten, "Persuasion coopérative," 385; cf. Frank Crüsemann, *The Torah: Theology and Social History of Old Testament Law* (trans. A. W. Mahnke; Minneapolis: Fortress, 1996), 277–78.

50. Joosten, "Persuasion coopérative," 395.

51. Ibid., 396.

52. Ibid.; cf. Deut 6:21–22.

53. Insofar as it purports to transmit divine speech (cf. the plenary transmission of revealed law in Exodus and Deuteronomy), we may speak of the priestly-prophetic dimensions of the levitical preaching in H. See also Joosten, "Persuasion coopérative," 396; and idem, "Structuration du pouvoir."

54. Joosten, "Persuasion coopérative," 397.

of scrupulous observance of the law without first being convinced of two things: (a) the international necessity of all-Israel keeping the law, and (b) that all-Israel has been commissioned, authorized, and empowered to fulfill its ethical-ritual mission.

B. Reconsideration of Cultic Roles in H as a Function of Social Tension

In view of the prominence placed on Aaronide leadership of the cult, one would not expect the Holiness Code simultaneously to hint at significant lay participation in that cult. Nonetheless, we find exactly that from the beginning of the corpus: "If anyone of the house of Israel slaughters . . . in the camp or . . . outside the camp and does not bring it to the entrance of the tent of meeting. . . . This is in order that the people of Israel may bring their sacrifices *that they offer in the open field*" (אשר הם זחים על פני השׂדה; Lev 17:3–5). Although the passage in 17:1–4 clearly seeks to outlaw indiscriminate slaughter, the recognition that laypersons do indeed sacrifice away from the central sanctuary concedes that such practices will continue. Therefore, the passage probably owes to the impractical expectation of elite priests. Although vv. 1–4 do not fit well in the interpretive horizon of H, they help link the P materials in the earlier chapters of Leviticus to H.

Throughout the corpus of the Holiness Code, there ensues a reconsideration of the institution of cultic leadership. The discussion takes shape in a less evident manner than in the office laws of Deuteronomy (see below). H at times presents a rambling (cf. 21:1–9 to vv.10–15 to vv. 16–23 to v. 24; 22:1–3 to vv. 4–7 to v. 8 to v. 9 to v. 10; 24:1–8 to 9–22 to 22–23), almost extemporized reassessment of theological premises, cult liabilities, and roles. The depiction of the community in the layered texts of H oscillates somewhat experimentally between leadership modes (or "offices") of various cultically competent persons—lay, priestly, and high priestly (especially ch. 22).

One senses both cooperation and tension in the "discourse," yet there is nothing here that compares with the open *mêlée* in Num 16, or for that matter the fiery ordeal in Lev 10. Although sociopolitical rivalry remains somewhat subdued in H, the audience/readership cannot but interpret it as reflective of the power dimensions accompanying a system that focuses intently on the religious performance of the entire community (cf. 17:2; 19:2; 21:24; 22:3, 18; 23:42), while at the same time reserving certain ministrations for professional priests. Attempts to reallocate religious leadership types would not be received with open arms, especially were the impetus to come from outside the elite sphere of hieratic leadership. Although we see a severe reaction to presuming on the sacred domain in Lev 10 and, equally late, theocratically revised texts in Numbers,[55] H's idealistic program seems to have survived reasonably intact. The survival of this program might be explained as a product of the intentionally innovative, yet remarkably durable, stabilizing components within its idealistic system, such as the fundamental importance accorded to cultic purity. It would seem that both the addressed and envisioned community in H shared the view that purity played a central role both in the formation of community identity and in the maintenance of right-standing with the deity. The model the Levites seek to institute in H, however, purports to move beyond the myopic perceptions regarding ritual purity that might otherwise descend into a pattern of excluding nonspecialists, on the one hand, and harboring and bestirring xenophobic tendencies on the other.

With the input of the community, assistance of community leaders, and likely supporters among the Aaronides,[56] the Levites successfully created the impression of a collaborative venture.[57] As part of their persuasive artistry, they drew upon shared experiences and communal knowledge of past events. They also presumed familiarity with the current state of legal matters. Joosten summarizes this technique of appeal:

> Enfin, les connaissances et le vécu de l'auditoire sont également sollicités en vue de la persuasion. Les grands chapitres de l'histoire nationale tels l'exode et le don du pays, ainsi que la sainte terreur qu'inspire la présence de Dieu dans son sanctuaries sont mis à contribution dans l'argumentation explicite du Code.[58]

The mid-level cultic personnel spearheading the composition of H employed aspects of the pedagogical approach they had refined in the field, that is, in local and regional cultic settings. The objective here, in contrast to that of the narrative of Neh 8:1–9, is not merely "énoncer la loi, ni dicter la loi,

---

55. Achenbach attributes the final edition of Numbers, which already included texts originating with HexRed and PentRed in Num 10–25*; 32, to three layers of theocratic revisions (*theocratischen Bearbeitungen*; ThB). These circles were responsible for Num 1–10; 26–31; and 33–36, texts usually attributed to P. It is the third stage of revision, ThB III, responsible for the "Korah-Levite revision" (e.g., Num 16:1, 5–7*, 16*, (17b), 19a, 20–22, 24b, 27, 33bβ, 41–45; 17:1–5, 6–10; 18) that vehemently opposes the involvement of laity in the cult.

56. I employ shaded terminology when treating the Israelite priesthood, emphasizing the "levitical" (Semitic *lwy*, originally a vocational term meaning "client of X," and later tribal affiliation) aspects of both Zadokites and Aaronides, hence my distinction between Zadokite-Levites (associated with Ezek 40–48, parts of Deuteronomy, and some theocratic *Bearbeitungen* in Numbers) and Aaronide-Levites (usually associated with P).

57. Doubtful of villager collaboration in the compilation of laws is Knight, *Law, Power, and Justice*, 99.

58. Joosten, "Persuasion coopérative," 397.

mais inculquer la loi."[59] Further, "l'acte du discours (l'acte illocutionnaire) est directif avec une forte composante de persuasion—on veut amener l'auditoire à l'assentiment, à l'appropriation des règles énoncées."[60] The rhetorical style is also imbued with the authoritative motivator "you should (not)... because (usually כי)" (thus the programmatic Lev 19:2; cf. the negative formulation [לא + imperfect] in, for example, 17:12–14; 18:10–11, 13; 19:20; 20:19, 23; 21:12, inter alia).

C. Israelite Laity and Ritual Purity

In the chapters following Lev 19 the writers of H present a series of *theologoumena*[61] that would persuade the audience, through the agency of rhetoric, to accept the responsibility for maintaining a holy community. The presentation connects the people's hesitation to embrace their priest-like calling—tied in part to a defeatist mentality acquired over years of protracted servitude (Exod 6:9)[62]—with Yhwh's affirmation of their election. Leviticus 20:25a asserts the provocative notion that the people are not only to assume the priestly calling, but also to demonstrate it on a fairly sophisticated and critical level. By divine command they are to distinguish between clean and unclean: "You [2nd pl.] shall therefore make a distinction [בדל *hip'il*] between the clean animal and the unclean, and between the unclean bird and the clean" (cf. Lev. 10:10). Verse 25bα assumes the lay quasi-priests' awareness of the cultic risks of profanation and v. 25bβ presumes their capacity for reckoning unclean (טמא *pi'el*) that which Yhwh has already declared to be unclean (cf. the use of בדל *hip'il* in Neh 13:3). Verse 25bβ, then, similarly to 19:2b, indicates the essential qualification for performing key priestly functions: Yhwh—and not cultic personnel[63]—has made known the critical distinction himself. A careful reading of this text reveals the following: the divine separator and sanctifier of people (cf. Lev 22:32b) (1) separated between clean and unclean animals,[64] and then (2) revealed this distinction to his people via apparently unofficial (i.e.,

---

59. Joosten, "Structuration du pouvoir" (emphasis added).
60. Ibid.
61. Milgrom describes the succession of holiness themes as having a "staccato emphasis" (*Leviticus: A New Translation with Introduction and Commentary* [3 vols.; AB 3, 3A, 3B; New York: Doubleday, 1991–2000], 2:1887).
62. Cf. Num 14:9–11, which directly connects disobedience and rebellion (מרד) to fear (ירא) of the surrounding nations.
63. "Priester spielen in Heiligkeitsgesetz nur eine untergeordnete Rolle" (Georg Steins, "Priesterherrschaft, Volk von Priestern oder was sonst? Zur Interpretation von Ex 19,6," *BZ* 45 [2001]: 20–36, here 33).
64. Grünwaldt, "Amt," 232–33.

unmediated through cultic officials), direct revelation.⁶⁵ This point deserves special emphasis, since direct revelation, disclosed to an assembly at a regional sanctuary (cf. Neh 8) heightens the uniqueness of the Yhwh–Israel relationship. Such unmediated revelation also serves to increase the level of its recipients' culpability. The same holds true for prophetically charged environments, where discerning between true and false "words" and teachings becomes a community-wide responsibility (see section IV below). Thus, from what we can gather from these textual witnesses, cultic competence and prophetic discernment were regarded as essential skills for the Israelite community to have.

D. Local and Regional Settings for the PRR by Yahwists

The *setting* of revelation in Lev 20:25 plausibly corresponds to the *original* local and regional venues for preaching, teaching, and worship in which the revelation of divine law (e.g., the Decalogue) reportedly occurred. The local experiences were later condensed literarily into one or two major events at the national level (Exod 20:18–22 [esp. vv. 18, 22]; 33:1–4; Deut 4:10–12, 33–37; 5:4, 22). Similar to our interpretation of Neh 8 (section II above), in which the single, plenary reading of the law actually condenses numerous public readings and sermons given by the religious personnel such as the levitical priest-prophets, the Sinai/Horeb receptions of the Decalogue condense numerous local and regional proclamations of laws and regulations delivered over time.

Stanley Stowers describes a similar phenomenon occurring in biblical depictions of temple worship, which "borrowed the everyday practices" of local worship settings. The local events were then "greatly elaborated and exaggerated ... to mark them precisely as not everyday." With regard to altar worship, biblical writers wanted to make local sacrifice something more: "it was not just an everyday dinner, but a sacrificial feast in the house of a god."⁶⁶

---

65. Cf. 11:44b, where Yhwh commands the people directly, without mediation; 11:44aβ emphasizes that the worshiper is to sanctify himself, in contrast to 20:25. Christian Frevel and Erich Zenger recognize the significance of 11:44–45 and 20:25–26 for the non-priestly community's religious life ("Die Bücher Levitikus und Numeri als Teile der Pentateuchkomposition," in Römer, *Books of Leviticus and Numbers*, 35–74, here 42).

66. Stowers, "Theorizing Ancient Household Religion," 12. P. M. Michèle Daviau emphasizes the crucial nature of finding and excavating temples for distinguishing between central and peripheral expressions of religion: "The relationship of the domestic cult to the official or national cult cannot be determined for the Iron Age kingdom of 'Ammon, since excavation has not yet revealed a temple where public worship was celebrated" ("Family Religion: Evidence for the Paraphernalia of the Domestic Cult," in *The World of the Aramaeans*, vol. 2, *Studies in History and Archaeology in Honour of Paul-Eugène Dion* [ed. P. M. Michèle Daviau et al.; JSOTSup 325; Sheffield: Sheffield Academic Press, 2001], 199–229, here 223). But differentiating between various types of roofed structures can be difficult.

Assemblies at these events most likely consisted of tribes, families, and individuals (cf. the resident alien) who aligned themselves with their warrior/deliverer god. Biblical tradition avers that this god revealed himself and his law to the people he brought near to himself (Ps 65:5a; Deut 4:7, 10–12a; 5:27). This deity's communicative propinquity finds radical expression in Deuteronomy. The following passage boasts of regular and direct knowledge of the will of God:

> Now what I am commanding you today is not too difficult for you or beyond your reach. It is not up in heaven, so that you have to ask, "Who will ascend into heaven to get it and proclaim it to us so we may obey it?" Nor is it beyond the sea, so that you have to ask, "Who will cross the sea to get it and proclaim it to us so we may obey it?" No, the word is very near you; it is in your mouth and in your heart so you may obey it. (Deut 30:11–14)

Given that the context here is the aftermath of Israel's banishment to the nations (v. 1), the assertion of prophetic potential (esp. v. 14) is unexpected. Yhwh's chosen underwent perilous initiations (cf. the typological reenactments of the exodus) and painful transformations associated with the occupation of the promised land. And yet, even with such momentous failure in (pre)view, vv. 11–14 posit the people's potential for ongoing, close communicative relationship (כי־קרוב אליך הדבר מאד; v. 14a) with their self-disclosing deity.

The nearness of God, whether the voice (קול) or the word (דבר), can be anxiety-provoking. Neither the Hebrew Bible nor the Christian New Testament lacks for communicative encounters between the divine and human realms, some of which involve instructions given to regular people.[67] That Lev 20:25bβ (and 11:44b) would report or allude to Yhwh having instructed the people directly should therefore not surprise us, though, admittedly, these reports run counter to the dominant presentations and interpretations familiar to scholars and students of the Hebrew Bible. Though the notion of an expected prophetic competence applies more overtly to the community in the office laws of Deuteronomy, post-P and post-Dtr texts such as H presume its importance in their conception of personal responsibility, for example, differentiating between Yahwistic and non-Yahwistic modes of inquiry.[68]

Edelman underscores the difficulty of differentiating between a god's house and a human dwelling "when the primary term that is translated 'temple' is the common word for 'house' and context alone determines which value the word [בית] is assigned" ("Cultic Sites," 89). In the case of Shechem, Bethel, Hebron, Beersheba, Salem, and possibly the transjordanian site of Peniel on the Jabbok River in Transjordan, we have "no explicit sacrifice being offered on any of these altars" (ibid., 83).

67. E.g., Gen 16:7–11 (esp. v. 9); 18; 25:21–23; Exod 24 (esp. v. 11); Judg 2:1–5 (esp. v. 2); 13 (esp. vv. 4–5); Luke 1.

68. Cf. the concept in Lev 19:31 and 20:6, which is less developed than Deut 18:20–22.

IV. Scenario Three: Deuteronomy 16:18–18:22 (The Office Laws)

A. The Intended Audience of the Office Laws

Our third textual scenario is situated within the framework of Deuteronomy. The portrait of the Israelite community in this text has some affinities with that of the community of H, in that it too describes a community of "brothers" (אחים; cf. Deut 15:2–3, 7, 9, 11; 19:18–19; etc.), in which a distinct group appears to have been set apart within the larger community (cf. Deut 18:6–7). The office laws emphasize that this "brotherhood" is a group of *summoned* individuals,[69] a group that in the law of the priest (18:1–8) appears to merge with the Levites, despite some variability in the actors' identity in vv. 1–8.[70]

Matters of the political freedom and responsibility of the citizen loom large in the office laws. The author emphasizes the importance of this omnipresent actor in the text, which is often addressed directly: the "you" is summoned by the discourse of Moses and embodies the citizen *constructed* by the legislator. In this we see the—perhaps early[71]—concept of collective responsibility of Deuteronomic law. Consider the opening verse in the office laws: "*You* [2nd masc. sg.] shall appoint for yourself judges and officers in all *your* towns which the Lord your God is giving *you*, according to *your* tribes" (16:18). The effort of the lawgiver to persuade his audience via direct address similar to live conversation here recalls the persuasive techniques in H, over against the persuasive technique evident in Neh 8. In the latter, authoritative law is promulgated through the detailed *written* description of the proclamatory event and the fetching and reading of the *written* law in vv. 13–18[72] (cf. 2 Kgs 22:8–11).

However, distinctions emerge as well between the respective self-authorization strategies characterizing the office laws of Deuteronomy and the Holiness Code. Whereas we have argued that, in the parenetic assemblage of H, priests are subject to the community, the regulations in the Deuteronomic Code are connected to a past founder (Moses) beyond the control of the people. The latter principle of self-authorization suggests a geopolitical context in which the past hero conceptually trumps the current forces of political power,

---

69. Jean-Marie Carrière, *Théorie du politique dans le Deutéronome: Analyse des unités, des structures et des concepts de Dt 16,18–18,22* (ÖBS 18; Frankfurt a. M.: Peter Lang, 2001), 47–48.

70. Ibid., 148 and n. 190.

71. So ibid., 47.

72. Note that in v. 18aα the root שטר implies that the judges are literate and therefore likely play a part in teaching the law. That the people are charged with selecting and appointing them (v. 18aα) recalls the role the people play in selecting and approving priests in H.

be they foreign or domestic. Moreover, as an authorized prophet (18:18), the Moses figure serves as a religio-political buffer between the citizen and the political powers. He has the potential to function as prophetic-political advocate for the citizenry in a capacity conceptually similar to Isaiah's service to Hezekiah (Isa 36–39//2 Kgs 19–20).

Although the office laws do not belong to the original Deuteronomic Code,[73] they bear many of its sentiments (e.g., the threatening experience of Assyrian aggression and dominance; negative experiences with Israel's monarchy), teasing out its inchoate musings while simultaneously adding new elements. For example, the post-P and post-Dtr addition to the office laws of Deut 17:18–20 depicts the Levites instructing the domestic king and establishing a system that would hold him and future kings accountable (cf. Josh 1:7–8). In this late text the Levites merge with Moses and the Mosaic office of interpretation (cf. Deut 31:9; 24:8). Levites also personify the citizenry both in H[74] and in the latest texts of the office laws. For example, the bulk of the office laws still envision a context in which a political leader remains a valid option for the future (so Deut 17:14–17). In Deut 17:18–20, however, we have reached a stage contemporary with H in which the cooperation of religious leadership with the citizenry—however idealistic that may sound—becomes key.

The office laws enshrine in a written charter a particular political form of freedom and its expression. The projection of a different kind of class impacts the definition of the citizen, which expressly includes women (e.g., Deut 17:2, 5).[75] The individual citizens summoned in the office laws are a legal force in the community the identities of which are not static. They take on various modes of leadership, identifying most clearly with Levites (Deut 17:15bα), but also with judges (16:18), prophets (18:15aα), and even the king (17:15bα).[76]

B. Authority and Charisma in the Office Laws

Christa Schäfer-Lichtenberger has written on the authority relationships in Deut 16:18–18:22. Analysis of the office laws' view of authority and charisma

---

73. Carrière, *Théorie du politique*, 49.

74. Milgrom, *Leviticus*, 2:1712. Similarly, in the P history, "Levites assume an intermediate role between the Aaronide priests and the people" (Dozeman, *Commentary*, 710). In Num 1–8 the Levites substitute for the firstborn.

A satisfying explanation for the citizenry envisioned in H must reckon with the liminal Levites' virtual presence in spite of their literary absence in the mostly late text of H. We are suggesting that the space left by the Levite lacuna may have to do, at least in part, with an innovative—perhaps experimental—notion of a *de facto*, quasi-priestly peoplehood, which is faintly perceptible opposite the larger-than-life, *de jure* institution of the Aaronide priesthood.

75. Carrière, *Théorie du politique*, 46 n. 85, and 47.

76. Lindblom, *Erwägungen*, 51.

elucidates the relations of authority recognizable in the topos of the Yhwh–Moses relationship. According to Schäfer-Lichtenberger, these relationships are "*all charismatically founded*" (e.g., Deut 18:14–22).[77] Schäfer-Lichtenberger comes close to dealing with the PRR in her analysis of the "law of the prophet" (Deut 18:9–22). For example, she recognizes the distinctiveness of Deut 4:1–40—a late composition—which advocates for the immediacy of the divine relationship with Israel (e.g., 4:4a, 7; cf. v. 13). However, she does not address the issue of whether the new citizens' relationships to the Levites and/or to each other are somehow "charismatically founded." The term "charismatic" lends itself to a plethora of meanings. Here it is used essentially to designate an extra-institutional power/influence that creates roles and or relationships in order to fulfill a critical purpose (18:18–19). One could also speak of a divine ordaining of relationships.

Because the office laws concern themselves with the prophetic, especially in vv. 14–22, we must also include the dynamic of the spirit (רוח, which speaks in Yhwh's name; v. 20aα) in our consideration of the charismatic relationship. Though it is impossible to measure or quantify spiritual aptitude, Elisha is said to have had a "double portion" of the spirit פִּי־שְׁנַיִם רוּחַ (2 Kgs 2:9–15[78]; cf.

---

77. These are "*alle charismatisch begründeten Beziehungen*" (Christa Schäfer-Lichtenberger, *Josua und Salomo: Eine Studie zu Autorität und Legitimität des Nachfolgers im Alten Testament* [VTSup 58; Leiden: Brill, 1995], 45).

78. In spite of the inheritance context of Elisha's request for a double portion from Elijah, the larger context suggests (as does the context in Deut 34:9 in which Joshua receives a full impartation of the spirit of wisdom [מָלֵא רוּחַ חָכְמָה] from Moses; vv. 10–12 foreground the prophetic and the miraculous, and the "face to face" encounter [v. 10] which is associated with supernatural feats) an abundant conferral of the spirit of Yhwh. Elijah chides Elisha for asking such a thing (v. 10a; cf. v. 2) but then concedes that the request may likely be granted—and very soon.

Second Kings 2 paints a portrait of a prophetically infused environment and, indeed, community; v. 5 suggests that Elisha already has notable prophetic gifting and insight, since he claims to "know" what is about to happen before the company of prophets announce it to him, and he commands them not to mention it again (גַּם־אֲנִי יָדַעְתִּי הֶחֱשׁוּ). It is possible that Elijah, like the other prophets, already recognized his student's special gifting and found it difficult to think that Yhwh would grant such an extravagant request—this on top of any conferral of the firstborn brother's share and his master's religio-political authority. Verses 11–15 then confirm that Elisha has received everything he asked for. The surprising outpouring reminds of an even more unexpected conferral of the spirit of prophecy on Eldad and Medad in Num 11:25–29. The spirit rests on them (וַתָּנַח עֲלֵיהֶם הָרוּחַ; v. 26), not in company with the seventy elders and Moses at the tent of meeting (= a major sanctuary) where the major infilling event takes place (v. 25), but rather inexplicably among the community in the camp. Here we see depicted popular, democratized notions of encounters with the holy alongside more institutional conceptions. Although v. 25bβ limits the seventy's prophesying to a single event ("they prophesied"; v. 25bα), Eldad and Medad both "prophesied" (וַיִּתְנַבְּאוּ; v. 26bβ) and "are prophesying" (מִתְנַבְּאִים; v. 27b) in the

Gen 41:38–39; Isa 61:6–7). Recalling our analysis of Lev 20:25bβ (cf. 11:44b) the idea that the people have received cultic training directly from the deity betrays an assumption of prophetic aptitude in the sense of a special perception or sensitivity. For musings on the democratization of revelation in postexilic Israel, the reader is referred to Gary Knoppers's recent essay.[79] He states in the conclusion that:

> The author [of Chronicles] affirms that a whole range of people—professional and non-professional, native and foreign—were employed by Yahweh to speak to Israel. The importance of the prophetic impact on society is enhanced, rather than diminished, by its diffusion through a variety of conduits."[80]

Deuteronomy 18:16 self-evidently has some conception of the PRR in view: it concurs lexically and thematically with the narration of 5:5, 25–26, and reflects on Exod 20:18–19,[81] which emphasizes the people's fear, inability to withstand direct encounter with Yʜᴡʜ, and, consequently, the urgent need for intermediation (PentRed). In sharp contrast, the PRR conception in 5:4 (HexRed or school of HexRed), which lines up with 4:10–12, 33–37; Exod 20:20, 22*, depicts a community capable of "taking their stand" before the numinous deity (à la Exod 19:17b; יצב hitpaʿel); in this conception Moses functions more as a lightning rod for, than mediator of, revelation (Exod 33:7–11a; e.g., פנים אל פנים in v.11a).[82]

Thus, Deut 18:16b's reference to the people's fear of direct encounter does not merely repeat the familiar (Exod 20:18–19). Verse 16b indeed revisits the

---

camp. Although some in the community found this objectionable, Moses fully supports the democratization. This depiction of Moses does not originate with PentRed, but rather with the school of HexRed and/or one of the theocratic revisions, though not the latest, which opposes the involvement of the laity in the cultic worship; see n. 56 above.

79. Gary N. Knoppers, "Democratizing Revelation? Prophets, Seers and Visionaries in Chronicles, in Day, *Prophecy and Prophets in Ancient Israel*, 391–409.

80. Ibid., 404; cf. 405: "One would think that the Chronicler would not place such a stress on the prophetic phenomenon in Judah in continuity with the promise of Yahweh to appoint successors to Moses in Deuteronomy, if he thought that such a phenomenon had come to a definitive end.... The different forms prophecy takes in the Chronistic depiction of the past may provide some clues about the kinds of prophetic activity that were occurring in his own time, as well as the types of prophecy he commends to his readers. The diversity is quite striking. There is a certain amount of democratization or diffusion in the means by which Yahweh speaks. The Levites prophesy while functioning as musicians, thus attesting to the phenomenon of cultic prophecy associated with the Jerusalem Temple."

81. Space constraints do not permit a thorough discussion of the function of the people's fear of direct encounter with their deity in this passage. I treat the issue in chs. 2–3 of my dissertation; see unnumbered note above.

82. Cf. the tradition appearing in *1 En.* 89 (in the Animal Apocalypse), which also describes the people receiving Sinai revelation directly, though with Moses in the vicinity.

report of the people's fear at the holy mountain, though here we find no mention of the need for a mediating shield as in PentRed texts (e.g., Deut 5:5; cf. vv. 25–26; contra 5:4, 22, and other HexRed texts supporting the PRR: Exod 20:18–22; 33:1–4; Deut 4:10–12, 33–37) that emphasize Moses' authority and *sui generis* role as intermediary. Instead of motivating the people to seek Mosaic protection and interlocution (as in the scenes at the holy mountain in Exod 20), the fear in Deut 18:16 imagines a greater dreadfulness than an immediate encounter with Yhwh. Verse 16 leads circuitously to the postexilic situation in which the prophet like Moses (vv. 18–19; cf. Jer 1:4–19[83]) is to be heeded above all.[84] Now the impending disaster following the community's incautious reception of illicit revelation (vv. 20–22) is what one should fear most. Deuteronomy 18:16 thus functions as a stratagem in the battle waged on the level of the proto-canon to a shift from pentateuchal legal hermeneutic to the post-pentateuchal *prophetic* hermeneutic (i.e., *Tradentenprophetie*;[85] cf. Jer 1:4–19) and postexilic leadership.[86] The latter hermeneutic presumes the community's collective reception and acceptance of the revelation conveyed by Yhwh's authorized prophet.

The heightened degree of discernment attributed to the priestly-prophetic sodality for distinguishing true from false prophetic leadership (esp. Jer 14:13–16) and avoiding the lure of the latter (Deut 30:17b; נדח *nipʿal* "are drawn away," "impelled," "beguiled") corresponds to the cultic competence enjoined on the hybrid (priestly-lay) sodality in H. Whereas in H the Levite-infused community asserts itself in the commissioning and (re)examination of professional

---

83. Jeremiah 1:4–19 evidently has the law of the prophet (Deut 18:9–22) in view. Along with Deut 34:10–12, this passage may intend to announce the end of Mosaic prophecy; see Eckart Otto, "Jeremia und die Tora: Ein nachexilischer Diskurs," in Achenbach et al., *Tora in der Hebräischen Bibel*, 134–82, esp. 136–38.

84. Williamson points to hidden the reality that Huldah, "and in her wake, Deborah have also become central, institutionalized prophets in the Mosaic succession. . . . It is to Huldah, not Jeremiah or Zephaniah, that Josiah is said to have turned" ("Prophetesses," 73).

85. See Otto, "Jeremia"; idem, "A Post-exilic Discourse: Old and New Covenant. A Post-exilic Discourse between the Pentateuch and the Book of Jeremiah. Also a Study of Quotations and Allusions in the Hebrew Bible," *OTE* 19 (2006): 939–49; idem, "Scribal Scholarship in the Formation of Torah and Prophets: A Postexilic Scribal Debate between Priestly Scholarship and Literary Prophecy—The Example of the Book of Jeremiah and Its Relation to the Pentateuch," in *The Pentateuch as Torah: New Models for Understanding Its Promulgation and Acceptance* (ed. Gary N. Knoppers and Bernard M. Levinson; Winona Lake, Ind.: Eisenbrauns, 2007), 171–84.

86. Ernest Nicholson ("Deuteronomy 18:9–22, the Prophets, and Scripture, in Day, *Prophecy and Prophets in Ancient Israel*, 151–71, esp. 168) asserts that Deut 18:9–22 "was familiar with a corpus of scripture that included Deuteronomy and its related literary corpus into which it had already been incorporated . . . as well as a series of prophetic books . . . [including] Isaiah and Jeremiah."

priests, in the office laws the levitically taught community avoids prophetic "contamination" by holding potential prophets' feet to the fire (e.g., Jer 28).

IV. Conclusion: The New Citizen in the Office Laws and H

It becomes clear through the juxtaposition of these texts that both the office laws and H envisioned a new kind of citizen summoned to participate in major aspects of the leadership of the community. This new breed of citizen inhabits a "middle ground" between proletariat and elite, benefiting from at least rudimentary religious education. It is important to remember that we are dealing here with part projection of an ideal figure and part concrete *job description* of the individuals YHWH has qualified and empowered to serve in his kingdom. The malleable (not necessarily by choice) Levite of history and tradition probably serves as the essential model and inspiration.

Similar to what we see in both H and the office laws, there is a palpable tension between existing social conceptions and structures, on one side, and what is now being projected and advocated for the future, on the other. During this time of reassessment and change, radical new social positioning is thought possible and projected as if it were imminent. Drawing from the work of Victor Turner on *communitas* in periods of transition and liminality, Jeremy Hutton summarizes:

> As the ideological but complementary opposite of structure, communitas entails a leveling of social class during the liminal period. The community's hierarchy temporarily breaks down, and social position goes unrecognized or is intentially ignored.... [I]t engages in a mutually enriching dialectic with structure. One cannot be fully grasped without recourse to an understanding of the other. Communitas at the same time embraces social structure as its mutually affirming and defining partner and pushes it away, as its ideological opposite.
>
> The transitional period, the time in which communitas comes to the fore, yields a disconcerting homogeneity or even reversal of political power....[87]

Both the office laws and H reflect a time of transition in which modes of authority are in flux and a middle-social class finds opportunity to emerge as a voice and as a force, a new citzenry that merges with levitical priest-prophets.[88] This new priest-prophet-citizen is imbued with religious aptitude, qualified, summoned into action, and held to a high degree of accountability. The call to

---

87. Jeremy M. Hutton, *The Transjordanian Palimpsest: The Overwritten Texts of Personal Exile and Transformation in the Deuteronomistic History* (BZAW 396; Berlin: de Gruyter, 2009), 20–21; Victor Turner, The Ritual Process: Structure and Anti-Structure (Symbol, Myth, and Ritual; Ithaca, N.Y.: Cornell University Press, 1969).

88. For example, the reenvisioned community of Third Isaiah (e.g., Isa 66:18; cf. vv. 19–24) in the reading of Nihan, "Ethnicity," 87.

action exceeds forensic concerns. It includes the mobilization of a group that will do the sovereign's bidding in both local and international contexts.

This new type of citizen differs from the figure of the ideal Israelite envisioned by readers of the Hebrew Bible, namely, that rare individual who rises above the pedestrian pattern of disobedience and acts justly, avoiding both the lure of self-aggrandizement and syncretism. Against the few success stories (e.g., Noah, Abraham, Joseph, Moses, Deborah [judge and prophetess], Samuel, David, Josiah), and irrespective of whether one wishes to emphasize personal or communal performances (such as the Nazirites or the Rechabites of Jer 35), most solutions are transitory.[89] What I am attempting to bring into relief—and what I believe levitical priest-prophets advocated—is a more effective and enduring social and political plan for Yahwistic adherents based on a combination of special election (manifested in ancestral promises, such as those given to Caleb, Rahab, and Ruth) and its accompanying endowments (*heilsgeschichtlich*-ritual sanctification à la Lev 22:32b–33,[90] חסד in the sense of Jer 31:3, wisdom, and a consecrated land). It seems that both the office laws and H have something like this in mind, and that the motivating forces behind this move are Levites cooperating with lay leaders and selected members of the elite religious leadership.[91] Not to be underestimated as an additional driving force during the Persian era would be resident aliens (גרים) living in close and friendly proximity to Israelites. The need for coexistence might be particularly great in non-urban contexts in which survival could depend on political and economic cooperation with locals and traveling merchants.

Scholars often credit the Babylonian exile for theological innovations that made postexilic Israelite religion something quite different from its preexilic manifestations.[92] By the same token, and though a startling development in view of the traditional, dominant perspective of animosity toward foreigners, Israel's Levites probably owe aspects of their alternative vision to their in-depth

---

89. Compare, for example, the "saviors" in the book of Judges, the few "good kings" in the Israelite monarchy, and intimations of community repentance at the preaching of the prophets as in Zech 1:6.

90. Grünwaldt, "Amt," 233–34; and see the present essay's final paragraph.

91. See Jean-Louis Ska, *Introduction to Reading the Pentateuch* (trans. P. Dominique; Winona Lake, Ind.: Eisenbrauns, 2006), 88. Except for contexts in which the Levites themselves become part of the elite, a situation of which Chronicles seems to know, and which the late text Josh 18:1–10* suggests, the support of the population would probably be insufficient to see traditions like the PRR included in the received literature (see p. 174 above). There is significant negotiation going on behind many of these texts. In H the involvement of the Levites behind the scenes, arguably known by the community, yet left unspoken in the text, may well have been the result of negotiation. In Exod 32 the Aaronides come up short and the Levites receive resounding praise. Note that in vv. 2–6 Aaron makes gross, "idolatrous" concessions to the people that recall that for which the Levites are condemned in Ezek 44:10–12.

92. See Leuchter, *Polemics*, 167–68.

dealings with non-urbanites and the diverse peoples they encounter on trade routes, at wayside shrines,[93] and in villages (Neh 13:10).[94] The vision, whose basic socio-religious contours are visible in HexRed narratives that emphasize the faithfulness of a number of foreigners opposite unfaithful Israelites[95] comes to fuller theological expression in the writings of the later school of HexRed responsible for the composition of much of H, as well as in texts such as Deut 31:12, which takes openness to the integration of pious aliens to a new level. Now, not only aliens but also women and children may enter the covenant, that is, the Moab covenant (Deut 28:69 [Eng. 29:1]) offered to the second (and doubtless diverse) exodus generation now living in the land.[96] The comprehensive theological system advocated by the school of HexRed is tersely and unapologetically summarized in Lev 22:32b–33 ("I am the Lord who sanctifies you, who brought you out from the land of Egypt, to be your God: I am the Lord") in conjunction with Lev 19:34 and with recourse to Exod 19:6.[97] The weight of the evidence presented in this study suggests a strong conceptual connection between the "new citizen" communities envisioned in the office laws and H—they need not be identical—and the community pictured in PRR passages, particularly those in Deuteronomy (4:10–12, 33–37; 5:4, 22).

---

93. Zevit, *Religions*, 340 (and n. 6 above); Davies, "Urban Religion," 108.

94. Christian, "Priestly Power That Empowers," 78–79.

95. Achenbach, *Vollendung*; see the summary of the profile of HexRed in Mark A. Christian, "Openness to the Other Inside and Outside of Numbers," in Römer, *Books of Leviticus and Numbers*, 567–608, esp. 581–83 and nn. 10–14; cf. 582: "Whereas the non-Israelite Caleb receives unabridged praise (Num 14:24), disobedient Israelites garner harsh criticism [15:32–36]. In contrast, even traditional enemies of Israel such as the Edomites come to be accepted once they acknowledge *Yhwh* (cf. the post-Dtr *qahal* law of Deut 23:8). Thus within the horizon of HexRed a deep divide exists between devoted—and delinquent—Yahwists. In contrast to Dtn/Dtr's patent aversion to aliens, HexRed allows for the possibility of integration." The *openness* to integration in HexRed would become *law* in the school of HexRed texts in H.

96. The previous, Horeb covenant had been associated with the taking of the land and with a largely unbelieving population that died in the desert; see Reinhard Achenbach, "Der Eintritt der Schutzbürger in den Bund (Dtn 29,10–12): Distinktion und Integration von Fremden im Deuteronomium," in *"Gerechtigkeit und Recht zu üben" (Gen 18,19): Studien zur altorientalischen und biblischen Rechtsgeschichte, zur Religionsgeschichte Israels und zur Religionssoziologie. Festschrift für Eckart Otto zum 65. Geburtstag* (ed. Reinhard Achenbach and Martin Arneth; BZABR 13; Wiesbaden: Harrasowitz, 2010), 240–55, esp. 246–55.

97. Klaus Grünwaldt, *Das Heiligkeitsgesetz Leviticus 17–26: Ursprüngliche Gestalt, Tradition und Theologie* (BZAW 271; Berlin: de Gruyter, 1999), 82–83. Space constraints do not permit elucidation of the connections between these passages or their significance for the postexilic conceptions of a diverse and priestly citizenry.

The Cultic Status of the Levites in the *Temple Scroll*: Between History and Hermeneutics

Jeffrey Stackert

Understanding the Levites and their cultic status in both biblical and postbiblical literature has proven a formidable task. Repeated and in-depth scholarly focus on Levites and their relation to the Israelite/Judean priesthood has fostered only limited consensus concerning Levitical origins, functions, and status in Israelite and early Jewish religious history.[1] One of the fundamental ques-

---

1. Beside commentary treatments, studies on biblical views of priests and Levites are multiple and diverse, including Julius Wellhausen, *Prolegomena to the History of Israel, with a Reprint of the Article Israel from the Encyclopedia Britannica* (trans. J. Sutherland Black and Allan Menzies; New York: Meridian, 1957; 1st German ed. 1878), 121–51; Yehezkel Kaufmann, *The Religion of Israel: From Its Beginnings to the Babylonian Exile* (trans. and abridg. Moshe Greenberg; 1960; repr., New York: Schocken, 1972), 193–200; G. E. Wright, "The Levites in Deuteronomy," *VT* 4 (1954): 325–30; J. A. Emerton, "Priests and Levites in Deuteronomy," *VT* 12 (1962): 129–38; A. H. J. Gunneweg, *Leviten und Priester: Hauptlinen der Traditionsbildung und Geschichte des israelitisch-jüdischen Kultpersonals* (FRLANT 89; Göttingen: Vandenhoeck & Ruprecht, 1965); Aelred Cody, *A History of Old Testament Priesthood* (AnBib 35; Rome: Pontifical Biblical Institute, 1969); Raymond Abba, "Priests and Levites in Deuteronomy," *VT* 27 (1977): 257–67; idem, "Priests and Levites in Ezekiel," *VT* 28 (1978): 1–9; Menahem Haran, *Temples and Temple-Service in Ancient Israel: An Inquiry into Biblical Cult Phenomena and the Historical Setting of the Priestly School* (1978; repr., Winona Lake, Ind.: Eisenbrauns, 1985), esp. 58–148; Rodney K. Duke, "The Portion of the Levite: Another Reading of Deuteronomy 18:6–8," *JBL* 106 (1987): 193–201; idem, "Punishment or Restoration: Another Look at the Levites of Ezekiel 44:6–16," *JSOT* 40 (1988): 61–81; M. D. Rehm, "Levites and Priests," *ABD* 4:297–310; D. Kellermann, "לוי; לוים," *TDOT* 7:483–94; Stephen L. Cook, "Innerbiblical Interpretation in Ezekiel 44 and the History of Israel's Priesthood," *JBL* 114 (1995): 193–208; Ulrich Dahmen, *Leviten und Priester im Deuteronomium: Literarkritische und redaktionsgeschichtliche Studien* (BBB 110; Bodenheim: Philo, 1996); Risto Nurmela, *The Levites: Their Emergence as a Second-Class Priesthood* (South Florida Studies in the History of Judaism 193; Atlanta: Scholars Press, 1998); Gary N. Knoppers, "Hierodules, Priests, or Janitors? The Levites in Chronicles and the History of the Israelite Priesthood," *JBL* 118 (1999): 49–72; Deborah W. Rooke, *Zadok's Heirs: The Role and Development of the High Priesthood in Ancient Israel* (OTM; Oxford/New York: Oxford University Press, 2000); Joachim Schaper, *Priester und Leviten im achämenidischen Juda: Studien zur Kult- und Sozialgeschichte Israels in persischer Zeit* (FAT 31;

tions with regard to the biblical material is, Were all male members of the tribe of Levi eligible to be priests, or was this right reserved for only a faction among them? The evidence for answering this question is wholly contradictory and thus regularly explained in terms of historical development. Postbiblical texts present additional, variant perspectives from the Second Temple period, most notably in the *Book of Jubilees*, the *Testament of Levi*, *Aramaic Levi*, Ben Sira, and the Qumran *War Scroll* and *Temple Scroll*.[2] It should be acknowledged that these respective literary sources in many cases do not accurately reflect historical realities either from the time that they purport to describe or from the time when they were written. Notwithstanding the danger inherent in making historical arguments on the basis of solely literary evidence, the quantity and range of these data do suggest a complex and multifaceted development of the Israelite priesthood from the First Temple period into the Greco-Roman era.

In this paper, I will focus on one historical moment in this history, a moment preserved in the legislation concerning Levites, priests, and priestly service and emoluments in the *Temple Scroll*. After briefly characterizing the biblical (especially Priestly and Deuteronomic) laws concerning priests and Levites, I will compare the *Temple Scroll*'s prescriptions with the biblical laws that it revises to show the nature of the *Temple Scroll*'s hermeneutical engagement with the biblical text. In so doing, I will propose a new explanation for the *Temple Scroll*'s unique view of non-priestly Levites. Specifically, I will argue that the *Temple Scroll*'s Levitical innovations represent an incomplete application and reorientation of the equality principles outlined in Deut 18:6–8. The result is, in effect, a "separate but equal" policy for priests and Levites that accords closely with Deuteronomy's portrayal even as it presumes the fixed boundary between these sacerdotal groups that characterizes biblical Priestly literature.

I will then attempt to situate this exegetical work sociohistorically. Evidence suggests that the *Temple Scroll* did not originate at Qumran;[3] this scroll's

---

Tübingen: Mohr Siebeck, 2000); Nadav Na'aman, "Sojourners and Levites in the Kingdom of Judah in the Seventh Century BCE," *ZABR* 14 (2008): 237–79.

2. For an overview of Qumran texts that mention Levites, see esp. Robert Stallman, "Levi and the Levites in the Dead Sea Scrolls," *JSP* 10 (1992): 163–89, and, most recently, Joseph L. Angel, *Otherworldly and Eschatological Priesthood in the Dead Sea Scrolls* (STDJ 86; Leiden/Boston: Brill, 2010), 278–95. For discussion of the priestly role ascribed to the Levites in the *Book of Jubilees*, the *Testament of Levi*, and *Aramaic Levi*, see, e.g., James L. Kugel, "Levi's Elevation to the Priesthood in Second Temple Writings," *HTR* 86 (1993): 1–64; Robert A. Kugler, *From Patriarch to Priest: The Levi-Priestly Tradition from Aramaic Levi to Testament of Levi* (SBLEJL 9; Atlanta: Scholars Press, 1996); Cana Werman, "Levi and Levites in the Second Temple Period," *DSD* 4 (1997): 211–25.

3. See, e.g., Baruch Levine, "The Temple Scroll: Aspects of Its Historical Provenance and Literary Character," *BASOR* 232 (1978): 5–23; Emile Puech, *Qumrân Grotte 4.XVIII: Textes Hébreux (4Q521–4Q528, 4Q576–4Q579)* (DJD 25; Oxford: Clarendon, 1998), 87;

ideology must therefore be located first outside of the Qumran community. In my view, the *Temple Scroll*'s simultaneous favor toward and restriction of the Levites may originate as part of a Qumran precursor group's attempt to garner Levitical support against the alternative views of the Jerusalem temple leadership. Its inclusion in the library of the splinter Jewish group at Qumran may reflect the latter group's similar objections to the Hasmonean priesthood, especially in light of the significant ideological accord between the *Temple Scroll* and other documents, including sectarian texts, found at Qumran, such as the so-called Halakic Letter (4QMMT), the *Damascus Covenant*, and the *Community Rule*.[4] Finding itself in a situation vis-à-vis the Jerusalem cult similar to that of the *Temple Scroll*'s authors, the Qumran community could easily co-opt this document and its overtures toward the Levites to further its own religio-political goals.

I. Levites in the Bible: Conflicting Characterizations

The biblical presentations of Levites, especially in their relation to the priests, provide essential data for understanding the *Temple Scroll*'s Levitical innovations. Most relevant are pentateuchal Priestly and Deuteronomic perspectives, as these serve as the main literary source for the *Temple Scroll*.[5] Yet other biblical texts also provide important contextual data. To summarize the biblical evidence briefly, Levites are almost wholly missing from the book of Leviticus, appearing only twice with regard to their irrevocable right to redeem Levitical cities (Lev 25:32–33). The issue of their cultic service is completely absent from this book. Numbers presents the characteristic pentateuchal Priestly source's division between priests and Levites, establishing the latter, for example, as carriers of the wilderness sanctuary and its furnishings (Num 4:4–15), and otherwise as lesser-status cultic officials who have no right to altar service (e.g., Num 16–18). An analysis of pentateuchal Priestly literature according

---

Lawrence E. Schiffman, "The Law of the *Temple Scroll* and Its Provenance," in *The Courtyards of the House of the Lord: Studies on the Temple Scroll* (ed. Florentino García Martínez; STDJ 75; Leiden: Brill, 2008), 3–18; Sidnie White Crawford, *The Temple Scroll and Related Texts* (Companion to the Qumran Scrolls 2; Sheffield: Sheffield Academic Press, 2000), 24–29.

4. See, e.g., George J. Brooke, "The Temple Scroll: A Law unto Itself?" in *Law and Religion: Essays on the Place of the Law in Israel and Early Christianity* (ed. Barnabas Lindars; Cambridge: James Clarke, 1988), 34–43; Crawford, *Temple Scroll and Related Texts*, 77–83.

5. For discussions of the various sources that constitute the *Temple Scroll*, see, e.g., Michael Owen Wise, *A Critical Study of the Temple Scroll from Qumran Cave 11* (SAOC 49; Chicago: Oriental Institute of the University of Chicago, 1990); Lawrence H. Schiffman, "The *Temple Scroll* and the Nature of Its Law: The Status of the Question," in idem, *Courtyards of the House of the Lord*, 33–51, esp. 42–43.

to its strata reveals that the Holiness Legislation (H) shows special interest in Levitical cultic status and provides the strongest confirmation of the Levites' subservient rank through its distribution of perquisites in Num 18.[6] H's increased focus on Levites in comparison with that of P accords well with the trend toward greater interest in Levites in later and postbiblical literature.

The Deuteronomic (D) source, by contrast, makes no distinction between priests and Levites with regard to their right to serve at its central sanctuary (Deut 18:1–8). Many scholars have viewed this insistence on a pan-Levitical priesthood as D's attempt to counteract an anticipated effect of cult centralization—namely, the loss of cultic status for priests serving outside of Jerusalem.[7] In other words, unlike the view of pentateuchal Priestly literature, where there is a divinely ordained and absolute distinction between priests and Levites, in D any difference is geographical and one of function, not identity. Moreover, as Deut 18:6–8 asserts, this distinction is made wholly on an ad hoc basis.

Among demonstrably exilic and postexilic texts, Malachi follows D by using the terms "priest" and "Levite" interchangeably (Mal 2:1–3:4), even as this prophet seems to know both Deuteronomy and pentateuchal Priestly literature.[8] However, Ezekiel (44:6–16), Ezra (6:15–18), and Chronicles (see, e.g., 2 Chr 23:6; 29:34[9]) each recognize the categorical distinction between priests and Levites, though they disagree on the degree of Levitical inferiority to the (Aaronid/Zakodite) priesthood. From the time of Wellhausen,[10] Ezek 44 has been viewed as a crux for solving the question of Levitical cultic status, for it purports to explain and thus justify the distinction made between priests and Levites, even as it uses the term הכהנים הלוים (Ezek 43:19; 44:15)—the same designation that Deuteronomy employs for its pan-Levitical priesthood—to

---

6. Israel Knohl argues that the Levites and their status vis-à-vis the priests in pentateuchal Priestly literature is the sole concern of the "Holiness School" (*The Sanctuary of Silence: The Priestly Torah and the Holiness School* [trans. Jackie Feldman and Peretz Rodman; Minneapolis: Fortress, 1995], 209–12). However, this conclusion may press too far (*pace* Jeffrey Stackert, *Rewriting the Torah: Literary Revision in Deuteronomy and the Holiness Legislation* [FAT 52; Tübingen: Mohr Siebeck, 2007], 191–98). It appears that P (as opposed to H) provides the basic narrative strand in the pentateuchal Priestly source, including the Priestly Korah rebellion narrative, with its focus on Levites (Num 16–17).

7. So Wellhausen, *Prolegomena*, 124, 146–47, which has been followed by many.

8. Malachi 1:6–2:9 appears to reuse the so-called Priestly blessing of Num 6 (see Michael Fishbane, "Form and Reformulation of the Biblical Priestly Blessing," *JAOS* 103 [1983]: 115–21), and Mal 2:8 seems to know Deut 31:29.

9. In Chronicles, the Levites are viewed more positively than in pentateuchal Priestly literature, even as the latter's distinction between priests and Levites is adopted/upheld in Chronicles. As a postexilic composition, one can see ideological similarities between Chronicles and postbiblical writings that elevate the status of the Levites. See, e.g., Nurmela, *Levites*, 165–75; Knoppers, "Hierodules, Priests, or Janitors?"

10. Wellhausen, *Prolegomena*, 121–51.

refer exclusively to the sons of Zadok (בני צדוק). Yet in spite of its suggestive claims, it is likely that Ezekiel's description does not accurately preserve the historical origin for the separation between priestly and non-priestly Levites.

II. Levites in the *Temple Scroll*: Hermeneutical Innovations

What is clear in this contest between pan-Levitical priesthood (D, Malachi) and intra-Levitical distinction (P/H, Ezekiel, Ezra-Nehemiah, Chronicles) is that intra-Levitical distinction gains the upper hand in the late biblical period. Yet this trend does not result in total loss for non-priestly Levites, for the same period that witnesses the ascension of the priests to a dominant position over the Levites also inaugurates the scripturalization of ancient Jewish texts and even the biblical canonization process.[11] This process, which is fundamentally anthological, undermines the distinctiveness of the competing positions juxtaposed in the nascent scriptural collection. The absolutist position of biblical Priestly literature with regard to Levitical inferiority is thus relativized. Such proto-canonical developments stand behind the presentation of Levites in Chronicles and also typify the various postbiblical texts in which the Levites also enjoy a favored cultic status, including the *Temple Scroll*. Yet in its unique halakic prescriptions, the *Temple Scroll* also affords the Levites special privileges otherwise unattested in the Second Temple period, and it is to these privileges that I now turn.

Including restorations, forms of לוי appear approximately twenty-eight times in the *Temple Scroll*. Of these, the majority refer to the subordinate cultic class the Levites, and only once is the term בני לוי attested in apposition to הכוהנים (63:3).[12] When compared with pentateuchal perspectives on priests and Levites, it is clear that the *Temple Scroll* endorses the categorical distinction between priests and Levites that typifies pentateuchal Priestly literature. Most significant in this regard is the injunction against non-priestly sacrificial officiation in its imagined temple. 11QT 35:4–5 states,

וכול איש מבני ישראל אשר יביא אותה והוא אין הוא כוהן יומת

---

11. For discussion of the process of canonization and its distinction from the "canon" properly so-called, see Eugene Ulrich, "The Notion and Definition of Canon," in *The Canon Debate* (ed. Lee Martin McDonald and James A. Sanders; Peabody, Mass.: Hendrickson, 2002), 21–35, esp. 30.

12. B. E. Thiering suggests that there are actually two classes of Levites (apart from the Aaronid priesthood) reflected in the *Temple Scroll*: the "sons of Levi," who are a secondary priestly class, and the non-priestly Levites ("*MEBAQQER* and *EPISKOPOS* in the Light of the Temple Scroll," *JBL* 100 [1981]: 59–74, here 63–64). This differentiation among non-Aaronid Levites seems unlikely and is based on questionable readings; see the critique of Stallman, "Levi and the Levites," 166–67.

Anyone from the Israelites who brings it (i.e., an offering) who is not a priest shall be put to death.

Line 5 here continues by specifying the precise identity of the priests who are permitted to present the offerings: they are "the sons of Aaron" (בני אהרון) and not simply any male of the tribe of Levi.

In light of this preference, it is somewhat surprising that the *Temple Scroll* nonetheless raises the Levitical profile vis-à-vis their rank in biblical Priestly literature. The full accounting of these privileges is well rehearsed and need not be repeated here.[13] Yet it is useful to highlight a few representative examples before turning with greater focus to the issue of altar service and sacrificial portions. According to 11QT 57:11–15, the Levites are to share equal representation in the king's council with the priests and the Israelite chiefs: twelve men from each group are to serve as the special advisers of the king. Similarly, the Levites are to serve as judges beside the priests and the lay Israelite judges (11QT 61:8–9), a hermeneutical innovation accomplished by inserting the Levites into a citation of Deut 19:17.[14] As in these administrative and judicial contexts, the *Temple Scroll* also raises the profile of the Levites in cultic situations. For instance, in the ritual protocols of its innovative New Wood festival, the tribe of Levi is assigned the right to sacrifice first among the Israelite tribes (11QT 23:5, 9–10).[15]

Yet most striking among the Levitical innovations in the *Temple Scroll* are its rules for the allocation of sacrificial portions, especially in light of its insistence that only Aaronid priests may officiate in sacrifice. It is well known that biblical texts that distinguish between priests and Levites, as the *Temple Scroll* does, never assign sacrificial meat to the Levites. Such offering portions are instead reserved for the priests alone (Num 18:8–20). Yet the *Temple Scroll*

---

13. See, e.g., Jacob Milgrom, "Studies in the Temple Scroll," *JBL* 97 (1978): 501–23, esp. 501–3; Angel, *Otherworldly and Eschatological Priesthood*, 280–88.

14. Milgrom, "Studies," 501–2. As Milgrom observes, the *Temple Scroll* author may here harmonize Deut 19:17 with Deut 17:9, which refers to הכהנים הלוים in a judicial context, inserting a *wāw* between הכהנים and הלוים, as in 11QT 56:1.

15. For treatments of the New Wood festival and offering, see, e.g., Jacob Milgrom, "Qumran's Biblical Hermeneutics: The Case of the Wood Offering," *RevQ* 16 (1995): 449–56; David Volgger, "The Feast of the Wood Offerings According to the Temple Scroll," *BN* 127 (2005): 21–39; Cana Werman, "The Wood-Offering: The Convoluted Evolution of a Halakhah in Qumran and Rabbinic Law," in *New Perspectives on Old Texts: Proceedings of the Tenth International Symposium of the Orion Center for the Study of the Dead Sea Scrolls and Associated Literature, 9–11 January, 2005* (ed. Esther G. Chazon et al.; STDJ 88; Leiden/Boston: Brill, 2010), 151–81. Note the caution of Michael O. Wise, who argues that the fragments containing the New Wood Festival should not be considered part of the *Temple Scroll* (but instead a proto-*Temple Scroll*; Wise, *Critical Study*, 50, 60; followed also by Stallman, "Levi and the Levites," 167–68).

strays from this biblical Priestly convention in its distribution of sacrificial perquisites.

11QT 21:1–5 and 22:8–14 each treat the allocation of perquisites from the well-being offering (שלמים):

11QT 21:1–5[16]

1 לכוהנים יהיה שוק התרומה וחזה
2 התנופה ולראשית ויתנו את האזרועות והלחיים והקבאות למנות
3 והיה להמה חוק עולם מאת בני ישראל ואת השכם הנשאר מן האזרוע
4 יתנו ללויים והיה להמה מאת העם לחוק עולם להמה ולזרעמה
5 אחר יוציאום אל בני ישראל

1. For the priests shall be the thigh of the offering and the breast
2. of the elevation offering and the firstfruit, and they shall give the forearms and the cheeks and the stomachs, according to the portions.
3. This will be an eternal portion for them from the children of Israel. The shoulder which remains from the forearm
4. they shall give to the Levites, and it shall be theirs from the people as an eternal portion for them and for their offspring.
5. Afterwards, they shall bring them out to the children of Israel.

11QT 22:8–14[17]

8 וירימו מן האלים ומן הכבשים
9 את שוק הימין ואת חזי התנופה ולראשית ואת האזרוע ואת
10 הלחיים ואת הקבה לכוהנים יהיה למנה כמשפטמה וללויים
11 את השכם אחר יוציאום אל בני ישראל ונתנו בני ישראל לכוהנים
12 איל אחד כבש אחד וללויים איל אחד כבש אחד ולכול מטה
13 ומטה איל אחד כבש אחד ואכלום ביום הזה בחצר החיצונה
14 לפני יהוה חוקות עולם לדורותיהמה שנה בשנה

8. They shall raise from the rams and the sheep
9. the right thigh and the breast of the elevation offering and the firstfruits, and the forearm and

---

16. The *Temple Scroll* texts cited in this paper are taken from Elisha Qimron, *The Temple Scroll: A Critical Edition with Extensive Reconstructions* (Judean Desert Studies; Beer-Sheva: Ben-Gurion University of the Negev Press; Jerusalem: Israel Exploration Society, 1996) (here 32). Qimron's texts are partially composite and reconstructed. All translations, unless otherwise noted, are my own.

17. Ibid., 35.

10. the cheeks and the stomach shall be the priests' portion according to their due, and for the Levites
11. shall be the shoulder. Afterwards, they shall bring them out to the children of Israel. The children of Israel shall give to the priests
12. one ram (and) one sheep, and to the Levites, one ram (and) one sheep, and to every tribe,
13. one ram (and) one sheep, and they shall eat them on that day in the outer court
14. before the Lord—eternal portions for their generations, annually.

These texts each draw from Deut 18:3 for the forearm, cheeks, and stomach portions, but they also innovate beyond Deuteronomy by designating the shoulder portion of the offering to the Levites. This sacrificial portion and its designation to the Levites are wholly unattested in biblical literature. Jacob Milgrom argues that the distinction between the forearm (זרוע) and shoulder (שכם) is based a Second Temple dispute concerning what exactly the זרוע entailed. The question was quite simple: Does the arm include the shoulder or not?[18] In Milgrom's view, by assigning the shoulder to the Levites, the *Temple Scroll* recognizes the pentateuchal Priestly distinction between priests and Levites, even as it accepts Deuteronomy's special regard for the latter. Implicit in this interpretation is the insertion of a *wāw* between הכהנים and הלוים in Deuteronomy's stereotypical designation of "Levitical priests" (הכהנים הלוים), with the result that each group receives part of the sacrificial portions.[19] Moreover, this innovation is accomplished without transgressing the letter of the Deuteronomic law: Deut 18:3 explicitly designates the arm, cheeks, and stomach to the priests, and the *Temple Scroll* author maintains this assignment. Because the Deuteronomic law does not address the shoulder, it is available for allocation to the Levites.[20] Indeed, according to the view that the shoulder is not part of the זרוע portion assigned to the priests, it would presumably be part of the sacrifice returned to its offerer for lay consumption. Milgrom concludes that the assignment of the prime shoulder portion to the non-priestly Levites represents a distinct preference for them not just in relation to biblical

---

18. Jacob Milgrom, "A Shoulder for the Levites," in *The Temple Scroll* (ed. Yigael Yadin; 3 vols. and suppl.; Jerusalem: Israel Exploration Society et al., 1977–83), 1:169–76.

19. Milgrom, arguing that the *Temple Scroll* exhibits a forerunner to the rabbinic method of *binyan 'āb*, even cites *Midrash Tannaim* to Deut 18:1, which reads the biblical הכהנים הלוים as "the priests and the Levites" ("The Qumran Cult: Its Exegetical Principles," in *Temple Scroll Studies: Papers Presented at the International Symposium on the Temple Scroll* [ed. George J. Brooke; JSPSup 7; Sheffield: JSOT Press, 1989], 165–80, here 173–74).

20. Milgrom, "Shoulder for the Levites," 171; idem, "Studies," 504–5; Stallman, "Levi and the Levites," 169; Lawrence H. Schiffman, "Priestly and Levitical Gifts in the *Temple Scroll*," in idem, *Courtyards of the House of the Lord*, 541–56, here 551–52.

Priestly texts but also in relation to their contemporary priestly counterparts,[21] and this view has achieved a relatively strong consensus.[22]

Milgrom's reading has much to commend it. Yet I would suggest that it does not take into account one of the basic issues that is driving the *Temple Scroll*'s innovations in this case. It seems to me that the division between the arm and the shoulder portions here is part of a larger attempt to build equality between the priests and the Levites. Informing this egalitarian push is Deut 18:6–8, a text that the *Temple Scroll* cites nearly verbatim. 11QT 60:10–15 states,

11QT 60:10–15[23]

10   כי במה בחרתי מ]כול שבטיכה
11 לעמוד לפני ולשרת ולברך בשמי הוא וכול בניו כול הימים
12 vacat וכי יבוא הלוי מאחד שעריכה מכול ישראל אשר
13 הוא גר שמה בכול אות נפשו אל המקום אשר אבחר לשכן
14 שמי ככול אחיו הלויים ישרת העומדים שמה לפני חלק כחלק
15 יואכלו לבד ממכר על האבות   vacat

10. for I have chosen them from all your tribes
11. to stand before me and to serve and to bless in my name—he and all his sons for all time.
12. And when the Levite from one of your towns in all of Israel who
13. is sojourning there comes at the desire of his soul to the place which I will choose to place
14. my name, he, like all of his brothers, the Levites, shall serve the ones presiding there. Equal portions
15. shall they eat, not counting what each inherits.

Lines 10b–11, as Yigael Yadin first noted, are based on Deut 18:5 (with LXX; see also Deut 10:8). In his view the modifications introduced in these

---

21. Milgrom states, "By all counts, these portions (i.e., the cheeks and stomach) are menial, if not miserable. How then could the entire foreleg, including the shoulder—one of the richest meats of the animal—be assigned to the priests? Thus in keeping with the modesty of the cheeks and stomach, the author reduced the size of the זרוע to encompass only a small portion of the animal's flesh" ("Studies," 505).

22. Robert Kugler, "The Priesthood at Qumran: The Evidence of References to Levi and the Levites," in *The Provo International Conference on the Dead Sea Scrolls: Technological Innovations, New Texts, and Reformulated Issues* (ed. Donald W. Parry and Eugene Ulrich; STDJ 30; Leiden: Brill, 1999), 465–79, here 468; Stallman, "Levi and the Levites," 169–70; Schiffman, "Priestly and Levitical Gifts," 551; Angel, *Otherworldly and Eschatological Priesthood*, 282.

23. For text, see Qimron, *Temple Scroll*, 85.

lines are primary evidence for the elevation of the Levites to full priestly status. He states,

> Interestingly, he [i.e. the author] has made two modifications of substance here, in addition to the change from the third to the first person: (a) "for *them* I have chosen" instead of "for *him* has he chosen." This change indicates that the subject under discussion includes priests as well as Levites, for the massoretic text might be understood as referring to the priests. . . . We can see that the change was intentional, as the author then reverts to the singular, as in the massoretic text; (b) "and *all* his sons", instead of "his sons." Apparently here, too, the purpose of the change was to emphasize that all the members of the tribe of Levi are being discussed. All this is further evidence of the emphasis the author lays on the status of the Levites.[24]

However, in view of the preceding text, which specifically outlines the perquisites of the Levites and then highlights an allocation of pigeons to the priests, Schiffman argues that 60:10b–11 refers to the priests alone and not to the Levites. In my view, Schiffman is correct: these lines are a justification for that special allocation of pigeons to the priests in distinction from the lesser allocation designated to the Levites.[25] Such observations point once again to the persistent differentiation between priests and Levites in this text and its reservation of altar service for the priests alone.

Yet lines 12–15 introduce additional complexity into the *Temple Scroll*'s view. Indeed, these lines prove to be the key to understanding the *Temple Scroll*'s allocation of perquisites and its reconceptualization of the role of non-priestly Levites. According to Deut 18:6–8, the Levite is to be "like all his brothers . . . those who stand there before Me," and he is to eat "like portions" (חלק כחלק יאכלו) to those enjoyed by the priests. The question might be posed, how is the Levite—and, in particular, his food—to indeed be "like" that of his fellow Levitical clansmen, the priests? I would suggest that by introducing the shoulder portion of the sacrifice, the *Temple Scroll* offers an answer

---

24. Yadin, *Temple Scroll*, 1:168. These alterations that the *Temple Scroll* introduces into its citation of Deut 18:5 cause the question of the identity of הכוהנים בני לוי in 11QT 63:3, who are "the ones I [i.e. God] have chosen to serve before me and to bless in my name" who participate in the עגלה ערופה rite. If this text, which cites Deut 21:5 and Deut 10:8, is read in concert with 11QT 60:10–11, where it is clearly the priests *and* the Levites whom God has chosen to bless in his name, 11QT 63:3 could be the only case in which the *Temple Scroll* calls the Levites priests. What militates against this possibility is the fact that the *Temple Scroll* never employs D's term הכוהנים הלוים, as noted already. Thus, it is likely that 11QT 63:3 alters the meaning of its biblical source, with the result that only the priests are meant here (with בני לוי accurately applying to them). Alternatively, it envisions both priests and Levites participating in this rite and has simply listed the different parties (הכוהנים and בני לוי) asyndetically.

25. Schiffman, "Priestly and Levitical Gifts," 555.

to this question and, with it, a specific fulfillment of this biblical mandate. It appears that the shoulder is chosen by the author because of its similarity to the priestly emoluments of Deut 18:3 in terms of both quality and quantity. The contiguity of the forearm and the shoulder and the rabbinic dispute over their distinction from each other both suggest that the one is "like" the other. Moreover, the division of shoulder versus forearm, cheeks, and stomach may be considered equitable, for the shoulder is the meatiest of the four portions outlined by the *Temple Scroll*. In other words, the shoulder may be considered both similar to the forearm alone in its basic character and equivalent in amount to the forearm, cheeks, and stomach(s) together.[26]

Such creative hermeneutical engagement with Deuteronomy's use of the preposition *kāp* in the comparison between priests and Levites is not limited to the *Temple Scroll*'s consideration of perquisites. It also characterizes this text's "Levitical" revision of the Deuteronomic judiciary, alluded to already. Deut 19:17 states,

ועמדו שני האנשים אשר להם הריב לפני יהוה לפני הכהנים והשפטים אשר יהיו בימים ההם

The two men who have the dispute shall stand before the LORD—that is, before priests and the judges who will be in office in those days.

11QT 61:8–9, however, inserts the Levites into this verse:

ועמדו שני האנשים אשר להמה ^{הריב} לפני ולפני הכוהנים <u>והלויים</u> ולפני השופטים אשר יהיו בימים ההמה

The two men who have the dispute shall stand before me—that is, before the priests <u>and the Levites</u> and before the judges who will be in office in those days.

In this case, it seems that the Deuteronomic claim of equivalence between the priests and Levites (indicated through the use of the preposition *kāp*), and perhaps also the use of the verb עמד in both Deut 18:7 and 19:17,[27] triggers the introduction of the Levites into the *Temple Scroll*'s revision of the latter verse. Especially notable in this revision is the fact that, though Deut 18 here refers only to altar service, the *Temple Scroll* generalizes the biblical admonish-

---

26. *Pace* Milgrom, "Studies," 505; Stallman, "Levi and the Levites," 169.

27. Note that while the verb עמד in each of these verses indicates a subservient role, the stance of the Levites vis-à-vis the verb עמד is quite different. In the case of Deut 18:7, the Levites are those who serve the deity (and thus stand in his presence). The Levites inserted in Deut 19:17, however, are in the position of authority, and the litigants stand before them.

ment to apply to priestly *judicial* service. In light of its earlier insistence that only Aaronid priests may offer sacrifices on the altar, the *Temple Scroll* here attempts to redefine the nature of the priestly service described in Deut 18:7 from the cultic sphere to the judicial sphere. Doing so again articulates the exclusive rights of priests to sacrificial officiation—a point underscored in the immediately preceding text of col. 61—while simultaneously accommodating the scriptural requirements of Deuteronomic law. It also justifies the designation of sacrificial emoluments in exchange for the Levites' "priestly" judicial service, even as the Levites remain barred from officiating in the cult.[28]

Yet the *Temple Scroll* goes even further. Most scholars have read 11QT 60:14 as basically consistent with its biblical exemplar, Deut 18:7.[29] However, as Milgrom observed in a study in which he revised some of his earlier conclusions, the *Temple Scroll* here makes a subtle change that radically alters the meaning of Deut 18:7:

Deut 18:7

ושרת בשם יהוה אלהיו ככל אחיו הלוים העמדים שם לפני יהוה

He shall serve in the name of the Lord his god like all of his brothers, the Levites, those standing there before the Lord.

11QT 60:14

ככול אחיו הלוויים ישרת העומדים שמה לפני

Like all of his brothers, the Levites, he shall serve those standing there before Me.

The *Temple Scroll* here replaces the biblical *weqatal* verbal form ושרת with the *yiqtol* form ישרת, a change that defies this text's regular practice of maintaining biblical *weqatal* morphosyntax when citing biblical texts. Yet this change permits greater latitude in the placement of the verb in the sentence, and the subsequent placement of this *yiqtol* verb proves to be a definitive

---

28. Ironically, the *Temple Scroll* may find a precedent for such designation of sacrificial portions to the Levites for non-altar service in the Holiness stratum of the pentateuchal Priestly source, which, like the *Temple Scroll*, denies the Levites the right to altar service. Numbers 18 (H) assigns the tithe to the Levites, a practice that the *Temple Scroll* accepts, and in so doing designates the tithe as a תרומה, a term otherwise used for sacrificial portions. See Stackert, *Rewriting the Torah*, 184–91.

29. See, e.g., Stallman, "Levi and the Levites," 170; Schiffman, "Sacred Space: The Land of Israel in the Temple Scroll," in idem, *Courtyards of the House of the Lord*, 290 n. 38; Kugler, "Priesthood at Qumran," 469.

syntactic choice. By placing ישרת between הלויים and the G active participle העומדים, the latter no longer serves as an attributive adjective modifying "the Levites." It is instead the object of the verb ישרת, which accords with Num 18:2.[30] In this way, the author achieves an entirely new meaning: "like all of his fellow Levites shall he [viz., the Levite who would come from an outlying town] serve the ones who are standing there before me [i.e., the priests; cf. 11QT 60:11]." In other words, העומדים are the Aaronid priests, and the Levite from an outlying town may come to the central sanctuary to serve *in an inferior role* to the priests like all of the other Levites who serve in this second-tier role.

In effect, then, after employing Deut 18:6–8 in a manner that elevates the Levites, the *Temple Scroll* author puts *the same text* to the task of subordinating them. No longer are the priests and Levites to be equated; instead, vv. 3–5 refer to the Aaronid priests alone while vv. 6–8 establish the subservience of the Levites to the priests.

III. The *Temple Scroll*'s Innovations: The Convergence of History and Hermeneutics

The foregoing analysis prompts the question, What motivated the *Temple Scroll*'s distinctive views of the Levites? Not surprisingly, scholars have offered several different explanations, both historical and exegetical, for this Qumran scroll's harmonization of biblical views and creative innovations regarding Levites. To begin with the historical, George J. Brooke argues that (at least) the sections that positively portray the Levites in the *Temple Scroll* are composed by the Levites themselves, and thus their improved status is the result of their own initiative.[31] In his earlier evaluation, Milgrom observes that the "quantity and thrust" of the *Temple Scroll*'s Levitical innovation reflect "the tensions and struggles among priestly families and between priests and Levites at the end

---

30. Milgrom makes reference to Num 18:2 but does not spell out its significance. Moreover, he suggests in a footnote that even in this context that the Levitical service of 11QT 60:14 could entail sacrificial officiation ("Studies," 503). Johann Maier follows Milgrom in the view that the Levites are subservient to the priests here (*The Temple Scroll: An Introduction, Translation, and Commentary* [JSOTSup 34; Sheffield: Sheffield Academic Press, 2009], 130), yet his translation on p. 52 does not reflect 60:14's alteration of Deut 18:7. One might prefer the *nota accusativi* prior to העומדים in the *Temple Scroll*'s rendering, but the author here makes his revision with minimal intervention.

31. George J. Brooke, "Levi and the Levites in the Dead Sea Scrolls and the New Testament," in *Mogilany 1989: Papers on the Dead Sea Scrolls Offered in Memory of Jean Carmignac*, part 1, *General Research on the Dead Sea Scrolls, Qumran and the New Testament: The Present State of Qumranology* (ed. Zdzisław J. Kapera; Kraków: Enigma Press, 1993), 105–30; see also Dwight D. Swanson, *The Temple Scroll and the Bible: The Methodology of 11QT* (STDJ 14; Leiden: Brill, 1995), 90.

of the Second Temple period."³² Using the sociological role concept, Robert Kugler offers a somewhat less positivistic, though similar, explanation to those of Brooke and Milgrom: in his opinion, the Qumran community, as a group of disaffected priests, identified with the Levites as a historically subordinated contingent of cultic officials. The *Temple Scroll* author thus elevates the status of the Levites in response to his own community's marginalization.³³ Joseph L. Angel has recently reassessed the various references to Levi and the Levites in the Qumran corpus and follows the view of Kugler.³⁴

Scholars also offer exclusively exegetical explanations for the *Temple Scroll*'s view of Levites. In a subsequent study to that just cited, Milgrom retracts his historical explanation of Levitical status in the *Temple Scroll*. In its place, he suggests that the author's method of "homogenizing" his biblical sources forces him to elevate the status of the Levites.³⁵ Schiffman similarly argues that the *Temple Scroll*'s author attempts to ground all of his rulings in the biblical text, and thus 11QT 60:1–11 is influenced both by Deut 18:1–8 and Num 18, as well as Num 31.³⁶

In my view, an approach that combines historical and exegetical features may better explain the Levites' unique cultic status in the *Temple Scroll*. This is as much a methodological conclusion as a finding based on specific historical data, which are quite sparse in this case. Early Jewish examples of harmonistic exegesis are certainly shaped and at times constrained by the perspectives in the texts they attempt to conflate. Yet each instance of harmonistic exegesis is achieved through both prioritization and sublimation of elements in its parent texts. The result is one conflation among many possible conflations, one novel interpretation that might easily be countered (and in many cases, as early Jewish interpretive literature demonstrates well, is countered) by alternative readings. Because multiple exegetical choices always exist in the practice of harmonistic interpretation, an appeal to a conflationary hermeneutic is insufficient to explain any particular instance of harmonization.

In the case of the *Temple Scroll* and other seemingly pro-Levitic Second Temple literature, the historical ascendancy of the priests over non-priestly Levites in the late and post-biblical periods is at least partially at odds with the trend toward harmonistic exegesis prompted by pentateuchal compilation and the growing scripturalization of biblical texts at this time. Thus, even apart from the particular historical situation of their composition, Second Temple

---

32. Milgrom, "Studies," 504.
33. Kugler, "Priesthood at Qumran," 478. Kugler gives brief attention to the exegetical arguments of Milgrom and Schiffman, arguing that such exegetical activity is ultimately motivated by the historical context of the author.
34. Angel, *Otherworldly and Eschatological Priesthood*, 291–95.
35. Milgrom, "Qumran Cult," 173–78.
36. Schiffman, "Priestly and Levitical Gifts," 554–56.

texts must navigate the competing interests of historical realities and conflationary hermeneutics in their treatment of priests and Levites. For each of the pro-Levitical Second Temple documents, then, something of a protest to cultic practice might be observed.

When we query the specific historical context of the *Temple Scroll*, we find that its halakic perspectives correspond in part to those of other Qumran texts (notably 4QMMT) and with some perspectives attributed to the Sadducees in later rabbinic literature. This affinity suggests that it too originates among a priestly group at odds with the Jerusalemite priests,[37] even if not the Qumran community.

Viewed in this light, the *Temple Scroll*'s allocation of unprecedented sacrificial perquisites to the Levites may represent an attempt to persuade the latter to side with its authors' position against the Jerusalem priesthood. Moreover, Deuteronomy's insistence that no distinction should be made between priests and Levites provides a prestigious veneer of authority to buttress what otherwise might be labeled opportunistic egalitarianism. Yet the true motivation for such changes cannot be hidden entirely: while the *Temple Scroll* engages in a rhetoric of equality and even makes some concrete concessions toward the same, the rights of cultic officiation remain the purview of the priests alone, that is, the rights of the *Temple Scroll*'s authors. At best, the new Levitical status can be characterized as "separate but equal."[38]

---

37. See, e.g., Schiffman, "*Temple Scroll* and the Nature of Its Law," 43; Hans Burgmann, "11QT: The Sadducean Torah," in Brooke, *Temple Scroll Studies*, 257–63. For a partial critique of claims for a tie between the Qumran community and the Sadducees, see Joseph M. Baumgarten, "Sadducean Elements in Qumran Law," in *The Community of the Renewed Covenant: The Notre Dame Symposium on the Dead Sea Scrolls* (ed. Eugene Ulrich and James C. VanderKam; Christianity and Judaism in Antiquity 10; Notre Dame: University of Notre Dame Press, 1994), 27–36; Eyal Regev, "Were the Priests All the Same? Qumranic Halakhah in Comparison with Sadducean Halakhah," *DSD* 12 (2005): 158–88.

In my view, it is unsurprising that there is a lack of full accord between *Temple Scroll* legal perspectives and Sadducean halakah, even if the *Temple Scroll* originated among Sadducees or a Sadducee-like group. Like all religious groups, these Jewish groups were characterized by internal diversity, even as their perspectives evolved over time. Such variability both complicates the issue of religious identity and cautions against doctrinaire assessments of the limited evidence available.

38. Cf. *Plessy v. Ferguson*, 163 U.S. 537 (1896), which enshrined the "separate but equal" doctrine in American law (only to be overturned in *Brown v. Board of Education of Topeka*, 347 U.S. 483 [1954]). In the *Temple Scroll*'s adjudication of Levitical rights, the bias remains more transparent than in *Plessy v. Ferguson*, however, for, as noted, no alternative altar is prescribed for Levitical service. The analogy is useful, however, for each instance relies on a construction of equality that proves insufficient to the circumstance it seeks to address. In the *Temple Scroll*, this task is as much hermeneutical, viz., in the adjudication of conflicting scriptural texts, as social.

Finally, the separation of the *Temple Scroll*'s authors from the Jerusalem temple likely contributes to the climate that makes its Levitical innovations possible, just as the Qumran community's separation from Jerusalem allows it to embrace such views. Though a major subject of the *Temple Scroll* is temple and sacrifice, the actual, *non-cultic* setting of its composition undermines the distinctions between temple personnel that are so fundamental to Jewish sacrificial worship and the distribution of perquisites that attends it. Elevation of the Levites, especially within the sacrificial cult, is possible especially when such innovations are hypothetical.

IV. Conclusion

In sum, the elevated status of the Levites in the *Temple Scroll* is best characterized as an attempt to build equality between Levites and priests while retaining for the latter the exclusive right to altar service—what I have termed here a "separate but equal" approach. This is accomplished hermeneutically through a creative engagement with the pentateuchal Priestly and Deuteronomic laws pertaining to the Levites and especially the laws concerning priestly service and remuneration in Deut 18:6–8. As demonstrated here, the result is a counterintuitive designation of sacrificial perquisites to the Levites in exchange either for non-priestly service or non-cultic, judicial priestly service. The impetus behind such legal innovation is likely the specific historical circumstances of the *Temple Scroll* authors, who may even be attempting to attract Levitical support for an opposition priesthood. It is certainly also abetted by the conflationary effect of a compiled and scripturalized Torah. In the end, it is this combination of historical and hermeneutical considerations that accounts most adequately for the unique Levitical perspectives in the *Temple Scroll* and its place in the Qumran library.

From Levite to Maśkîl in the Persian and Hellenistic Eras

Mark Leuchter

I. Introduction

The Levites remain somewhat of a mystery. Much effort has been invested in identifying their origins, the scope of their activity, and the way in which their lineage groups were orchestrated in different periods of Israel's history, and little consensus has yet been achieved.[1] However, one aspect of Levite function on which most commentators agree is their role as scribes and exegetes in a variety of biblical sources. Recent studies converge on the theme running through a diversity of texts that ascribes to the Levites—overtly or implicitly—the authority to compose, categorize, redact, read, interpret, and teach sacred literature to ancient Israelite audiences.[2] Of course, few would argue that Levites alone possess this role, and tabulations of the textual evidence reveal that other figures carried similar literate characteristics (e.g., Aaronide priests,[3] royal scribes, high ranking military officers, and even a limited spectrum of the lay aristocracy).[4] However, it is Levites that are most consistently and expressly identified with these characteristics and responsibilities. Legal, liturgical, poetic, sapiential, prophetic, and historiographic sources all point to Levitical activity in the production of texts for purposes spanning the spectrum of the mundane to the holy. Levites appear to mediate the different spheres

---

1. See especially Peter Altmann's contribution to this volume for a discussion of the current rifts in how European and North American scholars have approached the question.

2. See among others Karel van der Toorn, *Scribal Culture and the Making of the Hebrew Bible* (Cambridge, Mass.: Harvard University Press, 2007); David M. Carr, *Writing on the Tablet of the Heart: Origin of Scripture and Literature* (New York/Oxford: Oxford University Press, 2005), 120 n. 38, 139, 152; William M. Schniedewind, *How the Bible Became a Book: The Textualization of Ancient Israel* (New York/Cambridge: Cambridge University Press, 2004), 110–14; Mark S. Smith, "The Levitical Compilation of the Psalter," *ZAW* 103 (1991): 258–63.

3. Throughout this essay I use the term "priestly" or related variants with a lowercase "p" to refer to priestly status in general and "Priestly" with regard to the literary tradition and sacerdotal circles typically associated with Aaronide/Zadokite tradition.

4. Carr, *Tablet of the Heart*, 116–20. See also Ian M. Young, "Israelite Literacy: Interpreting the Evidence," *VT* 48 (1998): 239–53, 408–22.

of literary activity, both spatial (local/regional versus central/cultic) and conceptual (common/administrative versus sacral/covenantal).[5] This mediating role is a long-standing Levitical quality, as the textual and social-scientific evidence indicates that Levites had, from the beginning of their activity as a distinct caste, mediated between different kinship groups and social spaces.[6] And, contrary to a common misconception, scribalism had always had a place (albeit a limited one) in Israelite religious life even in the pre-state period as the Levite groups were beginning to form.[7] Given the numinous character of textuality attested widely throughout the ancient record, it seems only natural that Levites would have intersected with literacy and scribalism as part of their sacred duties.[8] However, it is in texts from the late preexilic and exilic periods—especially Deuteronomy and Jeremiah—that literacy and exegesis as Levitical hallmarks are most strongly attested. As is often recognized, Deuteronomy's emphasis on its own writtenness is expressed in the same breath as its presentation of Levites as custodians of the written law, its public proclamation, and the methods of its teaching and application.[9] The book of Jeremiah calls similar attention to its own literary character and strongly connects both the titular prophet and his scribal confreres with Deuteronomic prototypes regarding Levitical status and function.[10] In these works a Levite is, above all, a scribe whose role is to preserve the covenant dialogue with Yhwh through preserving that deity's written word.

These works develop an aspect of Levite function that, as I have noted above, may be traced back to much earlier periods and conditions, but package

---

5. A few examples of these polarities: the Levites read/teach the same law at the central sanctuary in Deut 31:9–13 that is to be read in the homestead (Deut 6:9; 11:20) or applied as civil regulation regionally (Deut 17:8, presupposing that the problematic local case is the exception to the norm). Likewise, the census or residence lists throughout Ezra-Nehemiah drawn from official records eventually form the basis for covenant inclusion facilitated by Levites (e.g., Neh 10 following upon the Levites' prayer in the previous chapter). See further van der Toorn, *Scribal Culture*, 90.

6. Jeremy M. Hutton, "The Levitical Diaspora (I): A Sociological Comparison with Morocco's Ahansal," in *Exploring the Longue Durée: Essays in Honor of Lawrence E. Stager* (ed. J. David Schloen; Winona Lake, Ind.; Eisenbrauns, 2009), 223–30.

7. On the early development of these Levite groups—drawn in large part from regional rural populations already in the Iron I period—see the classic essay by Lawrence E. Stager, "The Archaeology of the Family in Ancient Israel," *BASOR* 260 (1985): 27–28.

8. On the numinous dimension of literacy, see Schniedewind, *How the Bible Became a Book*, 24–34. For the (admittedly limited) availability of scribal resources in the pre-state period, see Ryan Byrne, "The Refuge of Scribalism," *BASOR* 345 (2007): 1–23.

9. Carr, *Tablet of the Heart*, 139; van der Toorn, *Scribal Culture*, 95; Mark Leuchter, "'The Levite in Your Gates': The Deuteronomic Redefinition of Levitical Authority," *JBL* 126 (2007): 417–36.

10. I have explored this phenomenon in detail in my book *The Polemics of Exile in Jeremiah 26–45* (New York/Cambridge: Cambridge University Press, 2008).

it in a particular and definite manner. Both Deuteronomy and Jeremiah present the Levitical production, proclamation, and interpretation of text as a basis for defining the boundary between order and chaos, between blessing and curse, and between social integrity and dissolution—in other words, the traditional concerns of priestly responsibility in extratextual contexts.[11] This tradition—which I would term the Levitical scribal tradition—was by no means an invention of the Deuteronomic and Jeremianic writers. As Karel van der Toorn has recently discussed, a similar shift is found in Mesopotamian religion preceding what we encounter in the Israelite Levitical scribal tradition.[12] Mesopotamian prophecy moves from a primarily oral context secondarily recorded in writing to a primarily written phenomenon, where the act of scribalism itself conveys the essence of divine wisdom and revelation.[13] Considering the influence of this literary tradition on Israelite culture in the late eighth through late seventh centuries B.C.E., it is fitting that a similar shift would occur in Israelite priestly categories.[14] This shift, as reflected in Deuteronomy and Jeremiah, placed Levite scribes at the center of Israelite concepts of the divine–human dialogue, offering new ways for Israel to encounter Yhwh's word and will. At a time marked by significant sociopolitical instability, the fixed nature of written works could help tether Israel to a baseline of ideological identity, but still remain adaptable and adjustable to the changing needs of the community.[15]

---

11. It is notable, for instance, that Deuteronomy consistently equates observance of the written law with enduring life in the land and the purgation of evil. Though the language is terse and utilizes legislative and treaty forms from Mesopotamian sources, the ideological content of this equation parallels aspects of the old combat myth where the chief deity subdues chaotic cosmic foes and thereby establishes order throughout the sacred landscape. The concept is most prominently attested in Exod 15, where following the defeat of the mythic enemy, Yhwh plants his people in his holy highlands. Consequently, the singing of the hymn in Exod 15 is a communal affirmation of that deity's hegemony. See my essay "Eisodus as Exodus: The Song of the Sea (Exod 15) Reconsidered," *Biblica* (forthcoming). The Deuteronomic law takes on the same role as Exod 15 vis-à-vis the public affirmation of divine hegemony throughout the land and the people's resulting tenure thereupon. The Jeremiah tradition follows suit: the late preexilic or exilic redactor behind Jer 9:11–12 makes clear that the abrogation of the law results in the presence of the cosmic foe Death wreaking havoc (Jer 9:20).

12. Van der Toorn, *Scribal Culture*, 206–21.

13. Ibid.

14. On the influence of the Mesopotamian literary tradition on Israel beginning in the late eighth century B.C.E., see Peter Machinist, "Assyria and Its Image in the First Isaiah," *JAOS* 103 (1983): 719–37; Eckart Otto, "Rechtsreformen in Deuteronomium xii–xxvi im mittelassyrischen Kodex der Tafel A (KAV 1)," in *Congress Volume: Paris, 1992* (ed. J. A. Emerton; VTSup 61; Leiden: Brill, 1995), 239–73; Lena-Sofia Tiemeyer, *For the Comfort of Zion: The Geographical and Theological Location of Isaiah 40–55* (VTSup 139; Leiden: Brill, 2011), 79–83.

15. Such is implied via the dynamic in Deut 17:8–13. So also the subtle adjustments

This emphasis on Levite scribes as the mediators of revelation as attested in Deuteronomy and Jeremiah did not surface without some challenges. There are indications that some Levites did not share in this suggested vision of self-understanding or the texts that delineate its terms (Jer 11:18–21), and older categories of oracular communication and teaching were preserved by supporters of the hierarchical status quo (Jer 18:18).[16] Finally, it is clear from the Aaronide priestly writings in P, H, and Ezekiel that written revelation was subordinated to older oral modes of priestly authority and teaching, even as such modes were communicated *through* the aforementioned Aaronide written collections.[17] By the mid-fifth century B.C.E., however, this conflict seems to have been somewhat ameliorated: Ezra-Nehemiah draws equally from both Deuteronomy and P, and Jeremiah's oracles are woven into the account of both Ezra's and Nehemiah's conduct and policies.[18] Perhaps new challenges such as the Golah community–homeland community conflict trumped the problem of earlier priestly fissions: in this case the reconciliation of Levitical-scribal and Aaronide ideology reflects the need for in-group cohesion among those returning exiles who sought to secure territorial and political primacy in Yehud. Against this background, Levite scribes could reconcile their positions and traditions with Aaronides as both formed the sacerdotal caste of the Golah community based in Jerusalem.

---

to Deuteronomic temple theology in Jeremiah's Temple Sermon; see Mark Leuchter, "The Temple Sermon and the term מקום in the Jeremianic Corpus," *JSOT* 31 (2005): 93–109.

16. See Stephen Cook's contribution to the present volume. Cook sees the conflict between Jeremiah and the Levites of Anathoth as one in which the former critiqued policies and ideologies that benefited the interests of the latter. It may also be the case that the conflict with the Levites of Anathoth reflects a different disagreement, namely, the latter's rejection of the Deuteronomic enterprise *en masse*. See my discussion in "Why Is the Song of Moses in the Book of Deuteronomy?," *VT* 57 (2007): 313–14. A mediating position between Cook's view and my own is entirely possible if one assumes that, like Jeremiah, there were members of the Anathoth community that supported Deuteronomy, members who rejected it, and members who agreed with Jeremiah's qualified critique and adjustment of its application. To pursue this point, however, goes beyond the scope of the present study.

17. Schniedewind notes that P never emphasizes its own textuality (*How the Bible Became a Book*, 115), and James W. Watts has recently argued convincingly that the textual form of Lev 1–16 was constructed to support the traditional oral/pedagogical authority of the Aaronide priests (James W. Watts, *Ritual and Rhetoric in Leviticus: From Sacrifice to Scripture* [New York/Cambridge: Cambridge University Press, 2007]). Finally, Ezekiel's literary sophistication does not hinder him from reversing the implications of Jer 36, where the divine word finds full expression in a scroll. For Ezekiel, the divine word in a scroll can only be obtained from the mouth of the priest-prophet who has consumed it (Ezek 3:1).

18. See my articles "Ezra's Mission and the Levites of Casiphia," *Community Identity in Judean Historiography* (ed. Gary N. Knoppers and Kenneth A. Ristau; Winona Lake, Ind.: Eisenbrauns, 2009), 173–95; and "The Politics of Ritual Rhetoric: A Proposed Sociohistorical Background to the Redaction of Leviticus 1–16," *VT* 60 (2010): 345–65.

If we are to accept the conventional dating of Chronicles to the mid-to-late fourth century B.C.E., the eve of the Alexandrian era saw Levites as a fixture of the Jerusalem temple's ranks. As many commentators note, the Chronicler's emphasis on Levites as integral members of this community speaks to their increased importance as mediators between the temple hierarchies and the communities that the Chronicler wished to include in his concept of greater Israel, especially those to the north of Yehud.[19] Legion are the passages that identify disparate Levite lineages with the foundation of the Jerusalem cult and its liturgy, and equally numerous are the passages that ascribe to Levites prophetic qualifications alongside their textual authority.[20] Yet it is also clear that their scribal duties, while strongly connected to the inner workings of the temple, are not restricted to this locus of activity, as the Chronicler mentions Levites teaching *torah* in the rural sectors (1 Chr 26:29; 2 Chr 17:7–9; 19:5–7; 34:13). For the Chronicler, the idea of Levitical scribalism promotes inclusion and social cohesion among populations distant from Jerusalem and is not limited to temple-based activity. This should be contrasted with what is found in Ezra-Nehemiah, where administrative literary charges are ultimately revealed to be ritually focused (Ezra 7) or the centerpiece of covenant ceremonies (Neh 8). This suggests that scribal exegesis—as a vehicle for defining order within the community and aligning it with divine will—was taking steps toward a new mythotype, one that saw the scribal act as maintaining a central place as a cosmic/sacral boundary marker but transcending the temple establishment.

All the same, a note of change must be detected here. Though Levites are without a doubt the outstanding scribal experts in late-Persian-era texts, the exegetical literary tradition they had developed by this time may well have been adopted by non-Levites who shared similar interests. One thinks, for example, of Nehemiah, a layman who is characterized in the Nehemiah Memoir as a supporter of the Levites but also as highly literate and fully capable of engaging in exegesis of a rather sophisticated nature.[21] It strains credulity that Nehemiah stands alone in carrying such qualifications; other administrative

---

19. On the Chronicler's more inclusive ethic regarding northerners, see Gary N. Knoppers, *I Chronicles 1–9: A New Translation with Introduction and Commentary* (AB 12; New York: Doubleday, 2003), 83–84.

20. Van der Toorn, *Scribal Culture*, 230; Carr, *Tablet of the Heart*, 152.

21. Nehemiah's prayers, for example, offer up prime examples, and the major commentaries have all noted the close engagement with antecedent texts in this regard. Though Jacob L. Wright has made a strong case for seeing these as mostly secondary entries into the Nehemiah Memoir ("A New Model for the Composition of Ezra-Nehemiah," in *Judah and the Judeans in the Fourth Century B.C.E.* [ed. Oded Lipschits, Gary N. Knoppers, and Rainer Albertz; Winona Lake, Ind.: Eisenbrauns, 2007] 344), the redactors responsible for their addition saw fit to identify them with Nehemiah himself and not a Levitical agent as is the case with the prayer in Neh 9.

figures in the Jewish communities of Yehud and beyond must have developed similar skills. That the Chronicler situates Levites in communities well beyond Jerusalem may indicate his recognition that lay factions cultivated traditions of sacral literacy and exegesis that rivaled those of the Levites associated with the Jerusalem temple establishment. Consequently, his placement of Levites as literate figures in the hinterland may constitute a suggestion that sacral scribalism even outside of the temple complex should be a Levitical imperative.

II. THE RESTRICTION OF LEVITICAL QUALIFICATIONS IN HELLENISTIC TEXTS

At the outset of the Hellenistic period, then, Levites remained firmly bound to the priestly faculty of the Jerusalem temple, assisting the Aaronides in the conduct of ritual, overseeing the collections of literature in the temple library, carrying out administrative duties and, most prominently, carrying scribal/exegetical authority.[22] But it is conceivable that these skills and their sacral dimensions were taken up by non-Levite elites outside the strictures of the temple hierarchy by suitably qualified individuals who possessed intellectual privilege and opportunity, and who may have challenged the sacerdotal circles in the temple. There is little in the way of direct textual evidence that the Levitical-scribal tradition was appropriated widely by non-Levites, but the indirect evidence is highly suggestive. It is in the third and second centuries B.C.E. that a renewed interest in the figure of Levi begins to surface in a variety of texts, all of which emphasize his own priestly status in the ancestral period.[23] This breaks with the antecedent pentateuchal traditions, which identify priesthood only with Aaron's descendants during the period of the exodus/wilderness. Against this, the Hellenistic texts such as *Aramaic Levi*, *Jubilees*, and, later, the *Testament of Levi*, repeatedly state that the Levite priesthood begins with the eponymous ancestor himself.[24] For these writers, Levite status is strictly a matter of hereditary qualification. Martha Himmelfarb has noted that while *Jubilees* presents priesthood as a wider province before Levi's consecration, it is restricted to Levi and his descendants thereafter.[25] A passage from *Jubilees* clearly conveys this concept:

---

22. Van der Toorn, *Scribal Culture*, 90.
23. James L. Kugel, *The Ladder of Jacob: Ancient Interpretation of the Biblical Story of Jacob and His Children* (Princeton/Oxford: Princeton University Press, 2006), 115–68; Robert A. Kugler, *From Patriarch to Priest: The Levi-Priestly Tradition from Aramaic Levi to Testament of Levi* (SBLEJL 9; Atlanta: Scholars Press, 1996). Kugel and Kugler date the compositional sequence of *Jubilees* and *Aramaic Levi* differently, but the question of this sequence is not immediately relevant for our purposes here.
24. Kugel, *Ladder of Jacob*, 123–36.
25. Martha Himmelfarb, "'A Kingdom of Priests': The Democratization of the Priesthood in the Literature of Second Temple Judaism," *JJTP* 6 (1997): 92–93. Himmelfarb

And the seed of Levi was chosen for the priesthood, and to be Levites, that they might minister before the Lord, as we, continually, and that Levi and his sons may be blessed for ever; for he was zealous to execute righteousness and judgment and vengeance on all those who arose against Israel. And so they inscribe as a testimony in his favour on the heavenly tablets blessing and righteousness before the God of all: And we remember the righteousness which the man fulfilled during his life, at all periods of the year; until a thousand generations they will record it, and it will come to him and to his descendants after him, and he has been recorded on the heavenly tablets as a friend and a righteous man. (*Jub.* 30:18-20)

Jubilees emphasizes that Levi's consecration rests on his father, Jacob, as the priestly authority who initiates him.[26] Ancestry lineage is the governing theme, and Levite tradition and responsibility are restricted to individuals of an ancestral line that could be traced to Levi; scribal exegesis akin to that promoted in Chronicles must similarly be restricted only to hereditary Levites connected with the temple. The author of *Jubilees* elsewhere specifies that this restriction was not to be taken lightly:

All this account I have written for thee, and have commanded thee to say to the children of Israel, that they should not commit sin nor transgress the ordinances nor break the covenant which has been ordained for them, (but) that they should fulfill it and be recorded as friends. But if they transgress and work uncleanness in every way, they will be recorded on the heavenly tablets as adversaries, and they will be destroyed out of the book of life, and they will be recorded in the book of those who will be destroyed and with those who will be rooted out of the earth. (*Jub.* 18:21-22)

From the perspective of the author of *Jubilees*, the sacral authority entrusted to Levi was to be carried forward by his "seed," that is, his priestly descendants. According to *Aramaic Levi*, measures needed to be implemented to preserve the genealogical integrity of this seed and the status it secured.[27] It is the descendants of Levi alone who are licensed to serve as "priests and Levites," presumably in the traditional capacities identified in the earlier biblical materials. Any non-Levites attempting to take up practices associated with them are reckoned transgressors of covenantal law and marked as enemies of the

---

observes that *Jubilees* is interested in extending priestly holiness to all of Israel akin to the H school of thought, which shows signs of what will obtain with later Pharisaic teaching (pp. 96-98). However, this is a matter of communal merit and not genuine priestly status, and I would argue that it constitutes a critique of contemporaneous priesthood as a sort of ideological *kal va-chomer* in reverse: if all of Israel is to be holy in this way, how much more should the priests who hold a unique status through their descent from Levi.

26. Kugler, *From Patriarch to Priest*, 161-62.

27. See the discussion in Himmelfarb's monograph-length study on the same topic, *A Kingdom of Priests: Ancestry and Merit in Ancient Judaism* (Jewish Culture and Contexts; Philadelphia: University of Pennsylvania Press, 2006), 25-28.

faith community. Though *Jubilees* makes the argument that certain restrictive modes of priestly conduct should be supported by all Israel, it restricts the role of legitimate scribes and exegetes of Scripture to hereditary Levites, effectively delegitimizing swathes of interpretive tradition that may have arisen from non-Levite/non-Priestly circles. The association of priests and scribes in the literature from this period is perhaps an attempt to extend priestly hegemony over the learned non-priestly classes,[28] and Ben Sira attests to this already in the early second century B.C.E. As Himmelfarb points out, Ben Sira is identified as a scribe, not a priest, but it is clear that he supports Priestly hegemony, and his own veneration of wisdom is bound up with his association of that principle with the priesthood.[29]

This view did not suddenly arise in the Hellenistic era. The appropriation of "Levite" texts for defining priestly rank involved a particular reading strategy of older texts witnessed already in Mal 2:4–7, as Robert Kugler has discussed.[30] The eventual and thorough incorporation of Levites into the temple faculty throughout the Persian period certainly reinforced such readings,[31] but this was also accompanied by an increased emphasis on genealogical qualification for sacerdotal office. The proclivity to restrict communal status to Golah lineage in Ezra-Nehemiah carries over into matters of priestly status as well, with limits placed on priestly intermingling with non-priestly kinship networks well before the composition of *Aramaic Levi* and its emphasis on this same idea.[32] However, with the challenges to the temple hierarchies that came with the transition from Persian to Hellenistic governance (and, subsequently, the shift from Ptolemaic to Seleucid rule) the notion of priesthood—including Levite status—deriving from strict lineage qualification proved a powerful rhetorical tool either as a claim to incumbent authority or among those who wished to question a priest's hereditary status.[33] What is more, literacy and

---

28. Himmelfarb sees the union of priesthood and scribalism as a democratizing impulse that subordinates priestly lineage status to the merit-based status of scribalism ("Kingdom of Priests," 103). This may be the case, especially at a time when priesthood was being questioned within the Priestly ranks. However, the hegemony of priests over the Jerusalem scribal establishment discussed by van der Toorn (*Scribal Culture*, passim), Carr (*Tablet of the Heart*, 201–14), and others suggests that the same concept may have been used for the very opposite purpose, that is, to reign in scribal autonomy as a subset of Priestly authority.

29. Himmelfarb, *Kingdom of Priests*, 30, 34–38. Himmelfarb does suggest that Ben Sira is also a priest ("Kingdom of Priests," 103–4), but this is not overt.

30. Kugler, *From Patriarch to Priest*, 18–22.

31. On this lengthy and complicated process, see the detailed discussion by Joachim Schaper, *Priester und Leviten im achämenidischen Juda: Studien zur Kult- und Sozialgeschichte Israels in persischer Zeit* (FAT 31; Tübingen: Mohr Siebeck, 2000).

32. See the discussion by Saul M. Olyan, "Purity Ideology in Ezra-Nehemiah as a Tool to Reconstitute the Community," *JSJ* 35 (2004): 5–8.

33. See the concluding remarks by Kugler, who notes that the *Testament of Levi* sup-

scribal skill are entirely restricted to those carrying Levite status. The authority to compose and interpret Scripture is an exclusive hallmark of the temple-bound priestly circles.

III. Daniel as an Alternative to Levite Scribalism

A strong challenge to this purview surfaces in the book of Daniel. Though emerging at a time proximate to the aforementioned Hellenistic texts,[34] Daniel emphasizes scribalism in a context as far removed from the priesthood and the Jerusalem temple as possible in Jewish imagination: the Babylonian exile and the early Persian-era Diaspora. In a recent study, Donald Polaski identifies the underlying political concern in Daniel regarding scribal exegesis, namely, that it was a fixture of the Jewish literati in relation to imperial administration.[35] For the authors of Daniel, text is part of a process that articulates utilitarian power structures within an imperial context and manifests the channels of authority that emanate from the foreign emperor as much as from the divine.[36] This rings of certain passages in Ezra-Nehemiah, but the geographic setting in Daniel divests it from the tradition rooted in the temple and Jerusalem. At the same time, while the emphasis on scribal exegesis within a wider social scope recalls Chronicles, the authors of Daniel move away from the Chronicler's emphasis on native institutions and locales as the setting for piety. Instead, they view the imperial context of their day as the locus for the production of new divine writs that are to be subject to scribal authority and interpretation (Dan 5).

The tendentious stance between Jewish and imperial life in Daniel, however, very much stands in the scribal tradition developed among the Levite (or pro-Levite) authors of earlier works such as Deuteronomy or Jeremiah that sought to maintain the boundary between chaos and order through textuality and the exegetical process. In those earlier works, it is the very act of writing, reading, preserving, and transmitting text that safeguards communal

---

ports incumbency while *Aramaic Levi* and *Jubilees* appear to challenge it (*From Patriarch to Priest*, 224).

34. Virtually all critical scholars see the final form of Daniel as emerging in the mid-second century B.C.E. See John J. Collins, *Daniel: A Commentary on the Book of Daniel* (Hermeneia; Minneapolis: Fortress, 1993), 37–38, 60–61. See also Rainer Albertz, who identifies an earlier stage in the production of Daniel but who recognizes that the final form of the book coincides with the Maccabeean period ("The Social Setting of the Aramaic and Hebrew Book of Daniel," in *The Book of Daniel: Composition and Reception* [ed. John J. Collins and Peter W. Flint; VTSup 83; Leiden: Brill, 2001], 175–79).

35. Donald C. Polaski, "Mene, Mene, Tekel, Parsin: Writing and Resistance in Daniel 5 and 6," *JBL* 123 (2004): 649–69.

36. Ibid., 668–69.

and personal identity and sustains divine blessing and safety from catastrophe.[37] Daniel's authors do not emphasize the role of Levites in maintaining this textual dynamic, but the tendentious stance between Jewish (socioreligious order) and imperial life (the potential locus of chaos and threat) in Daniel very much stands in the aforementioned Levitical-textual tradition. In the court tales, it is Daniel's own ability to discern patterns and signs in the "texts" provided for him that allows him to maintain a position within the royal retinue.[38] The wisdom gleaned by the scribal tradition is what affords him this ability, and it has routinely been noted that Daniel embodies the characteristics of a Jewish sage-scribe in the Hellenistic period, intimately familiar with the Mesopotamian intellectual culture that still flourished in the second century B.C.E.[39] But the authors of Daniel carry forward the function of scribalism as a vehicle for mediating between the ordinary and the cosmic. This is obviously the case with the highly mythological imagery permeating the entirety of the book (especially the visions in Dan 7–12), but the exegetical process is proffered as the conduit for this encounter. It is Daniel's scribal status that allows him to discern the mythic dimensions of the events in the court tales and to secure revelation concerning his own visions by a divine agent; the message of the book, then, is its own form of torah regarding the manifestations of Yhwh in history. But unlike the work of the Chronicler, who repeatedly stresses the place of Levites in the shaping of sacred history, the authors of Daniel refrain from overtly connecting their brand of instruction to anything Levitical.

Three examples of this strategy will suffice in revealing how the authors of Daniel carry forward the Levitical scribal tradition while simultaneously breaking from it, and the first occurs at the outset of the book itself. Daniel 1 takes up the annalistic form characterizing the redaction of the book of Kings and the similar historiographic sections of Jeremiah—enterprises that

---

37. E.g., Deut 6:9; 11:20; 17:18–20; 31:9–13; Jer 29:1; 30:2; 36:2, 4, 32; 51:59–64.

38. There is debate, however, as to whether the court tales constituted an independent collection secondarily joined to the apocalyptic visions in the book or if the original edition of Daniel incorporated both genres. For the former position, see Collins, *Daniel*, 35–37; on the latter, see Albertz, "Social Setting," 176–79. In the final form of Daniel, however, the court tales are fully incorporated into the book's logic. See Gabriele Boccaccini, *Roots of Rabbinic Judaism: An Intellectual History, from Ezekiel to Daniel* (Grand Rapids: Eerdmans, 2002), 171–72.

39. Karel van der Toorn, "In the Lion's Den: The Babylonian Background of a Biblical Motif," *CBQ* 60 (1998): 626–40; Paul-Alain Beaulieu, "The Babylonian Background to the Motif of the Fiery Furnace in Daniel 3," *JBL* 128 (2009): 273–90; Michael Segal, "From Joseph to Daniel: The Literary Development of the Narrative in Daniel 2," *VT* 59 (2009): 137–39. See also Alan Lenzi, who notes that the manner of scribal discourse in Daniel, especially the emphasis on secrecy, is a criticism of similar features of the Mesopotamian scribal tradition ("Secrecy, Textual Legitimation, and Intercultural Polemics in the Book of Daniel," *CBQ* 71 [2009]: 330–38).

repeatedly emphasize Levite sensibilities[40]—projecting their terms onto events leading to Daniel's place in Nebuchadnezzar's royal court:

> In the third year of the reign of Jehoiakim king of Judah came Nebuchadnezzar king of Babylon unto Jerusalem, and besieged it. And Yhwh gave Jehoiakim king of Judah into his hand, with part of the vessels of the house of God; and he carried them into the land of Shinar to the house of his god, and the vessels he brought into the treasure-house of his god. (Dan 1:1–2)

The historical inaccuracies in this passage are well known, and they cannot be reconciled with any of the extant biblical sources or, for that matter, the Babylonian Chronicle covering the same time span.[41] The purpose of this introduction, however, is not to recount genuine history but to call into question perceptions of the texts available not only to the authors but to their audience. The similarity to passages in Kings, Chronicles, and Jeremiah covering the same figures, events, and period of time is no coincidence, for those works enshrined and conveyed a distinctively Levitical scribal view of history, royal hierarchies, and the place of Yhwh in motivating events. But the break in content accuracy declares that what is to follow is a different sort of categorization of the past, a new chapter in scribal/exegetical methods in clarifying the meaning of history and the place of Jews in imperial contexts.[42]

It is also not a coincidence that the conclusion of Dan 1—where Daniel and his pious peers are sustained by resisting the royal foodstuffs—appears to offer a radically different view regarding survival from that in the conclusion to the book of Kings, where Jehoiachin is sustained by dining at the table of the Babylonian king (2 Kgs 25:27–30).[43] The resistance to the royal diet may

---

40. On the redaction of Kings as reflecting Levitical interests and very possibly deriving from a Levite historiographer, see Jeffrey C. Geoghegan, "The Redaction of Kings and Priestly Authority in Jerusalem," *Soundings in Kings: Perspectives and Methods in Contemporary Scholarship* (ed. Mark Leuchter and Klaus-Peter Adam; Minneapolis: Fortress, 2010), 109–18.

41. For a full discussion of the sources and inconsistencies in detail in Dan 1:1–2, see Collins, *Daniel*, 130–33.

42. The suggestion by the commentators noted by Collins (*Daniel*, 132 n. 25) that the authors of Daniel have confused the details in their sources misses the point entirely; the authors' great familiarity with these sources enables them to explode the conventional categories contained therein, an idea that surfaces with greater force in Dan 9 (see below).

43. This calls into question the view of Klaus Koch that the authors did not know Kings or consider it authoritative (*Daniel* [BKAT; Neukirchen-Vluyn; Neukirchener Verlag, 1986], 31). Matthew S. Rindge draws parallels between Daniel's refusal of the royal diet and the account of Joseph's acceptance of foreign royal accoutrements ("Jewish Identity under Foreign Rule: Daniel 2 as a Reconfiguration of Genesis 41," *JBL* 129 [2010]: 102–3), though the recalling of the annalistic form of Kings in the opening verses of Dan 1 invites a comparison with the former. For the difficulty regarding the common view that the resistance to

constitute a comment on the factions reacting to Seleucid rule in the authors' day. Daniel and his peers resist the royal diet and thus avoid the acquiescence of Jehoiachin at the end of Kings, yet the end result of their decision endows them with the wisdom required to survive equally well in the service of the foreign ruler. The authors may thus have advocated a mediating view between the Jews collaborating with the Seleucids, on one hand, and those who advocated violent resistance, on the other.[44] If the latter utilized the same earlier sources as the authors of Dan 1 to support their agenda, the authors of Dan 1 counter this with their proposed rereading of the past. What the audience knows of its past from the sources it possesses, the authors suggest, requires serious reconsideration. The playing with historical data in the opening verses of the book also suggests that the balance between chaos (collaboration or violent resistance) and order (the authors' mediating, negotiated piety) is revealed through careful reading of texts in light of a careful evaluation of the Seleucid present of the authors' day. This recalls some of the Chronicler's own strategies regarding the blurring of lines between traditions in response to contemporaneous threats and pressures, though the authors of Daniel move further and suggest that very perception of history itself required reexamination.[45]

That the authors of Daniel were perhaps aware of this dialogue with Chronicles is suggested by the second testament to Levite-scribal influence, namely, the meditation on Jeremiah's seventy-year prophecy in Dan 9. The hermeneutical formula or solution to the problem of the absence of true restoration—that Jeremiah's "seventy years" is to be viewed as seventy weeks of years—has received enormous discussion and is widely recognized as a masterpiece of early midrashic exegesis.[46] But what has not been as thoroughly discussed is that to arrive at this solution, the authors of Dan 9 have taken up the earlier exegetical joining of the Jeremiah and Leviticus material in Chronicles and, in the same breath, have dismantled it. We will recall that 2 Chr 36:20–21 identifies the concept of the exile as a Sabbatical rest with Jeremiah's prophecy;[47] rhetorically, the former equals the latter. The very fact that the character Daniel

---

the royal foodstuffs reflects concern with issues of purity related to Priestly law, see further Collins, *Daniel*, 141–42.

44. Albertz, "Social Setting," 201–2.

45. This may well show influence of the Enochic tradition, where history was viewed as degenerating against divine intention (Boccaccini, *Roots of Rabbinic Judaism*, 91–92). By retelling history using familiar forms but completely new/independent content, the authors of Daniel mediate between the Enochic and Priestly historical conceptions, suggesting degeneration of history but as the result of divine purpose (e.g., the interpretation of the dream in Dan 2).

46. Paul L. Redditt, "Daniel 9: Its Structure and Meaning," *CBQ* 69 (2002): 236–49 (with a review of scholarship on pp. 237–39); Collins, *Daniel*, 347–60.

47. See esp. Louis C. Jonker, "The Chronicler and the Prophets: Who Were His Authoritative Sources?" *SJOT* 22 (2008): 281–83, for an analysis.

FROM LEVITE TO MAŚKÎL 227

is troubled by the contradictions and lack of resolution in Jeremiah's oracle, however, reveals that the authors of Dan 9 considered the hermeneutical equation in 2 Chr 36:20–21 to be not only insufficient but inapplicable. The idea of interpreting Jeremiah's oracle in light of Lev 26 is presented in Dan 9 as a *new* insight despite the allusions to the Chronicler's earlier text:

> In the first year of his [Darius's] reign I Daniel meditated in the books, over the number of the years, that the word of Yhwh came to Jeremiah the prophet, that he would fulfill (למלאות) for the desolations (לחרבות) of Jerusalem seventy years. (Dan 9:2)

> And them that had escaped from the sword (החרב) he carried away to Babylon; and they were servants to him and his sons until the reign of the kingdom of Persia; to fulfill (למלאות) the word of Yhwh by the mouth of Jeremiah, until the land had been paid her Sabbaths; for as long as she lay desolate she kept Sabbath, to fulfill (למלאות) seventy years. (2 Chr 36:20–21)

The locution in Dan 9:2 involves word combinations not found solely in the Jeremianic source texts, so it is very likely that the authors knew and utilized 2 Chr 36:20–21 as a source.[48] But the authors of Daniel do not mention this source, and, moreover, the discourse in the first few verses of Dan 9 makes no mention of Leviticus, the other source lying behind the Chronicler's text. It is not until much later in the chapter (vv. 21–27) that the authors invoke Leviticus as the exegetical key to understanding Jeremiah's oracle, and this comes only as the result of Daniel's pious prayer (vv. 4–19).

Many scholars have noted that by engaging in a liturgy of penitence, Daniel's prayer secures the condition whereby Israel could be granted a reprieve from exile.[49] But it is also essential to recognize that this prayer falls into the category of penitential prayer recited by Levites in other contexts. This is the case not only in terms of language and form but also in terms of the prayer's redactional place in the chapter. The prayer in Dan 9:4–19 is widely regarded as an older composition redacted into its current context, similar to the penitential prayer in Neh 9.[50] The latter, a Levitical liturgy from the mid-sixth century, has been imported into a literary unit dating from, at the earliest, the late fifth

---

48. Collins indeed notes that the authors of Daniel already know and rely on material in 2 Chr 36 in their construction of Dan 1 (*Daniel*, 132–33). There is little reason to doubt that this same text was not known to the authors of Dan 9, especially if Dan 1 stems from a late redaction of an older collection (Dan 2–7) into the current form of the book (Albertz, "Social Setting," 179).

49. Collins, *Daniel*, 359–60.

50. Ibid., 347–48; Boccaccini, *Roots of Rabbinic Judaism*, 181–82; Redditt, "Daniel 9"; etc. One may also cite Ezra 9 as an antecedent, but Ezra 9 is itself a relatively late addition to Ezra-Nehemiah (Wright, "New Model," 344) and was probably shaped with an awareness of Neh 9 as an independent composition.

century, and likely considerably later than that.[51] Likewise, the authors of Dan 9 have worked a similar prayer with similar language into a later context. That this prayer follows the same form as the Levitical prayer in Neh 9 and that it is spawned by Daniel's meditation on the words of the Levite prophet Jeremiah points to the larger rhetorical point of the chapter: that the true understanding of history, revealed in an apocalyptic form to Daniel, is the result of emulating liturgical, hermeneutical, and compositional/redactional methods associated with the Levitical tradition.

The relationship between Dan 9 and the surrounding apocalyptic visions hinges on this very point. Daniel's apocalyptic form utilizes a standard of expression that had become popular among Jewish writers in the third and second centuries B.C.E, and several scholars have noted that the apocalyptic form is especially at home in priestly contexts.[52] If apocalyptic literature represents a medium point between mythic and sociopolitical thought, its place in the hands of the priesthood is natural, overlapping as it does with similar functions of the temple cult and Levitical scribal tradition. But it is essential to recognize that, like the court tales in the first part of the book, Dan 9 is disengaged from the cult.[53] There is no mention of priesthood or temple-based oracles; revelation via angelic intercession is secured through the study of text, penitential prayer, and scribal wisdom. Indeed, the author specifies that Daniel's revelation came at the very time of a regular evening sacrifice (מנחת ערב), but obviously in distinction from it (Dan 9:21). The implication is that Daniel's scribal authority is independent of temple circles. The Levite tradition that had earlier been fostered in those contexts has been completely abstracted and fixed in a new social location.

It is clear that the authors of Daniel recognized the ongoing vitality of penitence and supplication in securing divine favor, as well as the central role of orthodox text traditions as the point of departure for this form of piety. But it is the scribal process itself that channels and translates it into definable patterns and terms. In a sense, Daniel may be compared to Chronicles in terms of its understanding of scribal exegesis as a vehicle for ordering and sustaining national integrity under strained conditions. The authors of both

---

51. On the dating and provenance of Neh 9, see Lena-Sofia Tiemeyer, "Abraham: A Judahite Prerogative," *ZAW* 120 (2008): 61–63. On the late redaction of Neh 8–10, see Wright, "New Model," 344.

52. See, among others, Marvin A. Sweeney, *Form and Intertextuality in Prophetic and Apocalyptic Literature* (FAT 45; Tübingen: Mohr Siebeck, 2005), 239–47; Reinhard G. Kratz, *Translatio Imperii: Untersuchungen zu den aramäischen Danielerzählungen und ihrem theologiegeschichtlichen Umfeld* (WMANT 63; Neukirchen-Vluyn; Neukirchener Verlag, 1991), 279; J. C. Lebram, "Apokalyptic und Hellenismus im buches Daniel," *VT* 20 (1970): 523–24.

53. I do not wish to suggest that the authors of Daniel were specifically *anti*-temple (see further below), only that Daniel's exegetical methods are not rooted in the cult or limited to the priestly faculty in the temple complex.

works considered themselves the inheritors of earlier authoritative traditions that they could refract through their own compositions and, in so doing, reveal additional dimensions of meaning behind the surface features of Jewish society and the texts it preserved. But while the Chronicler sees the exegetical engagement of texts beyond the "Levite" curriculum fit for the enculturation of a society where Levites still held scribal roles, the authors of Daniel do not. Against the trend to particularize scribalism within the temple-based priestly ranks in *Aramaic Levi* or *Jubilees*, Daniel's recognition that the Jerusalem temple had been compromised led to a new understanding of how scribalism could survive as a conduit to the divine beyond its precincts.

The question of the authorship of Daniel is itself the final testament to the challenge to Levitical status and scribal authority. John Collins is certainly correct to see the authors of Daniel as intellectuals, but these intellectuals rival the priesthood as scribal mediators of revelation and the realm of the divine. Just as Ezekiel had envisioned the removal of the divine presence from the Jerusalem temple of his day (Ezek 1), the authors of Daniel saw scribal exegesis—the locus for the encounter with the divine—as fit for removal from the same institution in their own time. With Daniel, a new typology of cosmic mediation emerges in full flourish—that of the משׂכילים who stand beyond the cult but behind the production of the book (Dan 11:33–35 and 12:[1–2]3).[54] These texts alluding to these figures make clear that they are to educate the people, a role that had hitherto been Levitical (Deut 33:8–11; Neh 8:7; 2 Chr 35:3, etc.); the משׂכילים are positioned to succeed the priesthood as the disseminators of Yhwh's teachings. The abstraction of Priestly teaching for exilic audiences in Ezekiel's oracles served as a template for the authors of Daniel to abstract authoritative scriptural tropes in support of their own interests, including the tropes of Priestly literature. As scholars have often noted, the lexemes of Dan 12:3 present the authors of Daniel as inheritors of the role of the Servant in Isa 52–53 (see esp. Isa 52:13; 53:11).[55] Isaianic prophecies are deeply concerned with the sanctity of Jerusalem, but Dan 12:3 arranges its terms to claim mastery over the doctrines of the Jerusalem priesthood while maintaining distinction from it:

---

54. See Albertz, who sees the redactors of the final version of the book as among non-priestly circles ("Social Setting," 191–201).

55. See, e.g., Michael Fishbane, *Biblical Interpretation in Ancient Israel* (Oxford: Clarendon, 1985), 493. Ronald S. Hendel further notes the exegetical dependence of Dan 12 on the book of Isaiah; see his "Isaiah and the Transition from Prophecy to Apocalyptic," in *Birkat Shalom: Studies in the Bible, Ancient Near Eastern Literature, and Postbiblical Judaism Presented to Shalom M. Paul on the Occasion of His Seventieth Birthday* (ed. Chaim Cohen et al.; Winona Lake, Ind.: Eisenbrauns, 2008), 269–71.

And the wise ones (משכלים) shall shine as the brightness of the firmament (הרקיע); and they that turn the many to righteousness (ומצדקי הרבים) as the stars (כוכבים) forever and ever.

In Dan 12:3, the משכלים are not simply disseminators of righteousness; the locution suggests that through their actions, they democratize Zadokite sanctity to the masses (ומצדקי הרבים). Akin to the reframing of Jeremianic prophecy and Priestly thought in 2 Chr 35:25, the authors here utilize the tropes of prophecy to dislodge the fixed doctrines regarding the cosmos and the Jewish populace therein. The likelihood of this implicit meaning to the verse is amplified by the invocation of two images very much at home in Priestly discourse, namely, the association of the משכלים with the "firmament" (הרקיע) and the stars (כוכבים). Though these terms carry forward the cosmic rhetoric found throughout the book of Daniel, they also link the work of the משכלים to the P creation account in Genesis (cf. Gen 1:6–8, 14–18). This is hardly a matter of coincidental cosmic language, for the Genesis account makes clear that these celestial entities regulate history (Gen 1:14) and indeed rule over what unfolds therein (Gen 1:18), and the trajectory of history is one of the central themes in Daniel.[56] The scribal and exegetical authority of the משכלים, secured by their wisdom and the ongoing revelation it facilitates, competes with, counters, and trumps priestly hierarchy. The structure of the cosmos is grounded in Jewish society not through the cult but through scribalism independent of priestly status—including that of the Levite variety now subsumed within the temple faculty. History and its meaning are mediated through the teachings of the משכלים, not the priesthood.

III. Conclusion: From Levite to *Maśkîl* and Beyond

In stark contrast to the apocalyptic Enochic tradition that challenged the cosmic legacy of the Jerusalemite sacral curriculum, the משכלים affirm the literary and theological basis of the city's religious establishment. Yet in stark contrast to the wisdom espoused by Ben Sira, who staunchly advocated the Priestly social order as the basis for covenantal security, the wisdom of the משכלים demands a new understanding of who holds exegetical authority over sacred texts. It is not priests and Levites associated with the Jerusalem temple who secure divine blessing, but scribes who liberate Levitical modes of exegesis from cultic moorings and extend them to the masses. If Daniel is, as Gabriele Boccaccini puts it, a third way between these groups,[57] it exhibits the same mediating quality that other texts relying on Levite tradition exhibit

---

56. Boccaccini, *Roots of Rabbinic Judaism*, 176–81.
57. Ibid., 151–201.

in earlier times—only without any connection of Levite status. In the book of Daniel, the Levite has given way to the *Maśkîl*. Exegesis of text, the sustenance of piety, the expiation of sin and guilt, and the reification of the community over against potential social and cosmic disruptions are the province of sage-scribes, not priests or Levites.

Though the inclusion of Daniel in the Hebrew Bible suggests eventual priestly hegemony over its content and implications,[58] this also canonized the new social/intellectual typology that the book espouses. The authors of Daniel anticipate the rise of later forms of religious and intellectual leadership in subsequent generations, who were able to justify their own forms of exegetical authority by appealing to Scripture even as their own oral and literary tradition moved beyond it. To be a *maśkîl* meant that one was empowered to read and teach texts forged by Aaronide and Levite writers but now removed from their exclusive authority. With this, scribal exegesis in nascent Judaism was liberated not only from a narrow priestly-scribal typology but also from the narrow locus of their activity, forever breaking with the trends in the ancient world that had always restricted such sacral scholarship to sanctuaries and their itinerant clergy.[59] Thus, the shift from Levite to *maśkîl* serves as an important step along the way to subsequent innovations first conceived beyond an extant temple hierarchy, and then in the wake of its destruction.[60] In the post-70 C.E. period, Priestly and Levite heritage remained recognized on ceremonial grounds,[61] but the tradition of Levitical scribal exegesis evolved into an independent entity set free from ritual contexts or sacerdotal schools.[62] The rabbinic sages who took up the mantle of exegetical authority came to view

---

58. I follow here the suggestions of Carr (*Tablet of the Heart*, 260–72) and van der Toorn (*Scribal Culture*, 233–62) that Jerusalem priestly scribes are responsible for the shaping of the Hebrew Scriptures into their final, or at least penultimate, form.

59. Van der Toorn, *Scribal Culture*, 63–73 and passim.

60. Pharisaic tradition, for example, appears to have placed emphasis on oral tradition and scriptural interpretation as a basis for holiness beyond the temple, at least insofar as the description of the Pharisees in both the rabbinic and classical sources are concerned.

61. The Mishnah preserves a wealth of information demonstrating the distinctiveness of Levites in earlier times (*m. Qidd.* 4:1; *m. Soṭah* 7:5; *m. Šeqal.* 1:3; *m. Mid.* 1:1, 5; *m. Bik.* 3:4), but there is little in rabbinic discourse itself that highlights Levitical status as specifically bound to the scribal process. It is only with Maimonides' masterwork the *Mishneh Torah* that some inkling of this awareness is eventually broached (*Hilchot Shemittah Ve-Yovel* 13.12), and even this remains a lone and obscure reference within his work.

62. Alexei Sivertsev examines the points at which Second Temple priestly teachings were dislocated from priestly contexts as rabbinic literature formed in the decades following 70 C.E. See his monograph *Households, Sects, and the Origins of Rabbinic Judaism* (JSJSup 102; Leiden: Brill, 2005). That the rabbinic writers drew from priestly halakah indicates that priestly status still carried a degree of auspicious currency even beyond the destruction of the Second Temple.

the medium as the message in and of itself (*b. Qidd.* 49a), and memories of its origins and transmissions were shaped to circumvent priestly qualifications altogether (*m. ʾAbot* 1). With the passing of time, the memory of the Levite as the chief purveyor of scribal exegesis receded into relative obscurity, even as the effects of this contribution emerged as the preeminent characteristic of the Jewish intellectual tradition.

Contributors

SUSAN ACKERMAN (Ph.D., Harvard University) is Preston H. Kelsey Professor of Religion at Dartmouth College. She has authored several books and articles, including *Under Every Green Tree: Popular Religion in Sixth-Century Judah* (HSM 46; Atlanta: Scholars Press, 1992); *Warrior, Dancer, Seductress, Queen: Women in Judges and Biblical Israel* (Anchor Bible Reference Library 17; New York: Doubleday, 1998); and *When Heroes Love: The Ambiguity of Eros in the Stories of Gilgamesh and David* (Gender, Theory, and Religion; New York: Columbia University Press, 2005).

PETER ALTMANN (Ph.D., Princeton Theological Seminary) currently holds the position of Wissenschaftliche Mitarbeiter in Old Testament in the University of Zürich. He is the author of *Festive Meals in Ancient Israel: Deuteronomy's Identity Politics in Their Ancient Near Eastern Context* (BZAW 424; Berlin: de Gruyter, 2011).

JOEL S. BADEN (Ph.D., Harvard University) is Assistant Professor of Old Testament at Yale Divinity School. He is the author of *J, E, and the Redaction of the Pentateuch* (FAT 68; Tübingen: Mohr Siebeck, 2009); *The Composition of the Pentateuch: Renewing the Documentary Hypothesis* (Anchor Yale Reference Library; New Haven: Yale University Press, forthcoming); as well as of articles in *CBQ, HS, JBL, VT*, and other venues.

MARK A. CHRISTIAN (Ph.D., Vanderbilt University) has written *Torah beyond Sinai: A Study of the Plurality of Law and Lawgivers in the Hebrew Bible* (forthcoming) and has published articles in *Henoch, JHS, ZABR*, and other venues.

STEPHEN L. COOK (Ph.D., Yale University) is the Catherine N. McBurney Professor of Old Testament Language and Literature at Virginia Theological Seminary. He is the author of numerous publications, including *Prophecy and Apocalypticism* (Minneapolis: Fortress, 1995) and *The Social Roots of Biblical Yahwism* (SBLStBL; Atlanta: Society of Biblical Literature, 2004).

CORY D. CRAWFORD (Ph.D., Harvard University) is Assistant Professor in the Department of Classics and World Religions at Ohio University. He is the author of "On the Exegetical Function of the Abraham/Ravens Tradition in *Jubilees* 11," *HTR* 97 (2004): 91–97.

JEREMY M. HUTTON (Ph.D., Harvard University) is Assistant Professor of Classical Hebrew Language and Biblical Literature in the Department of Hebrew and Semitic Studies at the University of Wisconsin–Madison. He is the author of *The Transjordanian Palimpsest: The Overwritten Texts of Personal Exile and Transformation in the Deuteronomistic History* (BZAW 396; Berlin/New York: de Gruyter, 2009), as well as of articles in *ZAH, JBL, JNES, Maarav*, and other venues.

MARK A. LEUCHTER (Ph.D., University of Toronto) is Assistant Professor in the Department of Religion and Director of Jewish Studies at Temple University. He is the author of numerous publications, including *Josiah's Reform and Jeremiah's Scroll: Historical Calamity and Prophetic Response* (HBM 6; Sheffield: Sheffield Phoenix Press, 2006) and *The Polemics of Exile in Jeremiah 26–45* (Cambridge: Cambridge University Press, 2008); as well as of articles in *Biblica, CBQ, JBL, VT*, and other venues.

SARAH SHECTMAN (Ph.D., Brandeis University) is an independent researcher living and working in San Francisco; she has taught at Binghamton University (SUNY) and San Francisco Theological Seminary. She is the author of *Women in the Pentateuch: A Feminist and Source-Critical Analysis* (HBM 23; Sheffield: Sheffield Phoenix Press, 2009), as well as of "Women in the Priestly Narrative," in *The Strata of the Priestly Writings: Contemporary Debate and Future Directions* (ed. Sarah Shectman and Joel S. Baden; AThANT 95; Zürich: Theologischer Verlag Zürich, 2009).

JEFFREY STACKERT (Ph.D., Brandeis University) is Assistant Professor of Hebrew Bible in the Divinity School at the University of Chicago. He is the author of *Rewriting the Torah: Literary Revision in Deuteronomy and the Holiness Legislation* (FAT 52; Tübingen: Mohr Siebeck, 2007), as well as of articles in *CBQ, JBL, JANER, VT*, and other venues.

ADA TAGGAR-COHEN (Ph.D., Ben Gurion University) is Professor of Bible, Ancient Near East, and Jewish Studies in the Faculty of Theology at Doshisha University, Kyoto, Japan. She is the author of *Hittite Priesthood* (THeth 26; Heidelberg: Winter Verlag, 2006), as well as of articles in *AoF, JANER, JANES, VT*, and other venues.

Index of Passages

Biblical Writings

Genesis		49:33	106n16
1:6–8	230	49:28abα[1]	104n6
1:14–18	230	49:29–32	106n13
1:14	230		
1:18	230	Exodus	119, 183
1:27	230	1:2ff.	153n63
2:23–24	84n5	2:21	85
4:23–24	84n5	3:21–22	108
16:7–11	113	4:14	19n34
16:9	189n67	4:24–26	109
18	189n67	4:25	85
18:7	189n67	6:9	187
24:63–65	41	6:17	54
25:21–23	109	6:18	75
27:27	189n67	6:20	85, 88n21
29–30	109	6:23	88
29:31–30:24	153n63	6:25	88n21
30:14–16	152n63	11:2–3	108
31:54	109	12:14	183
34	43	12:17	183
34:30	103–116, 152, 153n63	12:35–36	108
34:31	114n35	13:6	166
35:5	112	14:31	14n17
35:16–26	108	15	106, 106n12, 217n11
35:22a	152n60	15:20–21	85
37:7	114, 114n37	16:23	179n29
38:11	109	17	110
41:38–39	85n9	17:1bβ–7	110, 110n26, 111, 115n39
46:1	193	17:1	106n16
48:8–25	43	17:2–3	110
49	153n63	17:4	110
	103–116, 138n9, 142, 142n23, 153n63	17:5–6	110
49:1b	104n6	18:2	85
49:3–4	104, 114	19–24	16n22, 109n22
49:3–8	114n35	19:6	176n11, 197
49:5–8	152	19:17b	193
49:5–7	103–107, 111–115	19:22	13n7
49:5	103	20	194
49:6–7	104	20:4–5	129
49:6	104	20:18–22	173, 188, 194
49:7	103	20:18–19	193

INDEX OF PASSAGES

Exodus (*continued*)

20:18	188
20:20	193
20:22	188
20:22*	193
24	189n67
24:1–2	110
24:9–11bα	110
24:11	189n67
25–30	118, 121
25:18	127
25:31–35	127
26:1	127
26:15–35	124
26:31	127
27:9–13	125
27:16	125
27:21	183
28:30	142n22
28:33–34	127
28:35	14n18
28:36	127
28:38	18
29	17
29:6	13n9
29:27	148n50
30:17–21	18
32–34	109n22
32	103–116, 128, 143n26, 196n91
32:2–6	196n91
32:20	109
32:21–24	109n21
32:25	109n21
32:26	110
32:26–29	109, 110n26, 111, 112, 112n32, 113, 115, 115n40, 116
32:26	109
32:27–28	109
32:27	110
32:29	109, 110
32:30–33	109
32:35	109
33:1–5	110
33:1–4	173, 188, 194
33:7–11a	193
33:11a	193
35–40	118, 121
35:2	188
36:20–30	124
38:9–13	125
38:18	125
38:21	103n1
39:24–26	127
39:30	127

Leviticus	17, 93n40, 176, 183, 184, 185, 201, 226, 227
1–16	218n17
1–7	25
1:5	25
1:8	25
1:15	25
1:11–12	25
2:2	28
2:8	28
3:1–17	25
3:7	183
6:18	183
6:22	93n40
7:6	93n40
7:11–18	93n41
7:22–27	25
7:28–36	25
7:31–34	148n50
7:34	93n40
7:36	183
8:8	142n22
10	185, 186
10:6–7	89n25
10:6	179
10:9	183
10:10	84n5, 187
10:14	93n40, 148n50
11:44–45	188n65
11:44aβ	188n65
11:44b	187n65, 189, 193
11:47	84n5
17–26	6, 25, 86n12, 176, 178, 182–189
17:1–7	25
17:1–4	185
17:2	185
17:3–5	185
17:12–14	187
18:10–11	187
18:13	187

19	187	23:42	184, 185
19:2	185, 187	24:1–8	185
19:2b	187	24:9–22	185
19:5–8	94n45	24:22–23	185
19:20	187	24:12	106n16
19:31	189n68	24:16	184
19:34	184, 197	24:22	184
20:6	189n68	25:14	184
20:19	187	25:22	14
20:23	187	25:32–33	103n1, 201
20:25–26	188n65	26	227
20:25	84n5, 188, 188n65	26:13	14
20:25a	187	26:15	19
20:25bα	187	27	93n39, 96, 96nn54–55
20:25bβ	187, 189, 193	27:30–33	96
21–22	87n15, 90n32		
21	88, 88n19	Numbers	177, 183, 186, 186n56, 201
21:1–9	185		
21:1–6	179	1–10	186n55
21:1–4	91	1–8	191n74
21:1	89	1–4	103, 103n1, 109, 112
21:3	91n34	3–4	17, 89
21:4	89	3:15	90
21:5–6	87n14	3:16	106n16
21:6	87n15	3:18	54
21:7–8	87	3:19	75
21:8	87	3:21	54
21:9	89	3:39	106n16
21:10–15	185	3:51	106n16
21:10	184	4:3	90n27
21:11	91	4:4–15	201
21:12	89, 187	4:37	106n16
21:13–14	87	4:41	106n16
21:15	87, 89	4:45	106n16
21:16–23	185	4:49	106n16
21:22	87n15, 90n32	6	202n8
21:24	185	6:20	148n50
22	93, 93n40, 94n45, 185	8	17, 103n1
22:1–3	185	8:11	14n17
22:3	90n32, 93n41, 185	8:14	176
22:3b	187	8:16	176
22:4–7	185	8:19–20	176
22:8	185	8:20	176
22:9	185	8:24	90n27
22:10	185	8:26	176
22:13	85n9	9:18	106n16
22:18	185	9:20	106n16
22:20–21	18	9:23	106n16
22:32b–33	196, 197	10–25*	186n55

Numbers (*continued*)		18:11	93n40		
10:8	183	18:17	25		
10:13	106n16	18:18	148n50		
11	110, 110n28, 115	18:20–23	46		
11:4–6	110	18:21–31	95		
11:13	110	18:23	183		
11:18–23	110	18:32	18, 96n53		
11:25–29	192n78	20:1	85		
11:25	192n78	20:2–13	115		
11:25bα	192n78	21:16–20	106		
11:25bβ	192n78	25	24, 116		
11:26	192n78	25:6–13	116		
11:26bβ	192n78	25:8	116		
11:27b	192n78	25:10–13	21		
11:31–32	110	26–31	186n55		
11:33	110	26	177		
12:1–15	85	26:32	50n17		
12:1–2	161	26:33	50n17		
12:7	14n17	26:58	54		
13:3	106n16	26:59	85		
14:9–11	187n62	27:1	50n17		
14:24	197n95	27:21	142n22		
15:15	183	31	212		
15:32–36	197n95	31:30	103n1		
16–18	201	32	186n55		
16–17	202	33–36	186n55		
16	21n39, 185	33:2	106n16		
16:1	186n55	33:38	106n16		
16:5–7*	186n55	35	72		
16:9	176	35:1–8	103n1		
16:16*	186n55	35:2	60		
16:17b	186n55	35:4–5	46, 47		
16:19a	186n55	35:8	46		
16:20–22	186n55	35:9–34	75		
16:24b	186n55	35:9–15	70, 75		
16:27	186n55	36:5	106n16		
16:33bβ	186n55				
16:41–45	186n55	Deuteronomy	26, 86, 94, 94n48, 96n53, 97, 97n59, 98, 99, 138, 140, 142, 146, 152, 152n61, 157, 157n4, 157–158n6, 158n7, 158, 159, 159n7, 161, 163, 165, 166, 167, 167n29, 169, 178, 184, 185, 186n56, 190, 193n80, 200, 202, 206, 209, 213, 216, 217, 217n11, 218, 223		
17	17				
17:1–5	186n55				
17:5	95n49				
17:6–10	186n55				
18	17-18, 24, 93n40, 96, 96n54, 103n1, 186n55, 202, 210n28, 212				
18:2	211, 211n30				
18:4	21n38				
18:7	21n38				
18:8–20	204				

INDEX OF PASSAGES

1:16	167	12:17–19	97
3:20	167	12:18	46, 97, 97n60
3:27	106n15	12:19	103n1, 163n18
4:1–40	192	12:27	146
4:4a	192	14	137n4, 149
4:7	189, 192	14:2	176n11
4:10–12	173, 188, 193, 194, 197	14:22–26	97
4:10–12a	189	14:27–29	97, 136n4
4:13	192	14:27	46, 103n1, 150, 163n18
4:15–19	129	14:29	103n1, 150, 163n18
4:33–37	173, 188, 193, 194, 197	15:2–3	190
4:41–43	75	15:2	146
4:45	140	15:7	167, 190
5–28	140	15:9	190
5:1	158	15:11	190
5:4	173, 188, 193, 194, 197	16	149, 166
5:5	193, 194	16:1–8	165
5:14	97n60	16:7	166, 166n26
5:22	157, 173, 188, 194, 197	16:11	46, 97n60, 103n1, 150, 163n18
5:25–26	193, 194		
5:27	189	16:14	97n60, 103n1, 150, 163n18
6:9	216n5, 224n37		
6:16	138n9	16:18–18:22	6, 140n17, 175, 178, 190–195
6:21–22	184n52		
7:6	176n11	16:18	190, 191
7:12	19	17	159
10:5	147n44	17:2	191
10:6	147n44	17:5	191
10:8–9	103n1, 109, 147, 147n44, 149, 149n51, 151n59, 154	17:7	159
		17:8–20	158n7
		17:8–13	145, 150n54, 158, 217n15
10:8	26, 138n9, 149n51, 207, 208n24	17:8–9	158
		17:8	216n5
10:9	156, 167	17:9	53, 136n3, 147n43, 150, 150n54, 159, 167, 204n14
11:20	216n5, 224n37		
11:31–12:7	146n39		
12–27	184		
12–26	136, 140, 148	17:9a	150n54
12	149	17:10	158
12:2	181	17:12	144, 158, 159
12:6	146	17:13	159
12:8–12	146n39	17:14–20	158n7, 166
12:11	146	17:14–17	191
12:12	46, 97n60, 103n1	17:15	158, 167
12:13–27	146n39	17:15bα	191
12:13–19	146n39, 150	17:18–20	158, 191, 224n37
12:13	146	17:18–19	159n7
12:14	150	17:18	53, 136n3, 158
12:15	150, 150n55	17:19–20	158, 167

INDEX OF PASSAGES

Deuteronomy (*continued*)			
18	147n42, 151, 151n58, 152, 152n60, 163, 163n18, 164, 165, 209	19:1–13	75
		19:1–7	75
		19:4	146
		19:7	209
18:1–8	6, 94, 103n1, 137, 139, 140n17, 145–153, 162, 164n22, 190, 202, 212	19:8–9	75
		19:17	150n54, 158, 204, 204n14, 209, 209n27
18:1–5	151n58		
18:1–2	163	19:18–19	190
18:1	53, 95, 136n3, 145, 146, 146n40, 147, 147n43, 150, 152n60, 154	20:1–9	148
		20:2–4	148
		20:2	144
		21	148
18:1*	149	21:5	103n1, 136n3, 138n9, 148, 148n49, 149, 208n24
18:2	146n41, 147		
18:3–5	211		
18:3–4	146n40, 148, 149, 154	23:8	197n95
18:3	25, 144, 146, 146n38, n40, 148, 150, 154, 206, 209	24:1–4	88n18
		24:8	53, 136n3, 145, 191
		24:9	85
18:4	146n40, 148, 148n50	26:3–4	144
18:5	26, 149, 151n58, 162, 207, 208n24	26:4	26
		26:11–13	103n1, 163n18
18:6–8	144, 147n43, 150, 151, 152, 152n60, 153, 153n63, 154, 167n29, 200, 202, 207, 208, 211, 214	26:13	96n53
		27	153
		27:9–14	152n60
		27:9	53, 136n3
		27:12–13	153n63
18:6–7	153, 190	28:69 [=ET 29:1]	197
18:6	150, 167, 182n42	30:1	189
18:6b	150	30:11–14	189
18:7	26, 151n58, 152, 153, 162, 209, 209n27, 210, 211n30	30:14	189
		30:14a	189
		30:17b	194
18:8	153	31	105
18:8b	167n29	31:9–13	216n5, 224n37
18:9–22	192, 194n83, n86	31:9	103n1, 136n3, 148, 148n49, 149, 152n60, 158, 191
18:9	146		
18:14–22	192		
18:15–19	161	31:10–13	181
18:15aα	191	31:11	181n37
18:16	193, 194	31:12	197
18:16b	193	31:16–22	105
18:17	144	31:25–26	158
18:18–19	192, 194	31:25	103n1, 152n60
18:18	191	31:29	202n8
18:20–22	189n68, 194	31:30	105
18:20aα	192	32	105, 105n9
19	70	32:45–47	106n10

INDEX OF PASSAGES

33	103–116, 136, 142, 143, 153n63	15:21–62	71, 71n116
		16:10	53
33:1–29	26	17:2	50n17, 52, 58
33:1–8	111, 112	17:3	50n17
33:8–11	105–107, 110, 111, 115, 115n40, 115n40, 116, 138, 138nn8-9, 142nn22–23, 143, 144, 229	17:8	57
		17:11–12	53
		18:1–10*	177, 196n91
		18:1	177
		18:7	103n1
33:8–10	138n9	18:8	177
33:8–9	105	18:9	177
33:8–9a	138n9	18:10	177
33:8	115n39	18:21–28	71
33:9b–10	138n9	19:1–9	71n116
33:9	110	19:22	73
33:10	26, 105, 158	19:35bβ	58, 59–60
33:11	105, 110, 138n9	19:38	73
33:17	105n8	19:40–48	61n68
34:1	106n15	19:40–46	56
34:2	192n78	19:47	56
34:5	106	19:48	56
34:6	106n16	20	60, 70, 70n108, 71, 75
34:9	192n78	20:1–9	75
34:10–12	192n78, 194n83	20:7	58, 69, 70
34:10	192n78	21	6, 45–81
34:10a	192n78	21:1–41	103n1, 177n20
		21:10	148n49
Joshua–Kings	2	21:11–40	70
		21:11–13a*	60
Joshua	45, 59n53, 67, 69, 76, 78n144, 145n33, 177	21:11	58, 60, 69n105, 70
		21:11*	60
		21:11aα¹*	60
1:7–8	191	21:11aα²β	60
1:8	179	21:12	60, 69n105
3:3	136n3, 138	21:13–40	60
8:33	136n3, 138	21:13–16	61
12:6	14n17	21:13	58, 60, 69, 69n105
13–21	177	21:13a*	60
13–19	57, 59, 71, 73, 73n124, 81, 13:3 50	21:15	61n67
		21:16	61n67
13:14	103n1, 156, 177n20	21:16b	68
13:18	58, 59	21:17–18	60, 167
13:33	103n1, 177n20	21:17	60n57
14:3	103n1	21:18	60n57
14:4	103n1	21:18b	68
14:4b	177n20	21:20–22	60
14:13–14	69n105	21:21	60, 70
15	177	21:21a*	58
15:13	60, 69n105	21:22	54

INDEX OF PASSAGES

Joshua (*continued*)

21:23–24	61
21:23	61n58
21:24	50, 61n58
21:25	50, 61n60, 61
21:27	60, 61, 61n61, 70
21:28–29	61
21:28	61n62
21:29	61n62
21:30–31	61
21:30	61n63
21:31	61n63
21:32	58, 59–60, 61, 61n68, 70
21:34–35	61, 61n64
21:36–37	58, 59, 61
21:36	60, 70
21:37–38	61n65
21:38–39	61
21:38	60, 61n66, 70
21:39	61n66
21:44	177
22	139n13
24:25	19

Judges

1:27	53
1:29	53
1:30	53
1:31	53
1:33	61n68
1:35	53
2:1–5	189n67
2:2	189n67
4–5	182n41
5	104
6:19	43n58
9	108n20
13	189n67
13:4–5	189n67
13:19	43n58
17–21	143n25
17–20	145
17–18	136, 136n4, 138, 138n8, 142, 142n22, 143, 143n26
17	103n1
17:5	142, 142n22
17:7–13	66
17:13	142, 142n22
18	56
18:30	21
19–21	138
19–20	139n13, 143
19:1	85, 103n1
21:19	39
21:33	61n68

Samuel–Kings 50n16

1–2 Samuel 26n5

1 Samuel

1–16	37
1:1–2:26	21n21
1:1–2	25–44
1:1	36
1:3	30n19, 31, 36, 37
1:4–5	28n11, 37
1:4	28, 42
1:7	41, 43n58
1:19	37
1:21	36, 37
1:24–25	37
1:24	42
1:25	28, 42, 42n57
2–4	28, 42n57, 43, 43n58
2:11	136n4
2:12–17	36, 37
2:13–14	27, 39
2:13	25, 28
2:15–16	19, 28, 41, 43n58
2:15	27, 28
2:16	27, 27n6
2:19	27, 27n6
2:27	38
2:27–36	19n34
2:28	26, 26–27n5, 162
3:3	26
3:10–14	19n32
3:11	162
7:17	162
8:4	30, 30n19, 37
8:5–6	37
8:11	158
9	146n38
	30n19, 31, 31n21

9:4	30n19	1–2 Kings	34, 224, 225, 225n40, 226
9:5	30n19		
9:11–14	30, 30n19, 31, 31n21, 32	1 Kings	126
9:12	30n19, 31, 32	1–2	136n4
9:13	31, 32	1:19	160n11
9:14	32	1:25	160n11
9:19	30, 30n19, 31n21, 32	2:26	19, 160n11, 162
9:22–25	30, 30n19, 31n21, 32	2:27	19, 162, 162n16, 163n18
9:22	30		
9:23	31, 42	2:35	19
9:25	32	3:9	158
10:17–27	160n11	4:4	19
10:25	19	4:12	53
14:41	142n22	6–7	121, 122n15, 127, 128, 130
15:27–28	160n11		
15:34	37	6	125
16:13	37	6:2–4	125
16:18	51n17	6:5–6	125
17:58	51n17	6:10	126n29
19:18	37	6:16	126n29
21	19	6:29	127, 127n32
22:6–23	163n18	6:32–33	127
22:17	160n11	7:2	126
22:18–21	162n16	7:17–20	127
22:18–20	162n16	7:25	127, 127n32
25:1	37	7:26	127
28	142n22	7:29	127, 127n32
28:3	37	7:36	127n32
28:6	142n22	8:24–26	14n17
		8:64	122n15
2 Samuel		9:15–17	53
2:4a	159n9	9:16	63
4:2	50n17	11:29–31	160n11
4:5	50n17	12	19–20, 128, 136
4:9	50n17	12:30–31	32
5:1–3	159n9	12:31	103n1, 143, 143n26, 163n18
6:10–12	51n19		
6:10–11	50	13:2	34
6:10	50	13:31	148n49
6:11	50	13:32	33
7	14n17, 131	13:33	33, 163n18
8:17	19	19:10	161
15:18	50	19:14	161
15:19–22	50	22:44 [=ET v. 43]	34, 35
18:2	50		
19:11–15	160n11	2 Kings	
21:19	51n17	2	192n78
21:29	50	2:5	192n78

INDEX OF PASSAGES

2 Kings (*continued*)		36–39	191
2:9–15	192	48:2	179n30
2:11–15	192n78	52–53	229
11	19, 20	52:1	179n30
11:13–18	159n9	52:13	229
12:4 [=ET v. 3]	34, 35	53:11	229
14:4	34, 35	56:7	18
15:4	34, 35	60:7	18
15:35	34, 35	61:6–7	193
16	128	61:6a	176n11
16:4	181	62:12a	176n11
16:14	122n15	66:18	195n88
16:17	128	66:19–24	195n88
17:9–11	33	66:21	103n1
17:9	33		
17:27–28	158	Jeremiah	33, 84n3, 161, 162,
18	128		162n16, 167, 167n30,
18:4	130n37, 163n18		168, 167nn29–30, 216,
18:22	163n18		217, 217n11, 218, 223,
19–20	191		224, 225, 226
21:3	163n18	1:4–19	194, 194n83
21:23–24	159n9	6:20	18
22–24	140	7:12–14	168
22	182n41	7:12	36, 36n32, 169
22:8–11	190	7:14	169
23	128, 136, 137n4, 144,	7:31	32n24, 33
	144n30, 151n58, 154,	9:11–12	217n11
	163, 165	9:20	217n11
23:1–3	159n9	11:13	174
23:4–8	58	11:18–21	218
23:5	33, 161, 161n13,	11:21	167, 167n30, 168
	163n18	11:23	167, 168
23:8–9	34, 136n1, 151, 167	12:6	167, 167n30
23:8	33	14:13–16	194
23:8a	58	18:18	218
23:9	139–140, 140n17,	19:3	162
	164, 165, 166	19:5–6	32n24
23:10–15	58	19:5	33
23:19–20	58, 161	20:10	167, 168
23:19	33	21:1	165
23:21	166	21:25–26	165
23:22	165	21:29	165
23:32	140	23:11–12	168
23:37	140	26:6–9	36, 36n32, 168
25:27–30	225	26:6	168, 169
		26:9	168
Isaiah	229n55	26:11	168
9:7	158	26:20	168n33
11:2–5	158	26:21	168

INDEX OF PASSAGES

28	140, 195	44:6–16	135n1, 202
29:1	224n37	44:7	25
30:2	224n37	44:10–12	196n91
31:3	196	44:10–16	53
32	162	44:11	29
32:6–15	167n30	44:15	25, 53, 136n3, 202
32:7–9	162		
32:7	165	44:22	85n9, 88n19
32:12	46n6	44:23	84n5
32:35	32n24, 33	44:25	91n33
33:17–22	162	45:4	89n26
33:18	136n3	45:5	47, 90n29, 103n1
33:21–22	103n1	48:13	103n1
33:21	14n17	48:31–35	153n63
35	196		
35:4	165	Hosea	33
36	218n17	5:1	51n19
36:2	224n37	6:9	161
36:4	224n37	10:8	33
36:5	168		
36:32	224n37	Amos	33
37:3	165	7:9	33
38:3–4	168		
41:4–5	180	Micah	
51:59–64	224n37	5:1–5	159n9
		6:4	85
Ezekiel	26n3, 33, 35, 47, 83n3, 85n9, 86, 90n29, 91, 119, 126, 136, 179, 203, 218, 218n17, 229	Haggai	84n3
		2:12	93n41
1	229	Zechariah	84n3
3:1	218n17	1:6	196n89
6:3	32n24, 33		
6:6	33	Malachi	202, 203
8	140	1:6–2:9	202n8
13:17–23	182n41	2:1–3:4	202
20:28–29	34, 35	2:2–3	18
20:29	33	2:4	103n1
22:26	84n5, 140	2:4–7	222
40–48	144, 186n56	2:5	18
40:46	148n49	2:8	202n8
40:49	126		
41:2	126	Psalms	
41:5	126	16	156
41:8	126	16:5	156
41:12	126	16:6	156
41:15	126	40:9	18
43:19	136n3, 202	65:5a	189
44	163, 202	72:1–4	158

INDEX OF PASSAGES

Psalms (*continued*)
78   36n32, 168, 169
78:9   169
78:59–61   169
78:60   36, 36n32, 169
78:60–61   163n18, 169
78:67–69   169
95:8   115n39
143:10   18

Ruth
1:6–8   85n9

Daniel   223–230
1   224, 225, 225n40, 226, 227n48
1:1–2   225, 225n41
2–7   227n48
2   226n45
5   223
7–12   224
9   225n40, 226, 227, 227n48, 228
9:2   227
9:4–19   227
9:21–27   227
9:21   228
9:24   179n30
11:33–35   229
12   229n55
12:1–2   229
12:3   229, 230

Ezra-Nehemiah   84n3, 179, 180, 203, 216n5, 218, 219, 222, 223, 227n50

Ezra   144n32, 147
2   180n34
2:40   153n63
2:61–63   153n63
2:63   142n22
3   180n34
3:8   103n1
4:17–18   178n25
6:15–18   202
6:18   103n1
7   219
7:24   103n1
7:25–26   179n31
8   154
8:15–20   147
8:28   179
9–10   179
9   227n50
9:2   179
10   88n18

Nehemiah
2:8   181
2:17   181
4:1   181
6:1   181
6:14   182n41
7   180n34
7:1   181
7:43   153n63
7:65   142n22
8–10   180n34, 228n51
8–9   181
8   6, 175, 178–182, 188, 190, 219
8:1–9   186
8:1–8   179
8:7   229
8:9–11   179
8:9   179
8:13–18   179, 190
8:13   180
8:18a   179
8:18aα   190n72
9   180, 219n21, 227, 227n50, 228, 228n51
9:1–5   180
9:1–3   180
9:3   180
9:4–5   179
9:4   180, 182
9:5   180
9:5aβ   180
9:6–10:1 [=ET 9:6–38]   180
9:6   180
9:14   179, 179n29
10   216n5
10:28   103n1
10:31   179
11:1   179
11:18   179

INDEX OF PASSAGES

12:27	181	6:53	54
12:47	103n1	6:54	50, 61
13:1–3	181, 182	6:55	61, 61n60
13:1	180	6:56	61, 61n61
13:1a	180n33	6:57–58	61
13:3	179, 187	6:57	61n62
13:10	197	6:58	61n62
13:15–22	179	6:59–60	61
13:22	179	6:59	61n63
13:23–28	179	6:60	61n63
13:30	103n1	6:61	61, 61n68
		6:62	61, 61n64
1–2 Chronicles	50n16, 51, 69, 84n3, 95n49, 136, 165, 193, 196n91, 202, 202n9, 203, 219, 221, 223, 225, 226, 228	6:63–64	61
		6:65–66	61
		6:65	61n66
		6:66	61n66
		7:8	71
		13:13–14	50
1 Chronicles	45, 67, 68, 69, 76	13:13	50
1–9	76	15	103n1
2:1–2	153n63	15:9	75
5:27–41	77	15:18	50, 51n19
5:28	75	15:21	50, 51n19
6	45–81, 103n1	15:24–25	50
6:1–38	77	15:24	51n19
6:2	54	16:5	50
6:5	54	16:38	50
6:14	54	18:16	19
6:23	75	19:45	50
6:35–38	77	20:5	50
6:39–66	68	23	54
6:39–41	61	23:12	75
6:40	69n105	23:19	54, 75
6:41	69n105	23:25–32	103n1
6:42–45a	68	24	103n1
6:42–44	68	24:23	54
6:42	69, 69n105	26:4	50
6:43	61n67	26:8	50
6:44	61n67	26:15	50
6:45 [=ET v. 60]	60, 60n57, 68, 167	26:23	75
6:45a	68	26:29–32	63
6:46	68	26:29	219
6:47	68		
6:48	68	2 Chronicles	
6:49	68	5:5	136n3
6:50	68	8:14	103n1
6:51–66	68	11:5–12	63n72
6:51–54	61	11:13–17	163n18
6:53–54	61n58	11:14	103n1

INDEX OF PASSAGES

2 Chronicles (*continued*)
13:9	163n18
17:7–9	219
19:5–7	219
19:8	103n1
23	20, 116
23:6	103n1, 202
23:7	116
23:18	103n1, 136n3
25:24	50
29	103n1
29:30	169
29:34	202
30:8	165
30:22	165
30:27	136n3
31:2	103n1, 165
31:4	103n1
31:19	93n40
34	182n41
34:5	161
34:13	219
35:2–4	165
35:3–6	103n1
35:3	229
35:17	166
35:25	230
36	227n48
36:20–21	226, 227

Luke
1	189n67

Acts
2:36–38	182n41

Hebrews
	118
8:5	118

Revelation
2:20	182n41

Hittite Texts

CTH
262	15n19
264	14, 16, 17n25, 22
264 i 21–26	16
264 i 34–38	16
264 i 38	18n27
264 ii 29	18n27
264 ii 34	18n27
264 ii 34–47	22n44
264 ii 50	19
264 ii 55	19
264 ii 57	18n27
264 iii 58	18n27
264 iii 64–68	18
264 iii 83	19

KUB
31.113	14, 15
32.133	14
32.133 lines 7–11	15
55.21	14, 15
57.29	14
57.36	14

Apocrypha, Pseudepigrapha, Dead Sea Scrolls

Community Rule	201
Damascus Covenant	201
Jubilees	200, 200n2, 220, 221, 221n25, 222, 223n33, 229
18:21–22	221
30:18–20	221
Aramaic Levi	200, 200n2, 220, 221, 222, 223n33, 229
Testament of Levi	200, 200n2, 220, 222n33
Ben Sira	200, 222, 230
War Scroll	200
4QMMT	201, 213
Temple Scroll (11QT)	199–214
21:1–5	205
22:8–14	205–206
23:5	204
23:9–10	204
35:4–5	203

35:5	204	m. Bikkurîm	
56:1	204n14	3:4	231n61
57:11–15	204	m. Middot	
60:1–11	212	1:1	231n61
60:10–15	207	1:5	231n61
60:10–11	208n24	m. Qiddušin	
60:10b–11	207, 208	4:1	231n61
60:11	211	b. Qiddušin	
60:12–15	208	49a	232
60:14	210, 211n30	m. Šeqalim	
61	210	1:3	231n61
61:8–9	204, 209	m. Soṭah	
63:3	203, 208n24	7:5	231n61

Josephus

Antiquities
7.83   51n19

Rabbinic Writings

Mishnah and Talmud
m. 'Abot
1   232

Midrash Tannaim
18:1   206n19

Index of Authors

Abba, Raymond — 53n27, 151n59, 199n1
Achenbach, Reinhard — 2n4, 136, 136n4, 137n6, 138, 142, 142n21, n23, 143, 143nn25-28, 144, 144nn29-32, 145, 145n35, 146, 146n40, 147, 147n43, n45, 148, 149, 149n53, 151, 154, 174n4, 178, 179n27, 183n45, 186n55, 197n95, 197n96
Ackerman, Susan — 4n12, 5, 36n32, 86n11, 91n35, 165n27
Ackroyd, Peter R. — 30n19, 37n38
Addis, W. E. — 107n18, 109n23
Aharoni, Yohanan — 63, 63n72, 125n26
Ahlström, Gösta W. — 3n7, 164n20
Albertz, Rainer — 139, 140n16, 223n34, 224n38, 226n44, 227n48, 229n54
Albright, William F. — 45, 51, 51nn19-20, 52, 52nn21-23, 54, 54n29, 55, 55nn31-34, 56, 56nn37-39, 62, 63, 72, 138
Allen, Leslie C. — 168n33
Alpert Nakhai, Beth — 33nn25-26, 39n45, 40nn47-49
Alt, Albrecht — 45, 57, 57nn42-45, 58, 58nn46-49, 59, 62, 63, 63n72, 73
Altmann, Peter — 6, 151n56, 215n1
Amit, Yairah — 30n19

Anderson, Gary A. — 28n11
Angel, Joseph L. — 200n2, 204n13, 207n22, 212, 212n34
Arie, Eran — 32n25
Arnold, Bill — 164n21
Arnold, Patrick M. — 37n39
Auld, A. Graeme — 50n16, 67n95, 67, 68, 68nn95-99, 69, 69nn100-103, nn105-106, 70, 70nn107-110, 72, 72nn118-120, 74, 75, 76, 77, 77n141
Avalos, Hector — 25nn1-2
Bacon, Benjamin W. — 104: n7, 106n11, 107n18, 109n 25
Baden, Joel S. — 6, 106n14, 109n22, 110nn26, 28, 117n, 120, 120nn8, 10, 121n12, 123n22, 141n20, 153n63
Baentsch, Bruno — 115n40
Barrick, W. Boyd — 32nn24-25, 33n26, 38n40, 164n20, n22, 166n27
Baumgarten, Joseph — 213n37
Beal, Richard H. — 22n44
Beaulieu, Paul-Alain — 224n39
Beckman, Gary — 19n33
Beckman, John C. — 164n21
Ben-Barak, Zafrira — 91n35
Ben Zvi, Ehud — 63n73, 70n108, 74n128, 75, 75nn129-133, 76n136
Bertholet, Alfred — 147n41;147n42, 148n50, 151n58, 152n61

-250-

INDEX OF AUTHORS

Beyerle, Stefan	115n40	Clements, R. E.	36n33
Biran, Avraham	32n25	Clifford, Richard J.	36n32
Bird, Phyllis	29n17, 42n53	Cody, Aelred	1n2, 2n6,
Blum, Erhard	107n18, 114nn		3n8, 28, 28n10,
	35-36, 121n11		29n14, 31n21,
Bocaccinni, Gabriele	224n38, 226n45,		53n27, 54n28,
	227n50, 230,		59n51, 65, 65n84,
	230nn56-57		66, 73-74n126,
Boling, Robert G.	52n22, 63n71,		n128, 139n15,
	64n 75, n77,		152-153n63,
	65n83, 66nn85-		167n29, 199n1
	87, 70n110, 80,	Cogan, Mordechai	20n35, 126n29,
	80n153, 157n4		127n32
Bowen, Nancy R.	91n35	Collins, Billie Jean	11n1
Braulik, Georg	28, 28n6, 42n53,	Collins, John J.	223n34, 224n38,
	43n57, 140n17		225nn41-42,
Braun, Roddy L.	63n73		226n43, n46,
Brettler, Marc Z.	26n5		227nn48-50
Brightman, Edgar S.	107n18	Cook, Stephen L.	2n6, 4n12, 6,
Brooke, George J.	201n4, 211,		53n27, 131n38,
	211n31, 212		145n35, 156nn1-2,
Brueggemann, Walter	168n32		157n3, n4, 159n9,
Budde, Karl	110n26		160nn10-11,
Buhl, Mary Louise	39n46		163n19, 169n35,
Burgmann, Hans	213n37		199n1, 218n16
Burns, Rita J.	86n11	Cortese, Enzo	70n110, 71n116
Busink, Th.	126, 126n30	Crawford, Cory	6
Byrne, Ryan	4n16, 216n8	Crawford, Sidnie White	201nn3-4
		Cross, Frank Moore	1n2, 26n4, 56n40,
Camp, Claudia	84n6, 92nn37-38,		74n128, 104n5,
	95n49		106n12, 120,
Carpenter, J. E.	104n7, 107n18,		120n11, 122,
	109n25		122n19, 123n20,
Carr, David M.	4n13, 107n17,		137n5, n7, 138,
	141n19, 215n2, n4,		138n9, 160n12
	216n9, 219n20,	Crüsemann, Frank	184n49
	222n28, 231n58		
Carrière, Jean-Marie	190nn69-71,	Daddi, Franka Pecchioli	13n13
	191n73, n75	Dahmen, Ulrich	53n27, 137n6,
Choi, John	164n21		142, 142n22,
Cholewiński, Alfred	183n44		143, 143n25,
Christian, Mark	6, 137n6, 157:		144, 145, 145n34,
	157n5;159n8,		146n38, n40,
	173n2, 176n15,		148, 148nn46-48,
	181n39, 182n43,		174n4, 199n1
	197nn94-95	Dalman, Gustaf	65
Chyutin, Michael	126, 126n30	Daviau, P. M.Michèle	188n66

INDEX OF AUTHORS

Davies, Phillip	4n15, 175nn8-9, 181nn38, 182n39, 197n93		125n26, 125n28, 157n4
Day, John	36n33	Friedrich, Johannes	23n48
Dearman, J. Andrew	65n78	Geertz, Clifford	79n149
Dever, William G.	32n25, 175n6	Gellner, Ernest	160n10
Dillmann, August	104n7, 107n18	Geoghegan, Jeffrey	2n4, 225n40
Douglas, Mary	84n6	George, Mark K.	118n1, 119, 119n5, 120, 123n23, 132, 132n42
Dozeman, Thomas	145n33, 176n12, 191n74	Gertz, Jan Christian	140n17, 150n54
Driver, S. R.	37, 37nn37-38, 42n57, 104n7, 106n12, 107n18, 109n25, 113n34	Gleis, Matthias	32n24, 33n26
		Gooding, D. W.	126n29
		Gottwald, Norman K.	51n19, 156n2
Duke, Rodney K.	53n27, 147n42, 151, 151n57, n59, 199n1	Gray, George Buchanan	103n2
		Gray, John	127n32
		Greer, Jonathan S.	123n21
		Grollenberg, Lucas	35n30
Edelman, Diana	3n11, 38, 38n40, 181n38, 182n39, 188-189n66	Grünwaldt, Klaus	178, 183nn46-47, 184n49, 187n64, 196n90, 197n97
Eilberg-Schwartz, Howard	84n6	Gunkel, Hermann	104n7, 107n18, 113n34
Eissfeldt, Otto	105n9		
Elliger, Karl	176n13	Gunneweg, A. H. J.	1n2, 51n19, 58n49, 111n29, 115n38, 199n1
Emerton, J. A.	32n24, 33n26, 53n27, 151, 151n57, 152n60, 154, 199n1		
		Güterbock, Hans G.	15n19
Esler, Philip F.	28n13	Haas, Volkert	11nn1-2
		Halpern, Baruch	35, 35n29, 36n34, 50n16, 56n40, 74n128, 164n22
Feinstein, Eve Levavi	87n16, 88n17, 89n23		
Feldman, Marian	129n34	Haran, Menahem	26n3, 30n19, 32n24, 45, 51n19, 66, 66nn88-90, 67, 73, 74n128, 95n48, 105n9, 106n11, 109n20, 109n25, 115n41, 117n1, 120, 120n9, 121n14, 122, 122nn 15-18, 123, 123n20, 131, 132, 132n41, n44, 199n1
Finkelstein, Israel	39nn44-46, 40nn47-51		
Fischer, Alexander Achilles	65n80		
Fishbane, Michael	116n42, 202n8, 229n55		
Fleming, Daniel E.	123n19		
Freedman, David Noel	104n5, 138, 138n9		
Fretheim, Terence E.	119, 119n6, 131		
Frevel, Christian	188n65		
Frick, Frank S.	156n1,		
Friedman, Richard E.	26n4, 104n7, 106n12, 108n18, 121n14, 124-125,	Harford-Battersby, G.	104n7, 107n18, 109n25

INDEX OF AUTHORS

Hauer, Chris	78, 78nn145-146, 79, 79n147	Jobling, David	67n90
Havrelock, Rachel	84n5	Jonker, Louis C.	226n47
Hayes, Christine	85n9, 87n16, 88n22	Joosten, Jan	178, 178n24, 183n47, 184nn49-54, 186, 186n58, 187nn59-60
Hayes, John H.	129n34		
Hendel, Ronald S.	229n55	Joüon, Paul	164n21
Hertzberg, Hans W.	27n6, 30-31n19, 37n38, 38n41, 42n55	Kallai, Zecharia	52n24, 55n36, 60nn56-57, 61n58, n61, 63n73, 67, 67nn91-94, 70, 70n110
Hess, Richard S.	123nn19-20		
Himmelfarb, Martha	220, 220n25, 221n27, 222, 222nn28-29		
		Kammenhuber, Annelies	23n48
Hobsbawm, Eric	131, 132nn39-40	Kartveit, Magnar	70n110, 77n143
Holladay, William	167n30, 168n33	Kaufmann, Yehezkel	45, 52n25, 53n26, 55, 55nn34-36, 56, 56nn37-39, n41, 57, 62, 63, 109n23, 112n32, 121n14, 138n10, 199n1
Holm-Nielsen, Svend	39n46		
Hölscher, Gustav	140, 140n17, 153n63		
Homan, Michael M.	122n 19, 123n 21, n 23, 124, 124-125n25, 125, 125nn27-28		
		Keel, Othmar	137n7
		Kellermann, D.	199n1
Hoop, Raymond de	103n3, 113n34	King, Philip J.	32nn25-26, 129n34
Hout, Theo P. J. van den	13n9, 15n19, 20n37, 21n38		
		Kitchen, Kenneth A.	122n19
Houtman, Cees	38n42	Klawans, Jonathan	87n16, 88n19, 133n45
Hundley, Michael B.	123n23		
Hutton, Jeremy M.	3n7, 5, 5n16, 45n, 53n27, 56n40, 65n80, 75n128, 80n152, 83n, 139n13, 154, 154n67, 155-156n1, 157, 157n3, 159nn8-9, 160nn10-11, 162nn16-17, 195, 195n87, 216n6	Klein, Lillian R.	43n58
		Klein, Ralph W.	30n19, 37n38, 38n41, 42n54, 51n19, 63n73, 76n138
		Klein, Samuel	49, 49nn13-14, 50, 50n15, 51, 51n19, 54, 62, 63
		Klinger, Jörg	13n12
		Knauf, Ernst Axel	140, 140n17
		Knight, Douglas	175n9, 186n57
		Knohl, Israel	1n3, 121n14, 178, 202n6
Ilan, David	32n25		
		Knoppers, Gary N.	2n4, 24n51, 53n27, 73n125, 76, 76nn134-135, nn137-138, 77, 77n139, n143, 78, 135n, 137n5, 165n25, 193,
Japhet, Sara	63n73; 76n138		
Jamieson-Drake, David W.	4n14		
Janzen, David	133n45		
Jenson, Philip P.	23n47, 87n13, 90n30, 93n42		

INDEX OF AUTHORS

Knoppers, Gary N. (*continued*) 193nn80-81, 199n1, 202n9, 219n19
Koch, Christoph 141n20
Koch, Klaus 121, 121n12, 225n43
Kratz, Reinhard 140, 140n17, 141n20, 228n52
Kraus, Hans Joachim 156n2
Kuenen, Abraham 107n18, 109n24
Kugel, James 113n34, 200n2, 220nn23-24
Kugler, Robert 136, 136n4, 137, 137n7, 138, 138n8, 139, 139nn11-12, n15, 140, 140n16, 144, 145, 147, 147n42, 148, 149, 149n52, 154, 200n2, 207n22, 210n29, 212, 212n33, 220n23, 221n26, 222, 222n30, n 33
Launderville, Dale 166n25
Lebram, J. C. 228n52
Lehming, Sigo 114n35
Lenzi, Alan 224n39
Leuchter, Mark A. 6, 27n5, 36n32, 83n, 95n48, 137n6, 164, 164n20, n 22, 166n27, 167n28, 176n15, 196n92, 216nn9-10, 217n11, 218nn15-16, n18
Levenson, Jon 117n
Levine, Baruch A. 86n12, 87n15, 90n28, 96n52, 200n3
Levinson, Bernard 2n4, 150n54, 158n6, 158-159n7, 165n24, 166nn25-26
Levtow, Nathaniel 129n35
Lindblom, Johannes 174n4, 182n42, 191n76
Lipka, Hilary 87n16, 88n20
Loewenstamm, Samuel E. 110n26
Lohfink, Norbert 140n17, 153n66, 158n7
MacDonald, Nathan 49n52
Machinist, Peter 217n14
Maier, Johann 211n30
Marzouk, Safwat 135n
Master, Daniel 79n150, 156n1
Mayes, A. D. H. 159n7
Mazar, Benjamin 45, 62, 62n69, 63, 63nn70-71, 64, n 77, 65, 73
McBride, S. Dean 161, 161nn14-15, 162, 165n23, 167n31, 168n32, 168n34
McCarter, P. Kyle 26n5, 27, 27nn6-7, 30n19, 37, 37nn37-38, 38n41, 42n54, n57
McConville, J. Gordon 151n59, 152n60, n63, 153n64, 158n6, 158n7
McKane, William 31, 31n20, 35n30
McKenzie, Steven 50n16, 156n1
McNeile, A. H. 109n25
Mettinger, Tryggve n D. 58n46, 63nn71-72
Meyers, Carol 38n41, 41n52, 42, 42n56, 43n58, 175n6, 182n41
Miano, David 26n4
Milgrom, Jacob 1n3, 19, 19nn29-30, 22, 22n43, 23n50, 28n11, 38n42, 39n43, 40n49, 46n3, 84n5, 87nn14-16, 88, 88n17, n22, 89n25, 91n34, 93n41, 94n45, 95n49, n51, 96nn52-54, 97n59, 178, 187n61,

INDEX OF AUTHORS

	191n74, 204nn13-15, 206, 206nn18-20, 207, 207n21, 209n26, 210, 211, 212, 212n32, 212n35	Olyan, Saul	3n10, 4n12, 29, 29nn15-16, 31, 31n23, 83, 83n, 83nn1-3, 84, 84n4, n6, 85, 85nn7-8, 86n10, 91n33, 93n43, 94nn46-47, 95n49, 98, 98n62, 99n63;137n7, 174, 175n7, 222n32
Miller, J. L.	16n22		
Miller, J. Maxwell	51n19, 63n72, 129n34		
Miller, Patrick D.	25n3, 30nn18-19, 31, 31n21, 32n24, 33, 33n27, 35n30, 182n41	Ornan, Tallay	129n33
		Otto, Eckart	2n4, 136n4, 144, 144n30, 157n6, 178, 179n28, 183nn45-46, 194n83, n85, 217n14
Miller, Robert D., II	79n150, 155n1		
Möhlenbrink, Kurt	1n2, 51n19; 52n22		
Na'aman, Nadav	70, 70nn110-111, 71, 71nn112-116, 72, 72n117, n121, 73, 74, 137n6, 145, 145nn36-37, 146, 147, 147n42, 152n62, 200n1	Pakkala, Juha	140, 140n17, 178n26
		Peterson, John L.	64, 64nn74-75, n77, 65, 65n79, n81, n83
		Pfoh, Emanuel	79n150
Nelson, Richard D.	26n4, 28, 28n9, 29, 29n14, 31, 97n59, 138n9, 146n41, 149n51, 150n55, 151, 151n57, n59, 152n60, 153nn64-65	Polaski, Donald	223, 223nn35-36
		Polk, Timothy	51n19
		Popko, Maciej	11n1, n2;12n7, 13n10, 21n42
		Propp, William	119, 119nn6-7, 120, 124n24, 125n26, 131
Neve, Peter	11n2	Puech, Emile	200n3
Nielsen, Eduard	114n35	Puhvel, Jaan	14n14, 23n48
Nihan, Christophe	178, 178n26, 183n44, 195n88	Pury, Albert de	107n18, 113n34
Nicholson, Ernest	194n86	Qimron, Elisha	205nn16-17, 207n23
Noth, Martin	57, 58, 58n50, 59, 59nn51-53, 60, 60n54, 62, 63, 65, 73, 74n124, n128, 81, 113n34, 115n38, 120, 120n11	Rad, Gerhard von	53n27, 113n34, 148n50, 151n58, 157n4
		Ramirez Kidd, José	178n23
		Redditt, Paul L.	226n46, 227n50
		Regev, Eyal	213n37
		Rehm, M. D.	199n1
Nurmela, Risto	53n27, 54n28, 84n3, 143n26, 199n1, 202n9	Rendsburg, Gary	26-27n5
		Rendtorff, Rolf	121n11
		Rindge, Matthew S.	225n43

Roberts, J. J. M.	137n7	Ska, Jean-Louis	196n91
Robertson, Amy Cooper	123n23	Skinner, John	104n4, 104n7, 107n18, 113n34
Robinson, Robert B.	51n19		
Rofé, Alexander	146n39, 180n32	Smith, Henry Preserved	37nn37-38
Rooke, Deborah W.	53n27, 54n28, 199n1	Smith, Mark	2n4, 215n2
		Sommer, Benjamin	141n20
Rose, Martin	148n50	Sparks, James T.	73n125, 76, 76n134, 77, 77nn140-142, 78n144
Ross, J. P.	68n95		
Rüterswörden, Udo	146n41, 149n51, 159n7		
		Speiser, Ephraim A.	107n18
Samuel, Harald	142n22	Spencer, John R.	53nn27-28, 75n129, 80n151
Sanders, Seth L.	5n16		
Schäfer-Lichtenberger, Christa	191, 191n77, 192	Spieckermann, Hermann	136n2
		Stackert, Jeffrey	6, 83n, 95n49, 96n52, 96n54, 97n56, 177n, 121n13, 135-136n1, 183, 183n44, n 48, 202n6, 210n28
Schaper, Joachim	2n5, 53n27, 84n3, 136n2, 137n6, 199n1, 222n31		
Schellenberg, Annette	83n, 135n		
Schiffman, Lawrence	201n3, n5; 206n20, 207n22, 208, 208n25, 210n29, 212, 212n36, 213n37	Stager, Lawrence E.	3n9, 21n41, 33nn25-26, 50n17, 51n19, 81, 117n, 129n34, 139, 139n14, 156n1, 160n10, 216n7
Schloen, J. David	156n1		
Schmid, Konrad	142, 142n23		
Schmidt, Brian	129, 129n36, 130		
Schmidt, Ludwig	75n131	Stallman, Robert	200n2, 203n12, 204n15, 206n20, 207n22, 209n26, 210n29
Schmitt, Götz	49n12, 50n15, 53n26, 58n50, 60, 60nn54-56, 61n61, 73, 73nn122-126, 74, 74n127		
		Starke, Frank	13n11
		Stavrakopoulou, Francesca	173n2
Schmitt, Rüdiger	174n6	Steen, Eveline J. van der	65, 65n82
Schniedewind, William	4n13, 178n25, 215n2, 216n8, 218n17	Steins, Georg	187n63
		Steuernagel, Carl	151nn57-59
		Steymans, Hans Ulrich	158n6
Schorn, Ulrike	114n35	Stökl, Jonathan	174n5
Schwartz, Baruch	108n19, 117n, 121, 121n12	Stowers, Stanley K.	182n40, 188, 188n66
Scott, R. B. Y.	126, 126n31	Suh, Myung Soo	123n23
Seebass, Horst	143, 143n24	Svensson, Jan	55n36, 72n117
Segal, Michael	224n39	Swanson, Dwight D.	211n31
Seitz, Gottfried	147nn41-43, 153n65	Sweeney, Marvin A.	228n52
Shectman, Sarah	6, 86n12	Tadmor, Hayim	20n35
Shiloh, Yigael	38n42	Taggar-Cohen, Ada	5, 12-13nn 3-8, 14n16, 15nn20-21,
Sivertsev, Alexei	231n62		

INDEX OF AUTHORS

Thiering, B. E. 203n12
Tiemeyer, Lena-Sofia 180, 180nn35-36, 217n14, 228n51
Tigay, Jeffrey 88n18, 138n9
Toorn, Karel S. van der 3n8, n10, 37n38, 38n40, n 42, 50n17, 143n26, 215n2, 216n5, n9, 217, 217nn12-13, 219n20, 220n22, 222n28, 224n39, 231nn58-59
Tsafrir, Yoram 61n61, n68, 69, 69n104, 72, 72n121
Tsumura, David Toshio 27n6, 30n19, 31n22, 37nn38-39, 43n57
Turner, Victor 195, 195n87

Ulrich, Eugene 203n11

Vanderhooft, David S. 50n16
Van Seters, John 109n25, 110nn26-27, 115n40, 121n11
Vaughan, Patrick 32n24
Vaux, Roland de 32n24, 51n19, 64n76, 65
Vogt, Peter T. 157n4
Volgger, David 204n15
Vos, Jacobus Cornelius de 177, 177nn16-22

Wall, Robert W. 88n18
Wallace, Anthony F. C. 79, 79n148
Walters, Stanley D. 43nn57-58
Watkins, Leslie 39n46, 40nn47-48
Watts, James W. 218n17
Weber, Max 156n1
Weinfeld, Moshe 14n15, n21, 21n40, 24n51, 36, 36nn35-36, 66n90, 132n43, 158n6

16nn22-24, 17n25, 18n28, 19n31, 20n36, 23nn45-46, n 49

Wellhausen, Julius 1n1, 5, 45, 46, 46nn1-7, 47, 47nn8-10, 49, 66, 104n7, 107n18, 117n1, 118, 118nn2-3, 119, 119n4, 120, 132, 135, 135n1, 136, 138n10, 151, 151n57, 163, 163n19, 164, 169, 199n1, 202, 202n7, 202n10
Wenham, Gordon J. 35n30
Werman, Cana 200n2, 204n15
Westermann, Klaus 107n18, 113n34
Whitney, J. T. 33n26
Williamson, H. G. M. 63n73, 182n41, 194n84
Willis, John T. 26n5, 30n19, 31n21, 35n30
Wilson, Ian 96n53, 97n58
Wilson, Robert R. 51n18, 165n23, 168n32
Winter, Irene 117n
Wise, Michael Owen 201n5, 204n15
Wright, G. Ernest 53n27, 151, 151nn57-58, 152n60, 199n1
Wright, Jacob 180n34, 181n38, 219n21, 227n50, 228n51

Yadin, Yigael 207, 208n24
Yakubovich, Ilya 12n6
Young, Ian M. 4n13, 215n4

Zenger, Erich 187n65
Zevit, Ziony 33nn25-26, 121n14, 174, 174n6, 197n93
Zobel, Hans-Jürgen 104n3
Zwickel, Wolfgang 181, 181n38

www.ingramcontent.com/pod-product-compliance
Lightning Source LLC
Chambersburg PA
CBHW021139230426
43667CB00005B/178